# LOST *for* WORDS?

A sermon resource for the Anglican three-year cycle

Compiled and edited by Jane Williams
*Editor of the Common Worship Living Word*

with a foreword by Denis McBride C.Ss.R.

A Redemptorist Publication

Published by **Redemptorist Publications**
A Registered Charity limited by guarantee. Registered in England 3261721.



First published November 2009

Layout: Rosemarie Pink
Cover design: Chris Nutbeen

ISBN 978-0-85231-369-5



A CIP catalogue record for this book is available from the British Library

Printed by Stanley L Hunt (Printers) Limited, Northamptonshire, NN10 9UA

Alphonsus House Chawton Hampshire GU34 3HQ
Telephone 01420 88222 Fax 01420 88805
rp@ rpbooks.co.uk www.rpbooks.co.uk

# Contents

# Foreword

*Dear Friends,*

Some days words come easily to us, and insights seem to spring up from some secret sanctuary to surprise and delight, leaving us wondering at hidden resources within. On other days we feel lost for words, with insight buried under a mountain of routine concerns. The telephone keeps ringing, people lean on the door with a litany of demands, the diary looks stuffed with tedious meetings, and the slates are slipping from the sacristy roof.

Sunday is approaching. Again. A congregation will assemble to hallow the name of the Lord, hoping that they might hear some good news. From you. You take a deep breath.

Having a word for your congregation, in season and out of season, for the high feast days and the spread of ordinary time, is no mean feat. Sometimes you might feel in sympathy with a tired priest who said to me: "People keep coming to me, but at the moment I feel like a shopkeeper with nothing on the shelves behind me. Sold out."

We all need help on dull days when reserves are low. This volume has been assembled not as a substitute for your best thinking, but as a humble help for those days when you feel a bit weary and out of luck. It aims to provide a line, an image, a thought – a trigger to set the mind in movement towards Gospel.

If this book achieves this, it will have fulfilled a wonderful pastoral purpose – helping you to minister to the people charged to your care.

*Sincerely,*

Denis McBride, C.Ss.R.
Publishing Director
Redemptorist Publications
Chawton
Alton
Hants GU34 3HQ

# Editor's Preface

For over a decade, Redemptorist Publications have been providing a Sunday homily for use with the Anglican lectionary. These homilies have been written by people who are not only biblical theologians, but also regular preachers. They may be lay or ordained, male or female, but they each bring their own perspective from their pastoral and preaching ministry.

Readers tell us that they use these sermons in a variety of ways. They can be preached just as they are, as a short, expository sermon. Or they can be customised by adding illustrations and comments to fit a particular situation. Some preachers read them to get their creative juices flowing, and then take the sermon off in their own direction.

It is extraordinary how, from the comparatively few pages of the Bible, endless insights can flow. Different readers and writers can help to bring to light fresh insights and new excitement about the work of God and the Christian life. Sharing prayerful, patient reading of the scriptures with each other is a creative use of the gifts of the body of Christ. The Bible is a book designed to be read together, explored together, so that we can share the riches that God gives each reader. The sermons gathered in this book are not only a gift from one preacher to another, but also an acknowledgement that all our gifts come primarily from the great Giver.

Drawn together here in one convenient volume are some of the sermon ideas from the last ten years, produced by regular writers for Redemptorist Publications' *Common Worship Living Word* team. With this book, the two volumes of *Common Worship Living Word Festivals* and *Common Worship Living Word Special Occasions,* no preacher need ever be lost for words again.

Thanks are due to all those who have contributed to the Anglican *Living Word* series over the years, to all at Redemptorist Publications who have worked so hard to make these resources more widely available, and, perhaps above all, to St Alphonsus, the founder of the Redemptorist order, whose vision of a missionary, teaching order lies at the heart of Redemptorist Publications.

Jane Williams
Editor

# Advent

*"Keep awake therefore, for you do not know on what day your Lord is coming."*
(Matthew 24:42)

**Illustration**

Most of us need an alarm clock if we are to wake up in time for whatever the day has in store. And many of us find it hard to respond when it goes off. We rouse ourselves just enough to hit the snooze button and give ourselves another five minutes of sleep.

On red-letter days, however, we may not even need an alarm clock, because we have gone to bed so aware of the next day's events that we wake up in good time anyway. What child needs to be woken up on Christmas Day? The expectation of cards and presents to unwrap, and of so much fun to be had, is all that is needed to ensure an early rising. The same thing happens on the days when we have an exam, or have to go into hospital.

Other kinds of alarm alert us to danger. The burglar alarm galvanises us into checking the doors and windows and counting the spoons; the smoke alarm causes us to get out of the house and dial the emergency number. Pressing the snooze button in those circumstances could mean the difference between life and death.

In all these cases the alarm is heard and attended to, either gladly or grudgingly. But, in contrast, all of us have heard the seemingly endless clamour of alarm bells that appear to alert nobody. They drone on in the background, causing annoyance, anger and frustration. If alarms are to be of any use, someone must be able to hear them and know what they are for.

**Gospel Teaching**

In today's first reading Isaiah celebrates his vision of the dawning of the day of the Lord. Then, he tells us, the Lord will exercise his universal authority over every nation and everyone shall walk in the light of the Lord.

In the second reading, Paul suggests that this time is getting closer even as we speak. "You must wake up now," he warns us. "The night is almost over, it will be daylight soon."

The Gospel passage also looks toward the return of the Son of Man, but there is a cutting edge to the words of Jesus. For the time of this coming is likened to the days before the Flood, when God saw nothing but wickedness on earth. It was only Noah who found favour with him. An element of danger is also introduced through the image of burglary: God's summons may catch us napping when we should have been alert. The image is clear: if you stay asleep while a burglar is in your house, you will lose everything you possess. If you stay asleep when Christ comes to judge the earth, you will lose even more.

So, the lesson is explicit: always be on the alert, because the Son of Man will come when no one is expecting him. And be careful – we may not be expecting him, but we do know he is coming. We don't really have any excuse not to be ready. If Jesus were to come today, and you were to say, "But Lord, I had no idea! Why didn't you tell me you were coming?" he would have to say, "I did. Time and again. But you pushed the sound of my voice to the background, like a warehouse alarm on a bank holiday weekend, that no one knows how to switch off."

**Application**

The message you have heard today is a very important sort of alarm. The Day of the Lord is a red-letter day, and we must be ready for it. Paul is right – it is getting closer all the time.

How can we ensure that we are awake and watchful when the Lord comes? Paul's letter to the Romans supplies the answer. We have no means of guessing at God's timing and it would be foolhardy to rely on a deathbed conversion. We must, he says, lead the kind of lives that can stand up to scrutiny by daylight. In other words, we have to give up our sinful ways (which we often hide from ourselves and others) and repent. The word "repentance" means turning back: turning back to the paths of the Lord.

In the season of Advent, the readings in church will constantly remind us that the Lord is very near. If we are to be among the welcoming party, we must translate our good intentions into action. Don't put it off until tomorrow – you may not have that long.

*"Jesus said, 'Beware, keep alert; for you do not know when the time will come.'"*
(Mark 13:33)

**Illustration**

In his famous novel *The Power and the Glory*, Graham Greene describes the last few hours of the life of a priest who was condemned to death during a time of religious persecution in Mexico. At first the priest had courageously resisted, but as time went on he turned to alcohol and became a drunkard, before having the chance of redemption.

Greene presents us with a scene in the condemned man's cell on the morning of his death. The priest is recalling all his lost opportunities, his inner emptiness and his loneliness. Above all, he laments his lack of vigilance and awareness of the presence of God in his life. The description of his last few moments is very moving: "He felt an immense disappointment, because he had to go to God empty-handed, with nothing at all. He felt like someone who had just missed happiness by seconds at an appointed place. He knew that in the end, only one thing counted – to be a saint." Most of us can identify with something of that feeling of disappointment, a sense that we are somehow missing out on something, or an uncomfortable fear, when we think about what we might feel if we were as close to death as the priest in Graham Greene's book.

**Gospel Teaching**

Today's readings are full of warnings about being vigilant, about not missing out on the coming of God into our lives. In the Gospel, Jesus urges his followers to prepare for an uncertain future – the only thing that is really certain is that the world will one day come to an end. We do not know when – that's why there is uncertainty – but we do know that it will happen. So, Jesus says, be ready to meet God at any moment.

Before you start to think all this talk about the end of the world sounds a bit far-fetched, consider this: we may not live to see the end of the world in our own lifetime, but we can all be sure that one day our own lives will end, and we do not know when that will be. We seriously need to be prepared for that. It is an interesting reflection on our society that the one thing about all our lives that is most certain is the one thing that we talk about the least and are most afraid of. Jesus came to take the fear out of death for those who believe in him. But we still need to be prepared, ready to meet our God at any moment.

The Jews prayed seven times a day that the Messiah might come among them. However, when he came, as their brother and their saviour and their friend, they did not recognise him. They expected a powerful leader. Instead, there appeared among them a simple human being, one of their own, someone with ordinariness stamped on his very being. It is his ordinariness, his humanness, that enables us to connect with him: in Christ God meets us where we are, as we are, and shows us tangibly what he is like. That is what we celebrate at Christmas.

**Application**

How did he enter our world at the first Christmas? Not in great majesty or power. He came as a helpless tiny baby. And now, we can meet Jesus in the smile of a child or in the neediness of a lonely old person. He is there in the beauty of a sunset or in the power of the wind or rain. He is there in the laughter of a teenager or in the healing touch of a nurse. We need not look far for him. However, it is so important that we learn to recognise him when he does appear in our midst.

God comes to you this Christmas. Do not miss his coming. Do not end up as that priest in Graham Greene's novel nearly did, empty and full of regret at the end. Do not harden your hearts by being caught up only in the material things of our world, failing to recognise him in the ordinary relationships and experiences of life. Seek to recognise him in the many different ways he appears in our midst. And as you become used to meeting with him day by day, so you will find you are prepared to meet him at the end of your life as well.

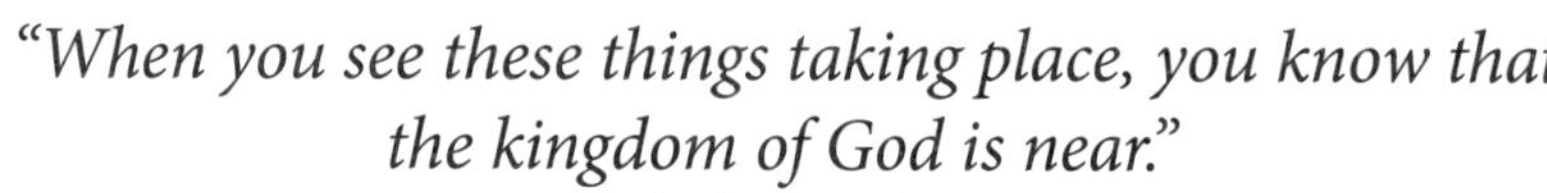

*"When you see these things taking place, you know that the kingdom of God is near."*
(Luke 21:31)

**Illustration**
Some time ago there was a series of television adverts for an insurance company. They portrayed a series of domestic catastrophes, and they all ended with the slogan, "We won't make a drama out of a crisis." So there was the harassed mother coming downstairs to find the washing machine flooding the kitchen floor. The man contemplating the remains of his car, crushed under a fallen tree. The family returning home to find the window smashed and the television and video gone. All they had to do, however, was to phone the insurance company, and the problem would instantly be sorted out. Because, "We won't make a drama out of a crisis."



**Gospel Teaching**
But making a drama out of a crisis is precisely what the Gospel writers do in the sections of their Gospels we read in Advent. So what is the crisis, and how does the drama help?

The words of today's Gospel reading are put into the mouth of Jesus, but they are being reported by Luke to a later audience. The first Christians had high hopes for the world after their experience of Jesus. They had seen his resurrection from the dead, and they fully expected him to return in power to judge the world very soon. However, his return did not appear to be coming soon enough to save them from trouble. They were living in a context that was doubly hostile to them, firstly because they were Jews, and secondly because they were Christians. So if they weren't in trouble with the Romans for being Jews, they were in trouble with the Jews for being Christians. Not long after the time of Jesus they had seen the Jerusalem Temple destroyed by the Romans. Their lives were precarious.

So there is a crisis for early Christianity. The Lord has not returned, and there is no predicting when he will come. Meanwhile, there is danger and persecution for his followers. These two factors contribute to a crisis of faith. Were they right to believe what Jesus said, when his promises do not seem to be fulfilled? Were they right in their assessment of who Jesus was, when he does not seem to have the power to save them from danger?

The Gospel writers take this crisis and make a drama out of it. Luke's drama involves signs in the sun, moon and stars, crashing waves, the powers of the heavens shaken and people quaking with fear. Jesus will return, Luke promises, in truly dramatic fashion. The troubles his followers are experiencing now are nothing compared to the upheaval that will herald his arrival.

What this drama does is to take fear and turn it into hope. Persecution and difficulty are no longer signs of Jesus' absence, but rather of his imminent arrival. The drama is there to energise Christians, to encourage them to hold fast to hope and to live as if every moment was the one when the Lord would return. The crisis for faith becomes a drama of expectation.

**Application**

Two thousand years have passed, and the Lord has still not returned. And if many of us are honest, we have mostly stopped believing that he will. In our context of faith and thought, Advent can be an embarrassment, with its language of heavenly darkness and shaking earth, and its promises that Jesus will return within the lifetime of the first believers. Many no longer take Luke's drama literally, so far down the ages.

But it is still important. The overall message which Luke and the other Gospel writers want to convey to their readers is echoed by St Paul, and it is this: live each day as if it were to be the day of the Lord's return. We are given Advent as a solemn season in which to examine our lives in the light of Christ's coming, to ask ourselves, if Jesus did return today, what would he find me doing? What would he think of my choices and my priorities? These are questions Christians may ask themselves all the time, but the drama of Advent sharpens them and gives them urgency. Much time may have passed since the first Christians looked to the heavens expecting to see Jesus returning, but the call of St Paul is still addressed to us: "it is now the moment to wake from sleep. For salvation is nearer to us now than when we became believers."

*"Repent, for the kingdom of heaven has come near."*
(Matthew 3:2)

**Illustration**

There are two completely different and unconnected meanings to the word repent. The one with which we are all familiar, from the French *repentir*, means to reject our sins in sorrow and return to God. When John proclaimed repentance he clearly used the word in this sense.

The second meaning of the word is more familiar to botanists and comes from the Latin *repere,* meaning "to creep". It describes plants which creep across the ground, their roots immediately above or below the surface. The bindweed which constantly threatens to take over our gardens as it strangles plants and the leaves of shrubs is one so-called repenting plant. The problem with bindweed is that you cannot ignore it. Spend half a day clearing the wretched stuff and then relax for a week, believing that it is destroyed once and for all, and it will return more vigorous than ever! If it is to be completely wiped out, every fraction of the root must be destroyed. In practice this is simply not possible. We can only do our best with the tools and time we have to eradicate this enemy of our gardens so that the fruit and flowers may grow to healthy maturity.

**Gospel Teaching**

John the Baptist emphasised the need for weeding out: "every tree therefore that does not bear good fruit will be cut down and thrown into the fire". His words seem harsh and uncompromising, possibly because he found himself confronted by the Pharisees and Sadducees at the Jordan. Like Jesus, John was far more gentle and sensitive with the ordinary people who came seeking repentance and healing.

In our own attempts at repentance we need to be both ruthless and gentle. Ruthless because sin strangles and destroys our relationship with God and the world, rather like bindweed throttles our garden plants. Our weaknesses need to be determinedly and consistently addressed, otherwise the new, fresh growth of love for God will be suffocated by their clinging tendrils.

But in the same way that ridding our garden of bindweed is difficult, so we can never totally root out our sins alone. This is why we need constantly to call upon God for help. We also need to be gentle with ourselves. We shall often fail on our pilgrimage, which is why Jesus persistently calls us to him to give us strength. Like developing a beautiful garden, repentance is a lifelong process.

**Application**

John the Baptist said: "Bear fruit worthy of repentance." The fruit from each of us will be different, according to the gifts God has given us, but we share similarities.

First we need to see those failings which are holding us back. Walking through our garden with our head in the air admiring the blooms of the climbing roses will not reveal the bindweed at our feet. We must get down on our knees for a closer look. So we need to learn to examine ourselves closely and honestly; not being too lax, but not too stringent either. We need to foster the desire for repentance and a steadfast spirit to change our ways, not overnight, but gradually, over the years, as we mature mentally and spiritually.

Like a gardener tending to plants, it may be necessary to get back on our knees more often. Prayer may be a bit like weeding: it needs to be constant, and attentive to detail. Repentance may be a turning away from sin but, more positively, it is directing our lives towards God who gives us the help we need. We can stretch out to him in prayer, sharing the details of our lives, accepting God's attentiveness and compassion, further developing that deep belief that God is always there and eminently worth turning to. Praying is like sitting on a bench in the garden, feeling the warmth of the sun on our face, eyes half-closed against its brightness. We deserve the time to relax in the balm of God's presence. When we do this God will take care of the half-destroyed bindweed at our feet.

We can begin today. Acknowledge the bindweed of weakness and failure and begin to root it out the best you can. Then sit calmly in the presence of God and let love's healing sunshine restore you and deal with what you cannot handle. Now IS the time for repentance – but now is also the time for love.

*"John the baptiser appeared in the wilderness, proclaiming a baptism of repentance for the forgiveness of sins."*
(Mark 1:4)

**Introduction**
A class of fourteen-year-olds was asked: "Who is John the Baptist for you?" One student put up his hand and replied: "He is a wild man – cool!" Asked to explain, he said he admired John for being able to live in the desert without any visible means of support, admitted some curiosity regarding his clothing, some amusement and "Eeew" factor at the thought of eating locusts, although the honey was "okay". The class consensus was that John was more interesting than many of the characters we read about in the New Testament, many of whom were seen as "goody-goody", while John had something of the anarchist about him.

The students were right to see John as the "wild man of God". John is a complex character whose life had several levels of meaning for the ministry of Jesus. But he also has several messages for us, too, partly because he represents an image of godliness we may not have considered, but also partly because much of what John is, and does, could well address our own vocation as disciples.

**Gospel Teaching**
We know already that John was special, born of parents blessed by a miracle which brought about his birth, as the Gospel of Luke tells us. His family was of priestly line and, though certain rigorous requirements were made concerning his upbringing, his family would have experienced a certain status in the community.

His parents knew from the angelic message that John must be dedicated to God and that his role would be key in the coming of the Lord among the people: that is, the arrival of the long-awaited Messiah.

The fact that he apparently threw up his birthright, and left his family, pursuing a life of asceticism, and proclaiming the coming judgement loudly and vividly, says something about him which his family was not prepared for. John lived his conviction that his role was to attract enough attention to transmit his message: that the time had arrived, the Messiah was imminent, the moment was now, there was no time to waste!

But John's appearance and lifestyle were not just a gimmick to attract attention: they were a preparation, a cleansing and a method of living out the very repentance that he preached as essential to others. God called him, and then worked from within John's apparent "wildness" and, in doing so, exposed a part of God that we rarely consider: that God too has a "wild" side, when the need arises. God does not always operate through Mr and Mrs "Nice", but sometimes chooses people whose attractiveness to some may, indeed, rather repel others.

God wants to appeal to the whole spectrum of humanity, not just the respectable and already godly, and so calls forth the appropriate types of evangelist to suit all groups and types. (Unfortunately it is now too often true that the Church itself limits this role only to those who fit a particular mould, those least likely to cause "havoc".) At the start of the Jesus movement, God needed strong, enthusiastic and sometimes fiery people with stamina and "grit" to energise the new Church, and God still needs such people today.

The seed of God's own wild Spirit planted in John enabled him to prepare the way for Jesus by gathering a group around him who, it is now believed, transferred their allegiance to Jesus when the time came. John was the key to the start of Jesus' ministry – perhaps such uncomfortable prophets are the key to the regeneration of the Church today?

**Application**
Living in the desert and dining so frugally is probably not what the practice of Christianity means for us; but stepping outside the mould which society and the Church create for us may well be.

John passed up his respectable life to follow God's path as his own. He taught by word and example, and told his message clearly and unequivocally; he lived, and stuck to, his own truth and, through his determination to be himself, showed us how to do the same. Perhaps it is this combination of attributes to which young people are drawn. John lived authentically his vocation as given to him by God. He encourages us to accept the invitation to be wild for God and, in being so, to permit God to be wild in the world, to shake it up, through us. Without John, Jesus would have been sorely deprived, and our students would have lost a "cool" role model.

*"The word of God came to John son of Zechariah in the wilderness."*
(Luke 3:2)

**Illustration**
Airport terminals are strange places. They have a mixed-up atmosphere that seems to come from the excitement of holidays, the weariness of the business trip, the anticipation of returning home, and the boredom of prolonged waiting at unearthly hours of the day or night. They have the clinical feel of a waiting room – except you have to buy your own magazines. Even the shops selling enticing things such as watches, souvenirs and huge bottles of whisky can't distract you for long from the fact that there is nothing to do except shop. And then there are those endless loudspeaker announcements trying to find people who have got lost somewhere between check-in and take-off. In an airport, you are in a kind of geographical limbo – it's as if you belong neither to the country you are leaving, nor the country you are going to. For however long you have to wait, you are neither here nor there, and there is little to do except listen eagerly for your gate to be called.

**Gospel Teaching**
The Bible has its own geographical limbo: the wilderness. Much more than a place of dust and rocks, the wilderness has a special spiritual significance in the relationship between God and his people. It is in the wilderness that God calls Moses from the burning bush to lead his people out of Egypt, and it is in the wilderness that the Israelites wander for forty years while they learn what it means to be the people of God. After his baptism, Jesus is led into the wilderness to be tempted by the devil, and filled with the power of the Spirit.

So when we read that the word of the Lord came to John son of Zechariah in the wilderness, we know that something of real importance is about to happen. John has spent the best part of his life in this geographical and spiritual limbo; just over a chapter earlier we read that he was in the wilderness from his childhood until the day he appeared publicly to Israel. Even allowing for the fact that we don't know how old John was, we can make a good guess that that's a long time to be hanging about in a desert. It was a measure of the importance of John's future work that he required the kind of spiritual preparation that only the wilderness can give. And when the word does come to John, it sets off something that will change the world.

John's call is the drum roll that announces that salvation is near, that something really new and really good is about to happen. It is a turning point in time, which is perhaps why Luke takes such care to locate this event in history, by giving us the names of the rulers of the day. John hears his call and sets off into public life to call people to repentance for the forgiveness of sins, and to baptise them as a mark of their decision to lead a new life. And so he becomes John the Baptist, preparing the way for the Lord.

**Application**
We all know what it's like to be in limbo: to feel that we are neither here nor there. Generally speaking, we are creatures who love to have a purpose, and we get restless and unhappy when we lack one. It may be that this "wilderness" is a stagnant time in our lives: a dead-end job or relationship. Some people talk of retirement as a time when they feel lost and useless after many years of work. Some parents talk of feeling strangely empty when their children leave home, and for some children the school years have a kind of aching boredom that can only be described as a wilderness.

Our experiences are all different, but the thing to note is this: that just like the airport, the wilderness is a place where things are about to happen, a place of preparation. It may be a long wait; it may seem painfully boring, it may seem pointless, but the wilderness is where the seeds of change are sown and nurtured. It may not be an easy time (although for some it may be too easy, and that is the problem with it) but it is a time to embrace. It is a time for waiting and listening carefully for the voice of God. And when it comes, who knows where God might lead us?

*"Yet the least in the kingdom of heaven is greater than he."*
(Matthew 11:11)

**Illustration**
Every part of our life is measured nowadays. We are tested at school and assessed at work. We compete with others or with ourselves to earn more money, find a better job, go on more exotic holidays, buy a bigger house, get fit, get slim. We've been sold the illusion that success somehow buys happiness. And indeed it might for a brief span, but the author of Ecclesiastes is not the only wise man to conclude that worldly success is ephemeral and all pleasure mere vanity. Like John the Baptist, we are all imprisoned in our mortality, awaiting the executioner. And that's when, as with John, doubts rise to the surface about the life we've lived.

**Gospel Teaching**
John was a successful prophet. He had a school of disciples and people came from all over Judaea to hear him prophesy against the Establishment. Jesus knew John well, knew of his oratory, his charisma and his courage, and clearly thought highly of him – in fact he says John is the greatest person who's ever lived! And yet, despite all that, Jesus still remarks that the Baptist is insignificant when compared with even the lowliest person in God's kingdom.

What is Jesus getting at here? Put his remark into the context we've described, where John is sitting on death row, wondering if his life has had meaning. He'd been a successful prophet, but to what end? He'd prophesied the advent of the Messiah, but did Jesus really match up to John's prophecies?

So he sends some of his disciples to ask Jesus if he's the one expected. In reply, Jesus simply points to what happens wherever he goes: the blind see, the deaf hear, the lame walk, lepers are healed, the dead are raised, and the good news is preached to the poor.

Jesus has two reasons for quoting Isaiah. The first is so that people draw the same conclusion as he himself had done when he'd read this passage in the synagogue at Nazareth (Luke 4:21): namely, Isaiah's prophecy has been fulfilled in his own person.

Jesus' second reason for quoting Isaiah, who prophesied eight centuries before John, is to indicate that he identifies John with the prophets of the Old Covenant. John is actually greater than Isaiah and all the other prophets but he's still one of them. He's the last of their kind, the forerunner of the New Covenant. Like Moses, John points to a new phase in human experience that he can't himself enter.

The very fact that John had to ask if Jesus was the one proves Jesus' point. John prophesied but couldn't himself read the signs. No matter what John did, how well he lived the Torah, he would still be baptising with water, as he himself admitted. He was able to prophesy the new life in the Spirit – that's why he was the greatest; but he didn't actually know what it would mean and could never experience it – that's why he was the least.



John and Jesus represent two dimensions, two different modes of being. The Isaiah prophecy quoted by Jesus makes that clear. We're not talking about blind people being happier in Jesus' world – no, they can see. Likewise the deaf aren't provided with better hearing aids in the kingdom – they can hear. The lame don't have new crutches – they don't need any crutches at all. The good news is preached to the poor not so they are more aware of their benefit rights, but because the poor – and all whose status had made them unacceptable – are welcomed into the heart of society wherever God's rule is applied. It's a sea change, a seismic shift that even the greatest person who's ever lived, John the Baptist, couldn't, in Jesus' opinion, begin to comprehend.

**Application**

And what about us? How willing are we to live the Gospel life? The last will be first? Give your spendthrift son the fatted calf? Stop to bind up your enemy's wounds? The last worker will get as much as the first? Welcome asylum seekers? Can such upside-down principles compete in our hearts with our drive to succeed, our desire to be the first no matter whom we hurt, our wish to consume even more as millions starve?

Thankfully, we don't face this challenge alone. We have the saints to inspire us, and those uncrowned saints working abroad and closer to home to bring God's kingdom on earth. And we have blessed communion in Christ's body, which feeds us and enables us to know that he is indeed the one.

*"He confessed and did not deny it, but confessed, 'I am not the Messiah.'"*
(John 1:20)



**Illustration**
In one of the episodes of the American television comedy *Friends*, Phoebe is challenged to do a good deed from which she derives no benefit at all. It proves much harder than she expected. Every time she does something kind or generous, somehow it always turns out to contain something for her, too. The serious question in the midst of Phoebe's increasingly desperate attempts to do something completely unselfish is whether there can really be a wholly altruistic act, or whether, like it or not, we always act only to benefit ourselves in some way or another.

**Gospel Teaching**
On the face of it, John the Baptist does seem to have achieved Phoebe's goal. It is very hard to see what John the Baptist gets out of his witness to Jesus. As we meet John at the beginning of the Gospel accounts, he is at the height of his fame. He has a great many disciples and people flock to hear him preach and to be baptised by him. He says what God gives him to say, under all circumstances, and without softening his message to suit important ears. He is not afraid to reprove King Herod for his immoral lifestyle, for example.

The religious leaders of his day are clearly impressed enough by John to wonder if he can be the Messiah for whom they are all waiting. He has all the right credentials. He comes from a priestly family, and his birth is surrounded by miracle and prophecy.

What's more, his message of judgement and his call to repentance are exactly what the religious authorities would expect the Messiah to say. All the prophets of old echoed John's warning to the people to repent or face God's judgement. Taken in conjunction with John's fearlessness in the face of authority, which would surely make him willing, if necessary, to take on the hated Roman usurpers of the nation's independence, it is entirely understandable that they come to ask John, point-blank, "Who are you?"

If there is any area of uncertainty in John, any deeply buried belief that perhaps he is, after all, God's chosen Messiah, the Gospels show no sign of it. He is emphatic in his denials.

We do not know quite how John prepared himself for this time, though tradition has it that he lived as an ascetic in the desert for many years before starting his ministry. Matthew's Gospel tells us that he wore clothes of itchy camel's hair, and lived on locusts and wild honey, all of which would seem to bear out the testimony to his self-denying lifestyle. But whatever he has been doing for the years since his birth, it has honed his vocation to this point, the moment at which he can say, forcefully, "I am not the Messiah."

As far as the Gospels are concerned, when John has baptised Jesus and recognised him and witnessed to him, his work is done. When John is later imprisoned and then executed by Herod that is a sad event but not a tragic one for the Gospel writers, because John has already fulfilled his life's purpose.



Humanly speaking, it is hard to see what satisfaction John could have got from his mission. A life of self-denial, brutally cut short; an influential ministry, remembered only in the context of someone else's far more important work – hardly the epitaph most of us would wish for.

But all the years of prayer and attention to God that allowed John to stand up and say with utter clarity, "I am not the Messiah," may perhaps have given him enough insight to know his own value in God's eyes. John was doing the thing for which he was born; he saw what all the prophets longed to see – God's Messiah coming to bring justice and peace to the whole world. So perhaps his altruism had its rewards, after all.

**Application**

John's calling is unique. He was born to stand on the cusp between the old world and the new creation in Christ. He was born to point forward to what all the rest of us can now receive. Thanks, at least in part, to his faithful witness, we do not have to wonder if Jesus is God's fulfilment or not. We know.

But now we have to take up John's mantle and bear witness to Jesus. John did it alone, and when no one else recognised Jesus, but he did what we are all born to do. He saw who Jesus was and he told the world. Now it's our turn.

*"One who is more powerful than I is coming; I am not worthy to untie the thong of his sandals. He will baptise you with the Holy Spirit and fire."*
(Luke 3:16)

**Illustration**

The book *Letters for Aunty Flo: Journal of a Reluctant Disciple*, by Graham Young, is humorous and challenging, daring its readers to let their lives be opened to the possibility of radical changes in their attitudes, values and activities. David, a young man who takes a job in a new town, writes of his experiences in regular letters to his Aunty Flo back home. His new church teaches him about a repentance that is more than the negative act of saying sorry; it is also the positive process of changing our minds, of going against the tide, the normal flow, of going "anti-flow" (which is where his Aunty comes in).

He is challenged about where he chooses to live, the kind of car he thinks he should be driving, how he spends his free time and his salary, the friends he identifies with, his reactions to injustice overseas and on his street, what peacemaking, racism and sexism mean, what he celebrates and prays for – in short, his life is turned upside down, the premises of his Christian faith radically exposed and his discipleship of Christ challenged. Personal repentance becomes radically life-changing for David and for the society around him. In short, David learns that to live out the salvation of God is to live life as an anti-flow person, a radical disciple.

**Gospel Teaching**

The salvation of God may not look like the salvation that the world tells us is our right, where external cleansing ceremonies are considered enough and sufficient to welcome home the Messiah. John the Baptist characteristically says it as it is – the Saviour is nigh, the crowds are not ready for him, and the need for repentance is urgent. For those unprepared, the coming kingdom will seem like wrathful judgement.

John sternly warns the people of the need for their unreal and sinful lives to be remade and restored. What is demanded is an internal repentance, a revolution of the inner nature, and, though he could point them to the urgency of their situation, and make it felt in his anger and in his baptism by water, John also knew that he was not the one who could bring deep change. He was not the one who was able to reach down to the inmost secret sin and bring freedom. John's baptism by water, then, is a symbol, an outward ceremony, a preparation for the reception of Christ's life within. It is not sufficient. John prepared his listeners for the coming fire of Christ's baptism with the Holy Spirit, a powerful fire to be unquenchably warming, searching and regenerating to those who are ready and open.

**Application**

To preach the Gospel of salvation is so much more than telling people of their sins, whether to wrap them up in guilt or to comfort them with the conformity of their lives to socially acceptable norms. We are encouraged into a one-sided view of the coming Lord Jesus in all the social events of Advent – the manger services with children dressed up as sparkling angels, cuddly sheep, caring shepherds, and cute Marys and Josephs; the cosiness of scenes of mulled wine, log fires and warm mince pies; the sentimental indulgence of present giving, especially to children. A complete picture of Advent must include the call to discipleship, the radical challenge of the prophets to the salvation of God, the turning we need in order to be restored, renewed and remade in the love and forgiveness of God, and so to turn our world upside down in his otherness, and with his saving power.

This year, let's not jump ahead too quickly to Christmas and the baby in the manger, but hear and respond to the challenge of the prophets in Advent. The voice of the world in Advent tells us extravagantly to multiply what we and our loved ones have; the voice of the Lord in John the Baptist tells us to divide what we all have and share with those who have not. The voice of the world encourages us into over-indulgence and over-satisfaction of our hunger; the voice of the Lord tells us to satisfy our neighbours' hunger. Why not consider some radical ways in which you and your family can give and share with the poor, whether in your neighbourhood or overseas, this Advent?

*"Joseph, son of David, do not be afraid."*
(Matthew 1:20)

**Illustration**

On 1st December 1955 in Montgomery, Alabama, Rosa Parks broke the law. A young black woman, she refused to give up her seat on the bus to a white man. Rosa Parks knew the law, but she was tired of being treated badly simply because of the colour of her skin, so, despite her fear, she broke the law. Rosa Parks was arrested, tried, found guilty and fined, but her actions raised global awareness of the injustice of racial segregation and effectively catapulted Martin Luther King to the front of the Civil Rights movement.

**Gospel Teaching**

Around two thousand years ago, Joseph, too, defied society's rules by accepting Mary as his wife. They were engaged to be married when Joseph discovered that his bride-to-be was pregnant. The law was very clear. It stated that if evidence of the young woman's virginity was not found, then the men of the village would bring the young woman out to the entrance of her father's house and stone her to death (see Deuteronomy 22:20-21).

But Joseph is described as a good man and he was not prepared to be responsible for any stoning, no matter how he had been wronged. Instead he decided quietly to end the contract between himself and Mary, something that he was required to do by law, since adultery by a woman was considered to be a heinous offence.

But then God took a hand in the story. Joseph had a dream in which an angel told him not to be afraid to take Mary as his wife, for the child she was carrying was from God. When Joseph woke up he obeyed the angel, apparently without a second thought.

It all sounds wonderfully romantic, but the reality was probably quite different. By agreeing to marry Mary, Joseph was voluntarily entering into her disgrace. There are hints in the Gospels that Jesus was always regarded as illegitimate, so the family may have had a difficult life. By agreeing to wed Mary, Joseph was setting himself up as a cuckold. No wonder the angel told him not to be afraid, for fear of public disgrace and ridicule is a powerful motivation.

Yet Joseph never hesitated. When he thought he had heard God speak to him in his dream, he acted immediately. He was commanded to name the child, which was in effect an instruction to bring up the boy as his own son. Joseph was told by God to defy both social convention and the law.

There is a neat postscript to the story. So that we are clear that Jesus was not Joseph's son, we are told that Joseph had no marital relations with Mary until after Jesus was born. So there was no opportunity for Joseph to evade the truth by pretending that perhaps Jesus might have been his. The truth was stark and clear and faced Joseph every time he looked at Jesus.

Interestingly, we are not privy to any of Joseph's words, for he does not speak in the pages of the New Testament. But his actions changed the course of history and enabled Jesus to grow up to be the Son of God. How different life might have been for all of us if Joseph had dismissed his dream. In the first century, the life of a woman alone with a child born out of wedlock would be almost impossible. Jesus would have grown up as an outcast in dire poverty, if he survived at all.

**Application**

It is easy to look back and condemn the attitudes of the past. We can look at Rosa Parks' action on the bus and throw up our hands in horror that black people were treated so badly. We can be shocked that, before his dream, Joseph actually considered getting rid of Mary because of her pregnancy. And we can condemn societies which cast out pregnant girls as not fit for human association. But it is much more difficult to discern the social injustices of our own time.

God still speaks to us today, calling us to Christian action. Sometimes God may call us to move beyond the accepted social conventions of our day to stand against our culture. The call to do this rouses fear in the strongest of us, so we need to remember the angel's words to Joseph, "Joseph, son of David, do not be afraid." Then, like Joseph and like Rosa Parks, we need to trust God and stand up for what we believe to be the right way forward.

*"Mary said, 'Here am I, the servant of the Lord; let it be with me according to your word.'"*
(Luke 1:38)

**Illustration**
Relationships are very delicate things. When they are healthy, they help us to grow in confidence and maturity and they free us to relate better to others, because we know that we are loved and valued. If our important relationships are healthy, we are able to think beyond our own needs and concerns and look to others. However, unhealthy relationships can be very damaging: they can actually make us more selfish and preoccupied with our own little world. They can make us feel very insecure, and insecurity can manifest itself in many different ways.

One of them, and it is a danger in any relationship, is the desire to own the other person, to control them, to possess them and keep them for ourselves. Whether it be a relationship between adults or children, as soon as we cease to treat the other with respect and just see them as an object to satisfy our own needs rather than as persons with needs and concerns of their own, then that relationship becomes unhealthy and damaging for all concerned. We do not love the other person as ourselves, but we are concerned only for ourselves.

**Gospel Teaching**
Today's readings give us an example of a healthy and an unhealthy relationship with God. David has an apparently natural desire to do something for God by building a Temple. But his motives are mixed: a Temple in his capital city would help him consolidate control over his kingdom. He tries to use God for his own political purposes, but God none too gently reminds David of who exactly is in control. We can all be tempted like David. He wanted to use God for his own ends. We, too, want a tame God, a God who doesn't challenge us or ask awkward questions about our lives. We prefer a God who acts as a crutch or support when we need him, but not one who makes us uncomfortable.

Contrast this with Mary. She was engaged to be married, she had her own plans for her future. Her life seemed settled, ordered. Yet she allowed God to enter her life and upset all her own hopes and intentions. This was no easy thing for Mary to accept – she is initially disturbed and confused by

Gabriel's message, and needs the angel to reassure her. She very naturally asks questions – she doesn't understand how what God wants can be done.

But Mary has a healthy relationship with God. She allows God to be a real person in her life, not an object who is there just to make her feel good. She allows her relationship with God to challenge her to grow as a person, to grow into the person God had created her to be. Above all, unlike David, she needs no reminding of who she is and who God is. She doesn't try to make God compromise. She simply acknowledges that she is God's servant: she makes God's will her own, not the other way round. And as she surrenders herself and her will and her whole life to God, so she begins to live the fullness of life that her son, our saviour, came to bring.

**Application**
As the great event of Christ's birth, Christmas, draws near, Mary offers us a timely example of how we can enjoy a healthy relationship with God and what the consequences might be. God will make demands of us because he wants us to grow into the people he has created us to be. He wants us to live life in all its fullness, and he knows how it can be possible. As with Mary, he wants our relationship with him to be life-giving both for ourselves and for others.

We too are offered the opportunity to say "Yes" to God. We too are his servants, we too can surrender ourselves and our lives to God. It may cost us everything, but it is the way to life in all its fullness, because as we surrender ourselves and open our hearts to God, so he will fill us with his love and presence. And God's love can continue to be made real in our world through our relationship with him and with those he gives us to love. That is what our heavenly Father wants for us this Advent.

*"When Elizabeth heard Mary's greeting,*
*the child leapt in her womb."*
(Luke 1:41)

**Illustration**
Greetings are an important part of our life. Every time we meet someone it involves some form of greeting. It may be a handshake, a smile, a wave, a cheery "Hi" or something more formal.

During the past few days or weeks most of us will have been choosing the special greeting which is to accompany each Christmas card we send. In some there will be just a simple line and in others a whole letter detailing the events of our past year. Our greeting depends upon the level of intimacy that we share with the recipient. We save our jokes for people who speak the same kind of language and our formality for those we either do not know so well or who are partially screened from us by status or great age. With friends and those who share our circumstances we can be completely open and free.

But this freedom may be realised in a simple word or phrase. Our language becomes almost a code expressing the secrets we share, full of mysteries which others would not understand or regard as relevant, as they do not know the history or belief which underpins the words. Every communication is important but some have a depth of meaning which speak of the foundations upon which the relationship is built, and, therefore, are a mystery to an outsider.

**Gospel Teaching**
The first chapter of Luke's Gospel is full of greetings. Mary is granted the angel Gabriel's "Greetings, favoured one! The Lord is with you." Zechariah is told: "Do not be afraid... your prayer has been heard." Zechariah is told the mystery of his future son's life in God and his responsibility towards the Messiah. Mary is told the secret of Elizabeth's pregnancy, which no one else knows, as proof of the angel's mission to confirm her own destiny. When she arrived at Elizabeth's door only Elizabeth would have known why her young relation had come. Mary must have known what others did not.

Elizabeth's reaction was immediate and spontaneous. Her own child leaped within her as John recognised the presence of the Lord, whose coming he would foretell. As the Holy Spirit filled Mary at her conception, so it filled Elizabeth, who became a living Pentecost long before Christ's mission was complete. The women shared their blessedness. They were women who shared a mystery. Their sons would change the world, they were utterly united in faith, anxiety, anticipation, trust and hope. Their acknowledgement of the great things which were happening to them would have been in their every touch and sigh, every look and most of all in their awareness of their shared maternity, the children within them, and their determination to brings God's will to fruition. Little wonder that Elizabeth exclaimed her joy at the way in which God shares his goodness with those who wait on him in trust and hope.

**Application**

Cultures which have developed out of religious beliefs often include blessing in their greetings and farewells. "God be with you" has been reduced to "goodbye" and we rarely consider its real meaning when we use it. However our relationships proceed, we always know when a greeting is not well-meant. Mary and Elizabeth recognised each other's worth in their exchanges, they were life-affirming for each other, each acknowledging the other's holiness. Their greetings said much more than "hello".

Perhaps we, too, could try to do the same with those we meet, especially at this special time of exchanging gifts and greetings. This is a good time for renewing true depth and real life-giving in our relationships. There may be people we have forgotten this year who would be warmed by our special remembrance.

Broken relationships we could consider mending, not necessarily by complicated explanations, but by a simple word, a recognition of their value. We might consider ways of exchanging greetings which catch some of Elizabeth's exuberance and blessing. In turn we may find ourselves receiving more than we expected this Christmas. Blessing and joy in the greetings given to us. A greater warmth, a deeper reality in our relationships. Friendships which better mirror the love which God has for us. The affirmation which is part of the gift which the Christ-child brings us in his coming. Reassurance that we are loved and valued so much that God would want to share our lives with us.

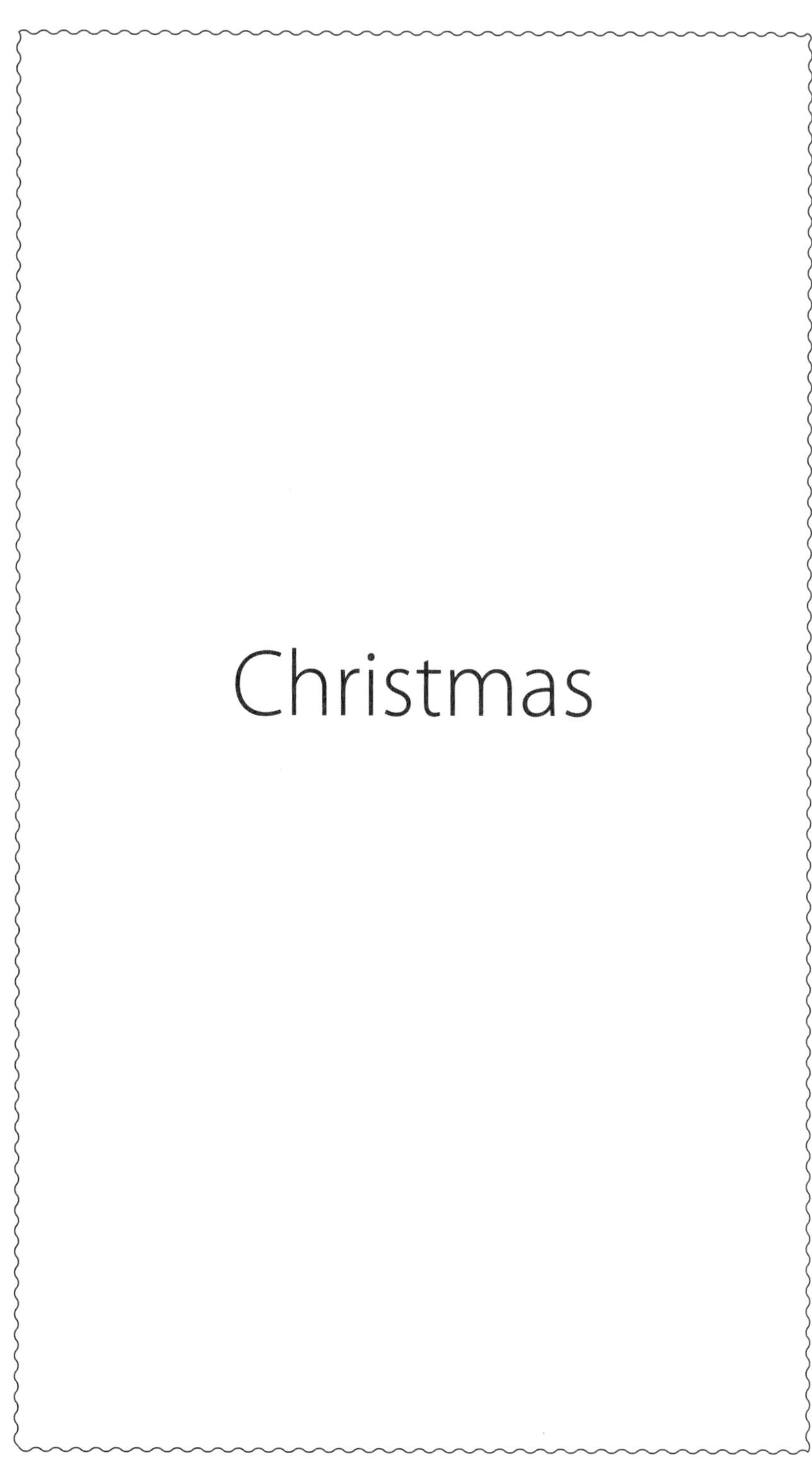

# Christmas

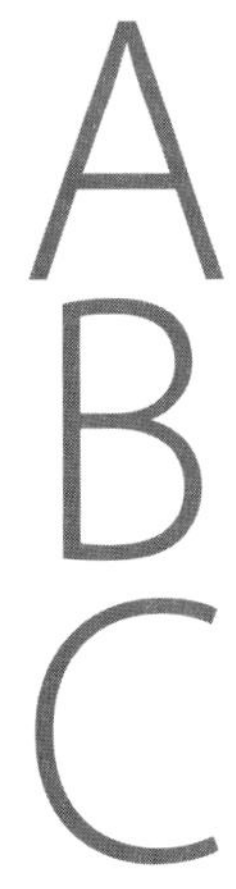



*"I am bringing you good news of great joy for all the people."*
(Luke 2:10)

**Illustration**
Well, here we are. How do you feel just now, I wonder. Is there a warm glow of joyful contentment; a sense of present-opened, turkey-loving satisfaction? Or perhaps there's anxiety over family tensions, or a sense that you never want to see another sprout again? Many of us today will feel a bit of relief, for all sorts of reasons, one of them being that we can at last stop buying things, or feeling the pressure to buy things. After all, we have been subject to a relentless marketing campaign that started sometime in September, and in that time we've spent more money than at any other time of year. It would take a saint to resist.

Marketing is big business these days; it's all about targeting the right people in the right places with techniques and tricks that get ever more sophisticated. One campaign a year or two ago famously sought out the "coolest kid in the playground" in order to give them a computer game console for free. The reasoning was that if the coolest kid had it, then everyone else would want it too. Apparently it didn't work too well, but it was a bold move, that's for sure!

**Gospel Teaching**
What a refreshing change, then, to read of Jesus' birth. While today's experts are finding cleverer and cleverer ways to target the right person in the right place, God targets all the wrong people in the wrong places. Instead of delivering their child among their friends and family, among people who might know a bit about the mysterious circumstances of Jesus' conception, or have heard Mary tell of what the angel said, Mary and Joseph have to deliver the saviour of the world in a town that they don't know, in an anonymous inn, among people who haven't a clue that the one that all Israel has waited for for centuries is tucked up in an animal-food trough next door. It's true that this unexpected journey to the town of Jesus' ancestors fulfilled the Old Testament prophecies and would ultimately help to cement his messianic credentials, but at this early stage, it doesn't look too good.

And the shepherds. Really, not a good choice for spreading the word. Shepherds were right at the bottom of the pile – the lowest of the low; definitely not the coolest kids in the playground. Not much chance of anyone wanting to believe or copy them. But God tells the greatest news that ever was, accompanied by angel choirs and celestial fireworks, right out in the fields where no one will see but a bunch of people no one will listen to. They'll just think they've been on the moonshine again. But then again, who better to tell than those who really need to hear the message: "goodwill and peace to all people; yes, you". The news of who Jesus was and what he was to mean to everyone didn't come to fruition for many years, but perhaps God did know what he was doing after all.

It tells what we really need to hear. As events started to unfold all those years ago in Bethlehem it didn't matter that, in terms of spreading the news, it was all in the wrong place and to the wrong people. God's concern was for those who were completely insignificant in everyday life. In God's eyes, the right people were the wrong ones. It just goes to show what kind of God we have: one who treasures the unloved, values the disregarded, listens to the lonely, lavishes attention on the ordinary and unsuccessful. This was the good news, and this is what the season of goodwill is all about.

**Application**

So as we enjoy the climax of that season of goodwill, and as we sit back a little and anticipate the adverts for summer holidays that will kick in about now, let's shake off for a moment all that advertising, all that marketing, and revel in the love of a God who sees the value in the most unvaluable people, and who is willing to spend the resources of heaven on bringing us close to him again, even if it's not good business. OK, so we've bought a lot of things. So be it. Let's enjoy the gifts given and received for what they are: not the fruit of a marketing campaign, but a symbol of another gift – a child born in a strange place, with just his mum and dad and a few shepherds who knew who he was – the greatest gift of all.

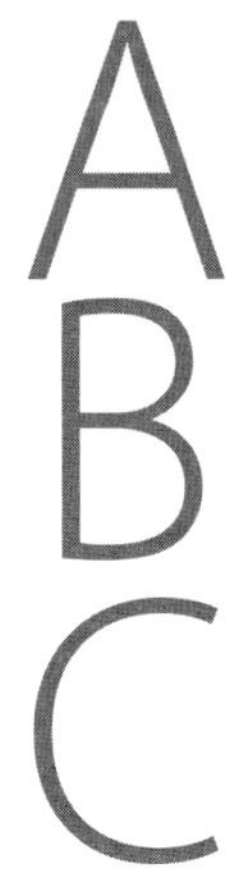



*"They went with haste and found Mary and Joseph, and the child lying in a manger."*
(Luke 2:16)

**Illustration**

There has been a great deal to do in getting ready for today. There has been much making of lists, much buying or making of Christmas presents, much buying, writing and sending cards, much organising. There have been Christmas plays at school or church, carols to sing and parties to go to.

And for many of us, after a while, as the day gets closer we begin to feel certain that we will never be ready for it. Or that if we are ready, we will be far too tired to enjoy it! And perhaps you are sitting here today, wondering if you have put the turkey in the oven at the right temperature, or worrying about the family dynamics of the day ahead. Or maybe you are so excited about all the presents under the tree that you can't wait to get out of church and back home to unwrap them. Or perhaps it is all over already – presents were opened before breakfast, and some are already broken or spoiled. Perhaps already there is a feeling of disappointment, a nagging disillusionment that this day is not as special as you had hoped.

**Gospel Teaching**

The shepherds of our Gospel reading were not expecting anything special. For them it was a cold, ordinary night. We know little about them. We are told they were keeping watch over their flock, but we do not know how diligently they were doing so. They may even have been doing the equivalent of sitting with their feet up, reading the paper. We have no reason to think they were deep in prayer. So why were they chosen by God to be given the honour of being the first people to be told the news of Christ's birth?

The truth is that God came to the world just as it was. He did not wait for it to be good enough or clean enough or holy enough. He shone his glory into the ordinariness of a day's work. Can you imagine all the angels of heaven bursting into your office? Or into your kitchen? How would you feel? "There is no need to be afraid," sang the angels. This is good news – the Messiah is here.

We do not know for how long those shepherds stood rubbing their eyes and staring into the sky after the angels had left them. They must have been grateful for each other – if the experience had happened to only one of them he might have considered it no more than a dream, and done nothing about it. As it was they left their sheep and rushed to find the stable where the newborn baby was, watched over by his young mother.

We have heard the story so often that we can forget its enormous impact. What was in the hearts and minds of the shepherds when they found everything was just as the angels had said? Perhaps a slow dawning that something life-changing and world-changing had really happened, even if they didn't fully understand what it was. As they stood in that stable, wearing their smelly work-clothes, faces shining with sweat from the exertion of getting there, they met with God. They told the baby's very young mother about the angels – and perhaps she needed that reassurance. She had just given birth for the first time, far away from her home and her family, in a dirty stable. Perhaps she wondered where God was in it all, and feared that things were not going the right way. The visit from the shepherds, and their message from the angels, would have reassured and comforted her at such a vulnerable time.

**Application**

You may not feel ready to meet God. You may not even have felt ready for today. The message of Christmas is that God, out of his great kindness, meets you where you are. You do not have to go somewhere special to find him. He knows who you are and he knows what you need. He is much more interested in the openness of your heart to him than he is in the tidiness of your house or the quality of your Christmas dinner. Let us invite him today into our ordinary lives, and let us pray that we may have the simple faith of the shepherds, the quiet trust of Mary and Joseph – and may we also know that same capacity for joy and wonder.

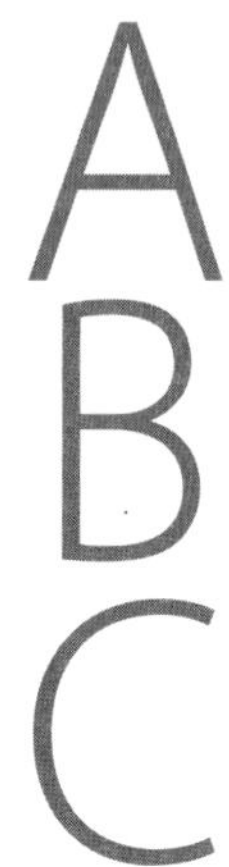



*"In the beginning was the Word, and the Word was with God, and the Word was God."*
(John 1:1)

**Illustration**
Van Gogh once wrote of seeing eternity in the sleeping, rested face of a child. But watch a child's face when awake – and not just in the excitement of Christmas morning! Words are often neither possible nor necessary for the myriad feelings of joy and hurt expressed in a child's face. She has not yet learnt to cover up and mask the power of her feelings, the flow of her thoughts, her joyful delight and her simple trust. Images of children's faces speak to us of fresh beauty and trusting innocence, whilst the sad, needy, tear-stained face of a child can break a heart, and encourage our response to reach out.

But if the faces of children can be powerfully expressive, so too can their words. It is enchanting to watch the young child as words start to come alive in her imagination. As we watch a child dance to sung words, act out poetry, become enthralled in a good story, listen wholeheartedly to an adventure or learn from a leading character, we see the power of words. And then, as the growing child exercises her mastery of words in discussing and analysing the plot, or finds the world opening up through learning other languages and other ways of communicating, we are reminded of how exciting speech is. We see words come alive, sometimes in ways we never knew, or had forgotten we knew. We can become so inured to words that we forget their magic. To watch a child's face as she comes to some new understanding, some first new steps towards faith, is beautiful.

**Gospel Teaching**
Human language and the limitations of our thought make even the inspired writing of John difficult fully to grasp in these few words which lay out the divine mystery for us again today. The mystery that God speaks today is the Word of God, revealing the eternal thoughts and being of God. That Word is Jesus, the true light and life for the world.

Just as we learn that words express our thoughts and ourselves, so we learn that Jesus, as God's Word made fully human with us, expresses God's nature and God's thoughts towards creation and all humanity. The eternal God has been revealed in the eternal Son, Jesus, the one who completely expresses all that God is to us. The love, power and wisdom of God are now revealed – it is as if the thought has become visible through Jesus, God's communication, and God's activity and presence in the world are now known as clearly as all is known in the light. As the one sent of God, reflecting the imprint of God's very being, Jesus makes known all the beauty of creation, of God's power, peace and love.

These abstract words about God begin to make sense when and as we look into the face of Jesus, who reveals to us, in his humanity and divinity, more clearly than we yet know or can express ourselves, that God is with us.

**Application**

Jesus, as God's Word to us and the world, reveals who God is, as the Holy Spirit reveals God's meaning, presence and thoughts towards and within us.

We pray, as we share in the words of our liturgy every week around the world, that we all may become more like Jesus, reflect more and more of the life and love of God's Son in our world, in our families and communities, in our personalities, conversations and activities. We also pray that our Church may speak words of truth, and communicate through lives that show the oneness of her being.

We fail and sin, but the Word remains the Word, remains the revealer of God and remains with us. Jesus is God's Word and reveals the Father's heart, presence and grace, but because he is also God's Word spoken in our human form, Jesus also knows us in all our humanity, and understands us perfectly, however we may be feeling, today, now, tomorrow, or any time. Whether we are happy or sad, surrounded by friends and family or feeling alone, celebrating or remembering, the birth of God's Son today reminds us that we are blessed always to have such a companion, such a friend.

To know and be known by love's Word and love's companion through all of life is the offer of the one born today for us, the gift which God has given us. God's Word – God with us, today and always.

*"So that what had been spoken through the prophets might be fulfilled."*
(Matthew 2:23)

**Illustration**
Good news for Librans – you can expect improved relationships next year; while Scorpios, you will be glad to hear, will receive pay rises. Meanwhile Capricorns will be heading up the career ladder, Aquarians will find the answers to their nagging questions, and Sagittarians are advised to exercise caution around their loved ones.

These rather sweeping generalisations are taken from a popular astrology website. Many famous people, including Ronald Reagan, Adolf Hitler, Winston Churchill, Princess Diana and the actress Shirley MacLaine, are said to have sought advice from astrologers – who were hopefully at least more convincing than the website. According to Marco Polo, Kubla Khan had no fewer than five thousand court astrologers, many trying to predict the weather, all living in fear for their lives if they got it wrong. The many newspaper column inches devoted to astrology forecasts are testament to its wide appeal.

Then again, you might think that the spoof predictions of UK astrologer Psychic Smith, writing in a weekly paper, make more sense, such as one in which he predicted his own demise: "The coincidence of Pluto's entry into Capricorn with an urgent heads of department meeting means I'm going to get sacked. Unthinkable, I know. But give it a fortnight and see if I'm not right." And of course he was.

**Gospel Teaching**
When you hear today's reading from Matthew's Gospel you could be forgiven for thinking that Mary, Joseph and the infant Jesus are being sent on a wild goose chase in order to fulfil ancient prophecy. It's almost as though they are pawns in a kind of divine chess game. You might think that the prophets were irresponsible and should have been more careful in their predictions. Perhaps, if it had been prophesied that Jesus would have an unadventurous infancy, none of this would have had to have happened.

You might also wonder why it matters that Jesus was raised in Nazareth. Is it God's way of proving his existence – to give the power of prediction

to the prophets and then fulfil their prophecies? However we look at it, perhaps we ought to admit that it's a puzzle. And it becomes downright sinister when you read the chilling story of what is sometimes called "the slaughter of the innocents". It's hardly surprising that this is a particularly controversial Bible passage. For one thing, there is the matter of who's to blame. If Herod were simply fulfilling his destiny, then he could hardly be held accountable for his actions. Yet it was an appalling act, one which surely must be condemned.

Some scholars turn to the history books and archaeological records, and say that there is not a shred of evidence of an actual killing of children, while other people try to demonstrate that each and every word of scripture is incontrovertible, divinely inspired truth. But can we seriously believe that it was part of God's plan that every baby in and around Bethlehem should die in order to fulfil a prophecy? What's more, the babies died pointlessly, even by Herod's warped standards, since Jesus and his family had already fled the area.

**Application**
Where does your destiny lie? Is it in the position of the sun, the moon and the stars? Is it perhaps in the tea leaves at the bottom of your teacup, or in the lines on the palm of your hand? Can you see what the future holds in a crystal ball, or through a tarot card reading? In such an uncertain world it is hardly surprising that we are desperate to know what lies ahead for us. But surely we want to believe in free will, for if we did not, what would be the point of getting out of bed each morning?

We can tie ourselves up in knots thinking about how and why ancient prophecies might have been fulfilled through the coming of the Messiah, but ultimately we will always be foiled in our puny attempts to unravel God's mysteries. For God alone holds the key to the future and we simply cannot know how and why. What the prophets knew and whether the Gospel writer painted an accurate picture – the answers are also hidden from us.

But this is not by any means bad news. On the contrary, we should be able to relax into trust. We don't need horoscopes or tarot cards, for the wonderful truth, the only truth that we need, is that we really have no choice but to trust our future to God.

*"But Mary treasured all these words and pondered them in her heart."*
(Luke 2:19)

**Illustration**
Are you one of those people who like to read the end of a book first, just to check out that you want to bother with the whole thing? Or are you one of those people who is tempted to throw your book at the person who interrupts your reading with "Can you believe that the butler did it?", and would never take a premature peek at the last page?

The thing is, that with the Christmas story, we know the ending, whether that would be our usual preference or not. We know it very, very well. And we know that with all its twists and turns, it is a happy one: the anticipation of Christmas is followed by the drama and joy of Easter. It's a sure thing.

**Gospel Teaching**
But for people who were in the first Christmas story all those years ago, there was no such certainty. To be sure, there were lots of hints at things to come: messengers from God, prophetic utterances; shepherds rushing off the fields to tell of an angelic choir singing that the saviour is born. Indeed, it says that the people of the day were suitably impressed.

But if the truth be told, there were still an awful lot of gaps in the picture, and plenty of ambiguity. People still argued about what the signs meant, or disagreed about the interpretation of the prophetic utterances, or just didn't notice what was going on at all.

All that ambiguity has its effect on Mary, and is encapsulated in those few words that describe Mary's response to the whole thing. Everyone else is amazed, but Mary is more thoughtful: "But Mary treasured all these words and pondered them in her heart."

What was she thinking? What did it mean to bear God's child? How will Joseph cope with this child? What did it mean that he would be called the Son of the Most High? Or that he would inherit the throne of his ancestor David? What does it mean to be Good News to all people? To be the Messiah? All these can mean so many things. And how do you bring up a child like this? Can you tell him off? Can you tell him anything?

What sort of career should he be steered into? Military training, a trade, scholarship? Will he be an outlaw; will he operate inside the system or outside of it? Will he be hurt? Will his family be hurt? Really, there's so much left unanswered, so much that is unclear about the way ahead. No wonder it says "but Mary".

There are quite a lot of "buts", quite a lot to treasure up and think about. It would seem that despite the clear and miraculous interventions in the day-to-day lives of this little community in Palestine, an awful lot was to be left to the humans involved. And that seems to be part of God's plan: the way that the story of salvation is woven with the story of humankind.

**Application**

Over the last few weeks, we have celebrated a familiar, well-worn and much-loved story. But let's take some time to stand in the shoes of those who didn't know how it would all work out, and who had only their faith to help them put together the pieces of the heavenly jigsaw that was being laid out before them. Often our own lives are a jumble of such pieces – some moments of great clarity, answers to prayer, signs from God and words of instruction.

But let's face it, these moments of certainty can be rather rare, and there are a lot of questions unanswered and uncertainties to face. And there always seems to be an awful lot of just getting on with it. But this is a great privilege. Rather than tie everything up with spiritual certainties, God gives us the space we need to allow the Christian story to unfold for each one of us.

We have been enriched by the story of Christmas as it has been retold. But there is space too to follow Mary's example and ponder not just the wonderful gifts God has given us, but the questions and uncertainties that those things raise. What does it mean, for each of us, here and now, to be a legacy of the Christmas child? We know the ending in a way, and it's a happy one, but there's so much to play for. It's exciting and it's rather scary, but it's our chance to take part in the greatest story ever told.

*"And all who heard him were amazed at his understanding and his answers."*

(Luke 2:47)

**Illustration**

Imagine that you are in a great cathedral, like Canterbury, admiring the architecture, reading about its history and soaking in the atmosphere of prayer which has evolved over centuries. Suddenly you come across a group of people obviously having a lively debate. You want to find out who they are and what they're talking about. You recognise the dean of the cathedral; the man in the purple shirt and dog collar is clearly a bishop; and all the others look very wise and knowing and, look, is that the archbishop himself approaching with speed and great excitement? At the centre is a boy, about twelve years old, firing questions at the older men and women about deep theological issues: the doctrine of the Trinity, transubstantiation, and the exact translation of a hard passage in the Bible. You realise this is no ordinary twelve-year-old, but who is he?

**Gospel Teaching**

Who is this boy? Jesus, aged twelve, is in the Temple in Jerusalem discussing religion with Jewish leaders and showing such knowledge and understanding that all who hear him are amazed. Later the question will be, "who is this man?" as all who hear Jesus continue to be amazed at his knowledge and authority.

For now, though, we're hearing about Jesus at the age of twelve, yet only a few days ago we were celebrating his birth. What's been happening in those years about which we know so very little?

It seems that Jesus has been developing a sense of who he is and of his special relationship with the God he will call "Abba". He has been acquiring knowledge and understanding of the scriptures. And now he's enjoying this opportunity to learn from others and discuss his own ideas and ask questions.

Just as we know so little about his first twelve years, so too we have very little information about the next eighteen years until he is thirty and embarks on his public ministry. What was happening during those years?

We are told that he grew in wisdom and perhaps he used this time to work out his own interpretation of the Law until he had a solid foundation on which to build that public life and ministry. The foundation that Jesus laid for himself was perhaps the summary of the Law which we hear him declare in the Gospels:

> "Hear O Israel, the Lord our God is the only Lord.
> You shall love the Lord your God
> with all your heart,
> with all your soul,
> with all your mind,
> and with all your strength…"
>
> "Love your neighbour as yourself."

"There is no other commandment greater than these," says Jesus. "On these two commandments hang all the law and the prophets."

**Application**

This is a time of resolutions and new beginnings: a chance to reflect on what it means for us to live out our faith.

Paul too thought through his faith and what it meant to live it out in the world. When he wrote to the Colossians he suggested ways in which we would live if we truly loved our neighbour as ourselves.

Loving our neighbour may sound straightforward, but the illustrations Paul offers show that it presents a challenge to us to rethink how we relate to people.

Loving our neighbour means showing compassion – compassion to people suffering through their own fault or who have shown no compassion for others. It means being kind – kind to everyone, not just those who are grateful and appreciative. It means being patient – patient when every fibre of your being is screaming out for action or change. It means forgiving others – forgiving even those we said we would never forgive.

Living out the commandments is not easy. Living the Christian faith requires commitment, discipline and a willingness to learn and grow.

It may sound daunting, but we are not required to do this on our own. As we seek to love God and our neighbour (and perhaps ourselves) we are in fellowship with others on the journey. We can learn from each other, share with and encourage one another.

Today is exciting. It's a day of new beginnings, the start of a new adventure. We can stay where we are, not wanting to risk the unknown. Or, like Jesus in the Temple, we can step forward, thinking, asking questions, exploring ideas, willing to change and grow. As we do so, we know that Emmanuel, God with us, is our companion on the journey.

*"And the Word became flesh and lived among us, and we have seen his glory, the glory as of a father's only son, full of grace and truth."*
(John 1:14)

**Illustration**

The kneeler Rosemary had made was wonderful. The rich, warm-coloured threads really brought the pattern to life. And the cross, and the script, "Glory to God in the Highest", stood out so clearly, just as she had intended. Yes, it had been a fulfilling task and she had so enjoyed doing it. It was a job well done, even though she said it herself. Her friends said much the same. Rosemary's church had plenty of colourful kneelers, all made by worshippers and other friends of the church, but, by general consensus, Rosemary's new kneeler was something special.

The attention it aroused caused her to recall the very day she had started the project. Her granddaughter had been visiting, and was very taken with what Grandma was about to use: the plain canvas backing, the lovely design Rosemary had sketched as the pattern for this kneeler and, alongside them, as yet untouched, the twists of brightly coloured thread. And now, here they were, all come together to create this wonderful picture.

**Gospel Teaching**

The opening section of John's Gospel is, perhaps, one of the greatest pieces of Christian writing ever crafted. In it are woven great themes: life and light, creation and glory, grace and truth, Christ human and Christ divine, woven like the richest threads into a wonderfully vivid tapestry, the most gifted piece of needlework ever.

The "Word" – we could almost say "thread" – which created the universe has taken human form in order to reveal God, and reveal his love and his purpose, to the world. In this passage John brilliantly tells us that Jesus, the "Word", was in the very beginning and yet is also eternal, everlasting. He affirms that from the beginning Jesus is the source of life and light for people everywhere, in every place and every generation, for you and for me, in this world and the next.

**Application**

It wouldn't be Christmas, would it, without a reading of the opening of St John's Gospel? Its beauty and splendour create a real sense of awe and

wonder, through which John unveils the "Word" – Jesus – so that we may all understand him better and come within his firm loving embrace. John makes clear that Jesus, the "Word", was in the very beginning with God, and that he is the source of life and light for all people everywhere, of every age – "all things came into being through him".

At Christmastime we rejoice in his coming to us as the baby born at Bethlehem, God-on-earth. Here, at the beginning of his earthly life, we see the blank piece of tapestry canvas. Then as we walk with Jesus, witness his ministry and hear his teaching, those coloured threads are woven revealingly into the tapestry. The tapestry takes shape, the picture becomes clearer. We begin to see who Jesus is, and why he has come to us. He is love, God's love, and comes to bring us that love.

In his teaching, in his care and concern for all people, in his holding out his arms to the outcast, in his healing of body, mind and spirit, in his love which knows no limits we see God in action, God-on-earth. Here are the threads.

And when those threads are woven together in, through and by Jesus we see the completed tapestry in all its glory. We see Jesus as he truly is, the Son of God, human and divine. We see – and begin to understand – his grace and his glory, the grace and glory of the cross, the grace and glory of his obedience to God's will and of his love, demonstrated in self-sacrifice.

"He was in the world… yet the world knew him not," John says. Do we really know him? Do we recognise him, in everyone, in every place, in all we are, and in all we do, here, now? The wonderful warmth, humanity and joy of the Christmas story helps us, inspires us, to see Christ – and his glory – everywhere and in everyone. Then do we truly begin to see God, and see the whole rich, wonderful, magnificent tapestry, from the crib to the cross.

And we are threads, part of the tapestry. We are called to add to its richness and vibrancy. What better time could there be for us to weave ourselves with our Lord Jesus? What time could be better than now, when we celebrate again the start of the earthly life of Jesus, the "Word", God-on-earth?

*"No one has ever seen God. It is God the only Son, who is close to the Father's heart, who has made him known."*
(John 1:18)

**Illustration**

Airports are the best places for "people-watching": all the comings and goings of the people of all nations and all ages. We can watch other people's greetings and homecomings with as much excitement as if we were personal friends. If a family is waiting with a huge "welcome home" banner, we can watch with real delight when the person they are waiting for comes through the arrivals gate and is embraced, even if we know nothing about their story. Who they were waiting for, why she had been away, how long – we don't need to know any of that to be thrilled by her obvious homecoming.

Or if you've ever seen a mother at an airport, collecting her children from the stewardess who has shepherded them on their flight, you'll see the smiles of satisfaction on all the faces around, as though they, too, had been reunited with their own children. The stewardess may have to do her job and ask for identification before she hands the children over, but really the faces of the mother and the children are the proper identification.

**Gospel Teaching**

In the opening verses of this Gospel, much would have startled John's contemporaries. Whether their picture of God came primarily from the Old Testament, or from the Greek culture that they lived in, they would have assumed that the divine being is mysterious, transcendent, largely beyond human knowledge and completely beyond human sight.

They knew the story of events on Mount Sinai and they knew that even Moses, God's much-loved leader who so longed to see God's glory, could hardly bear to see God's face. And when he had been speaking with God, Moses' ordinary human face became too bright for the people to look at. They certainly understood that no one could see God and live. And yet John now writes of having seen his glory. Moses and his people learnt of God's steadfast love and faithfulness. Now John writes of all this and more as the Son's glory. The law was given through Moses. Now John portrays God's grace and truth coming through the Son, Jesus Christ.

John is encouraging a new vision of life as God's people gathered into and filled with grace through Jesus. God's grace, forgiveness and power to live truthfully were now not just characteristic of God, but also of God's people. And the special activity of grace is to gather up all creation into life close to the Father's heart. All life: all memory, imagination and desire; all failure, wrong and ugliness; all that truly is. In the only Son, grace is seen as a homecoming to newness, beauty, strength, truth, a joyous growing into who we are in Christ. Grace shows us a past that needs repentance; it gives us a present that knows and lives in renewed and renewing love and is seen in reconciled relationships, and a future where, in God's Spirit, we become receivers and transmitters of the gift of grace. The gracious gift of homecoming is transforming, re-creating and strengthening – a gift made available and relevant to every human situation.

**Application**

What do grace and truth look like? It is God's grace that opens our eyes and hearts to glimpses of God's activity in life around us. The recognition of loving joy at airport welcomes is just such a glimpse, recognised by us because we recognise our own responses in those of others. In our lives, grace is seen in receiving repentance and the gift of forgiveness, the receiving of a child and the giving of a parent, the gathering embrace of people coming back together, the homecoming. Grace and truth are seen in the smallest protest against any poverty in our world which so many know as a place of loss, lies and namelessness. Grace and truth are our God-given gifts of life, given for us to give to others.

And, just as we all know in some part the loss and loneliness of our world, so we all long for the life of grace and truth, for the homecoming that God has for us. Airport scenes of welcome may bring tears to our own eyes, and imagining soap-opera lives of adventure and romance may mean we miss normal everyday truths. God opens opportunities to give and receive grace, to know and live in truth, and to be welcomed and gathered into those moments as we recognise the one who is waiting for us, offering all that there is, the one who sees the only Son in us.

*"The world did not know him."*
(John 1:10)

**Illustration**
One of the most striking, imaginative and moving memorials in the splendour of Westminster Abbey in London is the tomb of the unknown warrior. Westminster Abbey is the burial place of royalty, of politicians and poets, of people who have shaped their society and been thought worthy to lie in this hallowed ground. And there, right at the main door, is the unknown soldier, killed in the battlefield of the First World War. We don't know his name, or where he died, and it is important that we don't, because that way he holds the symbol for every soldier killed in every war.

**Gospel Teaching**
In today's Gospel reading, St John speaks of another unknown warrior – Jesus. Jesus comes to live, unknown, unrecognised, among his people, to save them. Like the unknown warrior in Westminster Abbey, he symbolises the human race.

But the bitterly ironic thing about this unknown human symbol, according to St John's Gospel, is that few people seem to know what it stands for, even with John the Baptist standing there shouting out his witness to Jesus.

John tells us with complete clarity exactly who Jesus is. In Mark's Gospel, we meet the human Jesus first, and we have to work out who he is as we follow him through the pages of the Gospel. Matthew and Luke do start with angelic messengers, making it clear what we are dealing with here, but they start the story with the birth of Jesus. John alone puts what is going to happen into the perspective of eternity.

The theme of choice runs through the whole of John's Gospel. Every person who meets Jesus must choose for him or against him, for the light or the dark. They do not, of course, all realise that that is the choice they are making. Those who reject Jesus do not realise that they are rejecting the maker and saviour of the world.

But they do know that they are rejecting a fellow human being, one who is good and truthful and who speaks for a new relationship between human beings, and a new relationship with God. They do know what this human being symbolises, at least to some extent, and that is what they reject. They reject any redefinition of human beings. They choose to keep the old ordering of humanity, where the rich win, where the poor and the sick and the vulnerable are of no importance, where God agrees with the powerful. They reject the vision of humanity that is offered in Jesus.

**Application**

The people who met the earthly Jesus met another human being. How could they possibly know he was also the presence and action of God? How can St John possibly blame them for not recognising the life and light of the universe in this man?

So part of what we decide when we choose to be for Jesus or against is what kind of a world we think it is. Jesus, the unknown human being, is prepared to stand with all ordinary human beings and see how people value him. He is prepared to be misunderstood, reviled, hated, killed, as well as loved, honoured, obeyed and understood. He is prepared to be the symbol for the whole of humanity, to live as we live, die as we die.

If people had known how important Jesus was, they might have gone out of their way to get on his good side. But because he was just an unknown human being, they treated him according to their own natures and purposes. They showed their true selves, kind or unkind, prepared to see into the depths of things, or preferring superficiality. All of this, Jesus called out of people, just by being a symbol of all human beings, known and unknown.

So we who do know who Jesus is now have a vital key to the world. It is not that we have cleverly found out that he is really important and so ensured positions of power and status for ourselves. Instead, we have learned that God values human life – every human life – so enormously that he is prepared to live, unrecognised, the life of an unknown human being in order to bring God's own life into contact with humanity.

That means that we now know how to value human life, too. Jesus is the well-known human being in whom every unknown human life is symbolised, and so made precious.

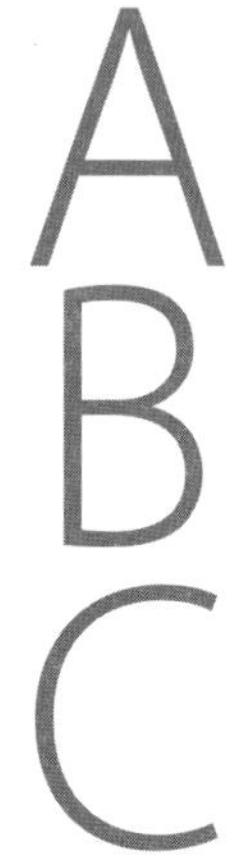



*"Where is the child who has been born king of the Jews?"*
(Matthew 2:2)

**Illustration**

How is it that sometimes someone else can see things so much more clearly than we can? Whether it is that we are looking for a place on a map or perhaps a product on a supermarket shelf, we can look and look and yet somehow it eludes us. We know it's there somewhere – or at least it usually is – but we just can't see the wood for the trees. And then, to our embarrassment and (ahem!) gratitude, someone else saunters up and picks out the elusive item without so much as a second glance.

**Gospel Teaching**

The magi – the wise men – play something of this role in Matthew's version of the birth of Jesus. In Luke's version, it is the shepherds who are the first to witness to the birth of Jesus. The little people – people who were always there, but not much noticed by anyone. In Matthew, it is the magi who recognise Jesus for who he is. People who were rich and important, but also outsiders and strangers. The last people you would have expected to know about the birth of a Messiah, let alone travel the world to find him and pay homage.

Matthew contrasts these well-travelled, well-informed strangers with the person who should have seen who Jesus was, but didn't – Herod. As the leader of a people who longed for a Messiah, he should have been the first to know that the new king had been born, and the first to pay him homage. But Herod doesn't see what is under his own nose. Not only is he ill-informed about the existence and whereabouts of the new king, he is frightened and threatened by the news that his strange visitors bring. If the magi were puzzled that Herod did not rush himself to see the new king, we do not know. What we do know is that they continued on their way, and, to their great joy, found what they were looking for.

Again, the differences from Luke's story are important. Luke has Mary and Joseph travel to Bethlehem because of a Roman census, and the shepherds witness a recent birth in temporary accommodation. In Matthew's account, Mary and Joseph are at their own home in Bethlehem. Jesus could be anything up to two years of age (we can guess this from Herod's order to kill the children aged two and under). There is none of the wonder of a new birth – it is just an ordinary, everyday scene. Apart, that is, from the well-travelled strangers bearing kingly gifts. What the magi did not find in Herod's throne room, they find in an ordinary house among ordinary people – the true king of Israel.

By rights it should have been different. The king of Israel should have been seen and recognised and worshipped by his own people, but, for one reason or another, it took a group of outsiders to respond to a strange sign and travel from a distant country to find what they could not, surely, have expected: the one king, the true Messiah, living unrecognised among his people.

**Application**

Whether it is in a situation that is fairly trivial – like the supermarket – or one that is desperately important, we all know what it's like to lose sight of what really matters, and to struggle to see the wood for the trees. It could be that we need a new way to look at a familiar situation, or a creative solution to a problem that threatens to overwhelm us. Whichever it is, we need to find Christ in the situation. We need the insight of the magi – a fresh pair of eyes to look at the problem and to provide a different perspective.

For some of us, we may actually need a different pair of eyes to see an answer – we may need to ask for help from a friend or a professional. For others, it may be that what we need is a break. It's not just coincidence that this is the time of year when the holiday brochures drop through our doors. It may be simply about making some space – a retreat perhaps – or an hour of quiet to think about something else. Whatever the right thing for each one of us, Matthew's message for us is that hope is there, right in the midst of us. We just need the eyes to see it.

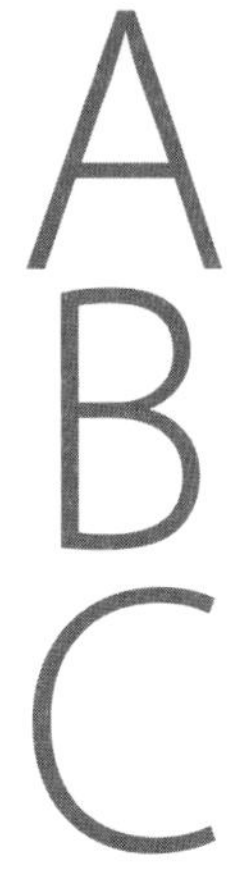



*"When King Herod heard this, he was frightened."*
(Matthew 2:3)

**Illustration**

All mothers are afraid. Fear goes with the territory. As soon as the baby is put in your arms, tiny, helpless, dependent, you know that fear is going to be your constant companion from now on. There is so much that can harm them. Some dangers you can protect them from. But there are illnesses, and accidents, and after a while they grow up and leave home and then they are out there, somewhere, doing who knows what, putting their precious bodies in the way of danger. Always, fear lurks at the back of the maternal mind.

**Gospel Teaching**

This mother is no different. First-century Palestine is not the best time and place for a child to be born. Many do not survive. Illness takes some, poverty others. Living under occupation poses its own dangers. This mother has good reason to be afraid for her baby. But here there is extra reason for fear. There is something special about this child, something provoking. This child is not going to live a quiet life out of harm's way, as every mother wishes. This child is going to get himself into trouble.

Already there are signs. The visitors, for example. It is normal, of course, for there to be visitors when there is a new baby in the house. Mothers do not always welcome them. They need time alone to get to know their new child. But still, it is natural for grandparents, aunties and uncles, friends and neighbours, to call in, wet the baby's head, bring gifts and good wishes. It is expected. But this baby receives unexpected visitors, strange and alarming. They are magi from eastern lands, they say, astrologers, scholars of the sky and the stars, of signs and portents. They have seen something in the heavens. They know that a king has been born, and they have come to bow before him. The signs have led them to this place, to this peasant baby and his frightened mother.

On the way, they have met another frightened person. Not a mother, but a king, and one who has seen a threat. The magi have gone first, not so wisely it turns out, to the royal palace to look for their newborn king. There they have met a tyrant, a weak and foolish king, who knows how tenuous is his hold on power, and lives in constant fear of the next rebellion, the next death threat, the poisoner in the corner, the stab in the dark.

The magi bring news of a replacement, perhaps a member of another branch of the family that claims to be royal, perhaps, perish the thought, a descendant of King David, ready to grow up and claim the old kingship, claim to be God's anointed, the Messiah. Yes, Herod is afraid, and fear breeds cunning, and violence. He will find the child, and will kill him, and the magi will unwittingly help.

The magi go on their way, and find the baby. They bring their strange gifts, not things for a baby, but symbols, of royalty, priesthood and death. The child's mother gazes at them, and wishes for a rattle and some flowers, safe and normal gifts. But in her heart of hearts she knows that nothing will ever be normal again. She is afraid, but in her fear there is also thrill. There is new life in the world, and anything could happen.

**Application**

Today the Church remembers the visit of the magi and proclaims Jesus as the "light to lighten the Gentiles". We are in a dark time of the year, and look forward to the return of light mornings and evenings. But light is not always benign. Bright light can blind. Intense light can slice through steel. Christ the light illumines and warms, but also judges. His coming brings fear. Herod is right to be afraid. He will have his day of slaughter, but he will not snuff out the light. This is no gentle glow, but a passionate fire that burns the cruel.

The baby receiving the strange visitors with the prophetic gifts will one day be killed by the fear he generates, but even then the light will not be snuffed out. For those who recognise and follow him, fear is mixed with a thrill of excitement. The light will burn eyes and hearts, it will drive out darkness and evil, and reveal God's truth.

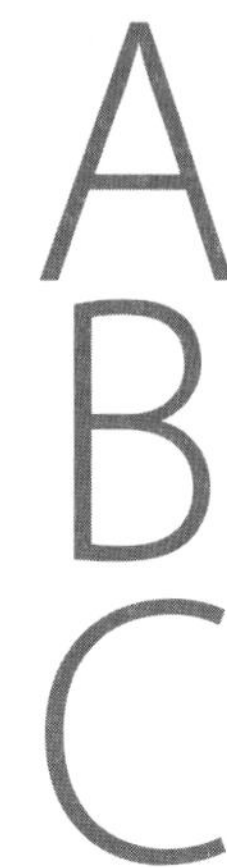



*"When they saw that the star had stopped, they were overwhelmed with joy."*
(Matthew 2:10)

**Illustration**

Iona Abbey is an imposing sight. This restored monastic building rises up on the remote Scottish island site where St Columba established a missionary community in the sixth century. Today it is a focus for the Iona Community, an ecumenical Christian community that actively links over two thousand Christians worldwide. Many pilgrims and visitors journey to this remote Scottish island, which is only accessible by a foot-passenger ferry running across the Sound from the nearby Isle of Mull.

One traveller was curious about how the locals regarded this spiritual landmark in their midst. He asked the ferryman what he thought about the abbey. "I don't know," was the reply. "I've never been." His listener was astounded. The ferryman had operated the service for over thirty years. Yet he had never walked the 150 yards or so from the landing place to see for himself the abbey that many of his passengers had come from so far away to visit.

**Gospel Teaching**

The good news was on their doorstep, yet they were unmoved. The most respected religious authorities in royal Jerusalem could quote prophecies foretelling the Messiah's birth in Bethlehem, just five miles down the road. Yet when learned strangers from distant realms appeared, speaking of significant sights in the heavens that pointed to a king's arrival on earth, the scribes showed no desire to investigate. They preferred to stay within the city's confines, rather than venture outside its walls.

Set against their apathy was King Herod's desperate fear. As one who wore a crown, he perhaps had more to lose. Placed in power by the Roman Empire, Herod was sensitive to the threat of being exposed as a usurper, and deposed by the Jews' rightful ruler. He used the opportunity to ascertain the newborn monarch's location for his own murderous motives, deceitfully exploiting the magi's insights, whilst appearing to help them. He was more concerned to preserve his position than bow to the truth.

It is the magi, those unlikely outsiders to Israel and its religion, who respond to God's activity. They were willing to leave their wealth and homeland to journey out into the unknown with gifts for a foreign king. Their humility in the face of cosmic events was marked, as was their obedience to God's voice, calling them on the way, or warning them to change their route home to avoid Herod.

Matthew's account of the magi is one of contrasts: he shows how God's salvation in Christ breached the division between Jew and Gentile. But it is the people on the margins, not the people who should have been central to God's purposes, who are open to the coming of the Messiah.

The vulnerability of the infant Jesus, "God with us" in our fallen world, is set against the backdrop of the Father's protecting providence. The appearance of the true king of God's people sets in motion Matthew's drama of the kingdoms of heaven and earth, as the Messiah's arrival provokes hostility from those whose own empires are threatened. As this Gospel reaches its climax, the title "king of the Jews" will be spoken again, but in accusation, not acclamation, over a dying king mocked by a crown of thorns. The bright star at Jesus' birth will be replaced by unnatural darkness at his death.

But Jesus' ultimate resurrection victory will seal God's salvation as open to all people, in all places and for all time.

**Application**
We can be humbled by how much those looking for God are willing to commit to their search. Sometimes those fresh to Christian faith can be more energetic and responsive in their spiritual lives than those for whom church life has lost its lustre. For the scribes in the story, the cutting edge of discipleship had been dulled by familiarity.

Perhaps Herod is a more challenging figure: we, too, may have our own personal patch, where we are king in our own lives, and we do not want to surrender our rule to the one who has a more rightful claim to our loyalties. Matthew urges us to regain our wonder and worship for the king, to learn from the wisdom of those who followed the star as it led them into the presence of the light of the world.

How far out of our own comfort zones are we prepared to go to meet with Christ – even if we are not quite sure of the way? And what will we offer of our material, emotional and spiritual wealth to the king when we reach him?

*"And a voice from heaven said, 'This is my Son, the Beloved, with whom I am well pleased.'"*
(Matthew 3:17)

The Baptism of Christ

**Illustration**

We may all have varying opinions about the importance of nature versus nurture, genes versus environment, when it comes to raising children – but how we love to see family traits in our children!

"Oh, he's just like his father!"
"She's got her mother's eyes…"
"She's the image of her grandmother…"
"They're following in their father's footsteps…"

All of these phrases are a way of saying that it gives us pleasure just to look at our children.

**Gospel Teaching**

At the baptism of Jesus, this is the most striking thing. It gives God pleasure to look at Jesus.

When Jesus came to John at the River Jordan for baptism, John was initially unwilling to baptise one whom he knew needed no repentance, and so needed no baptism. But Jesus says he wants to be baptised "to fulfil all righteousness". The Son of God was going to begin his ministry, his purpose for coming to our world, and he was to initiate this in a way that was going to show clearly and concisely who he was. Just as when the Jewish priests took up their office they were washed with water (Exodus 29:4), so too our great high priest begins his public work with his public baptism.

But, more than this, "to fulfil all righteousness" Jesus was putting the plan and will of God first, showing himself as Son, at one with Father and Spirit, sharing the will of God the Trinity for the world. As the reading from Isaiah 42 shows us, Old Testament prophecy spoke of God's servant, called to a new mission and a privileged relationship with God, and here was this servant bringing himself to the waters of baptism to receive the Spirit's affirmation and hear the Father's delighted love.

And, for us as witnesses, life-changing statements of awe-inspiring proportions are enacted. By his baptism, Jesus, the Son of God, identified himself with us – he willingly entered our world to offer salvation from,

and transformation of, our sin-filled lives with his own life. But also by his baptism, Jesus accepted the eternal mission of the Trinity – to save humanity, the image-bearers of God, to bring all of God's beloved creation, all that God had called "good" in the beginning, back to a knowledge of God's love and presence.

With this example of Jesus, baptism in the Church, Christ's body, takes on added meaning. It becomes not just a joyful duty, but an honour and privilege, a mark of our own sin but also of our identification with God the Son, who first identified with us.

Baptism is to us a sacrament, an outward sign of an inner reality – through belief in Jesus, we are forgiven; by baptism, we are included in God's mission in the world and in the Church. Strengthened by the presence of the Holy Spirit, and enabled to know Jesus, we are opened to recognising God's love and call in our lives and our world.

**Application**

Jesus' baptism is a source of great encouragement and comfort. As Jesus goes into the water for us and with us, he gives us images that are for all of us who believe and yet so often feel the need for peace, joy and consolation in our lives. When God spoke those words of complete acceptance and utter love for Jesus – "This is my Son, the Beloved, with whom I am well pleased" – God was announcing the Son's work as mediator between God and all creation, as the one who justifies those who have faith in Jesus, as the one who could perfectly offer us forgiveness and friendship with God, as the one who was to transform the world, beginning with us. Because of Jesus, we can know hope.

With the mission of Jesus accomplished in his death and resurrection, and by our faith and forgiveness, in God's sight we are counted as sons and daughters, friends and members of God's Son. God sees something of Jesus in us and in our lives, and is "well pleased".

We can know joy. To know hope and joy is also to know love, and to know and live love is to have something of the Father in our lives. To see God's activity in the work of members of the Church around the world, to learn to recognise Jesus in others' faces, to experience Spirit-filled worship in daily life is to understand just a little of the Father's pleasure in the continued mission of Jesus in our world.

*"A voice came from heaven, 'You are my Son, the Beloved; with you I am well pleased.'"*
(Mark 1:11)

**Illustration**
J.R.R. Tolkien's epic work, *The Lord of the Rings*, tells the story of Frodo, a hobbit, who inherits a magic ring that turns out to be an instrument of great evil. Frodo is given the task of destroying the ring by taking it to the volcano where it was forged, in the heart of an evil empire. He has many adventures on the way. At one point he is being pursued by ghostly black riders, and narrowly escapes them by crossing a river into Rivendell, the home of the elves. As he collapses he sees the river in flood, and a shining figure on a white horse riding on the waves.

When he recovers, Frodo asks for an explanation of what he has seen. The figure was Glorfindel, whom Frodo knows as a slender elf man. He is told, "You saw him for a moment as he is on the other side, an elf lord of great power." In the world that Tolkien has created, elves live in two worlds at once, the world of humans and their own eternal home across the oceans. Just occasionally the two worlds meet, and the elves' true power is seen.

**Gospel Teaching**
In the story the Gospels tell of the life of Jesus there are two moments when we see Jesus "as he is on the other side". Jesus, we are told, lives in two worlds at once. He is the eternal Son of God in heaven, and at the same time he is the human Jesus. The Gospel writers know this because they are writing their accounts of his life after the resurrection. Their experience of Jesus' death and resurrection has led them to believe that he is more than human. So they put into their stories brief moments when heaven and earth meet, moments which show the readers of the Gospels that something extraordinary is happening here, that Jesus is someone special.

Today we hear of the first of those moments, in Mark's version. John the Baptist has been out in the wild places around the River Jordan for a while, and has begun to attract crowds. People are looking for something new, something that will distract them from their dreary lives under Roman occupation. John offers a ministry of repentance, a new start. In him they recognise God at work. John himself, though, knows that he is only the beginning of something. The ancient prophecies speak of a forerunner, one whose presence and preaching will show that God is coming. With the benefit of hindsight, that is how the Gospels present John to us, as the one who paves the way for the arrival of Jesus.

And so Jesus appears among the crowds and is baptised by John. John's ministry comes to an end, Jesus' ministry begins.

But we, the readers, are told more. We are told that as he is baptised Jesus sees the sky open up and the Spirit fly down to him like a dove. And he hears a voice, saying, "You are my Son, the Beloved; with you I am well pleased." The next time these words will be spoken will be on the mountain of transfiguration, when Jesus has been teaching his disciples about his mission and destiny. Both of these stories are about moments when the two worlds, heaven and earth, meet, and Jesus is revealed, for a moment, as he is on the other side. They come at key moments – as he begins his ministry and as he prepares himself and his followers for his death.

And later still, as Jesus dies on the cross, God's words are echoed by the pagan centurion: "Truly this man was God's Son." It is in his death, ironically, that Jesus' destiny as God's chosen one is most completely fulfilled.

**Application**

The Gospels show us that Jesus belongs in both worlds. As we, like him, are baptised, we gain a home in heaven to add to our home on earth. We too live in both worlds. We become members of God's family, welcomed at God's table. And even now, in the ordinariness of our everyday lives, we may catch the occasional glimpse of the other world, if we are watching for it. Heaven may be closer than we think.

*"His winnowing-fork is in his hand."*
(Luke 3:17)

**Illustration**
The story is told of a king called Midas, who was granted a wish. King Midas did not need any more power. His kingdom was at peace. He had a beautiful daughter. But however powerful you are, you can always find a use for more money. So, the story goes, King Midas made his wish – that everything he touched would turn to gold. Soon there were gold leaves on all his trees, and gold flowers in his garden. He was rich beyond his wildest dreams. But the foolishness of his wish began to dawn on him when he tried to eat his supper, and found the food turned to inedible gold in his mouth. And then his daughter ran in to say goodnight and... you can imagine the rest. Midas had to get his gift removed. He had learned that you have to be careful what you wish for, because you might just get it.

**Gospel Teaching**
The people of God wished for a Messiah. They had been wishing for a Messiah for many centuries, ever since their land began to be attacked and overrun by the armies of more powerful nations. They told the stories of the glory days of the great King David, and longed for a new David, even more gifted and powerful, to rule them wisely, to fight off their enemies, and to bring in God's own reign of justice and peace. Their king would once again rule from Jerusalem, their wicked oppressors would be punished, and they would live in prosperity.

They had been warned. Their prophets had consistently told them that God's judgement was not partial, that the day of reckoning would be an unpleasant experience as much for God's own people as for their enemies. The coming of God's reign would involve a judgement on injustice wherever it could be found. But through long centuries of foreign oppression the people had kept their hopes alive by looking always for the coming of God's anointed king, and it was natural that they should imagine themselves restored and vindicated in the kingdom of God.

So John the Baptist seemed a likely candidate for Messiah. He preached repentance, and talked about judgement. He spoke of God's coming to his people. Amidst all the fervour and unrest of Judaea under Roman occupation, the rumour began to spread. Perhaps this was the one. Perhaps he could be drawn from his desert preaching to lead the resistance to Rome. But, as Luke tells us, John was quite clear that he was the forerunner rather than the Messiah. He talks about someone else, someone who is coming, someone more powerful, who will baptise with the Holy Spirit. Is this, then, the longed-for king, who will rescue his people and punish their enemies? Ah, but be careful what you wish for. Listen to how John describes him: "His winnowing-fork is in his hand, to clear his threshing-floor and to gather the wheat into his granary; but the chaff he will burn with unquenchable fire."

Like the prophets before him, John reminds his listeners that the coming of the kingdom of God is not an easy experience. The Messiah, when he comes, will challenge injustice wherever he finds it. The reign of God involves a purifying judgement, in which the fierce heat of God's justice will lay bare all human wrongdoing, so that it can be shorn of its power to harm.

So the Messiah finally appears, to be baptised by John and to begin his public ministry. In Luke's version, Jesus is just one of the crowd, involved in a mass baptism. There's no indication that the experience of God's commissioning is obvious to anyone but him. But from these quiet beginnings would come a revolution, a coming of God's kingdom in ways no one had expected, and in ways which would continue to reverberate till the end of time.

**Application**

It is easy for religious people to assume that God is on their side. But the story of Jesus should warn us that the reign of God is both much simpler and much more complicated than we think. Simpler, in that it straightforwardly demands justice. More complicated, in that we can never be sure on whom its judgement will fall. The man in the crowd steps out of the river to begin a revolution. One day, we are promised, it will come to its fulfilment. Do we wish for that day? We had better be careful what we wish for.

## *"What are you looking for?"*
(John 1:38)

**Illustration**

When teenagers gathered to hang about in the churchyard outside the church hall, the PCC was quite disturbed. They discussed the situation earnestly. One brave PCC member ventured out to chat to the youngsters but the chat was one-sided and did not last long.

Nonetheless, this PCC member was sufficiently concerned to come up with an idea. He and his wife suggested opening the church hall for the youngsters once a week, inviting them in for coffee and biscuits and allowing them to bring their own music. At least it would offer the teenagers somewhere to shelter during the cold winter evenings.

He told the youngsters his idea, promising that there would be no hidden agenda and no hard sell. They all grinned at each other and rather sheepishly agreed to come.

He and his wife opened the church hall once a week for a month, bringing along refreshments. But no teenagers ever appeared, so in the end the venture failed. The PCC shrugged. They realised that they had no idea what the youngsters wanted and suspected that the youngsters themselves had no idea what they wanted either.

**Gospel Teaching**

According to John's Gospel, when Jesus called his first disciples he asked them what they were looking for. Perhaps they had no idea, for they responded with a question of their own which appeared to have no relation to the question Jesus asked them. "Where are you staying?" they asked.

Jesus could have explained where he was staying, then continued his line of thought by striking up some kind of religious conversation with them. Instead, Jesus invited them to come back home with him to see for themselves where he was living. They stayed with him all day and, after that, they were hooked. They became his disciples and followed him for the rest of their lives.

When they first approached him, Jesus listened to Andrew and his friend and heard what they did not say. He heard that at this initial stage of contact they were not yet ready to discuss religion or to reveal what they thought. He heard that they did not know quite what they were looking for; although the fact that they were John's disciples indicated that they were searching for something spiritual.

Jesus heard all this from their one-line reply, "Where are you staying?", and started from where they were. He started by making a casual offer of friendship, an offer which could be accepted or refused without any difficulty on either side, and which carried with it no hint or suggestion of commitment. Then he made a relationship with them and it was as the relationship deepened that Andrew and his friend made their commitment to Jesus. Before long, they were introducing other people to him as well.

And no matter what their loyalty to John the Baptist, who had first stimulated their interest and started them on the road of religious exploration, as soon as they spent time in the presence of Jesus they recognised in him the ultimate fulfilment of their journey of exploration. In Jesus they found what they were looking for, even though they may not really have been aware of what that was.

**Application**

Part of our job as Christians is to bring other people to Jesus, knowing that once they make a relationship with him and spend time in his company, they will become committed to him.

But how do we do this? How do we strike the balance between overwhelming tentative searchers and smothering them with kindness, or ignoring them altogether?

In a recent Grove booklet (*Creating a Culture of Welcome in the Local Church*, by Alison Gilchrist) the author tells of a man who decided to test the welcome in churches for himself. Out of the 195 churches he visited he was spoken to only once by anybody other than the official welcomer, and that was to ask him to please move his feet.

If we want to bring people to Christ, perhaps we should follow the example of Jesus and offer newcomers not just a fleeting smile while passing the time of day, but genuine friendship which is prepared to spend time with them, getting to know them.

It has long been known that more people are brought to Christianity through friendship than by any other means. If we are able first to offer friendship to those who enter our churches, then perhaps they will find their own friendship with Christ. And when that happens, we will all find exactly what we are looking for.

*"Philip said to him, 'Come and see.'"*
(John 1:46)

**Illustration**
Keith and Jim had been friends since school and the friendship strengthened as the years rolled past, until the company where Jim worked was investigated by the Inland Revenue and Jim was accused of fraud. The papers were so full of it that Jim hardly dared leave the house. All his friends except Keith melted away. Jim was distraught, terrified that he might be sent to prison and deeply ashamed. At that point, his wife left him, taking the children with her, and Jim contemplated suicide. Then Keith asked him, "Why don't you come to church? It might help."

"What on earth for?" retorted Jim. "No religious claptrap is going to sort out this mess." But he went anyway. People were pleasant to him, treating him like a normal human being, and Keith helped him through the service. Jim did not understand much of the service and was unable to concentrate or to remember anything afterwards, but somehow it was a turning point in his life. Church became a lifeline for Jim which sustained him through his prison sentence and helped him to pick up his life again afterwards.

**Gospel Teaching**
Jesus did not directly call Nathanael to be one of the Twelve, he called Philip. It sounds from the Gospel reading as though Jesus actively sought out Philip to invite him to become one of the inner band of apostles, just as he had deliberately invited Andrew the previous day. In the Gospels of Matthew, Mark and Luke, Jesus calls people from their work to follow him, but here in John's Gospel Jesus calls disciples of John the Baptist to change their religious allegiance in order to follow Jesus.

Andrew brought his brother Simon to Jesus and in today's reading Philip seeks out his friend Nathanael, eagerly telling Nathanael that Jesus of Nazareth is the long-awaited Messiah. But Nathanael is highly sceptical and laughs in Philip's face. "Can any good thing come out of Nazareth?" he mocks, possibly using the words of a local proverb, since the people of Nazareth were universally despised. But despite his scepticism, Nathanael went with his friend and met Jesus.

As soon as Jesus spotted Nathanael he saw a young man who was straight and honest and upright, someone who might be outspoken in his views but who bore no malice and who would be a loyal and faithful supporter.

Perhaps it was this characteristic of open transparency which Jesus saw in little children. When Jesus was teaching his friends about the kingdom of God, he told them that in order to enter the kingdom, they must receive it just like a little child (Mark 10:15).

And just as a little child is instantly trusting, so Nathanael immediately trusted and believed in Jesus, simply because Jesus told Nathanael that he saw him standing under the fig tree where Philip found him. But Nathanael was instantly aware that this was much more than a clever display of clairvoyance. Nathanael was conscious that Jesus actually knew him through and through, even though they had never met before. That was enough for Nathanael. He did not bother to ask questions or to hedge his response with a fall-back position in case he was wrong; he gave himself wholly to Jesus and became exactly what Jesus foresaw, a loyal and faithful supporter.

Nathanael is not mentioned in any other Gospel, but is thought to be the Bartholomew of the other three Gospels and of Acts. It may be that bar-Tholomew, son of Tholomew (or Tholmai), was a surname, much as Simon's surname was bar-Jonah, son of Jonah. Nathanael/Bartholomew went on to become a missionary, carrying news of Jesus to Syria and Asia Minor. He was eventually martyred in Great Armenia and remains the patron saint of Armenia today.

**Application**

Nathanael came to faith through his friend. Philip did not urge him or cajole him into following Jesus, but merely shared his own excitement and invited Nathanael to see for himself. Philip did no more; Jesus did all the rest. As soon as Nathanael met Jesus for himself, he believed.

As Christians, all we are required to do is to share our excitement about Jesus and invite our friends to come with us. Once they meet Jesus for themselves, they too may believe, for Jesus does all the rest. Jesus can see the potential within every person and can bring that potential to fruition. But he needs us to say to our friends, "Come and see."

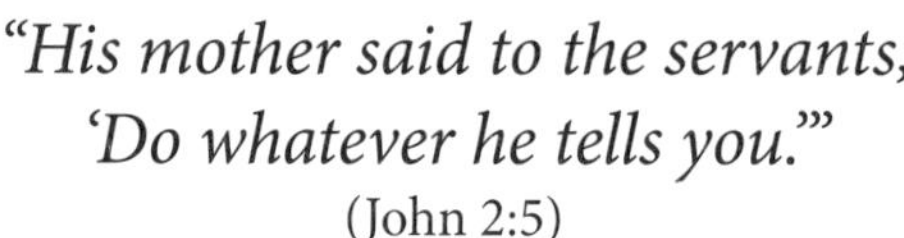

*"His mother said to the servants,*
*'Do whatever he tells you.'"*
(John 2:5)

**Illustration**

Tom was sixty-nine years old and had one ambition left in life. He wanted to have a go at abseiling. He had heard his grandchildren talking about it excitedly and longed to experience the thrill of climbing down a cliff face. A day's abseiling was arranged for Tom's seventieth birthday present.

When he eventually reached the top of the cliff, Tom was overcome with nervousness and feared that he might not be able to fulfil his ambition. The abseiling instructors sensitively appreciated Tom's anxiety. "You must trust in us completely," they advised. "Just do as we tell you and you'll be quite safe." Tom put on the safety harness and awaited his final instruction. Trusting the instructors completely and following their advice, he descended the steep cliff face slowly, cautiously and successfully.

Without total trust, Tom's ambition could not have been fulfilled. And it is that total trust in God that can help us to fulfil our life's purpose.

**Gospel Teaching**

We may often hear the expression, "Trust in God." It is easy to say but very challenging to do. Today's Gospel shows us that when we trust in God and do the Lord's will, his glory is revealed. Mary's trust and confidence in her son is shown when she advises the servants at the wedding in Cana to "Do whatever he tells you." Jesus had seemed reluctant to solve the wine shortage. "Woman, what concern is that to you and to me? My hour has not yet come." Mary's trust in the Lord was complete. She believed that something would be done. And the key to her confidence was that she knew him well. She could trust in Jesus because she knew him intimately, as a mother knows a son, she had shared with him, was comfortable with him, was close to him.

Throughout his ministry Jesus encouraged people to trust in God. His disciples grew close to him, they watched as he cured the sick, forgave the sinner and welcomed the outcast. Each encounter and experience deepened their faith. "He let his glory be seen and his disciples believed in him." They grew close to him.

If we wish to do the Lord's will we must first trust in him. To trust anyone it is important to know them well – no one trusts a complete stranger. The disciples' trust in the Lord grew as their friendship with Jesus deepened. Trusting in him, we are called to act on what we believe – to discern what is the Lord's will. When we follow the Lord's will we are taking great steps into the unknown. It isn't always the path the world wants us to follow. And as we go, it is important to remember that we may make mistakes. We can always start again.

Through doing God's will we reveal his glory and our lives will be a living proclamation of the Gospel.

**Application**

To trust in the Lord completely we need to know him well. Reading the scriptures on a regular basis, spending quiet moments listening to the voice of God as he speaks to us in the world around us, alert to what he is saying in the varied moments of our day, sharing in the lives of our fellow Christians: all these things help us to deepen our relationship with God. It is good to seek out a quiet moment when we can be alone with God, listening to what he asks of us. And as our knowledge of and closeness to God deepen, so will our trust in the Lord grow. We will have a better sense of discernment, helping us to work out what he wants us to do in the world.

We each fulfil God's will in a different way, as St Paul tells us: "Now there are varieties of gifts, but the same Spirit; and there are varieties of services, but the same Lord." We each have a particular gift which we are to use in fulfilling God's will in the world. No one else has our gifts, so it is up to us to use them – to act on what we believe. As we grow to appreciate the uniqueness of our own calling, we begin to appreciate more the unique gifts of each other person. We grow in love of one another as we grow in our love for God. In this way we are letting God's glory be seen and living the Good News.

*"Immediately they left their nets and followed him."*
(Matthew 4:20)

**Illustration**

One winter's day the great American evangelist D.L. Moody visited a prominent Chicago citizen, who was not a churchgoer. He was shown into the parlour where he was joined by his host. We do not know much about their conversation up to the point where Moody stressed the importance of the Church. His host objected that he could be just as good a Christian outside the Church as within it. Without a word, Moody stood up and walked over to the fireplace. He picked up the tongs and took a blazing coal from the fire. Then he simply stood there, holding the tongs and watching the coal. His companion also watched. In silence the two of them watched the coal smoulder and go out. "I see," said the man.

**Gospel Teaching**

Today's New Testament readings are both about the Church, though they give us rather different takes on it. Firstly, Matthew's account shows Jesus gathering the very first members of the Christian Church – his twelve disciples – around him. There is a real buzz – a sense of spontaneity and solidarity – as without hesitation Peter, Andrew, James and John leave what they are doing to follow in faith.

This is our first sighting of Peter, who will go on to become one of the most captivating characters of the Bible. Let us take a closer look at Peter – why does he capture our imagination? Well, for a start he is eminently fallible. We know his story well: the mouthiest of the twelve, he often pipes up with the foolish question, to receive a put-down from Jesus. And then, just when his Lord needs him most, Peter experiences a disastrous, total crisis of faith – when he is too ashamed and frightened to admit to knowing Christ – and denies him three times.

Yet many people believe that it was towards this imperfect, this very human man, that Jesus felt the most affection. It was Peter whom Jesus called the rock upon which he would build his Church, Peter he instructed to tend his sheep. Indeed it is from Peter, according to tradition, that the structure of the Church has rolled out down the centuries.

In contrast with the high-energy newborn Church in Matthew's Gospel, when we turn to Corinthians we see how quickly the rot can set in. The divisions in the Church at Corinth were mainly personality clashes and divided loyalties towards different teachers. As the Church's former chief antagonist, nobody knew better than Paul what a fragile structure it was, so it must have been exasperating to hear of infighting and squabbling. There is, as the saying goes, nothing new under the sun.

**Application**

Although we are talking about the Church as a body of people, it is also a collection of individuals. And it is individuals, after all, who give each individual church its unique identity within the wider Christian Church. Because the Church is a collection of individuals it is also an organic entity – one which changes from day to day, from Sunday to Sunday. And nobody, not even the minister, owns it. So each individual, including the committed churchgoer, the visitor and the occasional attender, has a vital and vibrant role to play.

We bring our personal joys to church – when we marry, or baptise our children – and we bring our sorrows – at funerals and memorial services. It is in church that we are most exposed, when we confess our sins. We might also feel vulnerable and self-conscious in confession, prayer or hymn-singing, or find it awkward to kneel in humility before a greater power. With so many personal emotions and anxieties stirred up, it's easy to see how a church can become inward-looking or divided.

So why do we come together as a body of people to stand upon the rock of St Peter, especially as we have seen how wobbly that rock could be at times? The answer is that we are all, like Peter, fallible, and we need to keep one another aglow in faith. As D.L. Moody demonstrated, when we are in the fire we crackle with energy and glow. Hopefully you have felt the deepening of the atmosphere at the Eucharist. Hopefully, when we pray or sing, you have felt the presence of the Holy Spirit. Today's reading from Isaiah tells us that the people, plural, who walked in darkness have seen a great light. We might walk in darkness, or lose the spark, but sometimes, hopefully, together we glimpse God's great light.

## *"You have kept the good wine until now."*

(John 2:10)

**Illustration**

Author Mary Wesley, who died at the age of ninety, was regarded as one of our finest authors. But she was seventy years old before her first novel was published, and her first commercial success, *The Camomile Lawn*, occurred when she was seventy-two. Her son described her as "a deeply feminine woman who wrote about being a woman in a way which had not been done before".

Mary Wesley wrote two children's books at the age of fifty-seven and said, "I have no patience with people who grow old at sixty just because they are entitled to a bus pass. Sixty should be the time to start something new, not put your feet up." Her last book, *Part of the Scenery*, was published in 2001 when she was eighty-nine years old.

Perhaps the whole of Mary Wesley's life was gradually leading to her calling as a writer, for she incorporated her own experiences into her work. She was a clear example of keeping the best until last, for her life reached its pinnacle in her latest years.

Perhaps this is true for all Christians. As we journey through life growing towards God and thus growing in maturity, perhaps God's plan is for our lives fully to blossom and flower in our later years so that people may see for themselves the huge difference that Christianity makes.

**Gospel Teaching**

Jesus' first act at the beginning of his ministry was to attend a wedding and change water into wine. This miracle of changing water into wine is one of the few non-healing miracles that Jesus performed and is only recorded in St John's Gospel. But it is given considerable prominence by John, who regards it as the first sign of glory pointing to the divinity of Jesus. It is given considerable prominence by the worldwide Christian Church too, for it occurs during each year of our three-year lectionary.

Why is this miracle so important? For John, it is the beginning of the gradual revelation of the divinity of Jesus. As we move through John's Gospel we discover several "signs of glory" which culminate in the ultimate sign, the resurrection of Jesus. But there are many more than recorded in the Gospel, so not all miracles are regarded as "signs of glory". What makes this miracle so special?

On this occasion, six stone jars were filled to the brim with water, producing something like 180 gallons of wine. That in itself must have been a pretty impressive miracle and was perhaps an over-the-top response by Jesus. They may have run out of wine at a relatively early stage in the wedding celebrations, but to be short by 180 gallons would indicate a very serious miscalculation indeed. But perhaps it is an indication of God's over-abundant response to all his children whenever they ask for anything.

The wine produced by the miracle was so fine in quality that the steward remarked on it, saying wonderingly, "Everyone serves the good wine first, and then the inferior wine after the guests have become drunk. But you have kept the good wine until now."

The best wine came towards the end of the wedding, when the guests may have been too drunk to notice the quality. But that was clearly irrelevant to Jesus who always gives top quality, no matter how late the request for help comes and no matter whether or not his gifts are appreciated.

As John is the only Gospel writer who fails to mention the institution of the Eucharist at the Last Supper, many scholars think that this story of the wedding at Cana is John's comment on the Eucharist. By the time John is thought to have written his Gospel, possibly towards the end of the first century, the early Church was firmly established in the practice of the Eucharist. Perhaps John is using the story to draw attention to the importance of that practice and to the quality and generosity of the eternal gift given to us there by Jesus.

**Application**

Those who receive Holy Communion receive this gift without having to do anything, for God's grace is freely given to us in the sharing of bread and wine. All we need is an open heart and the intention to receive the gift as it is meant, full of overwhelming love, support and care.

And we need to remember that Jesus keeps the best until last. Whatever the world may think, those who are in the latter years of their life are by no means on the scrapheap, for in Christian terms they are reaching the most mature point in their lives. We cannot all become authors at the age of seventy, but we can all allow those Christian gifts which we have received through the ages to be seen in all their glory.

St Paul described the "fruit of the Spirit" as love, joy, peace, patience, kindness, generosity, faithfulness, gentleness, and self-control (Galatians 5:22-23). Those who reach old age with these characteristics shining from them have truly followed our Lord and kept the best wine until last.

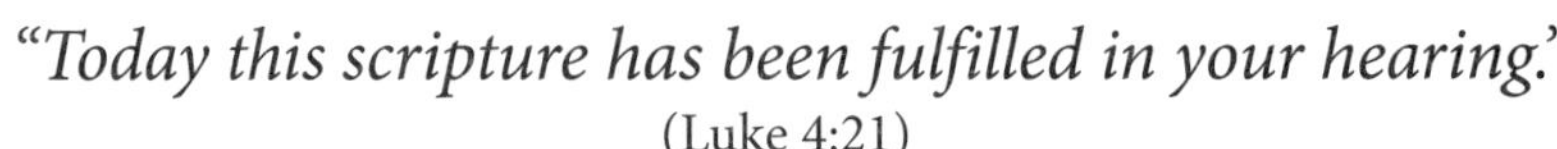

"Today this scripture has been fulfilled in your hearing."


(Luke 4:21)

**Illustration**

St Teresa of Avila lived during the sixteenth century. She was famous for her profound spirituality and her inspired writing which grew out of her intimate relationship with God. She founded the Discalced Carmelites, a strictly enclosed religious order (discalced = without shoes), opening several convents in Spain. She was a strong and determined woman who was investigated by the Inquisition and suffered at the hands of jealous clerics, but who was much loved by those who knew her and has been admired ever since, even earning the title "Doctor" of the Christian Church.

In addition to her mystical prayer life, she was intensely practical in her observances, a Martha and Mary both rolled into one, and she made a statement which invites us to share these attributes. She declared that she (and therefore we) must be the eyes and ears, the hands and feet of Christ in the world for, if we are not, then who will do Christ's work? Who will live the legacy Jesus left us? Who will spread the Gospel, speak for the prisoners, heal the sick and lift the burdens of the downtrodden, if not us?

**Gospel Teaching**

When Jesus stood up in the synagogue in Nazareth, and read from the scroll, it was not just to make a point about Isaiah's prophecy. It was not only to claim his rightful inheritance, the prophetic mantle, the authority which derives from being the Messiah whose arrival had been expected for more than a thousand years. Jesus was not bathing in the reflected glory of the scriptures, not even just to set himself off on the right track. This was, after all, the first time he had turned up in Nazareth since the life-changing events at his baptism and in the wilderness, when his true nature and vocation had become crystal clear.

No, what Jesus was doing, by acknowledging what had gone before, was to use this piece of scripture to declare unequivocally and openly who he was and as a ground plan and instructions for the future, immediate and long-term, for those who would become his disciples, then and now.

Jesus almost always taught *groups* of people, not just to utilise time and space more productively, but to ensure that everyone (or as many as possible) got the same message at the same time. In learning together as a group he encouraged them to begin the process of becoming the "Jesus movement", what we now call the Church, enabling them also to plan, build and act as a group.

This way of working was necessary to promote that measure of unity which enabled them to become what St Paul called "one body", acting in unison. For in unity is strength and the power to overcome the forces which would seek to diminish or destroy the purity of Jesus' message and the effectiveness of his action.

Jesus, when quoting Isaiah, was talking about himself, but his message was not solely repetition of the old law, in the synagogue where this was practised. Rather, it was the start of his teaching to us here today, in this place, and in every place where that teaching from the synagogue in Nazareth is still heard. It defined Jesus' mission as God's great act of liberation for his people, and it continues to define our mission today.

**Application**

In Nazareth, at the start of his ministry, Jesus became the pivotal point between what was and what is to come; enabling us to respect the past, but constantly turning us round to face the future; giving us the words which determine where we stand in relation to each other and in relation to his teaching and showing us what to do.

Jesus read that he was anointed by the Spirit of the Lord, and so are we at our baptism. To bring good news to the poor, proclaim release to captives, sight to the blind, freedom to the oppressed. This is the mantle, the responsibility, he took on and which is passed to us. This is what St Teresa meant. The work of Jesus is the work of the people of God. Individually, we are Christ's hands and feet, ears and eyes; together we are the whole body. This can be both a comfort and an awesome responsibility, to be an active part of the living scripture, from Isaiah until now. What a relief to know he shares it with us, and all his holy people, since that sabbath in the synagogue at Nazareth!

*"The servants who had drawn the water knew."*
(John 2:9)

**Illustration**

There are some words in our language that are used in many different ways and carry a range of meanings. One of these is "love", another is "know". At its lowest level, "know" is used without any meaning at all. So we begin a sentence with, "You know..." or equally we may end it "... you know", or "you know what I mean". In fact, it doesn't mean anything at all. We are simply using the expression to help along whatever it is that we are trying to express.

Equally, we may know a fact: that the battle of Hastings took place in 1066, or that Mount Everest is the world's highest peak. We may speak of "knowing" somebody. This may mean that we have met them a few times, and they remain a casual acquaintance. On the other hand, knowing someone may denote a friendship of many years' standing, a deep and mutually satisfying relationship which will bear confidences and the separation of time and space, perhaps over long periods. So we see that our "knowing" has come to take on a much more profound level of meaning. We "know" in the sense that we recognise at a deep, instinctual level the truth about ourselves, other people, and the situations in which we find ourselves day by day.

**Gospel Teaching**

If we look carefully at today's Gospel reading, we can see the same process at work. The wedding celebration was in full swing. The guests were enjoying themselves, and steadily working their way through the wine until there was none left. It was at this point that Jesus turned the water into wine. The chief steward of the feast had no idea how this had happened, and it was certainly no concern of the guests. But "the servants who had drawn the water knew". They "knew" in the sense that they could recognise the truth of what had happened, and had a deep conviction that they had witnessed something special – the first sign in which Jesus revealed his glory.

The Gospels tell the continuing story of Jesus revealing his glory, and there are many instances when those around him recognise the truth of the moment. On the mount of transfiguration, Peter is unable to do this,

although when Jesus asks him directly, "Who do you say I am?", Peter expresses the truth that he recognises deep within himself: "You are the Messiah, the Son of the living God." Mary Magdalene knows, and expresses the truth of the risen Lord in just one word: "Rabbouni", and Thomas almost as briefly, "My Lord and my God." Saul had his moment of knowing, on the road to Damascus, and even Pontius Pilate's wife seemed to know in some strange kind of way.

Jesus knew, too. He recognised his person and embraced his vocation. He spoke of God as his Father, and of the intimacy of that relationship. "The Father and I are one." But he also knew the cost of that vocation. We find him at an early stage of his ministry setting his face to go towards Jerusalem and all that lay before him there. "Father," he prayed in the Garden of Gethsemane, "remove this cup from me; yet, not what I want, but what you want." His knowledge of himself, of the moment, and of the will of God, was profound.

**Application**

However, not everyone was convinced. There were those who asked, "Who is this?" about his personal authority, his healing, his teaching. So it is important to notice that our Gospel reading ends with a phrase that is crucial to the development of the Gospel as a whole: "his disciples believed in him". What had taken place was for them, as well as for the servants, their moment of knowing. Many of us, too, will have our moment of truth which we recognise deep within ourselves. It is that profound level of knowing which is the source of our Christian commitment and all that flows from that.

We are now within touching distance of Lent. Underlying all the suggestions as to how we may profitably observe and use the time is the thought that we may come to know ourselves better, perhaps even love ourselves more, and with more understanding. As we do, we shall find that we come to know God more, love him more deeply and with greater understanding. So we commit ourselves more fully and openly and knowingly to the service of our Lord Jesus Christ.

*"They were astounded at his teaching, for he taught them as one having authority, and not as the scribes."*
(Mark 1:22)

**Illustration**
One friend was telling another recently of the large, inner-city comprehensive school where she had worked as a secretary for a number of years. This school served a very deprived area, one rife with social problems. The hard-working and dedicated staff strove to maintain a level of discipline that would enable them to actually teach and the children to learn; but it was an uphill struggle and staff absences through stress-related illnesses were commonplace.

"But", said the school secretary, "there is one staff member who never seems to have any difficulty. And she teaches RE – not usually the children's favourite subject! She's one of the youngest teachers we have and she's quite petite and very quiet – you hardly notice her in the staffroom. Most teachers find that they have to call the 'school patrol' at least a couple of times a term – they're a group who walk the corridors and who can be called on if things get a bit out of hand in a classroom. But this teacher has never had to call them, and when she's in the classroom you never hear a sound out of place – even with the toughest of classes. Most of the lads tower over her but she never even raises her voice; she has them eating out of her hand! I don't understand it – it doesn't make sense."

**Gospel Teaching**
Mark records this episode at the very beginning of Jesus' public ministry, setting the tone for all that follows. On the face of it the scene is a very ordinary one: Jesus and his disciples attend the synagogue on the sabbath. But there, the commonplace ends: rather than going to the synagogue to be taught, Jesus himself begins to teach. We are not told what his teaching was; only that "he taught them as one having authority, and not as the scribes". As the Gospel narrative progressed, it was not to be long before Jesus' teaching and his popularity with the crowds became a source of question and resentment amongst the religious hierarchy.

One of the people in the synagogue is a man with an unclean spirit. The man approaches Jesus, and the unclean spirit calls out in recognition: "What have you to do with us, Jesus of Nazareth? Have you come to destroy us?" Perhaps the greatest irony here is that, among all those in the synagogue that sabbath, the unclean spirit alone recognises who Jesus really is, and the source of his authority: "I know who you are, the Holy One of God". Jesus does not want or need that kind of acknowledgement and sternly rebukes the unclean spirit. But the crowd is captivated and Jesus' fame spreads.

**Application**

The nature of genuine authority is difficult to define, and it is not always to be found in the most obvious places. In our opening illustration, the slightly built, relatively inexperienced young woman teacher was the last person anyone would expect to be able to command the attention and respect of a class of rebellious fifteen-year-olds. And in today's Gospel a young Jewish man from an obscure background is recognised by his hearers as having an authority far beyond that of their usual, more experienced teachers.

So how are we to recognise genuine authority, and how are we to distinguish it from what is bogus? A key factor seems to be consistency: do this person's words match up with the kind of person they seem to be? There is a saying, "I can't hear what you say, because who you are is shouting too loudly." If the words we hear are at variance with the person speaking them, then those words will not ring true. There is a great deal of teaching in the New Testament about being alert to the possibility that some people – or spirits – may not be what they seem: "Test the spirits, to see whether they are from God" (1 John 4:1); "Not everyone who says to me, 'Lord, Lord' will enter the kingdom of heaven" (Matthew 7:21); "A good tree cannot bear bad fruit" (Matthew 7:18).

Amid today's clamour of competing voices, the need for wise and prayerful discernment has never been greater. And as we seek to discern that which is true in the world around us, so we seek also to discern the truth amidst the competing voices we find within ourselves. As humans we are weak, fallible and riddled with inconsistency. But in Jesus there is no inconsistency: the person and the message are one.

*"For my eyes have seen your salvation."*
(Luke 2:30)

**Illustration**
There are some well-loved children's stories by Arnold Lobel about the friendship between a frog and a toad. Although the two friends are so different, they complement each other perfectly.

In one story, Toad tells Frog that he has never, in his whole life, received a letter. Immediately, Frog runs home and writes a letter to Toad. He gives it to the postman to carry to Toad's house, and then runs back to Toad to tell him that, very soon, he will get his first ever letter.

In great anticipation, Toad sits down on his front porch to wait for the letter. Days pass, but Toad is not dejected. He knows the letter is coming, because he trusts his friend Frog. At long last, the postman – who happens to be a snail, hence the delay – arrives and hands over the longed-for letter. It isn't long, and it doesn't say anything that Frog could not have communicated in person, but it is everything Toad had hoped for.

**Gospel Teaching**
In today's Gospel reading, we meet two people who have been waiting even longer than Toad. But, like Toad, they have been waiting without anxiety, because they trust the God whose message is coming.

Simeon and Anna are only found in Luke's Gospel, and it is very typical of Luke that he gives us both a man and a woman. Luke is famous for his matched pairs of stories: think of the shepherd searching for a lost sheep and the woman searching for a lost coin, for example, or the man who sowed a seed and the woman who mixed the yeast with flour. Luke deliberately looks for stories that make it clear that women and men are both called to be disciples, and are both part of the new Church for which he was writing.

Anna is a striking and unusual figure. We are told that she has lived nearly all of her life dedicated to God, after just a few brief years of marriage. That was not a common or socially very accepted vocation; at this point in history, women were expected to marry and produce children, and fulfil their religious duty in that way.

So here are Simeon and Anna, both faithful people, waiting with longing for God to redeem the ancient promises to Israel. Simeon's words of praise and thanksgiving are an obvious echo of the book of Isaiah 49:6 where it says, "It is too light a thing that you should be my servant to raise up the tribes of Jacob and to restore the survivors of Israel; I will give you as a light to the nations, that my salvation may reach to the ends of the earth." Simeon is indicating the scope of Jesus' mission. It is not just to fulfil God's promise to Israel, but to bring all the nations of the world to know God and to be part of the salvation offered in Christ. Simeon lays out for us what is to be the theme of Luke's two-volume history, the Gospel and Acts: it is the theme of the universality of the Christian mission, the call to bring all peoples home to God, their creator.



Simeon and Anna recognise God's message, even in the form of the baby boy, because they have been preparing for it all their lives. Others will not be so ready to receive the good news: some will choose to reject it. Even Mary will have to choose: she will not automatically be part of the kingdom in her role as Jesus' mother. Luke tells us in Acts that Mary was with the disciples after the resurrection, so we know how she chose, but the sword that will pierce her soul is surely the living two-edged sword that the writer of Hebrews (4:12) mentions. Mary, like us, has to learn to be honest to herself and to God. That is why she is the model for our discipleship.

**Application**

Simeon and Anna waited trustfully for the whole of their lives and were rewarded with the message they longed for, the message of God's love and faithfulness, embodied in Jesus Christ. We are privileged to know Jesus already, but that doesn't mean that we can forgo the lifetime of learning about him more and more deeply. Like Mary, we need to lay ourselves open to that sword of truth, cutting away our deceit, our lack of trust, or ignorance and our laziness so that we really recognise and celebrate Jesus, the fulfilment of God's promises to the world.

*"And when the parents brought in the child Jesus, to do for him what was customary under the law, Simeon took him in his arms and praised God."*
(Luke 2:27-28)

**Illustration**
The argument at the dinner party became heated when the subject arose about involving children in a religious faith. The major consensus was that it was a bad idea. We hear this regularly, that we must not pass on to children what we believe (some call it "brainwashing") in case it limits their "freedom to choose".

"So are you averse to all knowledge, or just that which includes the name of God?" asked one of the quieter participants. The hullabaloo which ensued fervently reiterated that this was not a debate about knowledge, but about inflicting views.

She replied: "Don't we do this all the time? Pass on what we know and believe to be true, in all spheres of their lives, especially related to what we hold dear – relationships, morals, etc.? And don't we want our children to be part of something greater than themselves, family or community, providing a structure for living? Why should we not offer them preparation, a springboard from which to proceed, in matters of belief? Isn't it our responsibility to offer a framework for moral guidance, and a support system? Then let them decide in maturity whether or not they wish to continue within it?"

A deep silence followed and hung on the air like a thundercloud. Then someone suddenly remembered their babysitter, the rest looked at watches and made exit noises and the party broke up. Our present age creates ambivalence about faith which some people are fearful of addressing.

**Gospel Teaching**
This rich and beautiful Gospel story helps us to understand the depths and riches of faith; of honouring God, recognising the need for tradition, membership of a community and Jesus' place within all of them. Jesus was a Jew, of Jewish parents, with Joseph's heritage recorded as far back as King David. He was part of a religion based within a community of worshippers and part of a tradition which had rules for membership, some of which he brought into his Church, but he lived and died a practising Jew.

Jesus' parents were young and inexperienced but they knew their responsibilities. Whatever Jesus was to become, according to the message of the angel at his conception, he had to grow up knowing his roots, having a home in a tradition: a point of departure from which eventually to begin his ministry. His reception into the Temple, the purification of his parents with its accompanying rituals, continued the tradition of acceptance, which conferred the appropriate status upon the child as a member of his community. He would be included in the teaching available to male children, have a future in a known environment, a spiritual life, and the ministrations of the range of participants who made up close-knit society in first-century Palestine. In addition, he would have access to a common language with which to articulate his understanding of, and relationship with, God. This Gospel demonstrates that belonging to a spiritual community provides access to a wide range of people, of all ages.

It is no accident that Simeon and Anna, in their great age, declare Jesus' identity. It is from their deep spiritual longing and their experience that they can speak, conferring the sense of being part of something greater than oneself, past and present, roots which securely anchor our sense of self-respect in a safe harbour, among trustworthy people.

All of this is modelled by Jesus' reception into the Temple. He, of course, was so much more than an ordinary child. But he was still a child, like ours. His future would be very different, but it began with acceptance and blessing by holy people, within a faith.

**Application**

It is common to hear people declaring a belief in God but not in religion. This is often based on tired memories of, sometimes, outdated practices in stuffy surroundings, mostly directed towards an altar, and often solely controlled by clergy. Our modern understanding of Church – building supportive community, with all its benefits, living to mirror Jesus' teaching and example, in life and worship – is very different. Perhaps it is easier to dismiss what are remembered as discomforts than to recall the benefits.

So, the next time we hear someone suggesting they will let their children decide for themselves about religion, we might gently remind them where security, acceptance and love reside, the best foundations for a child's future. Maybe even offer them this lovely Gospel to read – for their children's sakes.

*"And a sword will pierce your own soul too."*
(Luke 2:35)

**Illustration**

In the early days of television advertising, commercials always showed immaculate homes and impeccably behaved families. Father was the breadwinner, always middle class, setting off to work with his briefcase. Mother was as neat and tidy as the house she spent her entire day keeping that way. Children were polite and well behaved. Everyone was happy and smiling. For many young couples bringing up their children, this must have seemed the way family life should really be: all sweetness and light.

Eventually, people admitted that these commercials did not reflect real life. Not only that, but they were doing real harm. People looking at these impossibly beautiful homes, these unrealistically happy families, compared them with their own and felt inadequate. Gradually, commercials have changed to reflect the complexities of family life – and not only because patterns of family life have themselves changed. These days, television couples occasionally argue. Children squabble, storm off and slam doors. There is a recognition that, even in the best-regulated families, life has never been all sweetness and light.

**Gospel Teaching**

Today's Gospel reading illustrates this. There is, admittedly, a lot of sweetness and light as we imagine the joy of Mary and Joseph, like any other Jewish couple of that time, seeking God's blessing on their first baby. First the purification of the mother, marking her re-entry into society after being shut away while pregnant, and then the presentation of the baby Jesus. It is a day of great celebration, joy and pride.

And there is joy for Simeon and Anna, too, as they recognise Jesus as the one who will bring salvation to God's people. Joy is the dominant theme in the story. A baby is born. The Lord has come to his Temple. And yet, there is a spectre at the feast. Mary is warned of sorrow to come, of a sword which will pierce her soul. The arrival of God's salvation, witnessed and celebrated here, is not the end. All is not sweetness and light.

Mary will suffer the agony of watching her son die upon the cross. Nor is that the only time when Jesus will bring her anguish. Luke's Gospel tells us more than the others about Mary, and it is Luke who records another visit to Jerusalem, when Jesus causes his mother great anxiety by slipping away from his parents before eventually being found with the teachers in the Temple. Later, in his ministry, Mary tries to see Jesus but cannot reach him through the crowd. Jesus must have caused his mother a great deal of heartache.

Salvation has come to the people of God in the person of Jesus Christ, but there is still, amidst the joy, suffering for those who love him and seek to follow him. Why? Because salvation is both now and not yet, already present in the life, death and resurrection of Jesus, remembered and celebrated in the Eucharist today, but still to come when he returns in glory, in God's good time. All will be sweetness and light, but not yet.

**Application**

In our Christian life, as in our private lives, there will be sorrow amidst the joy. Our families and our close friendships can be the source of great happiness, but because we invest so much time and emotion in them, and because we are flawed human beings, they can also cause us heartache, which in turn makes us feel inadequate. If we stop expecting the perfect relationships of the television commercials, if we accept that love can bring sorrow, our private lives will be more rewarding.

In the same way, our relationship with God needs to be realistic. If we turn to Christ expecting instant cures, a straight path, sweetness and light, what happens when we find that we still have doubts, or that life's problems have not all gone away? We suspect either that we have failed and are not "good Christians", or that God has let us down. Neither is true. We are merely caught in a time warp! In this life we are bidden to take up our cross and follow the one who was tested as we are. May we do so gladly, looking ahead to that time when God's salvation is complete. May we trust him to walk with us through sorrow and through joy, until we enter into his light and share his glory.

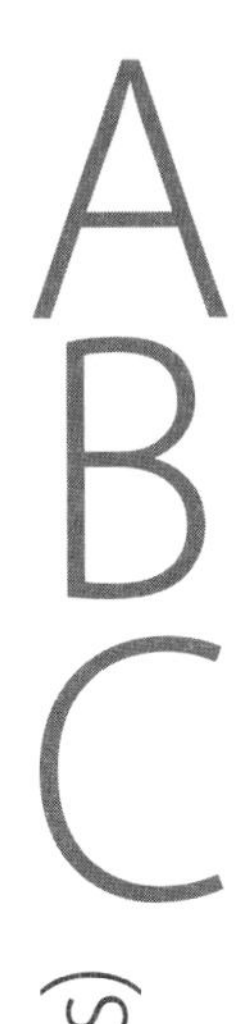



*"For my eyes have seen your salvation."*
(Luke 2:30)

**Illustration**

Kinetic energy grabs all the headlines. When anyone *does* something, they use kinetic energy. Kinetic energy runs and jumps and comes up with brilliant ideas.

However, before you can run or jump, you have to store potential energy in your muscles by taking in food.

Behind every action there is a story of how the potential energy was produced which made the action possible. These stories can be simple: in order for an arrow to fly, an archer has to store potential energy in the bowstring by pulling it back. But these stories can also be complex: when someone gets a degree, a lifetime of education has been needed in order to put that scroll in their possession.

**Gospel Teaching**

The presentation of Jesus at the Temple is another of these stories. Five people meet and there is an explosion of kinetic energy. But the passage is actually pregnant with the language of potential: consecration; waiting; promise; preparation; destiny. All five people are in the Temple for a purpose.

Let's look at all five, beginning with Jesus. He is a baby and also the Son of God. This is surely the most powerful example of potential that has ever existed. For baby Jesus speaks not just of his own future but of the rise and fall of many. Certainly Israel's potential to be glorious again lies stored in this baby, along with the chance of salvation for all people everywhere.

Joseph and Mary have brought this unique baby to begin the unfolding of his potential by consecrating him to God. His will and God's will are to be one. All that is needed now is for someone to recognise the potential for the energy to be released. That someone is Simeon.

Simeon is usually portrayed as an old man, but Luke doesn't mention his age. He is simply a devout and righteous man. He has become old in our minds by association with the aged prophetess Anna and because he was promised he wouldn't see death before seeing the Messiah.

It is surely more exciting to see Simeon as a man in the prime of life, his greatest triumphs still ahead of him, who is so devout that he has allowed himself to be enlisted into God's service. He will not be free to carry on with his life, as it were, until he has performed the vital and sacred task of recognising the Messiah. Picture Simeon with this one thing in mind as he tries to pursue his education and then his career: looking closely at every successful, important person he meets and asking himself, "Is this the one?"

Then one day the Spirit urges him into the Temple courts and suddenly Simeon finds the Messiah in the last place he would have expected: in his arms. Simeon bursts into song. His opening line quotes words which were spoken when a Roman master released a slave. Far from dying, Simeon is now free to live out the full potential of his devout life. And yes, he probably did begin by dancing round the Temple with God in his arms!

Anna is different. An old prophetess always in the Temple, she is a professional when it comes to recognising potential, so it's no great surprise when she supports Simeon's discovery.

Luke concludes by referring to the continued development of Jesus' potential, as he stores up wisdom and grace to be used on the journey to Calvary that awaits him.

**Application**

Are we fulfilling our potential as servants of God? Do we feel we have a part to play in the almighty purposes of the Lord? Or are we frittering away our divine energy, all the precious grace he has invested in us?

How are we to know? How can we recognise our divine potential? Simeon and Anna show us the way. Simeon is devout and righteous; and Anna spends her life in prayer. To see as these two people saw, we too need to wait upon God in prayer.

As Joseph and Mary consecrated their child to the Lord, so we should consecrate a time every day to an encounter with God in the temple of our hearts. By doing so, we begin to align our wills with God's will and so allow God's plans for us to unfold. Grandiose or humble, these plans will be worth singing about.

# Ordinary Time before Lent

*"Let your light shine."*
(Matthew 5:16)

**Illustration**

It was nearing Christmas 1993 in the town of Billings, Montana. It was also the Jewish festival of Hanukkah, and the Schnitzer family had stencilled a menorah symbol on their son's bedroom window. One night the peace was shattered when a rock was thrown through Isaac's window. Glass shards fell onto the boy's bed, but luckily he was unhurt. The police came, but, to the family's dismay, could only suggest they remove the menorah.

When Margaret MacDonald of the Montana Association of Churches read about it, she imagined having to tell her children they couldn't have a Christmas tree because it might provoke violence. She took action. Before long her church's Sunday school children had made menorahs for their own windows. The minister contacted other churches, and in the following weeks menorahs appeared in the windows of homes right across town, as people publicised their solidarity against bigotry. The local paper even published a full-page image of a menorah for readers to use as a template. The police chief was asked whether it might cause further criminal acts. "There's greater risk in not doing it," he said.

For a while the violence intensified. Bricks shattered the high school's windows, where an electric sign announced: "Happy Hanukkah to our Jewish Friends". A church's windows were broken because of its menorah display, and a shop window sign proclaiming: "Not in our town!" was shot at. But the people of Billings continued to take their stance against hatred. The following spring, a group of Christians joined their Jewish brothers and sisters for a traditional Passover meal. The bonds that were created in Billings that year were so powerful and extensive that they gave rise to a worldwide campaign called "Not in Our Town".

**Gospel Teaching**

Jesus does some plain talking in today's reading from Matthew. When he says, "You are the light of the world," it's a clear statement. Note the present tense. It's not conditional; not what you could become with a little tweaking or some adjustment. There's nothing to do or say differently; nothing to add; nothing to take away. You don't need a facelift, a rethink, or a change of heart. You simply, already, *are* the light of the world. Then he gives an equally straightforward command: "Let your light shine," and goes on to say – just as plainly – that the way to do this is through good works. As Julian of Norwich says: "Every act of kindness and compassion done by any man for his fellow Christian is done by Christ working within him."

It's clear that Christians nowadays go even further, in extending kindness beyond their fellow Christians. In displaying their menorahs, the Schnitzers were complying with God's command to publicise the miracle of Hanukkah, when one day's supply of oil burned in the Temple for eight days. In standing alongside their Jewish neighbours, and refusing to extinguish their menorahs, the Christian community of Billings were actively inviting the violence that the Schnitzers had experienced. In different ways they were all shining their light – which of course is to say that they were allowing God's light to shine through them.

**Application**

Most of us don't shine our light for one simple reason: we don't truly believe we have it within us. We might respond to hearing about the Schnitzers' ordeal with shock and righteous indignation – and leave it at that. By contrast, Margaret MacDonald found the inner resources, the courage of her convictions, the determination and stamina she needed to let her light shine out brightly into her community and further afield.

But, as she would surely agree, she's no Wonder Woman. So think about the steps that took her from reading a newspaper article to taking a bold stance against hatred. First of all, she needed to have the thought: "I can do something about that." That in itself requires a sense of self-worth which is, in its pure form, completely different from egoism. Next, she needed to draw on her God-given creativity to come up with an idea. Then she had to dig deep into her powers of persuasion and motivation – and you can bet she had to make a nuisance of herself at times.

Now you might not share Margaret's particular talents or skills, but with an open heart and mind, and the depth of faith that is only achievable through prayer and praise, it is possible to develop your own unique way of being the light of the world. Because it's simply what you already are.

*"Let us go on to the neighbouring towns, so that I may proclaim the message there also."*
(Mark 1:38)

**Illustration**

Direct mailing companies spend huge sums of money in developing junk mail that gets opened, instead of just being put into the bin. Packages arrive, and envelopes with exciting messages promising astonishing prizes, free gifts such as pens, plastic toys, on one occasion even two slices of bacon, all intended to grab our attention. The whole point of this exercise is to get a product noticed, to get people to read the message, be it for insurance, credit cards, or gas and electricity. Huge sums are spent on eye-catching posters, and armies of technicians make TV advertisements, all intended to catch the bored viewer or reader and to engage their interest with a view to selling a product.

Curiously, some of the best advertisements ever made were failures at selling the product they were hoping to promote. Most famous of these was a 1950s commercial for Strand cigarettes, an iconic short film featuring a lone man with a haunting theme, advertising a product which rapidly disappeared. The relationship between medium and message is a complex one. For works of art, the medium often is the message.

**Gospel Teaching**

Right at the beginning of Mark's Gospel we meet the curious phenomenon which has come to be known as the "messianic secret"; Jesus silences the demons because they know who he is and he does not want anybody to know that he is indeed the Son of God.

There are a variety of explanations offered for this phenomenon. One possibility is that Jesus does not want his identity to become more important than the message which he is carrying. As he says, he came to preach, and so he wants to move on throughout Galilee. If indeed he is known to be the Messiah from the outset of his ministry then that in itself would become the message, and would obscure the message of repentance and the news of the kingdom which he is carrying. People would want to know that the Messiah had come, but would not be interested in what the Messiah was saying to them, especially if the news which the Messiah was bringing was not what they expected to hear. The medium would obscure the message, and the mission would be like that of the Strand cigarette advertiser who made a classic film but failed to sell a product. If people knew that Jesus was the Messiah they would expect a message proclaiming the immediate triumph of Israel, whereas Jesus' messianic message is that Israel's triumph and God's kingdom are dependent upon people's repentance.

In the course of the Gospel, the identity of Jesus leaks out, but by the time that Jesus is able openly to accept his identity the mission to bring Israel to repentance has already failed, for his final acceptance of the title of Messiah takes place before the high priest when he is on trial for his life. The call to repentance has not been heard. By this time it does not matter if the medium becomes more important than the message, because the message has fallen on ears deliberately deaf. God's triumph in the resurrection of Jesus means that the message can continue, but the message then becomes the message about Jesus, rather than Jesus' message.

**Application**
The message has changed, for we are to proclaim Jesus himself rather than simply the message which he proclaimed; and the medium has changed, for Jesus no longer proclaims his own message, for the task of proclaiming his triumph has been given to us. And we are to proclaim that message not necessarily by preaching, but by living lives in which the triumph of Jesus, even in weakness and defeat, shines through.

What has not changed is the relative importance of the message over and above the medium. We are the means by which the message of Jesus is to be carried, but the point is not to do so in a way which draws attention to ourselves, but in one which allows the message of Jesus to be seen and heard. Jesus himself did not proclaim his identity, but was obedient to his purpose of proclaiming the kingdom. We are to be conspicuous as disciples of Jesus by being inconspicuous in the search for worldly recognition, notable for sanctity and humility, and not for sanctimoniousness and conceit, not in cleverness which courts admiration but in wisdom which only the Gospel can bring.

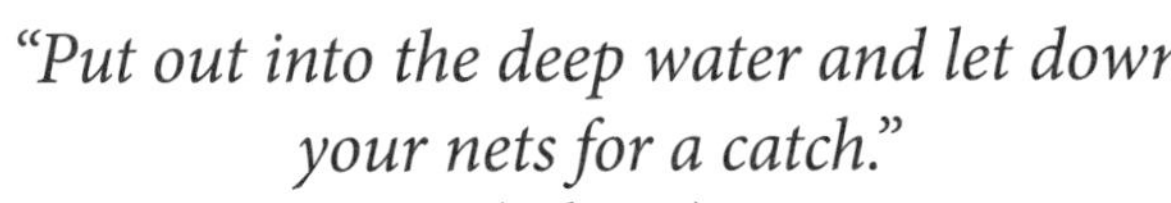

*"Put out into the deep water and let down your nets for a catch."*

(Luke 5:4)

**Illustration**

We have all done it, haven't we? We have been doing some simple, perfectly straightforward, everyday task – such as changing a wheel, or replacing a tap washer, emptying the vacuum cleaner, or baking a cake for a special occasion – and it won't go right, will it?

But we're determined it should. We've done it before, and we can do it again. With increased determination, our temperature (and blood pressure!) goes up. The odd oath may prove tempting.

And then, when we are most het up, along comes a friend, who jauntily and helpfully suggests, "Why don't you try…?"

Our immediate reaction may be to suggest that they take themselves off somewhere else – and quickly! A nanosecond later comes the stubborn desire to resist their suggestion and do things the way we always have. We are the ones who have been working at it. We know what the problem is – and we know how to solve it, if everything would just behave and fall into place.

Then, slowly, sanity begins to prevail. Yes, there is some sense in what our friend has suggested. Yes, what has been proposed will work. New eyes bring a new outlook; a new vision brings new understanding. We are able to see beyond the difficulties we've encountered. Yes, it works, we can do what we set out to do.

**Gospel Teaching**

Simon Peter was the expert. He'd been a fisherman all his life. He knew that there were plenty of good fishing trips – as well as the occasional fruitless one. He and his fishermen colleagues had just experienced one of these less fruitful nights. The nets had remained empty. And now here was this Jesus suggesting they go out and start fishing again.

We don't know what went through Simon Peter's mind. He might have been tempted to think, "Isn't he the carpenter? Does he know about fish and fishing?" True, he had seen Jesus heal his mother-in-law – an impressive talent, by any standards. But fishing wasn't about magic. It was about know-how.

But something – something about Jesus – made him respond. True, he pointed out the paucity of the previous night's efforts, but he responded, readily and willingly.

Could that something have been the impression Jesus had created earlier, when he innovatively sought the use of Simon Peter's boat as a floating pulpit, to teach those on the shoreline?

Here was a new approach. This man was prepared to tackle things in a different way. Here afloat on the shoreline Jesus put himself in touch with the people. And undoubtedly what Jesus had to say, and the way he had said it, made a very strong and incisive impression on Simon Peter. It was enough to induce Simon Peter immediately to call him "Master".

So when Jesus told him to cast his nets again Simon Peter was ready to do so, with amazing results, results that made him realise how stupid he had been to think, even for the blink of a second, that he might have known better than this very special man, the Master. Jesus gave him the chance to be a fisher of people and he readily grabbed it – as did James and John – and followed Jesus.

**Application**

Jesus' call was to ordinary folk, doing ordinary things. He wasn't looking for high-flying scholars or the sharpest intellectuals. He wanted ordinary folk, in touch with the ordinary and everyday world (the world we sometimes describe as "real").

That was the case two thousand years ago. It remains the case today.

Jesus calls ordinary folk – you and me – to help him in his mission and his ministry, to put him in touch with ordinary, real people. He wants to use our skills and gifts. He knows we can relate to those around us, and so we can link him with them, and them with him.

We too are called to be fishers of men, women and children. We are called to draw people into Jesus' presence.

We don't need theological degrees or to be members of Mensa to do this. We simply need to dispense with any doubts we may have – as did Simon Peter, James and John – and show our trust and faith in Jesus, in the way we speak, in what we do, in what we are, in the way we live our everyday lives.

## *"But I say to you..."*
(Matthew 5:22)

**Illustration**
There is a well-known children's story about a girl whose father has foolishly told the king that she can spin straw into gold. Of course she can't, and the king threatens to kill her if she doesn't do it. A strange little man appears, spins the straw, and saves the girl from death. But he asks for something in return. First it is a necklace, then a ring. And then he makes her promise to hand over her firstborn child when the time comes.

In due course the girl marries the king, and has a child, and the little man comes to make her keep her promise. However, she is so distraught that he gives her a second chance; she can keep the baby if she guesses his name. All such stories, of course, require a happy ending. The queen sends servants to find all the names in the world, and one of them happens upon the little man and discovers his name. So the queen keeps her baby, and Rumpelstiltskin disappears, never to be seen again.

One moral of the story is that it is unwise to brag or to make promises you don't intend to keep. But this is also a story about an impossible task made possible with a bit of the right kind of help.

**Gospel Teaching**
In what is known as the Sermon on the Mount, Matthew describes Jesus teaching people how to live. This kind of teaching is not new to the people Jesus is addressing. They are, after all, Jews. They have their law, given to them by God through Moses and interpreted down the ages, regulating every aspect of their lives. It prescribes how Jews eat, work and rest; how they marry and regulate their families; how they build their houses and grow their crops; how they look after the weaker members of the community. They are used to listening to rabbis like Jesus interpreting the law for them. "You have heard that it was said," begins the rabbi, "... but I tell you..." – and then comes a lesson on the law's contemporary application.

But what Jesus says is a little different from the norm. The law says do not murder; but Jesus says calling your friend a fool is just as bad. The law says do not commit adultery; but Jesus says looking at another woman with a

twinkle in your eye is just as bad. The law regulates divorce; but Jesus says divorce is the same as adultery. The law says don't swear false oaths; but Jesus says don't swear oaths at all.

What is going on here? Surely Jesus doesn't mean it? Surely a mild insult is not as serious an offence as murder? Surely a bit of flirting is not as bad as adultery?

What Jesus seems to be doing is challenging the people who are comfortable with their observance of the law. They have not murdered anyone, or committed adultery, or done any of the other things the law forbids. They are good-living, righteous people, who please God and care for their neighbour.

But Jesus tells them that they have no reason to be pleased with themselves. He pushes the law to its very limits, to the point where no one can obey it. There is no one who has not at some time expressed annoyance with another person. There is no one who has not looked at someone with desire. Obeying the law as Jesus expresses it is, it seems, as easy as spinning straw into gold.

Jesus is not saying that it is not worth trying. He recommends making efforts to live according to God's standards, but he points out that human beings will always fail. That does not mean, however, that all are equally condemned rather it means that all are equally in need of forgiveness and help.

**Application**

Too easily Christianity lapses into being a religion of good works. We try to be good people. And our very trying makes our religious observance all about us: our successes and our failures, our dramas and our crises. We come to the point where we are almost leaving God out of the equation, as though salvation is of our own making. So sometimes we need reminding of God's grace. We are God's people not because we keep God's law, but because we know that without help we cannot keep God's law. Our lives remain straw, until God turns them into gold.

*"Moved with pity, Jesus stretched out his hand and touched him."*
(Mark 1:41)

**Illustration**
Many people today are troubled by low self-esteem and a longing to be accepted. We now have whole TV programmes dedicated to plastic surgery, showing how to achieve a more "acceptable" body. Tabloids add to the pressure: scrutinising photos of celebrities, considering only the wrinkle-free, fat-free, blemish-free ones good enough.

Our struggles with acceptance and significance are nothing, however, compared to the experiences of the man in today's Gospel. He is referred to as a leper. This word is used in the Bible to cover a range of skin diseases, possibly not even including what we call leprosy today. Anyone diagnosed by the priest as having one of these skin diseases was considered ceremonially unclean and was no longer allowed to live amongst others. These people were expected to ensure that no one would ever approach them by making their leprous status even more conspicuous. If they were ever approached, they were expected to cry, "Unclean, unclean!" They were also expected to cover the lower part of their faces, wear ripped clothing and have dishevelled hair.

Shunned by society, even family and friends, and living in isolation, all this meant that these people were, in effect, treated as if they were already dead. In fact, in medieval times, lepers had the burial service performed over them while they were still alive!

**Gospel Teaching**
This leper showed great courage even approaching Jesus – having been forbidden from coming close to others. In great humility he begs, kneeling before Christ. What must this leper been have feeling? His stomach must have been a knot of nerves waiting for Jesus' response: would this holy man be horrified to be approached by someone unclean? Would he rebuke him for his audacity and send him away, rejected once more?

What is striking about the leper's request is that although he doesn't doubt Jesus' ability to heal him, he prefaces his words of faith with, "If you choose". Perhaps after a history of rejection, and resulting low self-esteem, he was unsure how important his plight would be to Jesus. He might have worried that this holy man would view his disease as punishment from God, the common thinking of the day.

Manuscript evidence differs over whether Jesus was filled with compassion or anger after the leper's request. If anger was his response, then perhaps it was at witnessing the intense suffering of this child of God, or maybe Jesus was saddened that the leper doubted his desire to heal him. He was certainly not angry that the leper had approached him, for he went on to perform the most compassionate act this pariah could have experienced: he touched him. We know that Jesus healed others without touching them, yet he chose to touch this leper, which according to the religious teaching of the day rendered Jesus unclean too.

How overwhelmed the leper must have been by this act of compassion – someone who embraced him when everyone else shunned him, and a holy man at that! This demonstration of love would have been almost as amazing to the leper as his consequent healing.

Jesus forbids the man from telling others about what has happened. The chaos that follows when the man ignores Jesus' words perhaps explains why. The Jews held the healing of lepers as a sign that the Messiah had arrived and most expected this Messiah to come and overthrow their Roman oppressors. Jesus was concerned here to keep his identity low-key, so as not to arouse civil unrest.

**Application**

Like the leper, many of us experience rejection of one sort or another and struggle with issues of acceptance and self-worth. Such experiences may encourage us to doubt, as the leper did, whether our holy God will love us and be interested in our worries and also lead us to fear that he will be angry at our weaknesses and reject us. But let's take comfort in the unconditional love Jesus showed the leper. Just as he reached out and touched him, so he embraces us and offers us acceptance.

Unlike the leper, though, we may be able to hide our uncleanness from others, keeping hidden the things of which we are ashamed. Like Adam and Eve after eating the forbidden fruit, we may unsuccessfully attempt to hide our shame from God too. But let's remember the leper's boldness in approaching Jesus while still unclean and be encouraged by Jesus' response to him. He was cleansed and given a fresh start: such healing and acceptance are there for us too.

*"Then he looked up at his disciples and said: 'Blessed are you who are poor, for yours is the kingdom of God.'"*
(Luke 6:20)

**Illustration**
One of today's growth industries is stress management. Schumacher College in the west of England runs courses on "simple living" for high-fliers. Its head, Satish Kumar, was quoted not long ago as saying, "People buy smart cars, big houses, yachts and all that, but they don't really have a life. They are so busy, so stressed, so guilty and pressured. They have no time to see their friends. They think they are rich. But if these things are bought at the expense of social, natural and spiritual values, then I'm afraid that I have to call this poverty."

He was putting into modern terms what Jesus says in our Gospel reading. We may have everything this world offers, yet still be spiritually and emotionally poor. By contrast, western visitors to countries in the developing world often discover that while people there are poor materially, they are rich in their strength of community and shared values. They know what faith and love are, in practice.

**Gospel Teaching**
Jesus' words, "Blessed are you who are poor," are sometimes understood to mean that material poverty is a special source of God's blessing. Certainly individuals who take vows of poverty in order to serve God often speak of his blessing and care. But material poverty isn't automatically a higher spiritual state than material wealth. Indeed, poverty is often a curse. Many are poor today because of other people's greed or violence. Those who are hungry or made homeless through accident, war or corruption can only be blessed if we help them and address whatever evils oppress them.

Jesus is not commanding us to sell everything and become poor. Rather, he's commending a spiritual attitude. The word "poor" here means someone who's at rock bottom, desperate. That may include people who don't know where their next meal is coming from. But it also includes those who feel passionately that life isn't worth living without God at the centre. They know their constant need of God. They're more hungry for him than for worldly goods. And they mourn deeply the sinfulness that hinders their spiritual growth. When they put God first in their lives, they're blessed. The word "blessed" is often translated "how happy", but it really means "how fortunate in the long term". The spiritually poor possess the kingdom of God. That is, they receive God's eternal love, care, gifts and power to serve him.

Jesus contrasts them with so-called "rich" people who are self-satisfied and who focus their lives on material things. They neglect God or move him to the margins of their lives. As a result, they know nothing of his forgiveness, and see nothing of his purposes. When they need him they may not find him. And those who reckon they are spiritually rich – who think their relationship with God is sewn up – will find their spiritual life drying up. Jesus, remember, was speaking to his disciples. A disciple, by definition, is one who knows there's always more to learn and is always aware of his or her spiritual poverty.

And the opposite of "blessed" is "alas". It means "how sad". When Jesus says, "alas for you who are rich" he isn't pronouncing a curse on people. Rather, he's grieving over their blindness and foolishness. He's sad that they've got their priorities wrong, that they're missing out on the most important things in life. They think they are rich, yet they are very poor.

**Application**
It's easy for us to agree with that! We're not like them; we've come in our spiritual poverty and hunger to worship God and to receive his nourishment in the sacrament. And yet, as soon as we think like that, we risk becoming self-satisfied, that is, "rich", and losing our hunger for God. It's not easy to stay spiritually poor.

One way is to keep focused on Jesus. He's perfect; we're not. He knows all things; we don't. He can do all things; we can't. He needs nothing; but we need him. Or think of someone you don't like too much; and remember that Jesus loves them as much as he loves you. Exercises like this soon show how poor we are, compared with him. And then we'll start to hunger for him and to weep for our sins – which is when we'll find his rich gifts to satisfy us deeply and, like tasty food, make us hunger for more.

*"Be perfect, therefore, as your heavenly Father is perfect."*
(Matthew 5:48)

**Illustration**

In Victor Hugo's novel *Les Misérables*, there is a famous scene in which a thief breaks into the bishop's house and starts to stuff the silver candlesticks into his pockets. He is caught by the police and waits, gloomily, to be carted off to prison. But the bishop says, gently, "I gave those candlesticks to my friend here, as a present."

It is hard to say who is more surprised by this statement, the thief or the police. Either way, the bishop seems to be someone who has taken to heart Jesus' teaching in the Sermon on the Mount.

**Gospel Teaching**

The Sermon on the Mount, in Matthew chapters 5–7, is often taken to be the moral teaching that most clearly and distinctively derives from Jesus. It is at every point obviously in dialogue with the Law of Moses, yet with its own unique twist.

But if this teaching sets out what Jesus really expects of his followers, then we are all doomed. Whether it is the warning, earlier in the Sermon on the Mount, that Jesus considers anger with a brother or sister to be as bad as murder, or the instruction in today's Gospel reading to love our enemies, we all know that we are going to fail.

It helps a bit, perhaps, to realise that today's passage is funny. We can imagine Jesus acting out the turning of the other cheek, or the gradual peeling off of garments to give them away. These are deliberately exaggerated instructions, cheerfully, cheekily, pointing to the deeper reality.

Jesus is suggesting that the real heart of the Law is not about placating God, or ensuring that we've ticked all the right religious boxes, and can present our forms at the Pearly Gates, all signed and filled in correctly. The Law is designed to make us like God. It is designed to form our characters, as individuals and as communities, until we can again be for the world what the creation story tells us we should be: the image of God.

So when Jesus says, frighteningly, that we have to be "perfect", like our heavenly Father, he means it. But this is not another codicil to the Law, not another instruction to be obeyed and ticked, as if that were ever possible. It is about re-imagining our whole life, and the life of our world, seeing it as God sees it.

**Application**

The Sermon on the Mount does indeed turn out to be utterly characteristic of Jesus and his understanding of morality. But not by adding yet another, more rigorous, layer of demands to those already expected of us, but by reminding us of what faith is for in the first place. It isn't primarily about our own personal morality, although that has to be part of it. It's about the world's salvation.

Jesus came not to teach a new ethic, but to reunite the world with its creator, and so to bring it back to its own true nature. A whole new way of behaving follows, because we suddenly see what we are for. We are here to live as the people who know the meaning of life, who know who we are: the brothers and sisters of Jesus, the Son.

And we are going to demonstrate that by being "perfect". "Perfect" is not "holier-than-thou", not separating ourselves from the sinners and preening ourselves on our good behaviour. "Perfect" is seeing the world whole, as God sees it. Jesus reminds us that God is indiscriminately caring to the good and the bad alike, giving sun, rain, life, impartially to all.

Does that shock us? Do we, with some part of ourselves, react as religious people reacted to Jesus in his own day? When Jesus said that he had come to call sinners, and to save the lost, many thought he was simply condoning immorality, and failing to set a strong moral example. But here, in the Sermon on the Mount, he explains exactly what he is doing: he is demonstrating the nature of God and the calling of all humanity.

That's why the bishop in Victor Hugo's story has really understood the Sermon on the Mount. He is not turning a blind eye to wrongdoing, but drawing the thief into his friendship, and giving him a chance to be a new person. He is being "perfect", like his heavenly Father. And that's our calling, too. We are privileged to see the world through the eyes of the God who created it, loves it and redeemed it, in Jesus.

*"...authority on earth to forgive sins."*
(Mark 2:10)

**Illustration**
In one of the Harry Potter stories, the young wizard and his friends are being threatened by some terrible creatures called Dementors. Dementors are security guards who control their prisoners by sucking the spirit out of them and leaving them in a state of abject despair. At one point Harry is alone and surrounded. But just as he is about to be overcome, a silver stag rides towards him, breaking the Dementors' spell and saving Harry. Harry recognises the spirit of his dead father.

Some time later, Harry's clever friend Hermione has been taught a way to travel back in time. She and Harry have gone back a few hours in order to put something right. Harry watches as he is attacked by the Dementors, and he waits for his father's magic to ride to the rescue. But nothing happens. Harry realises the truth just in time. The figure Harry saw wasn't his father at all: it was him, come from the future. Harry performs the magic himself, and rescues himself. It is the spirit of his father in him that has enabled him to perform such strong magic and overcome the Dementors.

**Gospel Teaching**
In today's Gospel reading, Jesus is in trouble. It is very early in his ministry, but already he is upsetting the religious leaders. He has gained a reputation for healing people, and so a man who is paralysed is brought to Jesus by his friends, lowered through a hole in the roof of the house where Jesus is because the crowds are too great below.

The dramatic entrance grabs everyone's attention, and all are waiting to see if Jesus can heal the man. They are quiet, waiting for Jesus to tell him to get up from his stretcher. But instead, Jesus says something surprising. He says, "Son, your sins are forgiven."

We don't know whether Jesus sees that part of the man's problem is sins that are weighing on him and hindering his healing, or whether Jesus is simply using the occasion to make a point. Whichever it is, elements in the crowd react. Only God can forgive sins. Jesus' declaration of forgiveness amounts to blasphemy. They are worried. Is this rabbi they have come to hear going to be trouble?

So Jesus addresses them. "Which is easier," he asks, "to say to the paralytic, 'Your sins are forgiven,' or to say, 'Stand up and take your mat and walk'?" Jesus then tells the man to get up and he does, healed. The crowd have got what they were waiting for, but they are also being expected to learn a lesson from what they have seen. Jesus has performed the miracle, he says, so that people may know that "the Son of Man has authority on earth to forgive sins".

Much scholarly ink has been expended on the meaning of the phrase "the Son of Man", which is in origin a Semitic way of saying "human being". But it seems that, at least in some cases, Jesus uses its traditional meaning. Here he seems to be saying that it is not the case that only God can declare forgiveness of sins: human beings can do it too. Human beings can look at their neighbours and tell them that they are forgiven and loved by God, that the wrong they have thought and done can be set aside, that they can walk out of the room leaving behind the guilt that has crippled them and start afresh.

This is not blasphemy. It is not a case of humans taking on a role that properly belongs to God. Rather it is humans taking responsibility for the well-being of themselves and others, a responsibility which God has given them.

The friends of the paralysed man loved him enough to bring him to Jesus, and make the effort to get him to the roof and lower him down. But they could not imagine making him feel forgiven.

**Application**
We can be like Harry Potter, waiting for our Father to ride to the rescue. But we, like Harry, have to learn that we have the authority to do things for ourselves. We can free ourselves and others from burdens of guilt and shame. We can be generous and forgiving towards our neighbours and towards ourselves. Then when we eventually meet our heavenly Father we will be able to stand upright, knowing that our sins count for nothing in the light of God's love.

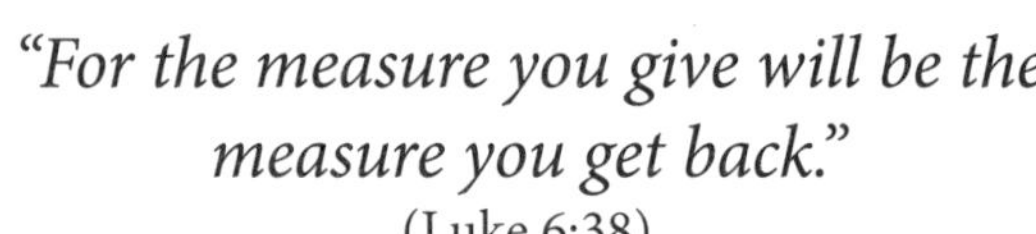

*"For the measure you give will be the measure you get back."*
(Luke 6:38)

**Illustration**

The words "spiritual" and "spirituality" are very popular nowadays. People often claim that, while they are not religious, they are spiritual. The National Health Service recognises a "spiritual" dimension in the process of health care and patient recovery. Bookshops have sections on "Mind, Body and Spirit", where books on crystals, myths, angels and meditation all rub shoulders together amicably.

So "spirituality" becomes another lifestyle choice. We can try different ones according to our mood. "Spiritualities" do not demand commitment or make tedious moral claims on our lives.

**Gospel Teaching**

In that sense, Christianity is not a "spiritual" religion, as today's Gospel reading makes plain. This is part of Luke's equivalent of Matthew's "Sermon on the Mount", and it is interesting to compare the two. At every point, Luke's version is more concrete, more demanding, less spiritualised, if that were possible.

Where Matthew's Jesus says, "Love your enemies and pray for those who persecute you," Luke spells it out to make it absolutely clear that this "love" is not a feeling, not a spiritualised, internalised approach to others; it is about what you do, and, in particular, what you do with your money and your possessions.

Luke's audience is used to a system of mutual benefits. If you lend somebody something, they are in your debt, and the debt must be repaid, in some way or another. But Luke says that we have a choice: we can go on belonging to the "I scratch your back and you scratch mine" system, or we join God's system, instead. God gets nothing from us, and yet he cares for all.

This leads, in Luke, into a brief discourse about forgiveness and its benefits. St Augustine of Hippo said that forgiveness ought to be one of the most characteristic things about Christians: we know that we have been forgiven and so we forgive. We know that we are constantly in need of new forgiveness, and so we know that our neighbours will be, too. This is the theme of the family prayer of all Christians, the prayer we call "the Lord's Prayer", which Jesus himself gave us: "forgive us our sins as we forgive others". It is a theme that certainly derives from Jesus himself, recurring in several parables, as well as in teaching like this.

"Forgive us our sins as we forgive others", "for the measure you give will be the measure you get back". We have here a picture of superabundance: pouring down in a steady stream into somebody's lap until they are almost buried in it. It is a joyful picture of generosity. But we tend to forget that what is to be poured into our laps is of the same kind as we have given to others. It's our choice whether it will be good things or bad, because it will reflect our own actions.

In Acts, Luke gives us the idyllic picture of the earliest Church in which possessions were held in common, and where rich and poor were all equally fed and cared for. Luke's first readers were not at liberty to think that Christianity was a "spiritual" religion. They needed to know that, if they joined this movement, it would make radical demands upon them, and change their whole understanding of how the world should run. God's mutual benefits system works very differently from the human one we have set up.

**Application**

It is extraordinary how we have managed to ignore so much of Jesus' teaching and turn our discipleship into another lifestyle choice which doesn't make too many demands upon us.

Few of us are called to follow St Francis who, when he heard Jesus' words to the rich young ruler read out in church, took them literally, and went and sold all that he had and gave it to the poor. But most of us are probably called to take the Gospel a little more literally than we do.

But this is not an attempt to send us all away depressed and guilty, because Luke's picture is a joyful one. It concentrates on what we get back through following Jesus' teaching: every time we give something, share something, try to treat our enemies with love, we know that that is what we will get back from God. And not just in some distant and spiritualised future, but now. Giving and forgiving are wonderfully releasing, vital actions. Let's all try them, today and every day.

2nd Sunday before Lent

*"Consider the lilies of the field, how they grow; they neither toil nor spin, yet I tell you, even Solomon in all his glory was not clothed like one of these."*
(Matthew 6:28-29)

**Illustration**
The *Little Book of Calm* was a best-seller for several months when it was first published. Its popularity revealed just how much worry and anxiety form part of our lives. There is so much to worry about – from money, to health, to relationships, to exams, to job interviews, to the future and it takes up a great deal of time and energy. Often when you're worried, you find you can't sleep – and then you get tired, and that makes everything seem worse. As Corrie Ten Boom, a writer and survivor of a concentration camp, said, "Worry does not empty tomorrow of its sorrow; it empties today of its strength."

**Gospel Teaching**
In today's Gospel reading we hear Jesus telling his disciples very specifically, "Do not worry." Jesus knew how much time could be wasted in worrying, and also knew that there were so many more important things to be thinking about and doing. Where do worry and anxiety really fit into a living faith? We are so easily distracted from what really matters. Our society encourages us to be distracted – you just have to look at all the advertisements lining the billboards around the streets to be deluged with information about things you do not need to know about, and to be given a sense of what life should be like – you should have a bigger house, a faster car, a certain type of bank account, a certain body shape. Our children should have the latest toys and wear the latest fashions; we should all be eating certain types of food.

It takes a degree of courage and insight to be able to stand back from all this pressure and hear Jesus saying, "Hey! Isn't life more than food, and the body more than clothing? Don't strive for all of this – instead, strive for God's kingdom, and his righteousness."

There are other things that worry us, of course: symptoms of ill health that scare us: a lump here, a mole there – possibly harmless, possibly deadly. We can put ourselves in the hands of the experts to tell us the diagnosis and to treat us as they think best, but the fear can still remain. In the face

of illness we realise that however much we may have achieved in terms of status, relationship or whatever else, we may have no control over what happens to us. And still Jesus says, "Do not worry about your life. Your heavenly Father knows what you need. But strive first for the kingdom of God and his righteousness."

He reminds his disciples that the God who takes so much care over making a flower beautiful and giving a bird wings will take much more care over each human being, because we are worth so much more than flowers and birds. The simplicity of the lifespan of a flower should give us pause for thought, however – all it does is follow the pattern decreed for it, putting all its energy into growing and into becoming what it is designed to be. Unlike flowers, we can choose how to grow and what path to follow. But we too will find our lives most fulfilled when we can grow to become the people God wants us to be.



**Application**

Jesus tells us not to get sidetracked, and not to waste our time worrying about all the things we think we need. Instead we are to strive for God's kingdom and his righteousness. That means allowing God to rule in our lives, rather than anything or anyone else. It means regularly asking ourselves: what am I trying to achieve in this situation? Am I trying to please the world or am I trying to please God? If it is the former, then you may as well get back to worrying about how you are doing and what you need to get next.

But if it is God you want to please, then remember that he looks at you as a unique individual, and that he knows and understands everything about you. He has everything in hand; you don't need to worry about it. He has planned a way ahead for you that will bring real peace, a peace that is unshakeable, whatever may change in the world around you. And as you seek God's will and God's way, so you will find that you are naturally working with him in bringing God's kingdom to the whole earth.

*"The Word became flesh and lived among us, and we have seen his glory."*
(John 1:14)



**Illustration**
There's a series of wonderful books for children which tell the adventures of Little Bear, who lives with Big Bear in the Bear Cave. One of them tells how one night Little Bear cannot get to sleep. It turns out that the problem is that he is afraid of the dark. Big Bear produces ever bigger lanterns but Little Bear is still afraid of the huge dark outside the Bear Cave. Eventually Big Bear takes Little Bear outside and shows him the moon and the stars, lighting up the sky, and then Little Bear falls asleep.

We can light up our own little world, but sometimes the bigger picture is frightening even for Big Bears. The world can seem a random and terrifying place, containing who knows what dangers, and threatening extinction in all kinds of horrible ways. Today's Gospel reading speaks to those fears.

**Gospel Teaching**
The readings set for today deal with very complex matters of faith. They speak of the creation of the universe, at the very beginnings of time, a time beyond the capacity of the human brain to imagine. And they speak of God incarnate, the creator of the universe somehow living a human life among us.

How can we speak of such matters? The biblical writers know well that only the language of poetry will suffice. Prose soon gets tangled in its own logic, and scientific language reaches its limits; only poetry can hope to convey the mystery of these huge ideas. So the prologue to the Gospel of John uses imagery to convey its message. The Word became flesh. The light shines in the darkness. We have seen his glory. The language is magnificent, and this passage deserves its fame for its poetry alone.

But the point it is making is one of deep significance. The author of the fourth Gospel uses the term "Word" for the one who became incarnate, echoing the Wisdom language of the Old Testament. By doing so, he reinforces his point that the one who becomes human and lives among us is no other than the one who was present at the foundation of the world.

The author echoes the language of the book of Proverbs, which describes Wisdom being beside God when he laid the foundations of the earth. And he also echoes the language of Genesis, which also begins with the phrase, "In the beginning".

So he makes the connections between God's actions in the beginning and his actions in Christ. The Word who became flesh "was in the beginning with God. All things came into being through him." The one who brought the very first light out of the dark wastes described in Genesis is the one who now shines in the darkness. The one who breathed life into the very first of God's children on earth is the one who now brings new life, "the power to become children of God".



**Application**

So how can such deep matters of theology speak to our fears? First, they show the consistency of God. Jesus does not appear from nowhere as a kind of random teacher and miracle worker, John's Gospel asserts. The incarnation of the Word is all of a piece with God's acts from the very beginning. Creation and recreation belong together. We can trust God, because it was he who formed our world and us in it and it was he who cared enough for our world to come and live in it. The God we worship today is that same creator God, known to us through Christ.

Secondly, order in the universe is asserted. We are not an accident and nor is our world. The creation of the world is purposeful, and so is its salvation. The world began when God spoke his Word, and it will not end until he says so. From the Greek for "word" we get our word "logic". There is a logic in the universe, and it is God's own logic, his purposes being worked out.

The world out there may seem a dark and dangerous and meaningless place sometimes, but we are assured that "the light shines in the darkness, and the darkness has not overcome it". It may be difficult to see God's purposes as more than a flickering candle in the dark, but the incarnation of the Word means that at least we have seen them in our own shape. In Christ incarnate we are given a glimpse of God's purposes in human form. "The Word became flesh and lived among us, and we have seen his glory." And that is enough.

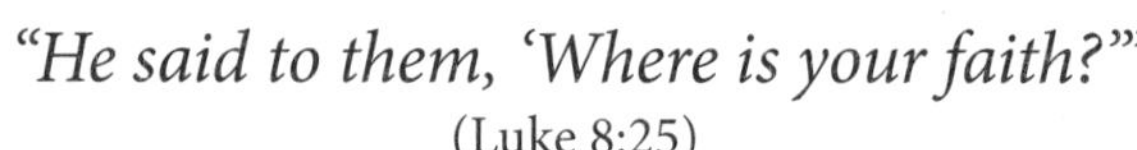

*"He said to them, 'Where is your faith?'"*

(Luke 8:25)

**Illustration**

Amid storms of bitter controversy threatening to overwhelm the Church and break it apart, a Christian leader was recently asked what was the one essential message that all its members needed to hear. You might have expected "Maintain the unity of the Spirit" or "Love one another", but his response was "Don't panic!" When we panic we stop trusting that God is present among us. But God is present in every storm and the way ahead for us always begins with trust. This is what the panic-stricken disciples of Jesus learnt when they were caught up in a storm on the Sea of Galilee.

**Gospel Teaching**

In the Bible, the sea is often thought of as a place of chaos and disorder, threatening God's good purposes. The people of Israel spoke of God stilling the raging of the waves and saving those in danger on the sea. Here the disciples see Jesus doing the same things: terrifying natural powers are tamed; life can go on in peace. And in his wider ministry Jesus calms storms not only at sea but also in the lives of those he heals and delivers from evil.

Such authority prompts the disciples to ask who this man is; gradually they will come to understand the fullness of God's presence and action in Jesus. There's also a hint here that the authority exercised by Jesus stems from his perfect trust in God; as the disciples rush around in panic achieving nothing, Jesus at first sleeps peacefully and then acts in power. The childlike trust in God which Jesus taught and lived out may appear impractical and foolish, but it is this trust which enables him to be a channel of God's action in the world.

This story illustrates the slow and painful progress of the disciples. They have left everything to follow Jesus; for some time now they have listened to his teaching and witnessed his power to heal; they acknowledge him as their master. But the storm on the Sea of Galilee seems to blow away everything they have learnt. "Where is your faith?" asks Jesus: panic has driven trust from their hearts. This isn't the only time the disciples fail in faith and understanding. Often Jesus rebukes them, but he perseveres with them and continues to entrust his mission to them.

**Application**

The God we see in Jesus is a stiller of storms; God wills harmony for the world and peace for all our hearts. But storms rage on, around us and within us. So why isn't the God who through Jesus stilled the storm more obviously at work in the world today? Although that question is notoriously hard to answer, our faith does offer us ways forward.

Storms in our own lives can all too easily undermine our trust in God and make us panic, like the disciples. But the disciples are rebuked for their lack of faith, not for calling out in their genuine need. So when our lives are in danger of being swamped by chaos or suffering of various kinds it's far worse to turn away from God in bitter silence than to cry out in faith (perhaps mingled with anger). We may then know some lessening of the storm about us or it may be that as the storm continues we are drawn deeper into the trusting relationship with the Father which we see in Jesus, who in this storm lies asleep like a child and trusts the Father through worse storms yet to come.

As we look beyond our own lives to the storms in God's world, it helps to remember that what we often call "miracles" are usually known in the New Testament as "signs". Signs point to something greater than themselves: when Jesus healed, fed hungry crowds, or calmed a storm, these were pointers to something greater, a foretaste of God's kingdom of lasting well-being, justice and peace. So in our daily praying for the coming of that kingdom there is both pain and confidence: pain because of the world's continuing storms; confidence because in Jesus God has stilled storms and the world is in the hands of this God. And sharing in the prayer of Jesus naturally leads to sharing in his work of stilling storms – a link well made in the prayer that asks God to make us channels of his peace.

*"Jesus took with him Peter and James and his brother John and led them up a high mountain, by themselves. And he was transfigured before them."*
(Matthew 17:1-2)

**Illustration**

Ask any mountaineers why they climb such heights and take such risks and you will receive a variety of responses. Among them are: because the mountains are there, for the challenge, the rush of adrenalin, the sense of achievement. But the more sensitive and enlightened climbers will also tell you: because it teaches you something about yourself; you are faced with yourself unlike in any other context.

Mountains have always fascinated people. They symbolise stability and continuity. They provide unparalleled vistas, a new way of looking at creation and our tiny place within it. Mountains have been places of refuge, and regarded by some tribes as being among the first created earthly things and, therefore, closer to God, by virtue of age and height. Moses went up a mountain to confirm his relationship with God; Peter remembered that Jesus had come down from the mountain and walked on the water. And even Julie Andrews in *The Sound of Music* went up a mountain to sing that "the hills are alive with the sound of music", as her character, Maria, found comfort and emotional and spiritual relief from the rather stultifying atmosphere of her convent. Everyone who climbs a mountain discovers something, even if it is only that they prefer sea level – but it is usually much more than that.

**Gospel Teaching**

Jesus was acting within a fine biblical tradition when he took his disciples up the mountain in order to teach them something special about himself, and themselves, as mountains have great significance in the history and geography of Palestine. When it came to important prophecies or teaching, or when God needed to impart something for the good of his people, a mountain was often the chosen location.

So why did Jesus take his disciples there and why, since he asked them to remain silent on the subject, do we need to know today? Because this event on the mountain happened six days after Jesus had told his disciples that any true follower must take up their cross and follow him. So, as

Peter, James and John went up the mountain with Jesus, so must we. On that mountain Jesus showed his friends exactly who he was and, as they witnessed his transfiguration, they began to realise within themselves exactly who they were. Jesus, no longer just another man with special powers, became confirmed as their Messiah. They became not just friends of this man with special powers, but true and complete disciples – fully informed about the extent of Jesus' role in relation to God and utterly committed to his person and his teaching.

In chapter 16 of Matthew's Gospel, Jesus asks the disciples who they think Jesus is. Peter responds that he knows Jesus to be the Messiah, the Son of the living God. Up until then this was inspired guesswork, based on the teaching and behaviour of Jesus. Peter's reward for his act of faith was Jesus taking him up on the mountain where he could witness the presence of Moses and Elijah in conversation with him and then hear the voice of the living God confirming Jesus to be exactly who Peter had thought he was. Suddenly Peter discovered something about his own identity and his destiny. He was no longer just the fisherman but the follower of truth in the company of the Messiah and the whole host of heaven.

**Application**

And so it is for us. This story of Jesus on the mountain is our story too, except that we do not have to keep silent, quite the reverse. From the moment when we truly acknowledge who Jesus is, our world changes. No longer just the sum of our worker or family roles, we become fully the disciples of Christ. We bear the strain and struggles of our lives, spreading his good news and changing the world. Because whenever Christians act for the good of the world, other people and the planet, in the name of Christ, so our world becomes a better place.

We may not have an opportunity to go with Jesus in person up a mountain, but the Gospel takes us there. What happened to the disciples then is for our enlightenment and ownership now. So, when you next climb a hill or mountain, remember Mount Hermon and God's message which confirms your discipleship, and open your heart to whatever else God has in mind for you.

*"He was transfigured before them."*
(Mark 9:2)

**Illustration**
This week's Gospel reading contains no words from Jesus himself. He is at the very centre of a major event, yet he has no comment to make, save to give an instruction to the disciples not to talk about it for the time being. So it is the event itself which must speak to us.

The Bible tells us that the creation of light was God's first move in the whole creative process. Light is a creative force in its own right. But it can be foe as well as friend.

For the person suffering from migraine, light may heap agony upon agony. The flashlight of a camera can, for a moment, blind us. The electric welder must use a shield to protect his eyes from the brilliance of the arc light which is the tool of his trade. The laser beam which can be the surgeon's instrument of healing can in other hands be an offensive weapon.

**Gospel Teaching**
The full glory of God is more than human eyesight can safely accommodate. We are told that Moses' face was so irradiated by a meeting with God that when he came down the mountain he put on a veil to safeguard the eyesight of those who looked at him. Even at second hand the glory of God has to be treated with care.

Jesus takes his closest friends to the top of a mountain. There, for a moment, they see their friend from Nazareth in a new light. Moses and Elijah come to talk with him. He is bathed in the glorious radiance of his heavenly Father. But the experience is only for a while. Moses and Elijah disappear. The light fades. Back to normal.

Peter, James and John recognise that they have witnessed a moment of special privilege. In a unique way the human Jesus has been revealed to them as the divine Jesus.

One of the glories of being human is that we are susceptible to experiences which lift us out of ourselves and put us on another plane. We have moments when we are specially vulnerable and specially receptive. Those who are musical may be transported by the inspired performance of a familiar work. Those who are sensitive to the visual arts may be captivated by a picture, a sculpture, a building. Those with an ear for words may find that a poem speaks for them unerringly. And all of us may be swept off our feet by some special experience or other – childbirth, perhaps, or the natural world in powerful uproar or tranquil peace. Our sensitivity to the world around us and to the ways in which it has been enriched by God's gracious gifts to his children is priceless.

But it is in the very nature of these experiences that they do not last. They may affect us permanently, but they are themselves transient.

Peter, James and John had to leave the hilltop. The memory of what had happened would be with them for ever, but the nitty-gritty world of everyday things was waiting for them at the foot of the mountain.

**Application**

The high points of everyday living are matched by similar special moments in our spiritual lives. Just at the time when our private prayers and our corporate worship may be going through a difficult patch – perhaps they seem arid, repetitive, lifeless – suddenly there's a spark. All at once, perhaps for no very obvious reason, something has set a light to our spiritual touchpaper. Perhaps it was the liturgy itself, either in elaborateness at a solemn liturgy or in simplicity at a Taizé-style act of worship. Perhaps it was a noisy, joyful acclamation, perhaps it was in silence. No matter. It's happened.

And suddenly a prayer monologue becomes a prayer conversation. Yes – there is indeed somebody on the other end of the line. Acts of Holy Communion, which for several weeks may have seemed more duty-driven than invigorating, suddenly come to life. "The body of Christ… the blood of Christ…" for me! We have caught a glimpse.

What matters is that we should take the glimpse with us when we move on. It will help us in the dog days, cheer us when we are feeling down, give us light when all around seems dark.

> "'Tis good, Lord, to be here!
> Yet we may not remain;
> But since thou bidst us leave the mount
> Come with us to the plain."

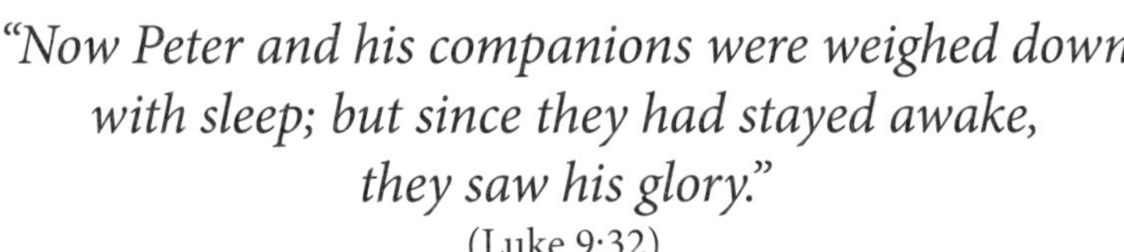

*"Now Peter and his companions were weighed down with sleep; but since they had stayed awake, they saw his glory."*
(Luke 9:32)

**Illustration**

It's probably true to say that the image of King Kong perched precariously on top of the Empire State Building, with "the queen of scream" Fay Wray struggling, and indeed screaming, in his hands, is imprinted on most of our minds. It might look a bit hammy now, but at the time the special effects were astonishing, and helped to give the 1933 film *King Kong* a firm place in our memories and imagination. The same is true of the special effects in the 2005 version of the film, although whether it will be remembered in the future with the same affection remains to be seen. To capture the imagination and make the unbelievable believable has been a major business within the film industry ever since it began. Every film director knows the power of the special effect to enthral and convince audiences, especially with imaginative plots that take place outside of the everyday familiarity of people's lives.

**Gospel Teaching**

Luke is a conscientious storyteller, scrupulous with his dates and history, but at the same time he shows the most delicate skill in weaving together the believable and unbelievable, the real and seemingly unreal. In this, he displays something of the film director's touch. With its virgin birth, miracles and resurrection, the Christian story is full of unbelievable things, and unlike the film director, who simply has to make that which is untrue believable, the greatest and most difficult task of every Christian is to convince others – and even ourselves sometimes – that the unbelievable is true.

And this is what the transfiguration is all about. It comes at a vital turning point in Luke's Gospel. Jesus has just ended his relatively popular ministry in Galilee, and is about to start a journey to Jerusalem and death. Peter has just declared that he believes that Jesus is the Messiah, and Jesus has begun to explain to his disciples that messiahship means betrayal and death, not glory and fame.

And it is at this crucial point of Jesus' ministry that he and three of his disciples go up a mountain to pray. While he is praying, Luke says, his appearance is altered, and his clothes become a dazzling white. No wonder the disciples don't seem to know whether they're awake or asleep, and they keep quiet about it afterwards. It's almost too strange to believe; like a little bit of Narnia in the middle of a documentary. Its purpose, though, is to clarify Jesus' identity and to cement his credentials for the task ahead. The presence of Moses and Elijah on the mountaintop – Moses as the greatest lawgiver in the history of the people of God, and Elijah the greatest of the prophets – shows that Jesus is much, much more than a Galilean carpenter with a way with words and a healing touch. He is the fulfilment of all the Law and the prophets; the long-awaited Messiah.

And as if to seal this point, a strange cloud descends upon the assembled group. In the Bible, clouds such as this mean one thing – the terrifying presence of God. It is meant to remind the reader of the giving of the commandments in the Old Testament, when just such a cloud descended on the mountaintop, and the glory of the Lord "was like a consuming fire". Jesus represents a new Law, a new commandment, anointed by God himself for the task.

**Application**

As we go through Lent, and towards the crucifixion, we are about to be confronted with some of the most faith-stretching parts of the Christian story. We will stand at the foot of the cross, and in front of the empty tomb, and reflect deeply on what they mean. Faith is seldom a question of lining up the facts and making a cold-hearted decision. Christianity asks us to believe the most unbelievable things, and therefore a little bit of hot-headed passion – even imagination – is required. Not the kind of imagination which makes the untrue believable, but that which makes the unbelievable true.

Luke wants us to comprehend the breadth of Jesus' identity: to see who he really is, and what he means for each of us. However rational and level-headed we are, we all have those moments when God asks us to declare our faith in his impossible story. Let's pray for God's gift of passion and imagination so that when that moment comes we will be able to respond with words of wonder and worship.

# Lent

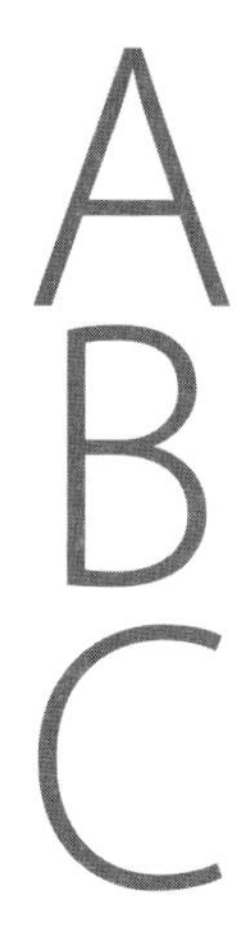



*"But store up for yourselves treasures in heaven, where neither moth nor rust consumes and where thieves do not break in and steal."*
(Matthew 6:20)

**Illustration**
John Connolly's novel *The Book of Lost Things* tells the story of a boy called David who escapes from unhappiness at home into the strange alternative world of the books in his bedroom. As David tries to find his way back home, he is forced to face up to his worst fears. As he does so, he grows from a boy into a man.

Finally David faces down and destroys the mysterious Crooked Man, the driving force in the alternative world. The Crooked Man lives for ever, drawing the life force from small children for his own use. He brings death and despair to all who encounter him. One of the cruellest things he does is to show people an image of when and how they will die. This knowledge blights the lives of those who receive it. They can no longer take any pleasure in life, because their death dominates all their thinking.

Human beings are not supposed to know how and when they will die. But knowing *that* we will die is a feature of our human life. We are aware of our mortality. We know that our lives are finite. We feel in our bodies the signs of ageing. In order to get on with our lives, we push the knowledge of our mortality to the edges of our consciousness most of the time. But occasionally we need to remember.

**Gospel Teaching**
Today is the day the Church gives us for remembering our mortality. In the context of our belief in Jesus Christ, we do have choices about what happens to us after death. In today's reading from Matthew's Gospel, Jesus tells his hearers that we make choices, day by day, about what is valuable, not always realising that those choices have ultimate significance. When we choose to store up our "treasures in heaven", we are not denying the reality of physical death, only its permanence.

If we follow the Church's tradition and receive ash on our foreheads, we hear the words, "Remember that you are dust, and to dust you shall return." We are reminded of the scene in the Garden of Eden, told to us by the authors of Genesis. Human beings are created from the dust of the ground, and have the life of God breathed into them. They live contented, unencumbered by awareness of their mortality, until they eat the fruit of the tree of the knowledge of good and evil. Then they become aware of who they are, in all their frailty, weakness and sinfulness. They know that as they came from the dust, so they will in the end return to the dust – as will we.

We are invited, today, to think about our death, to look it in the face, and not to pretend we are immortal. It is a painful process. But we are not left alone to despair. The words at the imposition of ashes continue: "Turn away from sin and be faithful to Christ."

Today, as we enter the season of Lent, we are reminded that Jesus was a human being like us. A more fully human person than the rest of us, in his ability consistently to put the claims of God above his human drives and desires; but human like us in being tempted to put self first. Jesus experienced our weakness, and our mortality. He knew for himself what it was like to be aware of death, and to be afraid. He lived, and died, as we do. But by doing so he gave us hope that our mortality is not the last word. Death did not, ultimately, have power over Jesus, nor does it over those who belong to him. So as we are urged to remember that we are dust, we are also exhorted to be faithful to Christ, to follow the one who shows us a way to face death and not despair.

**Application**

The awareness of mortality is both humanity's greatest tragedy and our greatest gift. It can lead us to despair, but it can also drive us on to greater heights of achievement. We can allow it to make our lives meaningless, or we can use it to remind us to make the most of the time we have. The season of Lent encourages us to be honest with ourselves and with God about who we are – weak, sinful, mortal, and in need of salvation. So we can choose to turn away from sin and be faithful to Christ, and live our lives, brief though they may be, to the full, in God's service.

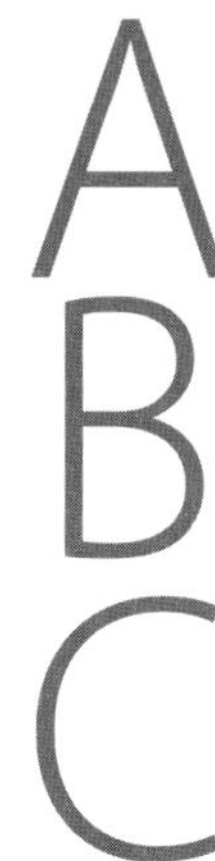



*"For where your treasure is, there your heart will be also."*
(Matthew 6:21)

**Illustration**

Today is the first day of Lent, and in Lent we give up things. Often they are things that we know we really shouldn't do anyway – swearing, perhaps, or eating too much chocolate. But the tradition began with more serious abstinence, with genuine fasting, and the wearing of sackcloth and ashes as a sign of penitence: hence, Ash Wednesday. Fasting, like prayer and almsgiving, is one of the marks of religious observance – common to Christianity, Judaism and Islam – which Jesus examines in today's Gospel reading.

"Giving up", of course, has another meaning in English. When we reach the end of our tether, when it all gets too much, there is a temptation to say, "That's it. I give up." Having tried everything, we decide that enough is enough and the situation really is hopeless.

Lent, when we recall the time that Jesus spent in the wilderness, is a vivid reminder that God never gives up on us. Jesus, faced with hunger and isolation and fear of the unknown, resisted the temptation to give up, to turn aside from his mission and surrender to the lure of worldly power and glory. He put his faith firmly in his heavenly Father. Alone in the wilderness, he fasted, prayed and prepared for his ministry and its inevitable outcome: the ultimate act of giving, laying down his life.

**Gospel Teaching**

The Gospel reading shows us Jesus preaching what he practised. Matthew records this teaching of Jesus, on the subject of almsgiving, prayer and fasting, right in the middle of the Sermon on the Mount. At its heart, in those verses omitted from today's reading, is the Lord's Prayer. Matthew's Gospel is very carefully structured; patterns like this are important. We can safely assume that, to Matthew, these verses, and the Lord's Prayer which they surround, represent the very kernel of the sermon Jesus preached.

Three times, using almsgiving, prayer and fasting as his illustrations, Jesus gives the same message: practise your faith in secret, and your Father who sees in secret will reward you. Not flaunting your faith, however, is not the same as hiding it. When Jesus tells his followers to pray in secret, to fast in secret, to give to the poor in secret, he is not saying to us, "Don't let on you're a Christian!" It is not our faith which we must keep from the world, but ostentatious display of it.

Whether it is almsgiving, prayer or fasting, Jesus tells us we should do it not for human admiration but for God. Then, the reward we are promised is not something transitory like public acclaim; it is nothing less than the love of a heavenly Father for his children. Repeatedly, Jesus speaks of "your Father". In the Lord's Prayer he urges us to pray to "our Father".

Worldly treasures like wealth, power and popularity are nothing in comparison with the heavenly treasures in store for us if our hearts are in the right place: with God. Throughout the Sermon on the Mount, Jesus reminds us that it is the heart that matters. True righteousness comes from within, from the secret part of us, the part where we can be with God.

**Application**

There is an organic relationship between fasting, prayer and almsgiving. In fasting, we deny ourselves luxuries which distance us from God; prayer brings us closer to God; and our love for God spills over into our dealings with others. Other people are then no longer those whose admiration we crave, but those with whom we want to share the love of God. When this happens, we gladly deny ourselves unnecessary extras, so that we have enough to give to others. And so it goes on.

In our fasting, we can give up all forms of conspicuous consumption, those things we really have no need of. In prayer, we can give up asking for ourselves and instead ask what God wants of us. In helping others, we can give up thinking in terms of charity, and see it as sharing all the good things God has given to us: not just our money, but our time and our talents. Every Eucharist commemorates again those mind-blowing events of Good Friday and Easter, the vivid proof that God never gives up on us. So let us make sure that our "giving up" in response is not just for Lent, but for life.

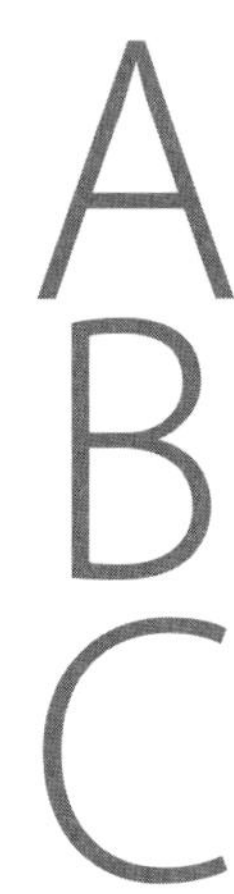



*"Let anyone among you who is without sin be the first to throw a stone at her."*
(John 8:7)

**Illustration**

A certain churchwarden, who was not enamoured of the vicar, was shocked to find that he was planning a wedding during Lent. And, like chilli peppers on a wound, flowers were to be allowed in church at the event. Not waiting to discover the poignant circumstances that made the wedding desirable at that particular time, the next Sunday the warden created a huge scene. Embarrassment and anger followed, which took many weeks to calm down. Surely our Lenten observances, precious as they may be, are not reasons for a bust-up.

**Gospel Teaching**

Jesus is teaching in the Temple, surrounded by the crowds who followed him everywhere. Is his popularity part of the cause of what happens next? His opponents would have said that they were defending the faith, but how truthful were they in that?

Some scribes and Pharisees appear with a woman who was caught in the act of committing adultery. There is no doubt that she broke the Law; the question is what to do about it. But the aim of these men is not to consult Jesus; they are testing him, "so that they might have some charge to bring against him".

What, then, is the test? According to Leviticus (20:10) and Deuteronomy (22:21-24), adulterers should be stoned to death. But the religious leaders knew well Jesus' emphasis on compassion to sinners and outcasts. So here is the trap. If Jesus upholds the Law of Moses he will contradict his own teaching and lifestyle, and be seen as a fraud. If he contradicts the Law he will be guilty of leading people away from divine religion, and should himself be disciplined.

Jesus doodles silently in the sand. Perhaps, as he doodles, he is meditating on the meaning and purpose of the Law and religious rules. The churchwarden wanted to uphold the rules and thought a major showdown was the way to achieve it. The scribes and Pharisees used Moses' Law as a means to trap Jesus. But for Jesus, salvation is the main concern and indeed the true purpose of the Law: "God did not send the Son into the world to *condemn* the world, but in order that the world might be *saved*" (John 3:17). So, without disowning Moses' Law, Jesus turns the tables, saying "Let anyone among you who is without sin be the first to throw a stone at her."

This response, which is both godly and politically astute, catches the accusers like a sharp stone striking the heart. One by one they melt away. The story of a woman caught in adultery has become one of men caught in hypocrisy. Jesus too declares that he will not condemn her, but adds the command to sin no more. God's grace is not only a matter of forgiveness of past sins, but a call out of God's deep love to men and women to sin no more and live a new and pure life.

**Application**

This story raises the subject of law and religious observance. The warden could not see beyond maintenance of the Lenten tradition. The scribes and Pharisees were not at all concerned about a woman whose life was in a mess; they thought of her as a worthless adulteress and made her a mere tool in their schemes. In both cases enthusiasm for the letter of the law came before respect for people and the desire for their well-being and salvation. Look now at Jesus. Yes, he is concerned for the Law of Moses, he frequently quotes it, but he is much more concerned that all people, precious in God's eyes, may be afforded God's grace and salvation.

Whatever our Lenten observances, let's be quite clear that they are not tools of our self-aggrandisement or manipulating others. Although our traditions may be worth guarding passionately, public rows are unlikely to further that cause. Instead we should approach Lent with serious joy, looking forward to growing closer to God. And while Lent can be helpfully inward-looking, should we not also look outward to the salvation of others?

And finally we do well to remember that no matter how carefully we may observe Lent we are all ultimately in the position of the woman in the story – in need of the grace of Christ. Indeed, as we hear God's forgiveness declared today, do we take it for granted? Or is it to us, as to the woman, the word of life and the reprieve of a death sentence?

*"Worship the Lord your God, and serve only him."*
(Matthew 4:10)

**Illustration**

In the fourth century, a powerful and influential movement began which has profoundly affected Christianity. Individuals and groups of Christians began to feel called to live out a life of extreme asceticism, often in the inhospitable desert. These desert fathers and mothers, as they are known, starved themselves of food, drink and companionship. They saw themselves as warriors on the front line of conflict between good and evil, and they trained themselves, through these feats of asceticism, to be dependent on the strength of God alone.

They did not set out to influence the rest of the Church or society. They lived lives of poverty, withdrawn from the centres of influence at court or cathedral. But somehow their witness energised even those who knew they could never imitate this hard calling. The battle in the wilderness brought victories not just for those directly involved, but for others, too.

**Gospel Teaching**

Matthew, Mark and Luke all know about the temptation that Jesus faced in the wilderness, though only Matthew and Luke have the details. All of them place it directly after Jesus' baptism and as the start of his public ministry. So Jesus goes into the wilderness, led by the Holy Spirit, with God's words of love and affirmation at the River Jordan ringing in his ears. But the wilderness is where he has to discover what it means to be the beloved Son of God.

It may seem an odd way to prepare for leadership, by starving oneself, alone in the desert. Jesus prepares for his ministry by making himself weak and utterly vulnerable, as though this is the only way in which he can be sure that the ministry he will exercise comes from God, and not just from his own strengths. He does not spend the time drawing up mission statements and identifying key people and setting targets. Instead, he reduces himself to barest essentials, leaving his character and instincts starkly exposed, with no externals to buttress them.

So when the devil comes to tempt Jesus, it is on these essentials of his being that the attack focuses. First, the devil suggests that Jesus should do a very simple, harmless miracle, of turning stones into bread. There is no one else there; it won't be showing off; it is just a practical suggestion. For the rest of his ministry, his miracles are to be one of the most characteristic things about Jesus. But here in the wilderness Jesus learns that miracles are tools, not vital parts of himself.

Next, the devil tempts Jesus to set limits to what God can demand of him. "Test how much God loves you," the devil suggests. "Test whether his love will keep you safe." Here, at the very start of his ministry, Jesus relinquishes that option, and so opens the way to the cross. He will not ask for personal security from God. He will make no bargains with God, but rely on God totally.

Finally, the devil offers Jesus power. As he goes about preaching, teaching and healing, one of the things that will most strike people about Jesus is his natural authority. He clearly has strong leadership qualities, and people yearn to follow him to battle, to victory. But because of this unseen victory in the desert, Jesus will not be tempted to build a personal army to put him on any throne. Instead, he will win God's victory for all of us, against sin and death.

What was being tested in the wilderness was the core of Jesus' being, stripped of all other defences. That core proved to be total dependence on God, his Father.

**Application**

We are not all called to go and live lives of harsh asceticism in the desert, like the desert fathers and mothers. But in Lent we are offered this challenge – what is at the heart and core of our lives? What would the devil offer to us to tempt us away from God? Do we even know what is essential to us and what is peripheral? Have we ever even tried to live without some of the props of comfort and security that seem to us so necessary?

Thanks to Jesus, we do not have to battle with the devil in the wilderness on our own. We are the body of Christ, and so share what he has already done, without any help from us. But perhaps occasionally we might be called to do our own bit of fighting against evil, for our sake and for others.

*"Jesus came to Galilee proclaiming the good news of God, and saying, 'The time is fulfilled, and the kingdom of God has come near; repent, and believe in the good news.'"*
(Mark 1:14-15)

**Illustration**
A celebrated television newsreader some time ago provoked a national debate on what constitutes news. He remarked in a speech that news broadcasts focused too much on bad news, and not enough on good news. In the discussion which followed, many people talked about what exactly is news. Do we presume that news is when something out of the ordinary happens, so that the commonplace is not worthy of comment? Or is news the description of events, and a commentary on their significance for society? One critic of the newsreader said that deliberately to balance the good news and the bad news was to intervene to an unacceptable degree in the reporting of the world as it is. And anyway, who can say what is good news, and what is bad news? Tragedy aside, what is good news for one person or one country is often bad news for another.

**Gospel Teaching**
Christian good news is quite distinct. Today's Gospel reading says that Jesus was proclaiming the good news from God. Jesus was proclaiming that God's will for the world was being fulfilled. The kingdom of God, the reign of God in which people are reconciled to God and restored to right relationship with him, is being established even as Jesus speaks. So for the Christian, good news is news that recounts the building of the kingdom of God. This is the message of Christ. His good news is the good news from God, the only good news that is good for all people. As disciples gathered around him, and as they heard and understood what this good news was, and why it would transform their lives, Jesus would send them out in their turn to make known the good news to all people.

**Application**
How do we recognise good news from God? Jesus' preaching of the good news was accompanied by forgiveness of sins and miracles of healing. The good news restores broken lives; it gives hope; it drives away fear; it promotes true peace; it is concerned for the well-being of others who cannot care for themselves; it is concerned with building up what is good,

and destroying what is evil. The good news is centred on Jesus – he himself was and is the good news that he proclaimed. He did not just talk about God: he was God, he is God. He drew people to himself and they found life in him. That is our testimony too – when we recognise God in our lives, when we respond to him and begin to relate to him, we will find life: life in all its fullness.

So our Christian life is to recognise the power of the good news; to see what it has done for us; to give thanks to God; and to bring other people to receive the news with joyful hearts. This may be by acting out the good news. It may be by speaking about God. It may be by our honest exploration of our faith with others. It may be by our prayer.

Proclaiming the good news involves us in it, and we become part of it: a people who are reconciled to God, speaking of a kingdom which we have glimpsed, and in which we long to live fully and completely. We are not all called to be celebrated speakers and preachers, though some of us may be. We are not all called to shout the Gospel from the rooftops and in the streets, though some of us may be. We are not all called to write eloquent articles about our faith, nor even to sell all we have and go to faraway places – though some of us may be. We are all called to live the life God has created us for, in living, dynamic relationship with him. In short, we are called to be ourselves, and we will truly find ourselves when we truly find God – our own good news.

Today is the first Sunday of Lent, and a good opportunity to reflect on our part in proclaiming good news. It is a good opportunity to reflect on the news our lives proclaim – are we telling only about ourselves, or are we telling the story of God's love, the good news of the Gospel?

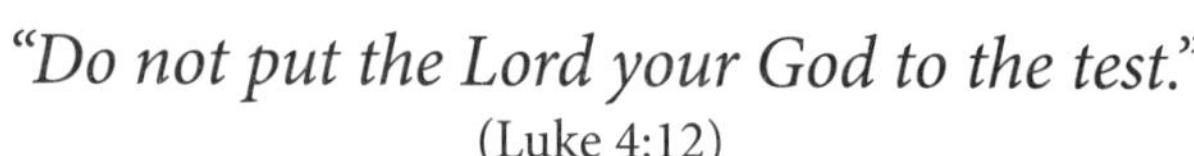

*"Do not put the Lord your God to the test."*
(Luke 4:12)

**Illustration**
A game which many of us enjoy in childhood is sometimes referred to as playing "chicken". The idea is to dare each other to do scary or illicit things and wait to see who will "chicken out" first. It relies upon the fact that everyone knows the rules and recognises that they may be punished if they are caught in the act: by parents, teachers, perhaps even the police.

But temptation for adults is often far more insidious than this sort of game. How many advertising agencies, for example, use temptation as their main selling stratagem time and time again: "Go on," they say, "you know you can have just what you want; we have it right here"... "naughty, but nice", or "because you're worth it". They encourage us to think that we are in charge. The difficult thing for us to accept is that practices which look innocent enough at the start can very soon take over our personalities, making us acquisitive and selfish.

We live in a time when denying ourselves anything is hard. But in Christ's temptations we may discover more of a shared experience than we might expect. At that moment all possibilities seemed open to him, as they often appear to us. Can we learn from his experience how to respond?

**Gospel Teaching**
Three temptations were placed before Jesus: the first prompted him to satisfy a physical need – hunger. The second – rather more daring, as is often the way with temptations – offered him seemingly great personal power, while the third urged him to prove his identity as the Son of God. The temptations were proposed, quite deliberately, by God's adversary – the devil. At this moment Jesus finds himself in the same position as Adam in the Garden of Eden. Can he resist, fulfilling God's true purpose for him, or will he succumb?

The first temptation entices Jesus to feed himself after a long period of fasting. Although that seems reasonable, he is being encouraged to flout the rules of nature in transforming stone into bread. Not only would Jesus be perverting the physical properties of matter, as ordained by God, but he would also, in performing such a transformation, be denying the humanity he shared with us. For none of us, I think, can make bread from stones.

The second temptation offers Jesus earthly power – the kind of kingdom he claimed neither to own nor to seek. Yet to gain it he would have to serve an unworthy master, and the power gained would be a mere illusion. Saying "yes" to such an offer would be, still more obviously, to reject the role God had given him – and failing to fulfil his purposes.

The third temptation calls on Jesus to assert himself: to prove who he really is. It is an appeal to the most fundamental weakness of human nature: egocentricity. Jesus is offered a chance to flaunt his own identity, to be revealed as a god in his own right. This foreshadows the ultimate test of Christ's obedience and faithfulness in God's service: for Jesus' response will be echoed in his passion and death.

**Application**

Living in the world presents us all with similar temptations, although most of the time we are hardly aware of them. Dragged along by the prevailing culture, we don't realise that we are still "playing chicken". It takes very little to get fully immersed in the game. For we routinely aim to satisfy our own physical needs and desires first and foremost; we often crave worldly status and power over others; and most of all we want to stress our uniqueness over against all other beings – mortal or otherwise. We are tempted to make ourselves gods.

Lent, however, offers one of the "sanctuaries" of the Christian year – a time when we can stand back from the hurly-burly of our usual activities and reflect. Are we the kind of people who try God's patience by thoughtless or wilful disobedience? How have we failed to be the people God made us to be? Can we change?

How seriously we attempt to encounter a spiritual wilderness, where our souls can be still, apart from life's encumbrances and distractions, is partly a matter of choice. Yet our most tentative prayer can open us to God; contemplation, however brief, may allow the prompting of the Holy Spirit. Perhaps one day we may discover that the winner in a game of "chicken" is usually the one who refuses to play at all.

*"No one can see the kingdom of God without being born from above."*
(John 3:3)

**Illustration**

The internet contains some wonderful information. For example, there is a facility called "Google Maps", with which you can get directions from one location to another, anywhere in the world. Entering addresses in New York and London, you are told to drive down to the quay. It then says, "SWIM 3,462 miles across the Atlantic Ocean." SWIM!? Is it a joke? Is it an error? Who knows; but one thing is absolutely certain: no one can get from New York to London without crossing a large body of water somewhere in the world. Without doing this it is impossible!

And Jesus said, "No one can see the kingdom of God without being born from above." Seconds later he repeated, "No one can enter the kingdom of God without being born of water and Spirit." Then again, a few seconds after that, he said it again: "You must be born from above." We usually think of Jesus giving invitations: "Come to me, you who are weary…", "…whoever comes to me will never hunger". Yet here, speaking in the shadows of the night to a deep-thinking yet fearful man, Jesus' tone is urgent and imperative.

**Gospel Teaching**

Nicodemus is mentioned only in John's Gospel and no one knows whether he ever fully came to believe. But at the very least he became a sympathiser, and here in John 3 we find him striving for faith yet sinking in the quicksand of fear.

The story begins with contradictory images: Nicodemus coming to Jesus at night. "Coming to Jesus" is what Jesus wants, if his invitations are anything to go by. Yet the "night" in John's Gospel is a symbol of uncertainty and confusion – a place in which a person can be thrown about in all sorts of ways. Nicodemus is caught between certainty and confusion: "We know you are from God," he says emphatically, yet the cloak of darkness he pulls around himself betrays fear of full commitment.

Reading on, the confusion continues, and underlying it is a question about the art of the possible. Nicodemus recognises Jesus' coming from God

by what he "can do". Jesus says, "no one can see… without being born from above". Nicodemus responds, "How can anyone be born after having grown old?" Nicodemus' eyes are open to what God can do in Jesus, but closed to what God can do through him.

Nicodemus is sometimes thought of as being a bit dense in this exchange, but perhaps he, too, is speaking metaphorically when he despairingly expresses the impossibility of entering again a mother's womb. As Bishop Westcott wrote, "How can he undo, or do away with, the result which years have brought and which goes to form himself?" Or, to put it another way, "How can I believe when I have spent all these years not believing?" Again we are faced with the art of the possible: "Can the accumulation of long ages be removed and the true 'self' remain?" (Westcott).

Jesus says this kind of rebirth can only come "from above… of the Spirit". And the Spirit must be received. He speaks with urgency because Nicodemus needs to step through doubt and fear into the light of a new life.

**Application**
Doubt is necessary for the creation of faith, but we can become paralysed by it. Jesus calls us to step beyond doubt and into belief – accepting his word and receiving his Spirit. In one of the most famous verses of the Bible, Jesus says, "God so loved the world that he gave his only Son, so that everyone who believes in him may not perish but may have eternal life." "Eternal life" is offered in the present – a life which starts now rather than when we die. But, likewise, to remain in fear is to be perishing in the here and now.

In the Gospel we see Nicodemus perishing in the quicksand of fear. Receiving Jesus' testimony meant making public his attachment to him and reordering his priorities; but it also meant cleansing and renewal, being found and being known. Jesus spoke to him urgently, and he speaks to us with the same urgency.

When we find ourselves caught between faith and fear, can we really believe? Jesus speaks to us urgently: do not be perishing, but believing! To see the kingdom of God, we may well need to lay aside the wisdom of our years and receive the Spirit as unborn children. In doing so, we emerge newborn into God's presence.

*"For what will it profit them to gain the whole world and forfeit their life?"*
(Mark 8:36)

**Illustration**

Last week, in our Gospel reading, Jesus was baptised by John and a voice from heaven, the voice of God, declared that Jesus was "my Son, the Beloved". After this act of commitment and affirmation Jesus was driven by the Spirit into the wilderness to work out the implications of his revealed identity and how to live out that identity in accordance with God's will.

Mark doesn't go into details of the temptations Jesus faces, but from Matthew and Luke we get an idea of what they were: the temptation to be a Messiah of miracles and dramatic signs; to perform superhuman feats to prove that God will protect him and to take for himself kingship and power over all the known world.

Jesus deals with each of these temptations in turn and holds steadfastly to his commitment to do things God's way and not his own.

**Gospel Teaching**

This week we see a similar pattern of events, this time involving the disciples of Jesus, especially Peter.

Peter has just made his memorable declaration that Jesus is the Messiah. His voice echoes the voice of God claiming Jesus as his Son, the Beloved.

Jesus now tries to teach the disciples what he understands the role of the Messiah to be: a painful understanding reached through hardship in the wilderness and a great personal struggle with temptation.

Peter has not gone through this process as Jesus has. For him, and the others, it is still quite inconceivable that God's Anointed One should suffer and die; it goes against everything they have always believed about the Messiah. Even after all these centuries, it is no easier for us to understand the strange form that God's victory takes.

Now Peter's voice echoes the voice of the tempter in the wilderness. Jesus once again hears that voice disguised in the voice of a friend which is perhaps much more difficult to resist.

Once again, Jesus turns on the one he calls Satan, who is using Peter to undermine his integrity and strength of purpose. Once again, Jesus insists

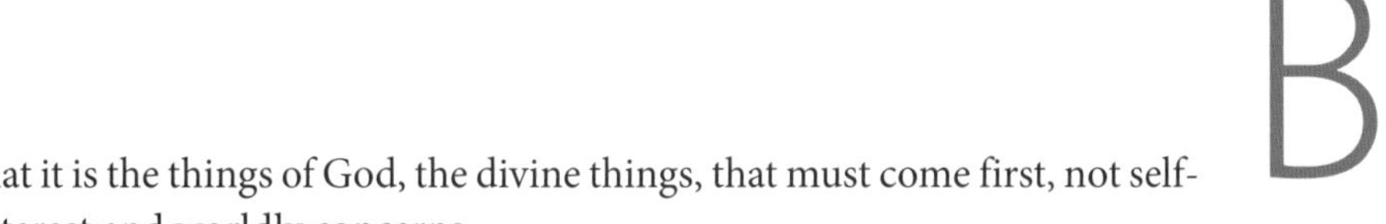



that it is the things of God, the divine things, that must come first, not self-interest and worldly concerns.

Then Jesus has to explain to his disciples, and to us, what it will cost to follow him and to try to live like him.

**Application**

Jesus says, "If any want to become my followers let them deny themselves, take up their cross and follow me."

Especially in Lent we perhaps tend to think that "denying ourselves" is something to do with giving up things we enjoy, be it wine, chocolates, music, dancing or television. Or we might even think of it as some kind of punishment for our sins. But perhaps there's a different way of understanding it.

We don't know what form "Satan" took when Jesus was in the wilderness, but it clearly was something Jesus recognised as being in opposition to God. In our Gospel reading it's the voice of Peter that tries to pull Jesus away from his intended path.

Now Jesus is saying to those around him, and to us, that if we're serious about following him we are going to have to resist our own inner voice which tries to distract us. And that won't be easy. Our own inner demons know only too well where our particular weaknesses lie and they may have nothing to do with chocolate, wine or time-wasting.

Perhaps our weaknesses lie in enjoying gossip, hearing and passing on rumours; making judgements without knowing the whole story; reacting with impatience when we're inconvenienced in some way, or breaking rules for our own advantage.

We each have our very own temptations and failures and these are what we need to deny ourselves: the things we need to recognise and bring to God asking for forgiveness, healing and the grace to begin again.

Jesus' message is that having everything we want and having everything going our way is worthless if in achieving that we have sacrificed our integrity, our honesty and our identity as God's beloved child in whom he is well pleased.

Similarly the message is that even if our lives in worldly terms seem lacking in achievement, possessions, or status, if we still have our integrity, are being our true selves and following what we believe to be God's will for us, then we have a life caught up in divinity and in the eternal kingdom of God.

*"Yet today, tomorrow, and the next day*
*I must be on my way."*
(Luke 13:33)

**Illustration**

Today's passage from Luke's Gospel is sometimes known as the "Lament for Jerusalem", and it is the inspiration for the English composer Sir John Tavener's work of the same name. It is written in the English choral style and was first performed in 2003. Tavener's *Lament* incorporates Christian, Jewish and Muslim influences. As the music rises in a crescendo of "cosmic laments" it takes on layers of meaning. One influence is "The rivers of Babylon", that mournful psalm sung by the Israelite exiles in Babylon. Another part is drawn from the Islamic poet Rumi's poem, *Masnavi*. Through its Jewish and Muslim references, the *Lament* becomes a heartfelt appeal for understanding, tolerance and love. And it reaches through the years to become a lament for modern Jerusalem – still the focus of so much religious and political strife. It is a universal lament, as human voices strive to create a divine sound, echoing the longing which all human beings feel so deeply – the longing to reach God, which lies at the heart of our every feeling, thought and action. The composer has described the work as "a love song, lamenting our banishment from home"; and, of course, our true home is with God.

**Gospel Teaching**

Just imagine that somebody told you your life was threatened by a powerful man – someone you knew had the clout and influence to carry out that threat. Anyone might be forgiven for fleeing to save their skin, abandoning any sense of a higher purpose, or a job left unfinished. But when the Pharisees tell Jesus that Herod wants to kill him, he is undaunted. Instead he stands his ground in defiance, and even throws a vivid insult Herod's way: "that fox".

Then comes one of those spine-tingling moments, which takes on a particular resonance in Lent: "on the third day I finish my work". There was so much going on during the ministry of Jesus, to those around him it must sometimes have seemed to be a dizzy whirl of miracles and parables. And doubtless they did not – could not – pick up on the true significance of his words: "on the third day". But hindsight is a wonderful thing and we, two thousand years later, have a privileged insight into the full meaning of what Jesus said.

But then, out of the blue, Jesus seems to crumble into grief. But why? What has got to him? Surely it's not Herod's threat – his faith in God's purpose remains absolutely unshaken. So is it really Jerusalem that Jesus is lamenting? The city certainly did, and still does, have special significance, and moves people to strong feelings. But above that, there is something universal in what Jesus says, as though Jerusalem were a symbol for all human failing and cruelty.

Perhaps, more than Herod's words, more than Jerusalem's flaws, Jesus is suffering under the weight of a burden he carries within. For, though he knows that Herod's immediate threat is empty, he also knows that he will face death before long. It must have been so lonely at times, knowing what was to come, while everyone around him treated his ministry like a party, and he the life and soul of it all.

**Application**

It's all too easy to see Jesus as an abstract symbol of divinity.That he was "fully human and fully divine" is a paradox we have to take on faith, but here, surely, is a glimpse of his true humanity. It reminds us that Jesus really did become flesh and blood, and experienced those emotions that we all do – grief, loss, yearning, fear, doubt.

The theologian Paul Tillich said: "Doubt is not the opposite of faith; it is one element of faith." And there is nothing shameful, weak or wrong in doubting, or even crumbling. What would be damaging would be to hide or deny it. Sir John Tavener interprets the lament for Jerusalem as a moment when Jesus loses sight of God, but he also sees that loss as temporary. For while Jesus knows he will suffer and die, he also knows that the third day will follow. When we are adrift on a swirling sea of uncertainty, we don't need to cling to a raft of conviction. On the contrary, if we let ourselves go into our fears and doubts, we are demonstrating an even greater faith: faith that God will ultimately find us and set us again on dry land.

*"Jesus said to her, 'I am he, the one who is speaking to you.'"*
(John 4:26)

**Illustration**

Most people who live in developed countries have got used to being profligate with water. It is just a never-ending natural resource. But global warming is forcing everyone to think about how precious water really is. Countries like Britain that have traditionally had regular and dependable rainfall are finding that they are ill-equipped to conserve water, and are having to learn to change their ways. Old-fashioned gardens are being replanted with shrubs that can withstand long dry periods, and water companies are being forced to invest heavily in better ways of conserving water.

**Gospel Teaching**

Jesus' society knew the value of water. Every drop of water had to be carried by hand from the well to the home, and used with the utmost economy. As in many parts of Africa today, that was mostly the job of women, like the Samaritan woman in today's Gospel.

There are quite a lot of romantic stories associated with wells in the Old Testament. Abraham's servant found a wife for Isaac by a well, when she helped him get water for his camels, and Moses met his future wife by a well when she needed to get water and was being prevented. Perhaps the Samaritan woman's heart beat a bit faster when she came to the well and found a strange young man sitting alone beside it.

At first, all seems to be going according to the woman's flirtatious plans. The young man is quite willing to talk, displaying no hostility or reserve, even though she is a Samaritan and he a Jew. Even when his conversation becomes a bit peculiar and incomprehensible, the woman doesn't immediately give up. She has wide experience of men, and has got used to putting up with the less than perfect.

Then the young man starts asking about her husband. Are things looking up? Is he trying to find out whether or not she is married? She flutters her eyelashes a bit and says she is not.

But, oh dear, things are not going to plan at all. It seems he is some kind of moral and religious fanatic. The woman quickly tries to get things back

onto a less personal footing. If he wants to talk religion, she can at least make sure that they are talking about the distant future coming of the Messiah, rather than her own personal morality.

"I am the Messiah," says the young man.

For once, the woman is silenced. She is not used to being at a loss for words. The man must be mad, mustn't he? But he seemed so sane. With relief, she hears a group of his friends coming, and she takes her water and runs back to the village. The sensible thing would be to forget the strange man and his even stranger conversation, but she can't quite get him out of her head. Although she knows that her neighbours don't think much of her, and is used to being laughed at and despised, she cannot resist telling them what has happened.

There must have been something about the way she told it that caught their imaginations. Her exchange with Jesus showed that she had a ready wit and a swift tongue, but her neighbours would have been used to that. Somehow, the peculiar quality of her encounter with Jesus came across, and they followed her to see Jesus.

As her neighbours escorted Jesus back to the village, as they hung on his every word over the next couple of days, the woman was proud to see that she had not been mistaken. There really was something about this man, and she had been the one to introduce him to the village. Naturally, they were not grateful. They said, dismissively, that it wasn't because of her that they had come to believe in Jesus, but because of the effort they had put in for themselves.

But the woman was used to that. She knew what had really happened. And now we do, too.

**Application**

Did her meeting with Jesus change her life? We don't know. But we do know that she used her water very wisely. She was offered the water of life and she used it to irrigate her village. Because of her, many people came to drink from the water that Jesus was offering, the only water that can truly satisfy.

That is all that is asked of us – that we use our water wisely and generously, since we know it is not ours, but was given to us when we met Jesus.

*"Jesus answered them, 'Destroy this temple, and in three days I will raise it up.'"*
(John 2:19)

**Illustration**
"The diffrense [sic] from a person and an angel is easy. Most of an angel is in the inside and most of a person is on the outside."

On a foggy November night in the East End docklands of the 1930s, a young man named Fynn found a neglected five-year-old girl named Anna. Fynn's profound and moving book, *Mister God, This Is Anna*, charts the course of their friendship over the next couple of years until Anna's death in an accident at nearly eight years old.

On one level, Anna was like any other five-year-old child: mischievous, energetic and endlessly curious. But on another level she was precociously gifted, with a depth of understanding and insight beyond her own – or anyone else's – years. In Fynn's own words: "At five years Anna knew absolutely the purpose of being, knew the meaning of love and was a personal friend and helper of Mister God. At six Anna was a theologian, mathematician, philosopher, poet and gardener."

Fynn paints a picture of himself as a young, intelligent adult willingly following in the wake of a remarkable child, struggling to keep up with the depth of her insights and perceptions. Anna's thoughts and words stop us in our tracks because they challenge our limited understanding, and because we instinctively feel that she is offering us a tantalising glimpse into the mind of God, just beyond our sight.

**Gospel Teaching**
Anna may remind us a little of Jesus at twelve years old, when he stayed behind in Jerusalem after the Passover festival. Baffling his worried parents with talk of needing to be in his Father's house, and amazing the teachers in the Temple with the level of his understanding, Jesus spoke with an authority that commanded the respect of his hearers.

In today's Gospel reading Jesus is back in the Temple, lashing out in anger at those who were trading there. This incident appears in all four Gospels: at the beginning of Jesus' ministry here in John, and associated with the Passion narratives in the Synoptics. A popular interpretation has been to see this as an example of Jesus' humanity – he got angry just like the rest of us! But in our eagerness to claim similarity between Jesus and ourselves, we are in danger of missing a far deeper truth. John does not have to "prove" Jesus' humanity; after all, he has already affirmed that the Word became flesh (1:14). Of far deeper import here is the authority that the fully human Jesus claims for his words and actions.

The traders that Jesus drove out were not gatecrashers into the daily life of the Temple; far from it, they were essential to the whole operation of the Temple cult. Animals and birds were needed for sacrifices, and the money changers were necessary because coins bearing the emperor's head were not acceptable within the Temple precincts. When the outraged Jews demanded to know by what authority Jesus did these things, he referred cryptically to his future Passion and death: "Destroy this temple, and in three days I will raise it up."

This was a revolutionary claim. For the Jewish nation, the Temple was the locus of God's presence amongst his people, the beating heart of their faith and worship. But by referring to the temple of his body, Jesus was effectively claiming that the cult of the Temple was past: the presence of God upon earth was now embodied, not in a building, but in Christ himself.

**Application**

The scandal and the challenge continue to this day. A great danger for the Church in any age is that it will fall into the trap of assuming that the Church's authority is the same thing as God's authority. When we think of our own Christian community, what are the "sacred cows" – areas that we have closed off, declared non-negotiable, made impervious to the indwelling and renewing action of Christ's Spirit? The danger is there for all of us, whether we are part of a long-established church community or a new fellowship.

The startling insights of Anna, and the authority-challenging words and actions of Jesus, jolt us, if we allow them, into new ways of seeing God and the ways in which he seeks to draw us more fully into the depths of his love. The scales fall from our eyes, and we see things as if for the first time. The yardstick for all our Christian communities must be the revelation of God in the life, death and resurrection of Jesus Christ. How open are we prepared to be?

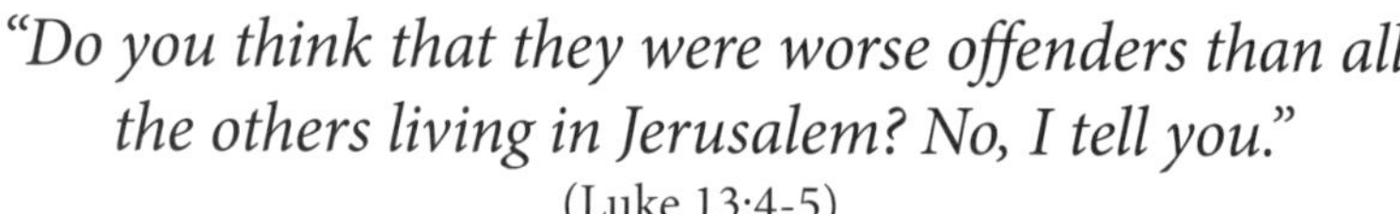

*"Do you think that they were worse offenders than all the others living in Jerusalem? No, I tell you."*
(Luke 13:4-5)



**Illustration**

Just imagine the furore which would arise if anyone suggested that the victims of the Holocaust, or innocent children killed by a paedophile ring, had "brought it on themselves"? And yet there was once a school of thought which assumed that if something terrible happened to you, it must be some kind of "payback" for past bad behaviour on your part, or on the part of your family.

Jesus confronted this question directly from one questioner, putting him right. The idea that innocence should be blamed for evil is abhorrent, going against everything we understand about justice. But in the past people had to find meanings for terrible things which happened. Even now, people generally dislike mysteries and uncertainties, unless they can dress them up in creative and beautiful stories, preferably with happy endings, which soften the anguish which uncertainty can generate. They often create meanings, or, worse, identify people upon whom blame can be laid: scapegoats, like people of a different colour or social class, ethnic group or religion. In ancient Israel it was the victims of disaster themselves. As if it were not bad enough to have been made an unintentional victim in the first place, to then be blamed for your own misfortune!

**Gospel Teaching**

Jesus tries to remove for ever the notion of personal blame through sin for accidents and unavoidable disasters, like blindness from birth. But he implies that if people do not work to change their lives, to accept his promises and have faith in God, they might end up worse off than those whose disasters he describes. Not because God will impose punishments upon those who stray (after all, elsewhere Jesus tells us about himself as a loving shepherd who goes out of his way to rescue a sheep which has strayed). But we call down upon ourselves all kinds of risks when we do not accept the best that is on offer. That is, Christ himself and his relationship with God, of which we are heirs and which contains everything necessary for happiness.

What he is asking of us is a light burden and may save us from a much worse fate. There is terrible uncertainty about living without God, with no foundation which will bear our weight when we need to lean on something or someone other than ourselves in time of trial. The foundation which Jesus offers, the strength which will carry us through when tragedy strikes, is love. Not the tabloid newspaper notion of love, which disperses like summer mist when the first trials occur. But the love which seeks justice, which tolerates hardship and welcomes difference, love which endures in spite of our weakness.

Jesus offers us both the opportunity to accept the love which strengthens and enables us to grow, and also the ability to see beyond the superficial in others and to love them unconditionally as Christ loves us. It is upon this foundation that a perfect world (the kingdom) will be built. It was love which designed the incarnation, love which inspired Mary, love which carried Jesus through his ministry to his passion and death. It was such love which conquered death, for him and us. But, Jesus makes clear, without adopting his brand of love, and following in his footsteps, we place ourselves and the future of the world in greater uncertainty and at greater risk.

**Application**
Jesus invites us to arm ourselves against possible disasters and to be able to cope when they occur. But even Jesus cannot make himself responsible for us and our safety if we ignore his warnings and his teaching, however much he might desire to do so. But he goes on giving us "another chance". One of the secure aspects of Christianity is that every day we wake, we can turn over a new leaf and try afresh to live well.

If we are serious in our intention to become the people Christ calls us to be, then love is our yardstick and action is our proof. Love is the measure of the Christian because Jesus loved unto his very death, which is about as far as it goes. The horrendous acts of people against their neighbour are not a failure of love on the part of the victim, but in the perpetrator who has ignored Christ and his warnings. We are made for love and it is this love which will save us and our world.

*"One thing I do know, that though I was blind, now I see."*
(John 9:25)

**Illustration**

One of the great riches of life is that we all have different ways of viewing the world. But a frequent problem for human beings is our mental "tunnel vision", when we have a particular way of looking at things and cannot understand or accept alternative approaches. This can be true in the habits of our daily lives, with its "messages" from our childhood: clean your teeth after meals, eat your greens, or even don't admit to anything! These are usually a mixture of the sensible, the quaint and the downright misleading.

We have a similar list for our deeper beliefs. The difficulty comes when we think our stance is absolutely right, without making sure that it is founded upon sound reflection and judgement. Without realising it, what we are doing is claiming our view is right because it is our view, rather than choosing it because it is right. The temptation is to assume that others are wrong, which is to devalue both them and their argument.

**Gospel Teaching**

In Jesus' time it was assumed that physical or mental disability was the result of some failure or sin perpetrated by the sufferer or their family. Jesus used the inaccuracy of this assumption to illustrate the deeper misunderstanding his listeners had of his own role and mission. Not only did Jesus heal the man born blind, but he did so on the sabbath.

The authorities had to declare such an action unacceptable. Being accomplished on the sabbath, when any work is forbidden, the action could not be from God. The man born blind was regarded as a sinner and, therefore, as a dishonest witness. The authorities were already committed to condemning Jesus and so anything in which he was involved would be turned into further evidence against him. Differences in their statements resulted in total contradiction. They were reduced to saying that what had happened could not have happened and certainly could not be recognised as valid because it infringed the Law. The blind man's answer exposed very simply the inadequacy of their argument: "One thing I do know, that though I was blind, now I see."

This story is not just about the blind man, but also about the prejudices that prevent the officials from recognising the true nature of Jesus and his actions. When the authorities asked at the end of the story whether Jesus was calling them blind, he replied that being blind does not matter. In itself it was a tragic but natural circumstance and carried no blame. In such a state, we would know we were blind, and we would yearn to be able to see. Guilt arises when we are interiorly blind, yet think we can see, and when we insist upon everyone else having to see the world from our own warped perspective.

**Application**

Some of our prejudices can be harmless: dislike for particular food or music or art. The difficulty arises when we make our opinions absolute or when we are led into a misunderstanding of what is right or wrong because of it. One litmus test can be how far our views lead us to discriminate against others. In the Gospel story people with disabilities were considered not just second-class citizens, but sinners.

In our society such discrimination still exists, despite many attempts at legislating for equal rights and opportunities. Across society there are other groups who are the focus for discrimination. For example, women and ethnic minorities often experience it from some white males who regard themselves as the social norm – see some of the language commonly used to describe people in general: "men", "mankind", "brothers". Many people cannot even understand how this creates an imbalance. To alter just this one fundamental prejudice in our society would demand profound changes in the way we think. It is one, among many, of the potential upheavals of our era, but Jesus implied that following him required us to change.

The crucial insight here is that the vision we think is clear can be impaired, and we must strive to see more clearly. With this attitude in mind we can become more open to what we do not at first see or comprehend, rather than jealously guarding our own corner. The Gospel is a dynamic message leading us always towards the light of truth. Struggling through the thickets of our prejudices, assumptions and misunderstandings is always humbling and certainly a very seasonal Lenten discipline and offering.

*"For God so loved the world that he gave his only Son."*
(John 3:16)

4th Sunday of Lent

**Illustration**

"The cat has brought in another mouse!" How many of us have heard that familiar refrain? And there it is, a small grey bundle of fear tucked trembling behind the cooker while the sleek, black cat prowls around and licks its lips in anticipation. Your kids cluster round, shooing the cat away, eyes wide with concern and pleading with you to save the mouse. "Okay," you say, "we'll catch it and put it back outside where it belongs." And then there follows a good ten minutes of planning to find a way of safely removing the terrified mouse. "Okay mouse," you say hopefully, "just you sit quietly and we'll get you back outside," and carefully, oh so carefully, you try and catch it in your hands. But, of course, the mouse isn't having any of this. He is just as distrustful of us as he is of the cat. Then, as the effort becomes greater and you wonder if the trouble is really worth it, your eyes turn heavenwards and you ask yourself why the stupid mouse won't let you help it.

**Gospel Teaching**

We can be like that mouse when God in his goodness and compassion tries to save us. Sometimes we seem to have the idea that God is out to get us – that he is the Judge, the one waiting to trip us up if we go wrong, the one who sees all our dark and secret sins which we would rather no one knew about. But if we are anxious it is because we are letting our false notions of God take over – we are forgetting the Gospel. God does see all we do, but his response is not to condemn us. He sees sin for what it is, the damaging and wounding force that causes us so much misery and distress. God's response to our sin is to look on us with great tenderness and compassion. Jesus did not come to damn us, but to free us, to liberate us from all that makes us less than what we really are, from everything that makes us less human, less loving.

This is why the Gospel today asks the exasperated question: Why on earth do people continually resist God's efforts to save the world when he is only trying to help? "Indeed, God did not send the Son into the world to condemn the world, but in order that the world might be saved through him."

That seems the hardest thing in the world for us to believe. And we so-called religious people seem to find it just as hard to accept that God really does not condemn us. He wants to rescue us. He offers us love.

But people clearly do resist the love of God. We still watch the news broadcasts full of war and greed and violence, of rich and poor, the well-fed and the hungry. We are still unable to do very much in the face of the rising tide of poverty at home and abroad. We still hurt our children, our mothers and fathers, our brothers and sisters. We still lash out at our friends and bully and torment those we don't like. We can look into our own hearts and see that there is a mixture of good and bad within us. All of us live ambiguous lives, sometimes living the life of God and sometimes destroying the vision that we are trying so hard to build. We are still in need of the healing grace of God if we are to fulfil our purpose.

**Application**
It does seem a hopelessly difficult task. In fact, if we depended solely on our own efforts it would be impossible and we might as well give up right away. But thank God it is not by our own efforts that we can start to live the life of the kingdom of God. God reaches in to pluck us out of our sin and fills us with his grace so that we are transformed. He takes away our sin and gives us his own life. He encourages us to nourish that life with word and sacrament. All we need to do is accept it and allow ourselves to change as we grow.

Giving ourselves up to the love of God can appear to be a frightening process. But if we can only let go of our fears and trust him, then we will not be disappointed. God is truth and his truth sets us free.

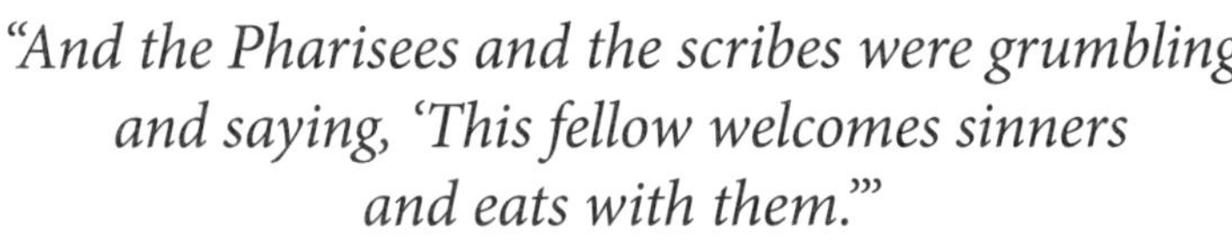

*"And the Pharisees and the scribes were grumbling and saying, 'This fellow welcomes sinners and eats with them.'"*
(Luke 15:2)



**Illustration**

If you have been a Christian for much of your life, it can be very hard to give your testimony. People who have had dramatic conversions, who have turned from wickedness and vice to follow God, tend to have much more to say than those who have never really doubted God at all. They can speak with real conviction about the power of God's love and forgiveness, in a way that puts a more steady, mundane faithfulness to shame. It's not that long-standing Christians believe they need no forgiveness, just that their sins can seem rather boring compared with the sins of the newly converted.

**Gospel Teaching**

Is it harder to be a black sheep or to be a boring good person? Black sheep often seem far more romantic. Books are written about them, and emotional energy is poured out in describing their wickedness and their salvation. This story in the Gospel is no exception. It is nearly always called the story of the prodigal son, rather than the story of the good brother. But perhaps, if it is read by churchgoers, it is the attitude of the older brother that is really significant.

The setting in Luke's Gospel makes it clear that this is primarily a story for those of us who believe that we are, fundamentally, good. We may realise that we are not perfect, but we do know that we have tried hard, for most of our lives, to do what we think God has asked of us. We have tried to follow the spirit of the Ten Commandments, and live in obedience to God, to our families and to our community. We believe, humbly, but confidently, that most people who know us would describe us as good people.

But, devastatingly, Luke tells us that it is exactly for people like us that Jesus told this story. Jesus was very well aware that many of the religious people of his day thought he had got his priorities wrong. He spent too much of his time with sinners, and he seemed to ignore, despise or even deliberately to insult good people. It is against the background of this murmuring that Jesus tells the story of the good brother and the bad brother.

As always, the bad brother gets the main storyline and most of the sympathy. As always, he gets all the attention, and everyone thinks the story is really about him. But it isn't, really. It's about us. It's about all of us who go to church regularly, and know that, even if we are not doing everything right, still, we are trying hard. We have never done anything dreadful, we have always acted with consideration, we are used to being greeted with mild affection and approval by all around us. Most of the time, that is all we ask for. But occasionally, we long for more. Occasionally, we long to know that we are loved for ourselves, we long to arouse passion in others, rather than the gentle love of those who can be taken for granted because we have caused no trouble to others, never made a nuisance of ourselves, never provoked anger and resentment, or demanded forgiveness and unconditional love.

So today's Gospel is really about the good son, who stays at home, and who is never quite sure what his father thinks of him. In his heart of hearts, he fears that his father loves his naughty, selfish, flamboyant son far more. Day after day, the older brother works away, dutifully, but without joy. What he longs for are the exaggerated words and gestures of love that his father offers to the younger brother. He longs for the kisses, the fine robes, the fatted calf, all the outward symbols of love with which the father greets the prodigal. For us, the punchline of the story is these words: "Son, you are always with me, and all that is mine is yours." They may not feel like words of extravagant love, but they are deep and true. They point to the life that the father and the older brother have shared, in which all that they are is embedded.

**Application**

If this is really a story for the good older brother, as the context in today's Gospel suggests, what might we conclude? Perhaps that what we have is what the prodigal son longs for. We have a shared life, shared goals, shared hopes. We can afford to be generous to outsiders. We will lose nothing, only gain brothers and sisters.

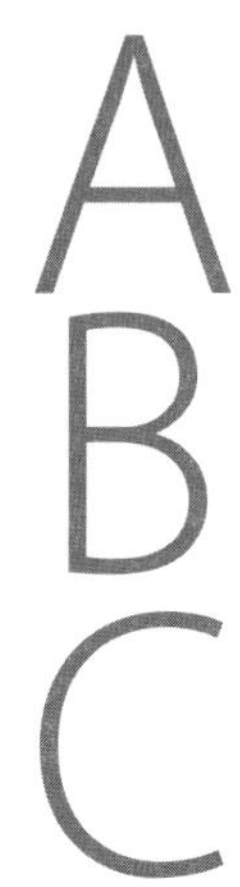



*"Here is your mother."*
(John 19:27)

**Illustration**
Jack frowned at the rack of greetings cards.

"Can I help you?" asked the shop assistant.

"I'd like a card for Mothering Sunday," Jack explained. "But they all say Mother's Day."

"Same thing," came the reply, but Jack shook his head.

"No, they're not. The lady I'm buying it for isn't my mum," he said. "But she's been like a mother to me."

Jack was right. Mother's Day and Mothering Sunday might fall on the same date, but they're not the same thing. One celebrates mothers, but the other celebrates mothering. Originally, Mothering Sunday had little to do with human mothers: it referred to the Church, and indirectly to God, as mother of us all. Part of the observance of Lent, on that day the Church required Christians to worship at their "mother" church, the one that had nurtured them. As a result, people working away, perhaps in service, could return home and spend a day with their families. They might take a posy of spring flowers for their mothers. Mothering Sunday gradually became Mother's Day.

**Gospel Teaching**
Today's Gospel reading indicates that mothering isn't restricted to our birth mothers. As Jesus approached his death on the cross, his compassion for those who loved him never failed. People often understand this scene only in terms of Mary being taken into the disciple's home and receiving his protection. But Jesus is also asking his mother to love his friend. Knowing that his mother and his closest friend would each need support after his death, he commended them to one another's keeping.

Jesus is saying to Mary, "Give a mother's love to my friend, be like a mother to him – mother my disciple." And to all of us who stand beneath the cross, and watch him dying for love of us, he says the same: "Mother my disciples." To the disciple, Jesus says, "Be like a son to Mary." Each would in some way be the son, the friend, the loved one, that Jesus had been on earth. Whether we are male or female, God calls us to share his love with others. We are called to be Christ to our neighbour, and to see Christ in our neighbour.

This Gospel reading reminds us, too, that mothering must have an object. The concept of mother only makes sense if there is also a child to be mothered: the "Here is your son" to Mary implies the "Here is your mother" to the disciple. There is a relationship here: a dynamic, not a status; a verb, not a noun. And it is a relationship, a dynamic that mirrors the very nature of God. The doctrine of the Trinity reminds us that God is loving relationship, the love of the Father for the Son and the Son for the Father, flowing through the Spirit and drawing us, too, into the very heart of God as the Spirit touches our own hearts.

A dictionary definition (*Chambers*) of the verb "to mother" is: "to acknowledge, adopt or treat as a son or daughter". The Bible tells us that this is exactly what God does to us: God sent his Son, born of a woman, so that we might receive adoption as children, and he sends the Spirit of his Son into our hearts so that we cry, "Abba, Father" (Galatians 4:4-6). Whether we use the word Father or Mother, we are reassured that God is a loving parent and we are acknowledged as his children. God mothers us.

**Application**

The love of a good mother for her children is an appropriate image for God's love for us. It certainly captures the way God puts up with our naughtiness, our sin, and yet still loves us. God himself gives us the pattern for parenthood. But it's also the pattern for all our dealings with one another: strengthening, encouraging and forgiving; serving, loving and surrendering.

Let's make a point of calling today Mothering Sunday, not Mothers' Day, because today isn't only for mothers. Nobody in church today should feel left out, because men can mother people, childless women can mother people. It's surely no accident that senior nuns are called Mother!

So today we give thanks: for our own mothers and all that they do or once did; for those who have been like a mother to us; and for God's mothering love for each one of us.

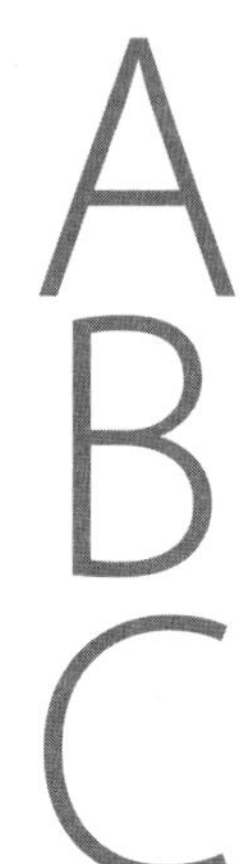



*"A sword will pierce your own soul too."*
(Luke 2:35)

**Illustration**

Have you ever bitten off more than you could chew? There are many times when parenting feels like this, especially in the early days: when she won't stop crying; when you can't get him to feed; and later when her boyfriend is not who you'd have chosen.

At times like this we know we have to hold on. But there are other occasions when parents have to let go; in fact, some of those are the same times as when we have to hold on: when our children make their own decisions, choose their friends, explore their interests, decide about their faith. This dynamic of holding on and letting go is a key aspect of parenting, and especially mothering. Many family problems are caused by getting it wrong through abandonment or overprotection. Perhaps you know someone who has been affected in this way.

But parenting is not simply about having human children. We all give birth in all sorts of ways: to ideas, projects, desires, hopes, intentions, plans, faith and worship. Sometimes we need to hold on to these things, but at other times we need to let them go.

**Gospel Teaching**

This episode in Jesus' life has a fable-like quality to it, but the connections we make with fairy tales shouldn't blind us to the fact that the activities of soothsayers and prophets were much more common in the ancient world than they are today. The historical nature of this event, therefore, need not be doubted. Nevertheless, Mary was hardly expecting it. With Joseph, she presented Jesus as a good parent. The reception by Simeon must have been a terrible shock.

He speaks of Jesus' destiny as a prophetic bearer of God's truth. People will reveal their hearts as they respond to the provocation of his word and being, and so Jesus passes through the world as a test and a judgement. Then Simeon says to Mary, "And a sword will pierce your own soul too."

The New Testament has two words for "sword". The first usually refers to a physical weapon, a blade, knife, or dagger; the second is metaphorical and is always connected to the word or judgement of God. Here the second word is used and Simeon says it will "pass through" Mary's soul. The phrase doesn't suggest a stabbing as our translation implies, but a movement across, like a sickle sweeping through a field (see Ezekiel 14:17).

Mary has come to the Temple as a devout parent, yet even her soul will be sorely tested by the presence of God's word in power. Luke often portrays Jesus as a prophet, carrying and embodying the word of God. His mission, which requires total focus on God, affects everyone around him. Mary must accept the destiny God has for him, releasing her son to fulfil his purpose. She could never abandon him, but she had to let him go. The process can never have been easy for her, but she rose to the challenge as the sword of God passed through the field of her soul.

**Application**

Mothering Sunday can lead us to think about our own mothering – not so much how, or how well, we were mothered, but how we ourselves mother, whether we're men or women, and whether or not we have human children. Today we can reflect on how we hold on to the things – and people – we give birth to; how we stand by them and how we let them go. And, in particular, how we allow God's purposes to affect our holding on and our letting go.

Ask yourself, "What is the thing right now that means the most to me?" It may be something really good you feel you're doing for God. It may be something bad you're pursuing but you know is wrong. Perhaps it's something at work. Perhaps it's a situation in your family. Whatever it is that's getting you excited or eager – take the opportunity of this Mothering Sunday to bring it before the Lord.

As you do this, listen for the voice of his Spirit. Perhaps God is telling you to hold on through a difficult time; perhaps God's telling you to let go and let him have his way. The important thing always is to let God be God. Everything good we birth is a gift from God. Everything bad we birth is the result of our fallen world. In each case we need to offer our lives to the purpose of God. Let's spend a few moments to reflect and pray about that right now.

*"Woman, here is your son."*
(John 19:26)

**Illustration**
Holy Trinity Church has tried a different approach to Mothering Sunday, dropping the sentimental celebration of "Mom" that crept in with the American Mother's Day invasion. Early in Lent, there was teaching about "kingdom kinship". Then, instead of buying flowers for their mothers, everybody gave to a fund which was spent at www.oxfamunwrapped.com. Then a banner was hung up in church which read: TO OUR MOTHERS. Pinned to it were pictures of a first-aid kit, a donkey, and a toilet, things that the collection of £110 had bought for the poorest in our world. People were so moved (especially mothers) that they decided to start fundraising so they could support "Build a Classroom" on next Mothering Sunday.

**Gospel Teaching**
On this day especially, we'd like to interpret today's Gospel as a dying son making provision for his mother. However, this is problematic for three reasons:

Firstly, because of Jesus' treatment of his mother hitherto. These lines from the cross echo Jesus' words at the wedding in Cana. On both occasions, Jesus addresses his mother as "woman", adding at the wedding: "What have I to do with you?" This was not an isolated incident. From the moment he began living in God's kingdom, Jesus ceased to be Mary's son in the traditional sense. We learn from an episode in Mark 3:31ff. that, for Jesus, anyone who obeyed God was his mother. The incident in the Temple when he was twelve (Luke 2:41ff.) suggests that he had a spiritualised view of kinship from an early age.

Secondly, there were traditions in Judaism that ensured family members were looked after, especially widows. If Mary had been dependent on the personal care of Jesus, then his handing on of that care would make sense. But nowhere do we infer this to be the case. In the Gospels we see Mary in the company of her other children (or stepchildren), presumably in their care.

Thirdly, it's significant which evangelist reports these words. John's Gospel doesn't tend to deal in mundane, domestic matters – especially when "the disciple whom Jesus loved" is involved. This disciple is referred to only when something central to Jesus' mission is happening, from the Last Supper onwards. We should expect these words of Jesus to contribute to

John's carefully constructed, deeply spiritual revelation of who Jesus is. Mothering Sunday or not, this is not the time to be distracted by sentiment.

There are two possible reasons why John includes these words of Jesus:

Firstly, to demonstrate Jesus' revolutionary view of kinship. Jesus is saying to his mother, "Look, as I've shown you throughout my life, I'm not exclusively your son. You love God and so does that disciple over there, so you two are mother and son, kith and kin, to each other." Typically, the Synoptic Gospels make this point in a dramatic incident (Mark 3:31ff.). In John's Gospel, equally typically, the same point is conveyed by a few words and, importantly, a meaningful act: John takes Mary into his home as a sign, an enacted parable, of this central tenet of Jesus' theology – kingdom kinship.

Secondly, John included these words because they link the Cana wedding and the crucifixion. We've already noted how Jesus addresses Mary as "woman" on each occasion. This is so striking that we make the link immediately. But there are other connections between the two events that John wants us to make.

At the wedding, God's glory flowed forth from Jesus' body in order to transfigure the wedding water into wine. He did this secretly because his hour had not yet come. He also did it reluctantly, and only because his mother pressured him into it – revealing how little she understood his mission.

Now, at his crucifixion, Jesus lets God's glory flow forth from his body for all the world to witness. God's glorification, a central Johannine theme, made much of by this evangelist in Jesus' farewell discourses at the Last Supper, is now a public demonstration.

And the reluctance has gone. Jesus glorifies God on the cross willingly, because now his hour has come. At the wedding of heaven and earth, his death and resurrection will transfigure the water of every person's dead religious life into the wine of a new spiritual life in God's kingdom.

**Application**

By doing something similar to Holy Trinity Church's scheme, we'd be as caring mothers to people in need. We'd also be celebrating that, as disciples whom Jesus loves, we're willing to take the world's poor into our hearts as if they were really our mothers.

*"I am the resurrection and the life. Those who believe in me, even though they die, will live, and everyone who lives and believes in me will never die. Do you believe this?"*
(John 11:25-26)

**Illustration**

In December 1939, Britain was experiencing the early, dark days of the Second World War. As part of his Christmas broadcast, King George VI offered these words, written in 1908 by the American social scientist and poet Minnie Louise Haskins:

> "I said to the man who stood at the gate of the year, 'Give me a light that I may tread safely into the unknown.' And he replied, 'Go out into the darkness and put your hand into the hand of God. That shall be to you better than light and safer than a known way!' So I went forth and finding the hand of God, trod gladly into the night."

**Gospel Teaching**

Mary and Martha have sent an urgent message to Jesus telling him of Lazarus' sickness, and urging him to come to them. Jesus delays his visit to Mary and Martha for two days, telling his disciples that Lazarus' illness will not lead to death but is rather for the glory of God. Wounded by Jesus' apparent failure to appreciate the urgency of the situation, Martha cannot contain her grief and distress.

She goes out to meet Jesus, and is unable to disguise her pain and frustration: "Lord, if you had been here, my brother would not have died." Jesus' reply is brisk, and to the point: "Your brother will rise again." Martha answers with a generalised statement of belief that her brother will rise again on the last day, eliciting a blunt response from Jesus. He confronts her with the narrow limitations of her belief and challenges her to trust him and to move "into the darkness" beyond. "I am the resurrection and the life… Do you believe this?"

Jesus' knowledge and understanding of Martha's character lead him to shape his challenge in a way which is exactly right for her, opening the way for her triumphant assertion "Yes, Lord, I believe that you are the Messiah, the Son of God, the one coming into the world."

Mary's opening words to Jesus are exactly the same as her sister's, but his response to her is very different. Seeing her distress, and the distress of the Jews who were supporting her, "he was greatly disturbed in spirit and deeply moved". After asking to be shown where Lazarus had been buried, Jesus himself began to weep, mourning the death of his friend.

And John's Gospel leaves us in no doubt about the actual, physical death of Lazarus. When Jesus eventually arrived, we are told that Lazarus had already been in the tomb for four days. Jesus commanded that the stone be moved away from the tomb. When Martha objected, saying there would be a stench after such a time, it brought forth a rebuke from Jesus: "Did I not tell you that if you believed, you would see the glory of God?"

For everyone involved in the Lazarus-event, this is strange, awe-inspiring territory. The other Gospels also record miracles where Jesus raised people from the dead (the synagogue leader's daughter in Matthew 9:18-26; the son of the widow of Nain in Luke 7:11-17), but there is something about this raising to life which moves us into a new dimension: one that prefigures the dying and rising of Christ himself.

Throughout this Gospel narrative, individuals and groups within it are challenged to take a leap of faith and "go out into the darkness" of this unknown territory, trusting that the God whom Jesus calls "Father" is able to transform their darkness into light, despair into hope and death into life.

**Application**

The raising of Lazarus, foreshadowing the resurrection of Christ, is for us a symbol of all those deep, dark places of our experience where hope seems absent and we are tempted to despair. In her book *Gateway to Hope* (St Bede's Publications, 1987), Maria Boulding speaks for all of us:

> "... as we teeter on the edge of despair, beset by every kind of temptation and feeling as though we had already fallen, the Spirit is released. This is his own place, the deepest place of our being where he is wedded to our spirit, where he can act and give life, where he can free us from all that hampers the true thrust of our will... Entombed Lazarus is a sign... of each one of us. In this hopeless situation, where you are nothing but stark failure, you know the miracle of grace. This tomb is the place of resurrection, and if you believe you will see the glory of God".

*"Unless a grain of wheat falls into the earth and dies, it remains just a single grain."*
(John 12:24)

**Illustration**
There's a poem by George Mackay Brown called *Elegy*. Its name suggests that it is a poem of mourning for death, but it is actually a poem about how life and death are inextricably intertwined. The poet speaks of the harvest crops as "risers from the dead", calling out "ripeness and resurrection."

Brown lived almost all his life in Orkney, a group of islands off the north coast of Scotland. It's a place where you cannot avoid nature. The darkness of the winter, and the long days of summer when it never grows dark; the seasonal comings and goings of the fish, the sand eels and the birds; the animals who are born, grow, and become the renowned Orkney beef; the crops sown, watered by the soft rain, buffeted by the winds, ripened by the warm sun, and finally harvested; the County Show, when the whole community gathers to celebrate another year of agriculture. Brown knew what city dwellers can sometimes forget: that we human beings belong to nature too. We are born, grow, live and die, like everything else on the earth.

Brown was also a Christian, and for him the turn of the seasons spoke not only of decay but of resurrection. The world turns, and there is death and new life.

On the whole, this is something we prefer not to remember. Our culture spends a lot of time and effort denying and delaying death. Medicine is there to mend the ills of old age; cosmetics reduce the signs of ageing. We pretend we are immortal. But the reality is, we die.

**Gospel Teaching**
Jesus had no time for sentimental notions about human life. He knew all its reality. According to the Gospel writers, he was aware that his own life would be cut short. The stance he took, the things he did, the people he consorted with, his outspoken attacks on religious and political authorities alike, all these things combined to make it certain that he would not be allowed to live to a ripe old age. In John's Gospel in particular, we find him

trying to break through his disciples' denial and misunderstanding, and prepare them for his death and what it would mean.

Like George Mackay Brown, Jesus and his disciples lived close to nature. Some were farmers, some fishermen by trade. They knew the cycles of nature, and human powerlessness in the face of nature's insistence. So Jesus turns to nature for a metaphor to try to help them understand. He speaks of a single grain. Held in the hand, it is useless. It needs to be put into the ground, where it breaks down as if it is dead. From that death, life grows, a plant with many grains that can be used for food. This is what his death is about, Jesus suggests. His effect on the world will be minimal while he is alive. But from his death will come enough new life for all the world. That is why he will not try to avoid his death. He knows that true life, for him and for those who come after him, only comes on the other side of death.

**Application**

Jesus is not just speaking of himself. He talks too about his followers needing to be ready to lose their lives in order to gain life. Being afraid of death, trying to delay it at all costs, trying to defeat the signs of ageing, all these things preoccupy people. The obsession with preserving our lives as they are prevents us from attending to the kind of life that really matters, life that is full and generous and truthful.

We, understandably, mostly want to take the road of avoidance, to forget about death until we can no longer ignore it, to cling on to youth and beauty and hope that cures will be found for everything that might kill us. It's hard to face up to death, both our own and that of those we love, and our society does not help us. We live with a nagging fear, buried deep inside us, which we push away rather than face up to. But facing up to it, Jesus suggests, is the way to real life, in which we know our limitations and can be honest about them, and not be afraid to take risks for the sake of love and truth. The result, according to our Gospel reading, is worth it. The result is eternal life, beginning now.

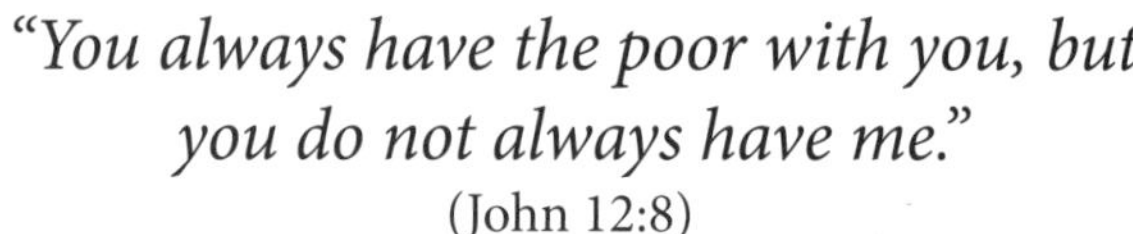

*"You always have the poor with you, but you do not always have me."*
(John 12:8)

**Illustration**

It's the stuff children's fairy tales are made of – seeing transformation. Look at "Beauty and the Beast", where a beautiful, kind girl unknowingly transforms the life of a prince who was turned into an ugly monster for his earlier unkindness. Or "Cinderella", where the poor, pretty orphan girl is treated like a slave by her stepmother, and transformed into a princess when a prince falls in love with her. Or even "Sleeping Beauty", who is awakened from her hundred-year sleep by a courageous prince.

The stories are all about knowing specialness and beauty, recognising reality, seeing the potential. They appeal to our hope for transformation, the promise of new life, and to our idea of ordinary people living out this vision. They encourage us to imagine life differently, to look for life in mundane or hard surroundings, and to reach out for life-giving transformations.

**Gospel Teaching**

Today's readings set out a vision for us to live within – the vision of our triune God's dream for creation and our part in it all. Forgetting what lies behind us – all the successes and failures, deserts and valleys, journeys and crises, who we are and where we happen to find ourselves – Paul urges us to fix our eyes on the vision God has prepared for us, salvation in Christ and life in God's kingdom. This vision was the secret of Paul's life for Christ, of all that he did, was and would be for Christ. It was also the vision that captured Mary, the woman who had listened deeply to Christ, who had recognised the profound value and timing of his presence, and loved him extravagantly with passionate service and devotion. Mary offered herself sacrificially as Christ's disciple.

What a contrast to Judas! Here was a man who had spent many hours and days, even years, in the presence of Jesus, heard his teaching on the kingdom of God, seen his miracles at first hand, been part of his chosen team of companions. But Judas had not even begun to see and understand. He had not begun to recognise presence, power and love in this man Jesus, God's Messiah. Judas pretended only to see the conflicts and needs of "now", refusing who Jesus was, and who he would be. The vision of God's dream – the prophecies, Jesus' life and words, the new life of God's kingdom – had not touched him. True, most of the disciples needed the evidence of the death and resurrection of Jesus to begin to understand, and the coming of the Holy Spirit to begin to know God's life. But Judas' heart was so untouched that he could even plan to betray this innocent man for a handful of silver. The one who complained at Mary's extravagance chose to gain from the jealousy, hatred and legalism which led to Jesus' death, the death for which he had accepted Mary's loving anointing.

**Application**

Mary and Judas present us with contrasting responses to Christ. It is not so very different for us all today either. There is still God's call to know him, and still so many of us miss the point, and need to be reminded. Christ's call to live within the kingdom, to see that which has come and is yet to come, to recognise Christ in our neighbours, in creation and in ourselves, and to live and work for the growth and glory of that kingdom and its king – all this is a work of God throughout the life of a Christian, and needing our open hearts, minds and eyes.

Mary shows us openness – letting love mould us and train us to live with our eyes wide open to the divine activity around us, and to be full of faith in our involvement. It is to see that to walk with the needy, lift up the weak, feed the poor, speak gently and love fully is God's call on all of our lives. It is to recognise that we need renewed hearts and minds to know the radical vision of Christ and experience the power of the promise of God.

Judas shows us the truth of living with a divided and loveless heart. We need first to be transformed for us to have a part in transforming the world. A vision of the kingdom of God brings together the call of personal salvation with political and social transformation; recognising the presence of Christ is to see both his lordship and friendship; knowing the promise and glory of God is the Spirit's work in us.

*"This is Jesus, the King of the Jews."*
(Matthew 27:37)

**Illustration**

On 16th May 1998, some 40,000 people gathered in Birmingham in England to call upon the leaders of the G8 summit to cancel the crippling debts of the world's poorest countries. It was one of the initiatives of the Jubilee 2000 campaign. At a particular time it had been arranged that everyone should hold hands to make a circle round Birmingham and make as much noise as possible for two minutes.

A woman joined in with her whole heart, clasping the hands of those next to her and shouting at the top of her voice. When the two minutes were up, she turned to her neighbour and asked, "Can you tell me what this is all about, please?" She had no idea – she had been in Birmingham shopping that afternoon and just found herself joining in. There must have been others like her in that six-mile circle of protesters.

**Gospel Teaching**

There must have been even more like her in the crowds making a lot of noise on that first Palm Sunday when Jesus rode into Jerusalem. People shouting at the tops of their voices, "Hosanna to the Son of David!" Jesus' journey was a significant one because it directly fulfilled an Old Testament prophecy. There had been signs all the time that Jesus was the Messiah, but this was more than a sign. Those who knew their scriptures knew that the king, of David's line, would ride into Jerusalem on a colt, the foal of a donkey.

And so it happened, exactly as the scriptures foretold. And the crowd went wild, following Jesus, following each other, shouting and chanting in praise. But there was confusion too – when they reached the city, people started asking, "Who on earth is this? What's going on?"

We might wonder what was in Jesus' heart as he rode along on the donkey. He knew the shallowness of much of the praise. He understood that many of the people who were proclaiming him king in fact just happened to be there that day, and were caught up in the crowd, like that woman in Birmingham. And he knew that this ride of triumph was in fact a ride towards his death, and that this same crowd who praised him would in a

few days' time be shouting for his crucifixion, with just the same ignorance and lack of understanding.

The majesty and triumph of the moment were laced for him with fear and sadness at the pain towards which he was journeying. Perhaps at one level he fervently wished that things could be different, for he was human; and humans usually try to avoid pain, not to walk into it.

But there was no turning back. And even if there had been a way out, Jesus would not have taken it. His mind was set on what was ahead, for he was motivated by love. And while, in this week of all weeks, we need to remember his pain and his suffering, we must not lose sight of the reason for it. When Jesus looked round at all those people shouting his praise, he loved them. Every single one of them. Even the ones who hated him.

Love was the reason why he was willing to walk into the hands of those who despised and misunderstood him so much that they wanted to murder him. Love was the reason why there was no turning back for Jesus.

Everybody failed Jesus; even the ones who loved him the most. His disciples fell away, even denied that they knew him. His family did not understand him. His community disowned him and the authorities killed him. Despite all that, Jesus went on loving. As St Paul writes in 1 Corinthians 13, "Love never ends. It bears all things, hopes all things, endures all things." Because of such love, the people who had failed Jesus were given new beginnings, and hopes that had died would be rekindled.

**Application**

When Jesus looks around at everyone on this earth, he loves us all, whatever our colour or creed. In all our confusion, in all our weakness and hypocrisy – he loves us. Even as we continue to cause him untold suffering with our selfish pursuit of material wealth, which may even be threatening the planet itself – he loves us.

Let us take hold of Christ's love this week, and let it take root in our hearts, so that as we follow Christ's journey to the cross we may experience his true resurrection when we celebrate Easter.

*"Those who went ahead and those who followed were shouting, 'Hosanna! Blessed is the one who comes in the name of the Lord!' ... Pilate spoke to them again, 'Then what do you wish me to do the with the man you call the King of the Jews?' They shouted back, 'Crucify him!'"*
(Mark 11:9; 15:12-13)

**Illustration**
Displayed in a showcase in the Great Hall of Lambeth Palace are the gloves which Charles I wore to his execution in Whitehall in January 1649. As he began to remove his outer garments, Charles gave his gloves to William Juxon, Bishop of London, who accompanied him to the scaffold. When Juxon later became Archbishop of Canterbury, he took the gloves with him, and they have remained at Lambeth ever since. Charles took great pride in his personal appearance, and dressed as carefully for his execution as for any other public occasion. It was a matter of honour that he should be seen to die well.

**Gospel Teaching**
In his first letter, St Peter tells us that Jesus also died well: "When he was abused, he did not return abuse; when he suffered, he did not threaten; but he entrusted himself to the one who judges justly." But for Jesus it was more than just a matter of honour. Peter is telling us of Jesus' complete and willing obedience to fulfil God's purpose.

Relatively early in his Gospel, Luke tells us that Jesus "set his face to go to Jerusalem". When Peter suggested there might be another way, Jesus reprimanded him angrily: "Get behind me, Satan!" It is the utter self-giving of Jesus, even to death itself, that restores, to those who have faith, our broken relationship with God. This is the drama which is played out through the events of Holy Week. We separate out those events in order to concentrate on the special meaning of each one of them, but we have at the same time to see them as a whole – Palm Sunday, Maundy Thursday, Good Friday, Easter Eve, Easter Day itself. The crowd in Jerusalem were witnesses to this unfolding drama, and found themselves caught up in it.

Crowds are notoriously fickle, and easily swayed. Those who had clamoured for the head of Charles I fell silent as the executioner raised his axe, and uttered a deep groan as the royal head was severed from the body. There was some kind of latent understanding that this was a unique moment. Never in the long history of England had the monarch been brought to public trial and execution.

Perhaps some similar kind of awareness permeated the crowd who welcomed Jesus into Jerusalem. They welcomed him in words reserved for, and applicable only to, the Messiah, the long-expected anointed one of God. But as the days passed, and events became ugly, the mood of the crowd changed. The voices that had been raised in welcome now called for his death: "Crucify him!" The soldiers made the most of their opportunity to beat up the condemned prisoner, and no doubt the crowd approved of what they saw. Even that was not enough for some. As Jesus hung upon the cross, "those who passed by derided him". The whole range of instincts and emotions which are at work within a crowd, even in our own day, were focused on Jesus during those last few tumultuous days of his life.

**Application**

We would naturally want to dissociate ourselves from any suggestion that we might be caught up in the mixed instincts of a crowd. We identify ourselves with the Good Samaritan, and condemn the priest and the Levite who passed by on the other side. Yet honesty demands that we recognise within ourselves the same fickleness which was at work amongst the crowd in Jerusalem. We may sing, "Thine be the glory", yet there is little glory in our lives. Or we may sing, "Make me a channel of your peace" – while conflict dominates our church or personal life. We want to believe, as did the crowd on Palm Sunday, that Jesus represents the answer to our hopes and prayers, while knowing that having faith does not protect us from life's problems. As we share the uncertainties of the crowd, we perhaps feel unworthy and discouraged.

But if we do, we load ourselves with unnecessary guilt and fail to grasp the meaning of Palm Sunday, Holy Week and Easter. "While we still were sinners," wrote Paul, "Christ died for us." And he rose again. Our response is one of faith. No matter how fickle that faith may seem, God accepts us through the crucified and risen Lord. So on this Palm Sunday, as we head together into this most holy week, let us be encouraged as well as challenged by our most holy Lord.

*"Father, into your hands I commend my spirit."*
(Luke 23:46)

**Illustration**
Dorothea was a pillar of her local church and her local community. She was at the centre of village life, interested in all that was going on and giving hours of her time to support worthwhile causes. She was greatly loved by the whole village and was like a steady rock, always there when needed. She also had a phenomenal knowledge of the village and its inhabitants, as she had lived there all her life. But one New Year, disaster struck. Dorothea suffered a massive stroke which hospitalised her for four months. After that she came home, but was bedridden and unable to move unaided. Worse, the stroke rendered her completely unable to speak. She could not utter a word. She changed from being a super-active person to being totally vulnerable and fully dependent on others for the slightest need, indeed, for life itself.

Yet, amazingly, Dorothea still had a vibrant ministry, albeit different. Once a month, half the church gathered around her bed at home for a Eucharist and this became a very special occasion. And despite the fact that talking to someone who is unable to respond verbally is difficult, visitors came in their droves and, after time in Dorothea's presence, somehow left feeling a lot better. Dorothea had given her spirit into God's hands and God was using her.

**Gospel Teaching**
At the Last Supper, Jesus gave his final instructions to his friends. He showed them that they should always serve one another and he gave them broken bread and outpoured wine as a special way of remembering him. Then he went with them for an evening stroll in the Garden of Gethsemane and, while they slept, Jesus spent the time in prayer, building up his strength for what lay ahead.

After that, Jesus did nothing at all. He became totally vulnerable and fully dependent on others for the slightest need, indeed, for life itself. That vulnerability was abused and Jesus was killed, yet perhaps his finest moment was when he was hanging on the cross in agony. It was this moment that dragged the admission out of the centurion that "Truly, this was the Son of God" (Mark 15:39).

What a contrast between this end and the beginning of Holy Week, with Jesus' triumphant Palm Sunday procession, so full of promise. On the first Palm Sunday, Jesus rode into Jerusalem as a king, but a king unlike any that had been envisaged. He rode not on a shining white charger with a huge military procession carrying flags and standards, but on a donkey with a ragbag of followers waving palm branches torn from the trees. It was a peasant procession, in direct and pointed contrast to the imperial entry into Jerusalem of any of the Roman officials. It fulfilled the prophecy of Zechariah that a king would ride into the city on a donkey and would bring not war, but peace (Zechariah 9:9-10).

In the eyes of the world, Palm Sunday's triumphant procession might be thought of as a much better witness to God than a man hanging in abject agony on a cross. But the centre of Christianity is not Palm Sunday but the witness of the cross – Jesus Christ dying for love of human beings. Perhaps this witness was so powerful and effective not simply because an innocent man was prepared to die for his beliefs, but because, throughout his life, Jesus gave his spirit into God's hands so that God was able to use Jesus in the best possible way. Jesus' final cry on the cross, "It is finished, Father, into your hands I commend my spirit", is a fitting finale which expresses the means by which Jesus achieved his perfect sacrifice.



**Application**

For many human beings, work has become that which defines their life. This may be voluntary work or paid work, but it means that for many people busyness is the most essential part of life. When that busyness is snatched away – through redundancy or illness or retirement or old age – people can feel useless and without worth. But all those who give their spirit into God's hands can be used by God in startling and unexpected ways.

For Jesus, the most powerful moment of his life was when he was completely helpless, hanging on a cross and utterly vulnerable. Dorothea's life, too, has become amazingly powerful since her stroke rendered her "useless".

Into your hands, Lord, I commend my spirit.

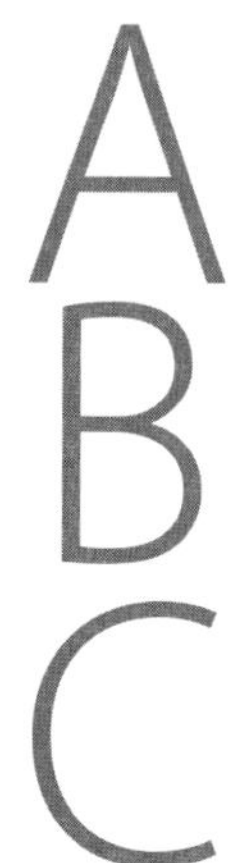



*"By this everyone will know that you are my disciples, if you have love for one another."*
(John 13:35)

**Illustration**

It's one of those quiz questions that will catch people out: "What's the state capital of California?" Many say Los Angeles, or San Francisco. But quiz buffs (and Californians!) know it's Sacramento.

The name was originally given to the Sacramento River by Spanish explorers – the city came later. When gold was discovered nearby in 1848 people flocked from all over the world, in what became known as the Gold Rush. As thousands of hopeful pioneers headed towards California in search of a better life, Sacramento was built to accommodate them. When California became a state just two years later, the town was already significant enough to be named state capital.

The name Sacramento means just what it looks like. Specifically, the Spanish explorers named the river after "the Most Holy Sacrament of the Body and Blood of Christ" – the Eucharist, or Holy Communion, one of the two sacraments instituted by Jesus and recognised by all Christians, however much they might squabble about the others.

**Gospel Teaching**

Today's Gospel reading shows us the Last Supper. While all the other Gospels record the origins of the Eucharist, John chooses to focus on another incident that occurred during the meal. And perhaps there's an allusion here to the other universally accepted sacrament: baptism.

The usual interpretation of this foot-washing scene is that it promotes service of others, in imitation of Jesus. It does! Commentators suggest it's a practical example of the "new commandment" that Jesus gives afterwards: to love one another as he loves us. It is!

But it's surely no accident that Jesus chose to use water, and cleansing, to illustrate his point. Master of the practical example, Jesus also had a gift for choosing the most telling one. Here, the comparison he draws between a complete bath and the washing of dusty feet is truly inspired! Whatever Peter's reasons for objecting (whether shocked by Jesus humbling himself, or merely offended that Jesus should think his feet are dirty!), his Lord and Teacher seizes on the teaching opportunity.

When we become Christians, our baptism into Christ cleanses us of the general sin that mars our fallen world. We go down into the water (either totally immersed or symbolically splashed!) just as Jesus will go down into the tomb on Good Friday. But then we rise again with him, cleansed by the power of his death and resurrection that together triumph over sin. Jesus predicts that Peter will only understand this "later". After the mind-blowing events of Easter?

Yet we all know that our daily lives are not totally free of sin. As we walk through the world, our feet pick up the dirt of doubt, anger, selfishness, jealousy… All we need do is allow Jesus to wash away these impurities, in penitence and prayer. We don't need to be baptised again. Is this what Jesus is suggesting in the exchange with Peter?

Rather than retelling the story about the institution of Holy Communion (which his readers would all know), John may be referring to the other sacrament that identifies us as Christians. But he records Jesus putting that into the context of loving service. People we meet can't see that we've been baptised, and if they're not in church they can't see us sharing Holy Communion. What really identifies us as Christians to the outside world is the practical outworking of our faith, loving others as God loved us in Jesus.

**Application**

How can we love others as Jesus loved us? How can we show people that we are his disciples? It begins in the Church, just as it began in the group around Jesus and later the community around John. If the world sees the Church embroiled in arguments over how many sacraments there are, in ungracious squabbles over women bishops or homosexual priests, what kind of image does that portray of Jesus? To identify ourselves as his disciples takes more than baptism and Holy Communion. It takes a readiness to listen to others and to celebrate difference. It takes genuine humility. Jesus washed the feet of all the disciples: the beloved disciple and the headstrong Peter – even Judas.

In the Gold Rush, pioneers trekked across America to Sacramento in search of a better life. In our Christian witness we can show people that the better life comes not from gold but from God. We, too, need to be pioneers, stepping out in faith, to encourage others to join us: not in a Gold Rush but a God rush.

*"I give you a new commandment, that you love one another. Just as I have loved you..."*
(John 13:34)

Maundy Thursday

**Illustration**

Never one to miss a photo opportunity, Archbishop John Sentamu of York made a sponsored parachute jump in aid of soldiers injured in Afghanistan. Safely back on terra firma, he faced TV journalists who quizzed him about his tendency to highlight "political" issues. After all, he had also cut up his clerical collar, live on camera, in protest at the political situation in Zimbabwe, and camped out for a week in a tent in York Minster, fasting and praying for peace in the Middle East. The archbishop's reply went something like this: "Christians follow a saviour who teaches compassion. We have a mandate to care."

What a vivid expression! Ironically, we associate the word "mandate" with politics. Election winners claim to have a mandate from the people, for their particular policies. But the word means more than just approval; it means "command", from the same root as Maundy. On Maundy Thursday we receive a command, a new commandment, to love one another: indeed, a mandate to care.

**Gospel Teaching**

Dr Sentamu is following his Saviour in more ways than one. Jesus, too, was a master of practical examples, vivid illustrations, parables in action. Often they, too, shocked onlookers. One of the most shocking of all is described in the Gospel reading for Maundy Thursday, an action only John's Gospel records.

At the Last Supper, Jesus removes his outer robe, ties a towel around his waist, and washes the disciples' feet. Can you imagine their horror? This was the most menial of tasks, performed by servants or slaves. This wasn't the sanitised version found in modern re-enactments, but real service, smelly feet.

In his usual role as spokesman for the disciples, Peter objects. But when Jesus convinces him this ablution is necessary, Peter's characteristic enthusiasm takes him too far in the opposite direction. Jesus could indeed have washed their heads and hands too if he chose, but he deliberately opted to focus on the most shocking, and therefore the most memorable, chore.

In case they missed the point, though, Jesus explained to his astounded disciples that he was illustrating something: "I have set you an example, that you also should do as I have done." Knowing their tendency to misunderstand him, he went on to anchor the specific example in a universal rule: "I give you a new commandment, that you love one another. Just as I have loved you..."

Who knows, without this further teaching, generations of Christians might have gathered... not to share in the Eucharist, on which other accounts of the Last Supper focus, but to wash each other's feet!

On this, the last night before he died, Jesus used not one but two vivid illustrations: the bread and wine of our Holy Communion, foreshadowing his death; and the foot-washing, a parable in action, giving his disciples a mandate to care, as he did, by serving others humbly, lovingly... and unconditionally, for Judas was present, too!

"Later," Jesus promised, "you will understand." After the events of the next three days, they would indeed understand – that his love for people, his care, his compassion, reached far beyond washing their feet. The ultimate practical example was his death, for us, on the cross: his blood would wash away our sins.

**Application**

The Church is frequently warned to stay out of politics; even some Christians try to keep them separate. Bishops should keep their noses out! It's inappropriate, some claim, that people in holy orders should make political statements. But Nobel Peace Laureate Archbishop Desmond Tutu famously announced: "When people say the Bible and politics don't mix, I don't know which Bible they're referring to. It's not the one I've been reading." Peace, justice, concern for those who are poor, oppressed or suffering – these all breathe through the Bible, which tells of a God who cares.

As for Archbishop Sentamu, as well as jumping out of aeroplanes he makes speeches. He has said: "Our society needs once more to rediscover the compassion and service at the heart of religion." For "society", read "politics". Governments should care. As Christians, how can we remind politicians of that? We can do so in high-profile ways (and you can't get much higher than 12,000 feet!) or simply by the careful, prayerful way we use our vote.

Bishops or lay people, how can we show that we are disciples of Jesus, if we forget our own mandate to care? That is the commandment we were given. In that sense, all of us are in holy orders.

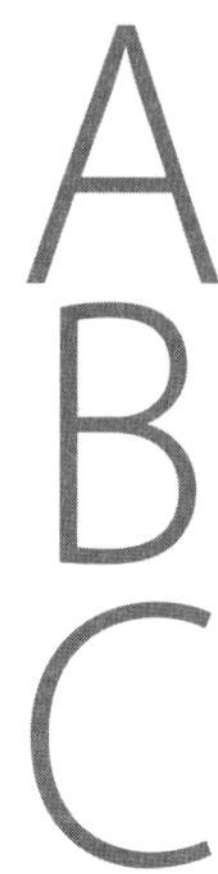



*"I give you a new commandment, that you love one another. Just as I have loved you..."*
(John 13:34)

**Illustration**
Imagine the scene. You are at a lavish state banquet at Buckingham Palace. The Queen herself presides at the top table, resplendent in silk and diamonds. Suddenly, in the middle of the meal, Her Majesty rises from her seat. Removing her tiara, she whips a flowery apron from beneath her chair, and ties it firmly around the royal middle. Then she moves swiftly along the line of chairs, reaching over the astonished diners to collect up their plates, scraping leftovers into a messy pile on the top one.

In the stunned silence, you glance at the guest beside you, who looks as horrified as you feel. Footmen come running, try to relieve Her Majesty of the task, but she shrugs them aside. "This is something one has to do," she insists. "Even so," mutters her consort, "one might have waited until one's guests had finished eating."

**Gospel Teaching**
At the Last Supper, the disciples were as stunned as the Queen's guests at that (purely fictitious!) banquet. It was unthinkable that their hosts should so demean themselves; it was also an odd time to indulge in such behaviour. Plates at a state banquet are collected at the end of a course, by servants; at the time of Jesus, feet would have been washed, by servants, before the meal began. Yet John's Gospel tells us that Jesus undertook this strange activity "during supper".

The timing is significant. During the meal itself, where other accounts of the Last Supper focus on the institution of the Eucharist, John shows us Jesus removing his outer robe, tying a towel around his waist, and washing the disciples' feet. Had he gone mad? Peter certainly struggled to understand. Headstrong as ever, embarrassed, and possibly even offended ("Are you trying to tell me my feet smell?"), he argued with Jesus. Eventually convinced that this ablution was necessary, his enthusiasm demanded even more of a good thing!

Quite what the Queen wanted to show by her actions in the fable above must be left to the imagination. Perhaps she, too, was making a point.

Jesus, however, openly explained to his astounded disciples that he was illustrating something: "I have set you an example, that you also should do as I have done..." And, lest they misinterpret this simply as an order to wash feet, he issued the universal rule which his specific action had illustrated: "I give you a new commandment, that you love one another. Just as I have loved you..."

On this last night before he died, Jesus instilled into his disciples the need to serve others humbly, as he did. The events of the next three days would add an extra dimension to this instruction. His love for his disciples stretched beyond washing their feet; he would die for them, to wash away their sins. He laid aside his heavenly identity to die upon the cross, just as he laid aside his outer robe to wash their feet. And just as he put on his robe again afterwards and returned to the head of the table, so he resumed his identity as Lord and God, rising from the dead to return to his Father.

**Application**

On this Maundy Thursday, we commemorate the new commandment (Maundy derives from the Latin "mandatum", a commandment) as we await the events of Good Friday and Easter, which give that commandment its full meaning. Sunday by Sunday, at Holy Communion, we recall these events, in remembrance of him. But we also need to love others, in remembrance of him. Sacrament and service: one is meaningless without the other.

The commandment to love was not new, since it was already a part of Jewish religious practice: "Love your neighbour as yourself." What was new about the commandment Jesus gave us was the reference to himself as pattern and example, and the reason for following it: so that others would know we are his disciples. We, too, are called to love others in imitation of Christ's love for us: self-giving, and not clinging to our dignity. And this love is practical, active, not sentimental; affection cannot be commanded, but loving service can. We are not commanded to like everyone we meet, but we are commanded to serve them, to see to their needs, in the name of Jesus: so that others may see the love of Christ in all we say and do, and may come to love him, too.

*"Pilate handed him over to them to be crucified."*
(John 19:16)

**Illustration**

It's a common story in many parts of the world. A young man is arrested and taken to court. He is charged with inciting rebellion and with some obscure religious crimes. Witnesses give their testimony, but the court has already made up its mind. He is convicted of treason, and sentenced to death. As is often the way, the sentence is carried out with indecent haste. There is no time for appeals. The execution is brutal and public, the better to provide a lesson for other would-be insurgents. The young man dies, the crowd disperses. Nothing very unusual has happened, on a Friday afternoon in Jerusalem.

**Gospel Teaching**

So that's the end of the story. It's one way of telling the story we're gathered here for today. But there are other ways to tell it. Let's start again, from the beginning.

In the beginning, God created the heavens and the earth – and the stars and the sea, and plants and animals, birds and fish, and human beings to care for the world and to be the friends of God their creator. But it was not long before the humans began to make a mess of things. They exploited the earth instead of caring for it. They exploited and killed one another. They refused to be friends of God, and to love and care for his world. They preferred hatred to love, exploitation to care.

God thought of ways of dealing with the situation. This was not what he had intended. He sent a flood of water to clean the world and make it fresh and new, but human nature did not change. So God tried something different. He chose one family, one nation, and concentrated on helping them to understand his purposes for the world. When they ended up as slaves in Egypt, he rescued them, led them through the desert, gave them some laws to help them live as his people, and gave them a land to live in. But human nature was not to be won over. Still God's people would not listen to him, would not accept his offer of friendship, would not love and care, refused the riches and the glory that were there for the taking simply by getting to know their creator.

So God realised that something more radical was called for. There was only one way to win his children back: to become one of them, to live their life and their death, to speak their own words to them face to face, to love them in ways they could understand. And so in Jesus God lived a human life, a life of goodness and love, a life such as only God could live, a life that touched others and transformed them, a life that challenged the powers of fear and hatred that had stopped human beings turning to God. And the fear and hatred fought back. They got him arrested and tried and convicted and executed. And on this day, God lived to the very end the human life he had chosen, putting himself wholly in the hands of his children and dying their death.

And from that moment, the world changed. On this day God proved his love and commitment to the world he made, beyond all reasonable doubt. On this day God went where we must go – to the end of life, and into death. God now knows all that it is to be human, even our mortality. Our life is for ever God's, and God's life is ours.

**Application**

So today is a solemn occasion for the Church. We mourn the death of the one who committed his life to us. We mourn the death of God at the hands of his children, and we grieve that our fellow human beings could do such a thing. We acknowledge all the wrong in our world that led to that execution and leads still to other executions.

But at the same time this is a joyful occasion. Today we celebrate the miracle of God's love for us despite all the wrong of our world. And we remind ourselves that in that terrible death lie the seeds of hope. God has gone where we must go, into death, into nothingness, but we know that this story is not yet at an end. And we wait with bated breath for the miracle to come. Because although today we remember the end of life, this end is also a beginning, of new life for all of us in relationship with the God who created us, redeemed us, and loves us beyond measure.

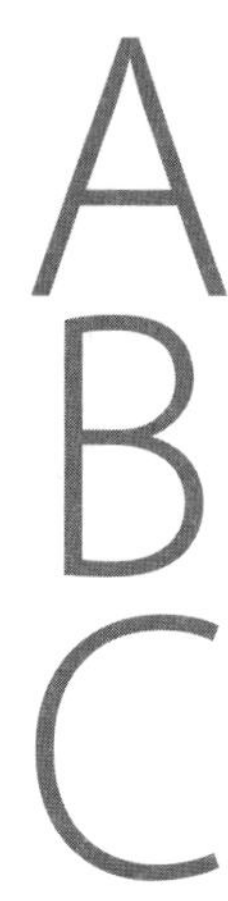



*"Then Jesus, knowing all that was to happen to him, came forward and asked them, For whom are you looking?'"*
(John 18:4)

**Illustration**
The TV presenter posed his question to the audience, "Why do you think Jesus died?" A lady in pink tentatively raised a hand. "It's the usual story: good man killed by bad people. What chance did the innocent Jesus stand in this evil world?"

"He miscalculated, didn't he?" a young man retorted. "Jesus wanted to reform Judaism but didn't expect opposition. Once he realised his life was in danger, it was too late!"

"I think he was just in the wrong place at the wrong time," offered an elderly gentleman. "He lived in a time of political and religious chaos and he simply got caught up in it. It was a tragic accident!"

Was Jesus powerless in the face of his enemies? Was he surprised to find himself facing death? Was his crucifixion simply an unfortunate accident? Our Gospel reading strongly refutes these views.

**Gospel Teaching**
In our reading, we are told that Jesus knew exactly what was going to happen to him and even the kind of death he would face (18:32). When Judas and the soldiers approached, Christ did not flee. We are told that, knowing "all that was to happen to him" (18:4), he stepped forward to reveal himself, believing this was all part of God's plan. Rather than Jesus being afraid, it is he who strikes terror with the very authority of his words into those seeking to arrest him (18:6).

The Gospel writer believed that the events of the Passion were not only foreknown to Jesus, but fulfilled the Hebrew scriptures. He shows that the disciples' escape, the casting of lots for Christ's tunic, the cry of thirst from the cross, Christ's unbroken legs and the piercing of his side were all predicted many years before. (See 18:9; 19:24, 28, 36-37.)

The religious authorities are intent on crucifying Jesus, yet he is not portrayed as a powerless victim and neither is evil shown to have overpowered good. All is presented as part of God's foreordained plan.

Indeed, Jesus corrects Pilate's assumption that he is the one influencing his fate: he states that Pilate only has power in the situation because God allowed it to be so to fulfil his purposes (19:11).

We are told that Jesus carried his own cross, which scholars believe again emphasises his control over his destiny. The Gospel even implies that Jesus controlled the actual moment that he died, bowing his head and giving up his spirit only once he was sure that his mission was accomplished (19:30). This reflects Christ's words in an earlier passage, "No one takes my life from me, but I lay it down of my own accord" (10:18).

**Application**

So, the Gospel author is adamant that Christ began his ministry in the full knowledge that it would end in his death and that, despite this knowledge, Jesus willingly chose this: he was not forced into it.

Knowing this can greatly encourage us. Jesus chose the path of suffering for our sakes. He did not stumble upon suffering by chance. How absolutely immense must his love be for us, to be prepared to suffer as he did! At any point in his ministry he could have taken a different way and avoided the pain. He chose not to.

Realising this will also motivate us in the choices we face as Christians. Just like Jesus, we are not forced to follow God's way: we can choose otherwise. However, when we realise the full extent of his love for us, we cannot fail to be grateful, and that gratitude can motivate us to keep going when the way gets tough, just as Christ's selfless example inspires us to persist and endure.

When we do suffer, remember that ultimately good is not overcome by evil. Jesus was not crucified because God was unable to defend him against wickedness. Neither were God's plans thwarted: Christ's death had been predicted in scripture and what appeared to be defeat was, in fact, victory.

Similarly for us, when we suffer it is not because God has forgotten us nor because God is not powerful enough to help us. The Good Friday message is that no matter how things may appear, God has the victory in the battle against evil. This is summed up from the very start of the Gospel with the words: "The light shines in the darkness, and the darkness did not overcome it" (1:5). Today, that light still shines, is still not overcome. May this knowledge inspire us and may God's immense love encourage us, as we take up our own cross and follow Christ.

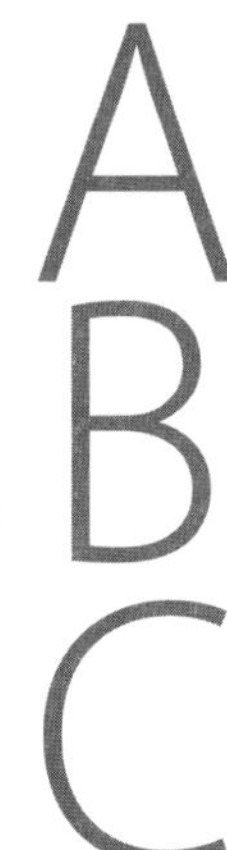



*"He who saw this has testified so that you also may believe."*
(John 19:35)

**Illustration**

It's hard to imagine a Good Friday service without "When I Survey the Wondrous Cross" by Isaac Watts. Charles Wesley admired the hymn so much, he said he would rather have written that one than all of his own put together. Even today, it features in many lists of favourite hymns. What makes it so special? The words themselves are very simple: in the standard four verses, the vast majority are just a single syllable. Only twenty of the words have two syllables. And just two words, two very important words, have three syllables: sacrifice; amazing.

Simple words, great poetry; rather like the Gospel of John, written in simple Greek, but conveying great truths in memorable language. And for the same reason: because, like John, Isaac Watts was an evangelist. Not in the sense that he wrote one of the Gospels, but in the sense of writing to spread the good news of Jesus Christ.

**Gospel Teaching**

Today's Gospel account of the crucifixion, like all of John's Gospel, was written to help the young Church understand who Jesus was, what was achieved on the cross, and what this means for each Christian. Watts continued this tradition in his hymn, one of the first in the English language to use the word "I" and focus on personal religious experience, on the effect on each one of us, as we look at the cross of Christ.

Critics sometimes say this hymn is too personal, focusing too narrowly on only one aspect of the cross: our emotional reaction to the example of Christ. They say it illustrates the "moral influence" theory of the atonement, at the expense of other aspects. You'll find no mention here of the victory of the cross, they say. Nothing about the cross setting us free from our sins. Nothing about Jesus as our substitute, our representative, the sinless Son of God doing for us that which we sinners could not do for ourselves.

Yet, like a true poet, Watts has covered all of this in a single word: "wondrous". It seems a very odd choice of word: Jesus died a bloody and excruciatingly painful death on the cross, so why does Watts serenade it as "wondrous"? The very wrongness of the word draws our attention to the fact that it's a shorthand, for all those achievements of the cross. Only when we consider everything that happened there could we possibly see the cross as wondrous: only when we remember that there, on the cross, God brought to fruition what he had begun in a stable in Bethlehem, and planned long before.

Today's Gospel reading stresses the fulfilment of scripture, the power of God and the acceptance by Jesus of his identity and his purpose: "I am he." Jesus hung on the cross, taking our sin upon himself: not a scapegoat, the innocent victim of a jealous God who demanded satisfaction, but God himself, who loved us so much that he was prepared to go through the agony of the cross, for us. To heal the breach between God and humans, God became human. To put an end to death, he died. The cross is nothing less than the meeting point between earth and heaven, between God and us: wondrous.

**Application**
The hymn is personal – in the best sense. It applies to each of us. We can't contribute anything to our salvation, but we can and must respond to God's love for us, for you, for me, so vividly portrayed on the cross: "Love so amazing, so divine, demands my soul, my life, my all."

The Gospel of John was the result of one person's response to that love. So were the other Gospels, and all the books of the New Testament. We must be grateful to their writers for recording the story of the cross. And to all those other Christian writers, like Isaac Watts, who have responded to the love of Christ through the centuries, by writing books, hymns, prayers and poems which help us to focus on the events of the first Good Friday: to survey the wondrous cross, to understand some small part of what took place. Enough to believe that Jesus is the Son of God, and that, through believing, we might have life in his name.

We're not all writers. But we all have gifts which God can use to spread the good news. What will we do in response to such amazing love?

# Easter

*"Do not be afraid."*
(Matthew 28:5)

**Illustration**
There is a delightful book by Martin Waddell and Barbara Firth entitled *Can't You Sleep, Little Bear?* Little Bear's problem is that he is scared of the dark. Big Bear provides bigger and bigger lanterns but nothing helps. Little Bear knows that outside the cave there is a lot of darkness, and the lanterns make no difference. Eventually Big Bear takes Little Bear outside to look up to the sky and face his fears. When Little Bear sees the moon and the stars, shining far above, splitting the darkness, he is at last able to fall asleep.

**Gospel Teaching**
It's natural to be afraid of the dark. But Matthew's story of the resurrection tells us about people who were afraid of the light. Sometimes, the darkness is easier to cope with.

The disciples of Jesus had lived through a roller coaster of emotions during that first Holy Week. They had been carried along by the cheering crowds of Jesus' entry into Jerusalem. They had spent the festival vigilant in the face of the risk to Jesus from the authorities, Jewish and Roman. They had experienced the intimacy of eating and drinking with Jesus and one another at the Passover supper; and then the fear, the shame, the despair and the grief of Jesus' arrest, trial and horrific death. In those circumstances, the deadness of grief seems welcome. It offers the chance to retreat into the dark and to stop feeling for a while. There is comfort in the dark, and a certain bleak peace.

So two women called Mary go early in the morning to a tomb they know to be secure and guarded. They go to grieve. The bright light of a Jerusalem morning may be shining around them, but there is darkness in their hearts. And perhaps there is comfort in that. Now that it is all over and the adventure of travelling with Jesus has come to an end, they can do what women do – weep for the dead, and tend to the living. They are sad, of course, devastated even, but they are not afraid, not any more. When the worst you feared has happened, there is no more reason to be afraid.

So it is not the darkness that scares them out of their wits, but the light – the light from two figures who ought not to be there. One is from another world, an angel, who should not exist in the real world of a Jerusalem garden. The other should be dead. Both break into the darkness of grief and despair with a searing white light of hope and joy. And the women are afraid. Grief they understood, it has its rituals and its expectations, and they know what is expected.

But this new thing, this unexpected joy, this painfully bright light, this is terrifying. In their grief, the walk to the tomb has been long and slow. Now all is movement. They run from the angel and from the empty tomb, not knowing whether to scream or sing. And they run headlong into Jesus. Little wonder that they fall at his feet. And his first words to them echo the message of the angel earlier: "Do not be afraid; go and tell."

Each of the Gospel writers tells the story of the resurrection in a distinctive way. None of the Gospels attempts to tell us what happened to Jesus between Good Friday and Easter Day. That remains a mystery. Instead, the Gospel writers show us the effect of the resurrection on those who were there. Matthew's account describes an earthquake and an angel like lightning. But he is not alone in describing the first reaction of those who experienced the resurrection as one of fear.

**Application**

As we sing alleluia on Easter Day, it is probably not fear we are feeling. But perhaps it should be.

The women at the tomb were right to be afraid. A bright light had pierced the gloom of the world, and nothing would ever be the same again. Dark death had been overcome. All the old, comfortable certainties had failed. The world had been turned upside down. And there were consequences. No returning to the safety of domesticity for the two Marys, but a commission to spread the news. And no safety for us either, if the light pierces through our lives and into our hearts today, but a life committed to the truth. Perhaps we should be more afraid, in order to hear the risen Jesus speaking to us: "Do not be afraid; go and tell."

*"Then the disciples returned to their homes. But Mary stood weeping outside the tomb."*
(John 20:10-11)

**Illustration**
It isn't always possible to predict how people are going to react. Some people who seem very ordinary and timid most of the time turn out to be superb in a crisis, while the person we all thought would be brave goes to pieces completely. Some people cope philosophically with sadness and loss but are totally thrown by unexpected happiness or good fortune, as though it somehow disturbs their whole understanding of how the world is supposed to be. Some people can only be at ease when they are in charge of a situation, and some can't cope with responsibility at all but are fine if they're told what to do. People are all different.

**Gospel Teaching**
So it is only to be expected that people reacted very differently to the death and resurrection of Jesus. Some of Jesus' followers had clearly been expecting the worst for some time before the crucifixion. It sounds as though some of the women, at least, had already made preparations for his death, had brought the spices they would need to anoint the body, and had detailed someone to watch out after the crucifixion and see where Jesus was to be buried.

Perhaps this group of people never really expected that Jesus would succeed. They loved him and believed in him, but they knew the world too well. They knew people's cynicism and selfishness, and so they knew that Jesus would be rejected and killed, eventually. Sad, but not surprised, they set off to take care of the corpse.

So they are thrown into disorder and terror when they find the empty tomb and the angel. Hope and new life were not part of their plan.

Other disciples were sure, right up to the last minute, that Jesus would pull some spectacular trick out of the bag and save himself. They had seen him do so many miraculous things, after all. So as it became clear that nothing was going to happen to save Jesus, that he really was going to die, their world was turned upside down, and they scattered in devastated disarray.

People's reactions to the resurrection are just as varied. In John's Gospel this morning, the empty tomb means very different things to the two sets of people who see it. For Peter and the beloved disciple, the dark mouth of the cave is a channel for the rebirth of hope. They had been right about Jesus: he did have one more spectacular miracle to perform after all. They see the tomb and run to spread the good news.

But for Mary, the black hole of the empty tomb is still about loss. Where is the dead body on which she had intended to lavish her loving tears? She is so far gone in the grief that she had been expecting for so long that she cannot feel hope until she sees Jesus with her own eyes.

Mary is sometimes called "the apostle to the apostles" because she was the first to see the risen Jesus and to tell others what she had seen. But other disciples, like Thomas, or the two who were walking to Emmaus, or Peter, who had betrayed Jesus, all needed to meet the risen Lord, too. Each of them needed something slightly different in order to believe. Mary needed to see, Thomas needed to touch, the pair on the road to Emmaus needed to see how it made sense in terms of the scriptures, Peter needed to be forgiven and given responsibility. Each one was different, and to each one, Jesus appeared.

**Application**

People are all different. Jesus knew that, and treated them accordingly. God knows that, because he made us. But we who want to proclaim the good news of the risen Lord don't always remember how different people are.

What makes each one of us come to faith in Christ and go on believing and trusting in his new life will vary from person to person. Jesus can be encountered in many different ways. Our task, on this Easter Day and always, is to discern what it is that people need in order to meet the risen Christ, and to try to help them in that need. Some need to meet Jesus in grief, some in hope, some in human touch, some in rational argument, some in anger at the cruelty of the world. Jesus wants to meet everyone where they can find him, so that all may share in his risen life. There isn't a package deal, only new *life.*

## *"Supposing him to be the gardener..."*

(John 20:15)

**Illustration**

It was an easy mistake to make. Garden, gardener. Early morning, before the fierce sun made manual work impossible, was the time to be tidying up, sweeping the paths. Who else would be there at that hour, among the dead?

**Gospel Teaching**

She was there to get away, as much as anything. So much had happened, so fast. The supper, the arrest, the hasty trial, the rush to execution, so much fear and grief in such a short time. And then the confusion of finding the tomb empty, and Peter and John no use, having a look, going away again, no efforts to find him.

She knew he wasn't there, but still she stayed. It was quiet, and empty. After all the noise, the rush, the emotion, now there was nothing, nothing but the still air, the dark space in the cave, and, away in a corner, the gardener doing whatever gardeners do.

He had rescued her. She had been ill, despised, an outcast, a woman with no friends, stared and pointed at in the street, living on the edge. He had drawn her into his circle of friends, his new community, where people who were nothing gained infinite worth. Under his gaze she had blossomed. She had learned of the new world where God reigned, where all the rules and regulations that had so oppressed her were overturned, where the poor were rich and the humble exalted, where the sick found healing and the tormented found peace, where even death could be challenged. But then they had come for him, as the powerful do for those who stand up to them. And now he had gone, leaving behind this empty space, this nothingness.

There was no going back. He had loved her, and, once you have been loved, the world is different for ever. She had a job to do, she knew. There was his mother to console. There were his friends to support while they decided what to do now. And then there was a future to find, a way of hanging on to it all. The new world of God's reign was too precious to lose.

The gardener was nearer now, disturbing her peace. Suddenly she was angry, that someone had taken the body away, denying her a last look, a quiet goodbye. Roman soldiers perhaps? The religious authorities? Misguided disciples? The gardener might know.

But then there was the voice. “Mary,” he said. The voice that had called her home into his family, calling her again. Even through her tears, she knew him. Not the gardener, then. She should have known, of course. How could she have believed for one moment that death could defeat him? Had he not shown them that love was stronger than death? How could she not have seen? How could she not have felt, in the quiet, in the emptiness, creation holding its breath waiting for his reappearing?

It was an easy mistake to make. Garden, gardener. A stupid mistake, perhaps. Or perhaps not. Because the garden was changed now. No longer the patch of scrubland carved from the dusty city. Now there was a new creation, and the garden was that garden from long ago, when the new human beings enjoyed the fresh dawn of the world where fruit fell from the trees and God walked in the evening cool. In the cool of this dawn God walked again, the world’s gardener, coaxing from the dust of death the growth of fresh new life.

Like Eve, she had to leave Eden. She would have loved to stay, enjoying his company all to herself. But there was a whole world out there that didn’t know that Eden had returned. Most would not believe her, but some would. They would take the message of the new creation until the seeds of Eden were planted all around the world.

**Application**

Mary’s story helps us to see the resurrection of Jesus through one person’s eyes, someone to whom Jesus had been immensely significant, who grieved his loss desperately, and who had the courage to believe the resurrection message and act on it, taking the news of death’s defeat to the traumatised and sceptical disciples. Through Mary we too receive the news. Death no longer has the last word. The seeds of Eden are here too. There is new life, eternal life, for those who are willing to take it. Love has proved stronger than hate, life stronger than death. Today the gate of Eden is open, and all may go in.

## *"I send you."*
(John 20:21)

**Illustration**

In *Bleak House* the author, Charles Dickens, has one of his characters, a Mr Chadband, say with great emphasis: "What is peace? Is it war? – No. Is it strife? – No. Is it lovely and gentle and beautiful and pleasant and serene, and joyful? – Oh yes!"

And what is it for us? We have uneasy peace when opponents watch each other over a gun barrel. We have peace because the children are not making a noise. We "need peace", we say, when perhaps all we need is a short sleep.

**Gospel Teaching**

But what did Christ give to his disciples when he said: "Shalom" – "Peace be with you"? Twice he said it and then breathed on them the Holy Spirit. An ordinary greeting suddenly became one of enormous significance.

The disciples were afraid. They had seen what the wrath and power of the high priest could do. The Master they so loved, who spoke with authority, who raised others from the dead and seemed himself so indestructible, was subjected to a mockery of justice and put to death with criminals. What hope for them if he could not defend himself? And so they gathered in fear, behind closed doors. Only when Jesus greeted them and showed the wounds he still bore did they allow the joy of recognition to surface. St John tells us little of what was happening in this room, except that the doors were shut. And that detail reinforces the reality of the resurrection. For here was Jesus, able to pass through the barrier of those doors and stand in their midst.

But Thomas was not there. One can imagine him in grief and disbelief, in doubt which could easily excuse him from commitment, refusing to take their words as truth. He would need proof of his own, he would need to see and to touch. He found acceptance at face value difficult – had he not asked how they could possibly find the "Way" Jesus had spoken about when he had not mapped it out for them? And the response then: "I am the way", Christ had said.

So now, with palpable love, Christ offers Thomas the proof he needs; offers him evidence of his wounds, the certainty of his physical presence.

Then, speaking into the future, Christ's words are to each one of us in our doubts and our questionings. We can almost hear the appeal in his voice, the longing to be real to all of us. "Blessed are those who have not seen and yet have come to believe." Another beatitude for his Church to take with it to the end of time.

And so he breathed on them. The same word is used as when God breathed life into Adam. Christ breathed life into his fledgling Church which now, certain in his resurrection, was ready to carry his peace into the world outside that room.



**Application**
But what of us who must believe without the physical contact, but who need his peace and the breath of his Spirit? Where can we touch him, see him, hear him?

We have that great leap of faith, which enables us to know that in the Eucharist, doubly hidden, is the risen Christ. Hopkins, the Jesuit poet, says in one of his poems. "And [I] fled with a fling of the heart to the heart of the Host" – the heart of Christ.

We touch Christ, too, whenever someone is hurt or in need. When we listen with patience, when we comfort a child, value the elderly, or infirm. When we take hold of each day of our lives and give him what we do. We are with him, too, in what we enjoy and love, in sights and sounds which give us pleasure, in both happiness and sorrow. The gift and the giver are one in Christ. Through such experiences, we receive Christ's peace, his comforting presence. This peace does not lull us into laziness, but gives us the confidence to share Christ's resurrection with others, as Thomas did.

Louis MacNeice has written a poem imagining St Thomas in India, where tradition says he carried the Gospel message. He speaks with envy of those he had converted, who believe without seeing, who have "a gift that was not mine". And yet it was Thomas', wasn't it? And the invitation of Christ called from him that prayer of utter faith: "My Lord and my God!"

## *"My Lord and my God!"*
(John 20:28)

**Illustration**

It is Caravaggio, the seventeenth-century Italian artist, who captures most vividly the moment when Thomas makes his declaration of faith in the risen Christ. Jesus has loosened his garment. In the dim light of the spluttering candle, he grips Thomas by the wrist. Thomas extends a distinctly grubby forefinger which Jesus guides into the loose flesh of the gaping wound in his side. Thomas' brow is deeply furrowed with doubt and incomprehension. His eyes follow the direction of his extended forefinger. This is the moment of decision. Can he believe what he sees? He can, and he does: "My Lord and my God!" It is a life-changing moment for Thomas. It remains a crucial moment for the many who would come after him in the course of time, "who have not seen and yet have come to believe".

**Gospel Teaching**

Because of his initial reluctance to believe that Jesus had risen, Thomas has given his name to all who find it difficult to believe, or experience moments of doubt. Yet Thomas was one of the original twelve whom Jesus sent out to proclaim the Gospel with very little to sustain them. When there were threats on Jesus' life, it was Thomas who encouraged the others: "Let us also go, that we may die with him." So we need to look again at the circumstances surrounding his declaration of faith.

As we are presented with Thomas' disbelief, we have to ask, "Why should he have believed?" We know very little about the disciples. We cannot know what went on between them, or what bound them together. We do know conflicts existed, as over which of them would be the most important. So when the others told Thomas they had seen the risen Jesus, it could have been that they were having a joke, in the worst possible taste, at his expense. Nor could he know they had already seen Jesus' wounds for themselves.

But the appearance of the risen Jesus confirmed that the disciples had not been joking. They had been genuine, and now Jesus was actually there amongst them again. Having greeted them all, "Peace be with you", it was to Thomas that he turned. "Put your finger here and see my hands. Reach out your hand and put it in my side."

This is the scene Caravaggio captured in his painting. The setting is commonplace, simply the house where the disciples met and locked the doors for fear of their enemies. The artist gives us no shining lights or angels waiting at the edges of his canvas. Yet it is a profoundly religious moment, lit by Thomas' declaration of faith. He is confronted by Jesus in person, a different person, yet essentially the same, who addresses him directly: "Do not doubt but believe." Thomas has to make up his mind, reach his decision. The evidence of the resurrection is there before his eyes. There is only one conclusion he can come to: "My Lord and my God!" Thomas is declaring his faith in the risen Christ, acknowledging Christ's claim upon his life from now on, and committing the whole of his life to proclaiming the Gospel of the dying and rising of Jesus. Ancient tradition has it that this took him as far afield as India.

**Application**
Nevertheless, Thomas' negative reputation lives on. His name stands for doubt, rather than faith. This means that we do Thomas a grave disservice. He has left an abiding and positive legacy to the Church, to all who would seek to follow the risen Christ. In many ways he stands for all of us, represents all of us. Many of us have followed his pattern. We have experienced the same struggle to believe, to come to terms with the Christian faith, to make a commitment to the risen Lord.

There is ample evidence in the Bible of the many who have heard God's call, and felt that it could not be so. How could God be calling them? For ourselves, we may also feel, or have felt, that it must at best be a mistake; at worst, a joke in poor taste. Like Thomas, we have to weigh the evidence, reach our own conclusion, make our own decision. Only then can we make our personal declaration of faith, and all that it implies for our belief, and our commitment to service in the name of the risen Lord. Like Thomas, we have to be able to say, at some stage, and in our own way, "My Lord and my God!"

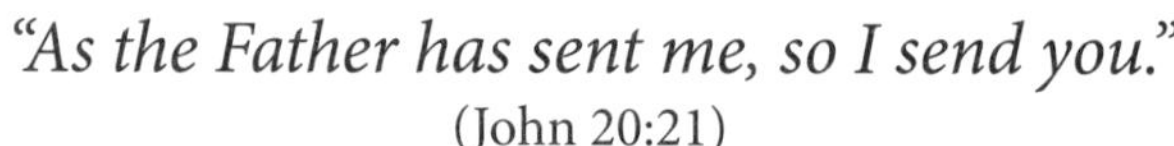

*"As the Father has sent me, so I send you."*
(John 20:21)

**Illustration**

To smooth the path of social communication we have various stock phrases to show that we really mean what we say: "I give you my word"; "My word is my bond", and so on. In courts of justice, a Christian reinforces an oath with the action of placing a hand on the Bible as proof of meaning what is said. Sadly we live in a world in which people's words, even promises, are frequently not enough to convince. Marriage vows can be broken. Business contracts are fractured, sometimes even by deception and fraud. The course of legal justice can be hampered by dishonest evidence, even that given under oath. Experience teaches us that words are fine, they can be given freely and often honestly. We can want to be convinced, especially when the speaker means a lot to us. But marriage vows made in all sincerity can later become broken under the strain of a failing relationship. So ultimately for people in uncertain situations it is concrete proof that convinces. Since we can never be really sure of someone else's ability to remain faithful to their word, can we blame anyone asking for proof?

**Gospel Teaching**

In today's Gospel narrative we hear how Thomas is faced with two problems. The first was listening to his friends telling him that he had missed the most incredible event of their lives, and having to decide if he trusted them enough to believe them. (And even perhaps feeling annoyed or hurt that he had been elsewhere when it happened.) The second was accepting the staggering possibility that his Lord Jesus had risen from the dead. The apostles said they had seen Jesus in the flesh. How could he have been sure that this was so? The consequences of what they were saying were incalculable. The last time he had seen Jesus he had been dragged away to be crucified. Of this much he was sure. This was hard evidence. It would take more than words from his excited friends to convince him. After all, how would we feel to be told that a dead loved one was alive again? It defeats logic.

When they met face to face, Jesus offered Thomas the evidence he sought. Jesus did not seem to mind that his previous appearance had not been sufficient to convince Thomas; he knows our weaknesses. But for Thomas the meeting was much more significant than an exercise in overcoming his doubt. The fact of Jesus arising from the dead said more about his true identity than any word or action during his ministry. Only God can raise or be raised from death, only God has the key to life. Thomas recognised Jesus fully and completely as "My Lord and my God!" Words alone could never have convinced him of this, only a personal encounter with the risen Christ. An encounter which changed his life for ever.

**Application**

People today will not generally simply accept our word for the reason for our hope, and their scepticism is understandable. Words could never properly describe the power of a relationship with the living God. Jesus may send us out, just like Thomas and the other disciples, to continue the work of bringing God's love into the world. But we have to offer our listeners something other than verbal assurances that there is more to life than that which they already experience.

But how are people to know that Jesus is alive unless they encounter it in our lives? Why should people believe us when we say that new life, eternal life, is on offer to all unless they see evidence of this in the way we live? How can people trust that God loves them unless we manage to make that love tangible, not just empty words?

Talk is cheap. The message of new life, of love or hope is credible only if people can actually experience it through us. Jesus did not send us out simply to tell others about the Gospel: he asks us to live out that good news, to give it flesh and blood, just as he did. When we do that, then we too become people whose joy, trust, hope and fearlessness are magnetic and infectious, drawing others to Christ through what they see in us. We become people whose word can be doubly trusted, as people see how we live that faith which gives us such abundant life, and how that faith is grounded in God.

*"He took bread, blessed and broke it, and gave it to them. Then their eyes were opened, and they recognised him."*
(Luke 24:30-31)

**Illustration**

At the time of the First World War, the principal morning service in most Anglican churches in England was Matins. This proved to be a problem for chaplains in the trenches who were trying to bring the presence of God into those mud-filled, blood-filled holes in the ground. It was a problem because many of the young men in uniform were unchurched. The glories of the *Te Deum* led by a parish choir, however humble, had not become a window onto the numinous for these boys. But more fundamentally, with the exception of the Psalms, Matins didn't speak to the soldiers' ghastly situation, where suffering and death were all around, fear and despair endemic.

What did speak to them was Holy Communion. The men didn't need to be familiar with the liturgy, for they soon came to recognise God in a body broken for them and blood poured out for them. Communion brought them the comfort of God's real presence and hope for life even there where death seemed to rule.

**Gospel Teaching**

As Cleopas and friend walked to Emmaus in the company of a stranger, they were certainly not in a situation comparable to that of soldiers in trench warfare. Or were they? Perhaps it would be wrong to underestimate the despair of those two disciples. Their country was occupied by enemy soldiers, who crushed any opposition ruthlessly. Mass crucifixions were common. And then a man called Jesus had brought them hope of liberation. Cleopas refers to him as "a prophet mighty in deed and word before God and all the people". And when he adds that "we had hoped that Jesus was the one to redeem Israel", you can feel the disappointment weighing on him like a million shrouds. He and his friend weren't just mourning the death of a friend, which would be bad enough, but the death of the dearest hope of a whole nation.

Although the stranger walking with them was, in fact, the Jesus whom they mourned, they didn't recognise him. He gave what must have been the most accomplished exposition of scripture, proving that the Messiah

was meant to "suffer these things and then enter into his glory", but still they didn't recognise him. It was only when they invited Jesus to stay with them, and he sat at table with them and broke the bread, that the veil was lifted and they knew that Jesus was Lord and he had risen indeed.

**Application**

What about us? We aren't fighting in trenches nor do we live under an occupying power. Or do we? Isn't that a perfect description of sin? An occupying power? And are we immune to doubt and despair? Clearly not. We walk the road to Emmaus on many a day of misgivings, when more bad news on the world's scene makes us question if God's in his heaven, when reading our scriptures brings God no closer and our prayers ring hollow.

Sometimes our hearts are filled with the kind of complaints that concerned the two disciples on the road to Emmaus. Like them, we are tempted to tell each other all the terrible things that have been happening to us in the last few days – in our case, perhaps, domestic quarrels, troubles at work, the loneliness of life – and all these things so fill our minds that we fail once again to recognise Jesus.

This is why Holy Communion is such a miracle of grace. Holy Communion has the power to lift us off the wearying Emmaus road, to still the questioning, to place our troubles at the foot of the cross, as we hold out our hands for the bread of heaven and the wine of the new covenant.

So yes, we can lose sight of Jesus in our questioning, in our biblical interpretation and even in our pastoral work – after all, even unbelieving social workers or biblical scholars engage in these activities.

But gather round the Lord's table for bread and wine and there is the defining moment of our discipleship. We know Jesus lives, not because a scholar has told us, not because of rumours of resurrection appearances, not because of all the work we've done in his name, but because, quite simply, we meet him where he's always been, in the broken bread and shared wine.

In the trenches of our fear and despair, nailing our occupying forces to the cross, he is recognised – if only for a fleeting moment. But it's a moment that can sustain us through the coming week.

*"Look at my hands and feet; see that it is I myself. Touch me and see; for a ghost does not have flesh and bones as you see that I have."*
(Luke 24:39)

**Illustration**
"From ghoulies and ghosties and long legged beasties and things that go bump in the night, Good Lord deliver us." So says the old Scottish prayer, and so perhaps say a good many of us, for we can easily feel uncomfortable and frightened by talk of spirits and ghosts and other strange things that we do not understand. Then there are the science fiction programmes on television that have sent many a child diving for shelter behind the sofa, or requesting the comfortingly solid presence of an adult. And as we read today, the disciples were not made differently from us. When they saw Jesus appear among them, standing before them, very much alive, and they had seen him die only days before, they were terrified. It must have been very confusing.

**Gospel Teaching**
They had stood gathered about the two disciples from Emmaus who had walked and talked with the risen Christ, who had failed to recognise him in the fading light; but who had known him instantly in the breaking of the bread. But all of them, when he came and stood amongst them, took fright. They thought he was a ghost. The Greeks saw reality in terms of concepts, of universal truths, but to the Jews, reality was particular and concrete. And so the resurrection was particular and concrete, not just a concept. Jesus really did come and stand with his disciples, risen from the dead. Thomas famously had need to touch in order to believe, and Christ understood that need. "A ghost", he said, "does not have flesh and bones as you see that I have," and, for final confirmation of his physical reality, he asked for some food. They gave him a piece of fish and watched him eat it.

There is a playfulness and humour in Jesus' words and actions, as he asks, "Why are you frightened? Never before seen a dead man eating?" The way Jesus teases them is part of what helps them to accept that it is really him, really alive.

This sense of Christ's reality, this absolute certainty that he had risen from the dead and was with them again, came before the strengthening and deepening understanding which was the gift of the Holy Spirit. Unless they were sure, how could they preach with conviction? The faith of those who came after them would be based on that certainty.

In the first reading, which jumps ahead of the Gospel story, we see Peter, in the new-found courage of the Pentecostal Spirit, reminding the Jews that they had disowned Jesus, the same Jesus whom he too had disowned before a serving maid. But now he knows and we hear the confident affirmation of this faith – a faith that has transformed his life in every way. And 1 John 2:2 attests that this Christ is the sacrifice which has taken away our sins and that we too can know him if we keep his commandments.

What a marvellous promise is contained in these words! When Christ is revealed, we will be like him, for we will see him as he is. It reminds us too of who we are – we are children of God, with all the promises of inheritance that come with that status. As believers we are not just acquaintances, not just friends, but children, members of the family: we are meant to be here; we belong.



**Application**
We do not have to do anything different or special. In our ordinary daily events, our walking and talking and working, if we do all these according to what we believe to be right, then Christ is risen and amongst us. He will live in our hearts, speak through our words, see with our eyes and reach out to others through the touch of our hands. The three years of his ministry are extended into the lives of all who believe in him, in whom God's love is coming into perfection.

It is an awesome thought to understand that people may see Christ in us, because of our status as children of God, because of our relationship with him. We have our part to play in the ever-extending family of God, in helping people to see that they too can be children of God, they too can find eternal life through Jesus. Let us be encouraged and awed as we contemplate some of the tremendous implications that come from a living faith in Christ.

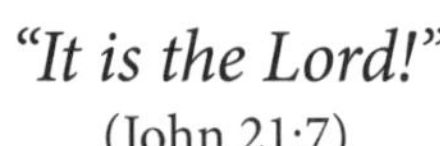

# *"It is the Lord!"*

(John 21:7)

**Illustration**

During the Second World War, a soldier said goodbye to his wife and two children to rejoin his regiment overseas. They were heartbroken at having to part. She promised to write every day to keep him in touch with what she and the children were doing. He agreed to do likewise when circumstances permitted, but asked her to remember that in whatever she was doing he would be there with her, and to look forward to his homecoming.

Weeks went by with the wife writing letters containing the days' activities and details of the children's development. She included thoughts and feelings and decisions to be made, asking his opinion, including him as a part of each day. She lived by faith that he would receive them and occasionally she received a reply reassuring her of their continued closeness and of their being reunited.

One day, after the usual queuing and shopping for essentials, she was travelling home on the double-decker bus with the children, plus bags and pushchair, wondering how she would manage everything, when down the stairs came her husband, completely unexpectedly. He had been given forty-eight-hour leave without prior notice. She was speechless and rooted to the spot, unable to believe her eyes. Later she told him how often she had imagined him there, involved in her ordinary daily activities, so much so that when he appeared it had seemed like a trick of her imagination. But the sense of his "presence" even during his absence was what had kept her going.

**Gospel Teaching**

In today's Gospel we hear how Jesus appears to his friends in one of their old familiar haunts, the Sea of Tiberias, while they are fishing, albeit not very successfully. Imagine their shock at seeing their beloved Lord in such mundane surroundings.

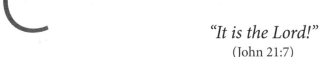

They knew Jesus was risen from the dead because they had been with him and had been commissioned for their ministry, but who would have expected the risen Lord to appear there? The disciple Jesus loved recognised the stranger on the shore and precipitated impulsive Peter to hurl himself into the water rather than wait for the boat to land. We are not told how the other disciples responded – probably like the soldier's wife: delighted that old times seemed to have returned, even if for only a brief time, some comforting familiarity in the midst of tragedy and uncertainty.

The disciples had seen their new life's work all but destroyed when he was crucified, and then partially restored at the resurrection. Jesus wanted to reassure them, and what better way than by appearing in the context they knew best and in the actions of a loving Lord? He had fed thousands during his ministry; now he was feeding them. He was no apparition, but their Lord who could sit and eat with them. Even his commissioning of Peter to continue the leadership of his new movement took place in these humble surroundings. Jesus always took people exactly how they were and wherever he found them, and he still does.

**Application**

It is crucial to remain in close touch with those who are important to us to maintain the relationships. Our relationship with God is no different. This will be nurtured by frequent prayerful references during our ordinary daily round and especially through regular worship together.

We also find God through our contact with other people, in our work with and for them; in the application of Jesus' teaching throughout every aspect of our lives and the daily events which seem to us so very ordinary. When we act like Christ we bring him into our lives in a powerful and effective way. He comes to us in many guises: the refugee, the destitute, criminals, the sick. Jesus is in our workplace, at the welfare department, at home, parish, school and football club. Wherever we are, God is. We need never worry that we have lost sight of him, for his love encompasses us at every moment in every place.

Listen for him as you are busy at your work. Think of him and talk to him in the mundane tasks, ask his advice in difficult situations. Acknowledge his presence, for he is the unseen partner who longs to share your life with you. Then, like the disciples, we shall recognise him as the true Lord who will guide us here before eventually leading us to heaven.

*"I came that they may have life, and have it abundantly."*
(John 10:10)



**Illustration**

Significant numbers of the working population in the UK are migrant workers. Many come from former Eastern bloc countries like Poland and they come to seek better conditions and a more realistic rate of pay. They take on jobs which are difficult to fill, because those jobs are dirty, cold and sometimes dangerous, as the scandal of the cockle pickers who drowned while working in unsafe conditions in Morecambe Bay in 2004 showed. And migrant workers are sometimes abused, receiving a very low rate of pay from which a large percentage is taken to pay for accommodation, even though that accommodation may be in appalling conditions.

Since they have no claim on any UK support system, it is little wonder that migrant workers occasionally resort to theft or break out into fights. Migrant workers have a bad press and are often despised and ostracised by UK residents.

**Gospel Teaching**

In first-century Palestine, shepherds had just such a press, especially if they were hired hands. Flocks were only allowed to be kept in the wilderness, since any sheep that was found between Jerusalem and Bethlehem was considered to be a sacrificial victim. So shepherds spent their lives in the wilderness scratching for food for their sheep and facing the danger of wild beasts.

Consequently, those who were poorly paid hired hands tended to lead their flocks onto other people's land, and had a reputation for pilfering. Because they often worked for months at a time without supervision, they were frequently accused of stealing from the flock. The pious were warned not to buy wool, milk, or kids from shepherds, on the assumption that it was stolen property. Shepherds were not allowed to participate in the judicial system, not even as witnesses. Polite society considered that there was no more disreputable occupation than that of a shepherd; and Philo, a Jewish philosopher of the day, wrote about shepherds, "Such pursuits are held mean and inglorious." So when we call Jesus "the Good Shepherd", we may be saying something much more revolutionary than we realise.

In today's Gospel reading Jesus refers to himself as something that sounds even lowlier than a shepherd: the door of the sheepfold. But in the ancient Middle East the door to the sheepfold was provided by the shepherd himself, who would lie across the open entrance at night in order to keep the sheep in and wild beasts out. This entrance was the only legitimate way into the sheepfold, since any other entry involved climbing over the wall, a route taken by thieves.

Having thus referred to himself as a caring shepherd and therefore the one whom the sheep rightly trust to keep them safe and lead them to good pasture, Jesus tosses a final insult towards the religious leaders of the day. He implies that they are nothing more than hired hands, by asserting that all who came before him were thieves and bandits caring nothing for the sheep. Therefore, says Jesus, the sheep failed to listen to these religious leaders. But Jesus affirms that the sheep instantly recognise him, hear his voice and identify him as their shepherd.

**Application**

By acting as the gatekeeper, Jesus both encourages his sheep into the sheepfold when necessary, but also leads them out to roam freely in the pasture. If the Church is the sheepfold, then perhaps we need to remember that its purpose is as a shelter to which we return to rest and recover. Our shepherd, Jesus, cares for us and keeps us safe from harm. But most of the time, he encourages us out into the world beyond, where we are to roam freely. And it is interesting that the sheep are mostly nourished not in the fold, but outside the fold. The sheep need to go out to find their own sustenance and, since the pasture outside the sheepfold is a wilderness, that may not be an easy task.

So our place is to rest and relax here in church, knowing that we are kept safe by Jesus, but then to go out into the world. Fortunately, we have a good shepherd. Jesus will guide us out to the places where we need to be and will gather us back into the fold, keeping us safe. If we hear his voice and go out and come back in through him, we will find our nourishment in the most unexpected places. And when that happens, then all of us, migrant workers included, begin to experience life as God intended.

*"The hired hand runs away because a hired hand does not care for the sheep. I am the good shepherd."*
(John 10:13-14)



**Illustration**
At the end of one of the Harry Potter films the hero's headmaster, Professor Dumbledore, says: "It is not the abilities you have that make you what you are – it is the choices that you make." Thus a modern amusing film suddenly takes on the nature of a morality play!

**Gospel Teaching**
It would be quite wrong to assume that just because a person is paid to do a job, they have less interest and less dedication. But we can all recognise the truth of what Jesus says. We often complain that levels of service are "not what they were", and we get infuriated when we are forced to listen to recorded messages on our telephones. We want something extra, beyond what is efficient or economic. We want something that we can describe as good.

This is what Jesus describes as the qualities of the good shepherd. He knows his sheep. He protects them from the wolf. He is prepared to lay down his life for them. This word that Jesus uses – "good" – describes the difference between the able person and the one who chooses to give love and service. Jesus is not talking about one occupation – although the image of a shepherd makes us think about pastoral care. He is speaking about an attitude which should be an essential part of life for those who follow his teaching. Naturally we think that Jesus is speaking of himself as the shepherd, and the Church as his sheep. We are those who get lost, who run into danger, and who become scattered.

First, there is a message to the Church in this. We must try and avoid losing contact with our master. We must try and keep together, rather than fragment our church into little groups that need to be brought into one flock. We must recognise the gifts that the good shepherd displays – the pastoral gifts which we are all called to show. Pastoral care springs from our faith in a loving, caring God. We do not employ a vicar, rector, or minister to carry out this task alone (a hired hand!). We are all called to share in the "shepherding" of the flock.

Second, there is a message to us all in the work we do each day. We are called to be good as well as competent. There is an extra responsibility that demands the commitment shown by the good shepherd: a care for those around us; a willingness to show integrity, and honesty, to go the extra mile. That is what makes the difference between the ones who are just doing a job because they are being paid for it, and those who are fulfilling their calling – whatever that may be. We are all able to recognise that difference in others. Do they see it in us?

Third, there is a message to us in our homes. It is at home that we may be impatient and intolerant, where we can acknowledge that we are tired, and let our behaviour show it. The good shepherd had to return home at the end of his tiring day in the fields and on the moors: Jesus would certainly not have suggested that he then could forget his principles and cease to care for others – to drop his attitude of care and love.

**Application**
The picture that Jesus gives of the shepherd of his day is one that still applies to us, whatever our work and occupation. The concept of good work, done with honesty and integrity, is one that we can recognise. We can contrast it with jobs that are done grudgingly and with what we call "ill grace".

That is a very appropriate term to use. Those who follow the teaching of Jesus, the good shepherd, work and live with grace – not with ill grace! These are virtues that we can show in our church, in our daily work and in our home. In each of these places today we see the need of the grace of God. In our churches we know that we should be one: one within each worshipping community, and one in the whole Church of God. In daily work, and in international politics, we know the need of truth and of healing. In our homes we know the need of honesty and purity. All of us who try to follow Christ are taught that we need to have, in every part of life, the qualities of the good shepherd.

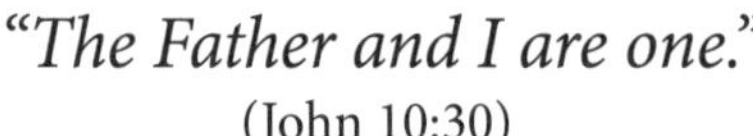

*"The Father and I are one."*
(John 10:30)

**Illustration**
How's your waltz these days? What about your salsa? Are you one of the many people who can be spotted tripping the light fantastic in an old school hall on a Thursday night? Formal dancing of all kinds seems to be undergoing a popular revival, partly, no doubt, because it's a little more interesting than the gym, and a great way to keep fit. But more than that, the recent revival of TV programmes that feature dancing, in one way or another, shows that even those who can't or won't take to the floorboards can enjoy watching it being done. There is something rather wonderful about the spectacle of a good dance: the glamorous costumes; the pace and movement; the way that two people can move so close and so quickly, and yet somehow manage not to step on one another. It's no wonder it makes great TV entertainment.

**Gospel Teaching**
But not only is it great entertainment: the image of a dance is an ancient and sometimes forgotten model that has something useful to bring to some of the claims Jesus makes for himself, such as the one we read at the end of our Gospel reading. "The Father and I are one," he says. Just six little words that sum up what John's Gospel is all about. John wants us to know that Jesus relates to God in a different way from that in which humankind had related to God before and that, because of this, the universe will never be the same again.

But the fact that Jesus can sum up his relationship to God in six little words does not make it easy to understand. The question of who Jesus was, and exactly how he related to God, stretched past Jesus' day into the first hundred years of the Christian faith and beyond. Right up to the present day in fact. When Jesus said, "The Father and I are one," he laid out a blueprint for the transformation of our lives. But he also set off centuries of debate about what this actually meant, and what it means for us.

And this is where the image of the dance comes in. As the early Church debated what it all meant, one of the models that they came up with in order to explain the relationship of Jesus to God was the dance. In a dance, the participants move as one, but they remain separate individuals with a distinct part to play. Before Jesus, the relationship of God to humankind had been characterised by a kind of awesome separation. God was too holy, too completely other, to be approached directly. Those who did come close to God generally tended to fall flat on their faces and fear for their lives. But in the God/man Jesus, all that is changed. For the first time in history, a human being was able to stand before God without flinching – in bold and lively partnership in fact. "The Father and I are one," Jesus says, and the world is changed for ever. The relationship of God to his people is transformed from an awesome separation to an intimate independence.

**Application**

We do not have those qualities that Jesus had – his divine qualities – that enabled him to bring about this shift in divine/human relations. But if we believe, then the unique nature of Jesus' relation to God changes the way that we relate to God too. This is a shocking truth that many, many Christians do not have the courage to claim for themselves: in Christ we are partners in the dance. It's not unusual to hear Christians talk of our relationship to God as if we were infants – completely dependent on God, with little life and thought of our own. And while this may be a suitable metaphor for some of us at some time in our lives, it does not do justice to John's Gospel, and the relationships he is trying to describe.

Through belief in Christ, we enter a partnership with God that is characterised by intimate independence. Think of those dancers on TV, sweeping round the dance floor. Sometimes they move together as one person. Sometimes they part for a few moments as each of them moves on their own. Always they are together, but each has something special to do. So it is with us. Because we believe, we can stand tall before God, just as we are, and rise to the challenge of his call as partners in the divine dance.

*"If you know me, you will know my Father also. From now on you do know him and have seen him."*
(John 14:7)

**Illustration**
In Jane Austen's *Pride and Prejudice*, Elizabeth Bennet says, laughingly, that she first realised that she loved Mr Darcy when she saw his wonderful estates at Pemberley. Although Elizabeth is mocking herself in admitting that she is not unaffected by Darcy's wealth, there is more to it than that. At Pemberley, Elizabeth sees Darcy in his own setting, in the place where he really belongs, for the first time. She sees him with people who love him and whom he loves, people who have known him since he was a child and are able to testify to his real character. So Elizabeth's love comes not just from seeing the rich Mr Darcy, but also from seeing the true Mr Darcy.

**Gospel Teaching**
The disciples would probably have said that they knew Jesus very well. They had, after all, spent a considerable amount of time in his company, day and night, travelling, eating, sleeping side by side, talking for hours on end, working together. The disciples must have been pretty confident that they had seen the real Jesus.

Of course, they were probably aware that they didn't always understand everything he said. They knew that he had his enigmatic side. They didn't entirely understand his relationship with God or his vision for their joint mission. But they may have thought that Jesus himself was a bit confused, in need of their friendship and guidance, even. He was undoubtedly their leader, but sometimes he just had his head in the clouds and needed the help of practical men like themselves.

But now, in this time before the crucifixion, the disciples get quieter and quieter, and their questions, when they venture to question at all, get more and more perplexed. There is a kind of grim certainty about Jesus that they do not understand, and he keeps talking about a time when he will no longer be there.

They begin to see that, important as they are to Jesus, and genuine as their friendship is, there has always been another Jesus, there has always been someone who knew Jesus much better than they did, and whom Jesus knew with an intimacy and a lack of misunderstanding that was simply

of a different quality from their relationship with him. And that someone was the God whom Jesus had always called "Father".

But if the disciples were tempted to feel jealous of this relationship, so much deeper and older than their own friendship, Jesus did everything he could to reassure them. His relationship with the Father would help them to know him better. It would bring him closer to his friends, not separate him from them.

All those things about Jesus that the disciples had found hard or incomprehensible were now to become clearer, because of the light cast by the relationship between him and the Father. They had often found it difficult to follow Jesus' instructions because they just didn't understand them or see where they were going. But now, because they could see the Father, the guiding principle behind all of Jesus' actions, they would be able to enter into Jesus' mission.

Far from taking Jesus away, the Father was offering them his own friendship, as well as his lifelong knowledge of Jesus, so much more profound than the knowledge they thought they had of him. And that knowledge is the disciples' way home, and ours, too. As we get to know the real Jesus, we get to know our true home with God.

**Application**

It is so hard to imagine ourselves into the position of Jesus' disciples. We come to Jesus already knowing what is said about him and who he is in relation to God the Father. But the disciples had to make a huge imaginative leap as they realised that the relationship with the Father was the defining relationship for Jesus. Until they saw him there, in his own setting, where he really belonged, they could not love the real Jesus, because they did not know him truly.

Jesus tells his disciples that following him and keeping his commandments will bring us into his relationship with the Father. But this is no mere mechanical obedience that is being asked of us. This is the obedience born of comprehension.

We can only understand Jesus when we see him with his Father. But the minute we see that, with the help of the Holy Spirit, we are part of it. This is not exclusive relationship, but utterly inclusive. The love between Father, Son and Holy Spirit has room for us, too.

*"My Father is glorified by this, that you bear much fruit and become my disciples."*
(John 15:8)

**Illustration**
God wants us to be happy, in spite of what many people who are outside of the Christian community believe about us. "You are a Christian!" they may say. When challenged on what they mean, people often quote the tired old stereotypes of rigid thought, suffering for the sake of it (one view of Jesus), religion as a "crutch" and the fear of a God who looms over us like a fantasy magazine monster. They sometimes find it hard to understand the extent of the love which we experience. In our dislocated Western world, where individuality rules, unity is often regarded as inhibiting, and the duties of relationships may be seen as claustrophobic. Reliance on God is, at best, foolish and, at worst, dangerous.

Yet we are surrounded by people who feel insecure, who turn to external means to satisfy their need to feel relevant, confident and able to compete with others whom they admire. For those with the means, life becomes bigger and better than that which went before, but so too does the emptiness inside them which alienates them from their true selves and which no amount of goods can fill or satisfy. But still they remain suspicious of our unity with God, which seems to give us something which money cannot buy. One of our tools for explaining our delight in God is given to us by Jesus in today's Gospel.

**Gospel Teaching**
Jesus wants us to be happy. In this beautiful Gospel passage Jesus is "owning" us, making us a part of him, allowing us access to that which God gives him. He will love us and value us, respect us and never let us go. In him we shall find our authenticity, our confidence and our relevance to God and to the rest of our world.

A vine is a remarkable plant. As it grows, a vine develops a very thick, winding stem from which the branches emerge. They can grow such that it can be hard to determine which is the original branch and which are the developed branches. When Jesus says, "I am" (God's own name, given to Moses) in relation to the vine we know that he speaks from his divine nature. He, Jesus-as-God, is the vine. The vine, and the wine which comes from it, are symbols of love, his love in the form of his blood poured out for us and given to us as the sacramental wine at Communion. He is the visible source of love in his ministry on earth and he invites us to become a part of that vine, a part of that love.

But it is important for us to remember that even though vine branches at first glance look alike, no two are exactly the same. They may weave and curl in similar ways, they may produce similar fruit after the same pattern, but each is unique. And this is symbolic of Jesus' call to each of us. He calls to us in our uniqueness to become joined with him in a similar purpose, that of spreading the love of God wherever we are. We produce the same fruit from our individual branch; we are integrally united with the original stem. Whether or not we are fruitful vines depends upon us. And there is a cost, of course, just as Jesus' life had a cost.

**Application**

The Holy Spirit wants us to be happy. Holy Wisdom which comes from God's right hand is God's special gift which strengthens and inspires us to hold fast, and to remain faithful and fruitful, both when we are challenged by the world and in our personal hardships – indeed, when we are "pruned".

But the wider our experience, good and bad, the deeper our understanding; sometimes, even, the more we suffer, the greater is our appreciation of life as a precious gift. And so the better we see others through Jesus' eyes and the greater value we place on them. Our little branch becomes an active extension of Jesus. From this grows a greater love for God and each other and the expansion of love throughout our world. The result of this love is joy which Jesus wants to lavish upon us. To let his joy permeate our lives, to be expressed in our daily doings, may in unexpected ways attract others to explore our cause for joy and discover how easy (and inexpensive) it is to acquire.

*"I give you a new commandment, that you love one another."*

(John 13:34)

**Illustration**

It occurred in a small village in France in 1943. The village was occupied, but the local people felt sorry for the enemy soldiers. They were young men, far from home, on short rations, so each day the parish priest would go from door to door with two large baskets begging food for them. Local produce would emerge, a few eggs, some bread and vegetables. Then one day the local resistance movement blew up a strategic bridge. The commander of the occupying forces demanded reprisals and ordered that every man in the village between the ages of sixteen and sixty-five be taken to the village square. There, in front of wives, mothers and girlfriends, they were shot.

The distraught and angry villagers turned on the priest: "If you come again asking for food for these murderers we shall kill you." On the day of the funeral the little church was overflowing, every family had lost someone. The old priest stood up and read from the Gospel of John, the passage we heard today. "I give you a new commandment, that you love one another. Just as I have loved you, you also should love one another. By this everyone will know that you are my disciples." Later that day he stood in the village square, with tears in his eyes, watching the local people filling the baskets he had placed at his feet with food to feed the enemy soldiers.

**Gospel Teaching**

This most simple-sounding commandment is probably the most difficult to carry out. It is easy to give it notional assent. It is fairly easy to recognise the wisdom of it. However, it requires a great deal of courage to put it into practice, and it cost Christ his life.

He died because he continued to remain true to this fundamental precept, to love every human being, regardless of their response to him. He was hated and treated unjustly by his enemies and yet he still loved them. Not in an emotional, sentimental way, but by understanding them and absorbing the fear which made them react against him; by concern for their well-being in spite of their actions; by recognising the basic humanity of each one which makes them precious in God's eyes.

This is the vocation of the Christian. The early Church accepted all who came in spite of their past, their disabilities, their faults. The enthusiasm of the early Church in the Acts of the Apostles speaks of the generosity of those followers who dedicated their lives to spreading this universal message of love and forgiveness.

Jesus did not say it would be easy. He simply stated the necessity for this radical new departure in human behaviour, because it is the only way in which the world can reflect the kingdom of God. Whether or not we personally, or collectively, succeed or fail to change the world, it is in the struggle to love that we draw closest to Jesus and, together with him, we may affect our world more than we think possible.

**Application**

When we think of the forgiveness and generosity of the villagers in the story, perhaps we may feel we could never match such an action. If we had seen a loved one murdered we might think that it is impossible to forgive. However, it is important to remember that this kind of love and forgiveness does not come naturally to most people. It is a gift from God. These villagers managed to make a superhuman effort after attending Mass and hearing the Gospel proclaimed.

Paying close attention to the word of God can have remarkable results. The ability to love without self-regard is a very radical call. But it is made possible by the gift of supernatural grace from God. Our present society would often have us believe that it is easy to love. But that is a different brand of love from Jesus'. To love like him is to surrender the needs and desires of the self to ensure that those of others are met, regardless of whether or not they are deemed "worthy". Knowing all the time that we too are precious to God, in spite of our own failings, is to know that we are a gift worth giving. This is the challenge of today's Gospel, both simple and profound. It is as fresh a call as it was when it came from the lips of Jesus: "Love one another… just as I have loved you." And he walks alongside us as we do his will.

*"If you love me, you will keep my commandments."*
(John 14:15)

**Illustration**

Most of us have seen the type of picture which can be looked at in two ways. One famous example is of the profile of a haggard old woman, with a big hooked nose and lots of wrinkles. Unless you know that there's another way of viewing this picture, all you will see is the ugly old woman. Even when someone tells you that it is possible to see something completely different – a full-length picture of a beautiful young woman – it's not always easy to make it out. However, once you see it, once it falls into place, it's hard to imagine how you could ever have missed it. Indeed, often it can be difficult to make out the original picture of the old woman.

**Gospel Teaching**

The Christians of today's Gospel faced a similar problem with regard to the rest of the world. Everyone knew that Jesus had been crucified and had died – that much could be seen by all. But the first Christians insisted that this was not the full story. There was much more to it than that. Though the world could not see Jesus, his followers believed that he was with them still – that he had not left them orphans – because, as he had promised, he had sent his Spirit to help them, to guide them, to console them, and to remind them of his teachings. Most of all, the Holy Spirit was simply present with them, and had made his home with them. He helped them to believe, and he helped them to work out their belief through their love for others.

We can imagine their sense of frustration that the world around them did not understand their experience, and simply could not see things in the way that they could. They saw the same picture but interpreted it very differently.

In many ways, we face a similar situation to those early Christians. We live in a world that is either hostile or simply indifferent to the Gospel message. Many people, even people of obvious goodwill, fail to see the importance of Christ for humanity, and are ready to dismiss as wishful thinking any claims of having a spiritual life or an experience of God. For many, life is a meaningless span of years, which they try to make as painless as possible until death finally puts an end to it.

**Application**

How are we to respond to this view of life? Jesus' answer to his disciples is still valid today: "If you love me, you will keep my commandments." He summed up the commandments by saying that the most important thing is to love God with our whole hearts and to love our neighbours as ourselves. If you want to know how to live as a Christian you would do well to concentrate your thoughts on those two central commandments. Because following Christ is not about being very religious – anyone can be religious but that doesn't mean they love either God or anyone else. We are called, even commanded, to love – but you cannot love what you don't know. We need to get to know God, and to love him with all our hearts. People who truly do so find that love for others, and a right love for themselves, flow naturally from them.

Loving as Jesus loved means asserting the value of every single individual, working to build up the community, and leading a life of loving service, even if it may cost us dearly. When Christians live as Christ commanded, we offer the world an alternative and more enduring vision of what life can be for those who are willing to accept the Spirit of truth and to allow him into their hearts.

We cannot force people to do this. We cannot make them see the truth. The old proverb says, "You can lead a horse to water but you cannot make him drink" – not until the horse understands what water is and understands and acknowledges that he is thirsty. But if we love in the way Jesus commands, then we demonstrate the reality of the Christ we believe in, and our world will be continually confronted by Christ and his Gospel, and will be able to look again and to decide. Then some will see a different picture of Jesus and will accept his offer of eternal life. And they will understand it not as a list of tenets of religion, but as a living relationship of love.

*"This is my commandment,*
*that you love one another as I have loved you."*
(John 15:12)

**Illustration**

Since 1965 the Royal Air Force's Aerobatic Team – the Red Arrows – have completed over four thousand displays. If you've seen them, you'll know that the breathtaking precision of their manoeuvres is an excellent antidote to thinking the world is full of bungling idiots. They are part of a tradition of highly skilled airmen and women whose proficiency and poise in high-risk situations are a good reminder of what human beings, given the right training and experience, are capable of.

It is more than sixty years since another group carried out an airborne feat of amazing precision and boldness during World War II. The attacks on German dams on 17th May 1943 used a specially developed "bouncing bomb". The dams had been identified as prime targets for the Allied Forces, but the technical problems were thought to make it impossible, until engineer Barnes Wallis invented a drum-shaped bomb capable of spinning and skimming on the surface of water. An accurate drop could bypass the dam's protection, but to pull this off from a height of only 60 feet, while flying at 240 miles per hour, required the bang-on precision and nerves of steel shown by members of Number 617 Squadron – or the Dambusters, as they're better known.

**Gospel Teaching**

Jesus says something which is both astonishing and moving in today's reading from John: "I do not call you servants any longer… but I have called you friends." But something else he says might take us aback: "You are my friends if you do what I command you." Now we don't tend to think of friends as issuing rules, and we don't think of friendship as dependent upon keeping them.

So let's think about the Red Arrows again for a moment. To get to that level of precision and skill takes years of training – and of course training requires obedience. So with such high stakes you can bet that fighter and aerobatic pilots take obedience extremely seriously – because they know their lives depend upon it. Of course we're fine, down here on terra firma. Since we don't have earth spinning towards us at hundreds of miles an hour, we don't have to obey commands in order to save our lives. Or do we? Throughout the Gospels Jesus spells it out with stark warnings and parables – the slave who fails to use his talents, the wicked vineyard tenants, the unproductive fig tree – they all end up cast out of heaven because they disobeyed God's commandments. So in fact our eternal lives also depend upon obedience – the stakes could hardly be higher. And it would be a poor friend who didn't do anything in his power to save our lives – even if that meant laying down the law.

**Application**

One problem we, in our modern, individualistic age, have is that we confuse obedience with spineless submission. But it depends who we're obeying and why. We don't think of the Red Arrows as being spineless in obeying orders during training or manoeuvres. We admire them for their dedication and discipline and understand that, when it's a matter of life and death, obedience is essential.

Another problem is that we tend to think it's dull to be obedient. The answer to this dilemma can be found in today's reading from 1 John. We hear that God's commandments are "not burdensome", and get a tantalising glimpse of obedience leading to faith which, in turn, leads to victory.

A third problem is that we don't think we're very good at obedience, so we give up before we've tried. What's at the root of this crisis of confidence? Perhaps it's because obedience involves a deep faith commitment. Søren Kierkegaard said: "It is so hard to believe because it is so hard to obey." The deeper we go into the Christian life, the more we find that faith and obedience are inextricably intertwined. Because obedience is not a sideline to faith, but a key element of it – it is no less, in fact, than faith in action.

Obedience is not simply saying "yes" to everything, but making a deeper commitment to live in faith and, above all, to obey Jesus' commandment to love one another. It's a skill like any other. In order for it to work for us as individuals we have to make it our own, incorporate it into the very fabric of our lives, and that takes training. But as our eternal lives depend on it, the stakes could hardly be higher.

*"Those who love me will keep my word, and my Father will love them, and we will come to them and make our home with them."*
(John 14:23)

**Illustration**

"What the world needs now, is love, sweet love. It's the only thing that there's just too little of," goes the song. But definitions of love are many and varied. "Actions speak louder than words" and "it's the thought that counts" seem to have diametrically opposed ways of judging love, for example. Does love have to be proved with actions, or are thoughts without any visible outcome enough?

**Gospel Teaching**

On the face of it, Jesus' definition would seem to lean towards the former. He says, "Those who love me will keep my word", and he doesn't seem to mean just preserve it in a glass case to be viewed occasionally but never used. Jesus' followers "kept his word" by active witness to the world, often at the cost of their own lives.

But what today's Gospel passage has to say about love doesn't stop there. The love that Jesus requires from his disciples does involve obedience, just as Jesus' own love for God requires obedience on his part. The whole of these "Farewell Discourses" in John 13–17 is full of the knowledge of what Jesus is about to do, in obedience to his love for God. But it is all too easy only to see the obedience and not to see that it is born out of love. Jesus goes to the cross not out of fearful obedience to a God who demands it of him, but because he loves his Father, and he knows that he is loved by the Father. Jesus' death is a joint decision, a shared action, accepted by Father, Son and Holy Spirit, not imposed by a stern God on a helpless victim.

Now, as Jesus gets ready to leave his disciples, it is this basis in love that he wants them to understand. When the disciples, out of obedience and love, keep Jesus' words, they will find that they are sharing in the love of God, Father, Son and Holy Spirit, who will come and "make our home with them". The disciples will only be able to keep Jesus' words because they know that they are loved by Jesus, just as Jesus is able to carry out his earthly mission because he knows he is the beloved Son of the Father. Jesus calls his disciples friends, not servants, because they act with him, out of shared love and understanding, not just out of blind obedience. And always with them is the Holy Spirit, the Advocate. St Augustine calls the Holy Spirit "the bond of love", the one who makes love real, strong, a force that can hold people together, even in hardship, adversity and death. Jesus does not promise that this will make everything easy for his disciples. Quite the contrary. He is perfectly frank in telling them that they may well be called to share his own fate. Is there, perhaps, a touch of irony as he tells them that the peace he is giving them won't bear much resemblance to the kind of peace that the world offers? If you want a religion of prosperity and harmony, one that will lead you to a quiet and revered old age, one that will allow you to view the world with quiet detachment and enjoyment, don't choose this one, Jesus seems to say. The peace Jesus offers is the peace of loving companionship every step of the way, and the peace of knowing that they are doing the will of the Father, as Jesus did.

**Application**

Although we are often called to walk in obedience, without fully understanding why God asks us to do what we have to do, still we must never forget that we are friends, not slaves. We are called to witness to the love of God in Christ Jesus, and we do this not only with words but also with our lives, and particularly with our lives together, in our friendship, shared and offered. We live as people with whom God has come and made his home, and now we have a home to offer to the lonely and homeless world. We don't have a manual for mission, or a set of forms to complete, but a life to live in God's world. And everywhere we go, we take our own strange peace, which the world won't always understand, unless it longs for friendship with God, and catches a glimpse, in us, of what it is like to be at home.

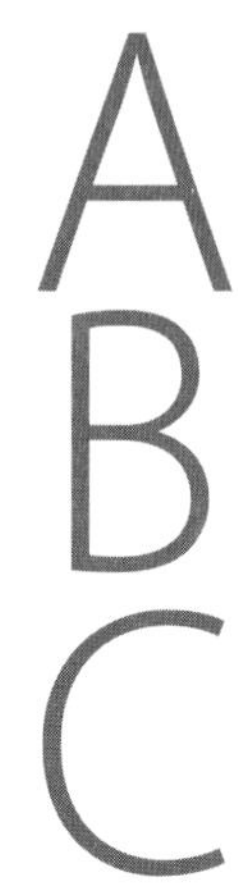



*"See, I am sending upon you what my Father promised."*
(Luke 24:49)

**Illustration**
It was a terrible crime, and the newspapers were full of it. The trial was headline news for weeks. "Evil monster!" shrieked the headlines, "inhuman". Crowds gathered outside the court, shouting abuse as the defendant arrived and left each day. The conviction was greeted by a chorus of approval, and calls for the restoration of the death penalty. The perpetrator was a monster, inhuman, not deserving to live, not one of us. When she committed suicide in prison, there was general rejoicing.

**Gospel Teaching**
What does it mean to be human? We are quick to define humanity to exclude people whose lives and crimes threaten us. We label some as "inhuman" so that we don't have to think of them as like us, or face the idea that in other circumstances we could be like them. We create a definition of being human that reflects the way we like to think of ourselves and excludes people whose actions make us face our potential for evil.

Some of our most serious ethical debates tackle the question of the nature of humanity. Is human life so important that it must never be taken in war, whatever the circumstances? Are we entitled to create it in a laboratory, to clone a human being? We can value human life so highly that we treat the needs of human beings as paramount, ignoring the good of other forms of life; or we can value it so cheaply that we can blow up innocent people in a cherished cause. We can take to ourselves so much power over the world's destiny that we want to engineer a future for the planet, or we can run away from our responsibility to care for the world. Working out what it means to be human in our world is a complicated business. But as Christians we have help in an unexpected place.

Today is the feast of the Ascension, a day when we celebrate humanity. The story of the ascension relates what happened to Jesus after the resurrection. Jesus rose from the dead as a fully human person, recognisable as the same Jesus as he was before his death. Yet clearly he did not stay around in Palestine for ever. There came a time when God's presence with the disciples was experienced differently, in the form of what they came to call "the Holy Spirit", and Jesus was no longer seen walking on the earth. Luke uses the ascension to explain this change in story form.

That's the story. But the doctrine of the ascension is very important for our understanding of what it means to be human. The picture language about Jesus disappearing up into the clouds tells us that Jesus, the man, returned to God. Humanity has become part of God for ever. After the resurrection and ascension, Jesus did not stop being human. All that he was, all that we are, was taken into the nature of God. It is miraculous enough that the Bible tells us that we are made in the image of God our Creator. The ascension shows us that we are closer to God even than that, taken into his very being. Human beings were always God's creation, God's children, but the ascension casts us in a different light; now we are truly in God. That means that we share God's responsibility for the world; but also that all our struggles, all our weaknesses, are acknowledged and affirmed.

**Application**

So we are encouraged to value humanity rightly. We are not perfect. We are capable of the utmost cruelty and violence. But at the same time, we are infinitely valuable, because God is in us and we are in God. We are worth redeeming, worth sending the Spirit to, worth taking up into the Godhead.

Valuing humanity rightly has huge ramifications. If humanity is part of God, we are not entitled to deny humanity to any of God's children, no matter what crimes they have committed. And we must take the hard ethical questions extremely seriously, because they concern the humanity that God has taken to himself.

We can be realistic about human nature, but we can be optimistic about it too. Our future is bound up with God's future, and the possibilities are endless. In fact, one might use Luke's picture language and say, for humanity, the sky's the limit.

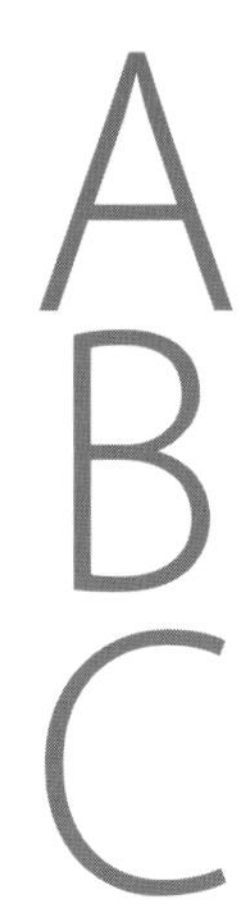



*"While he was blessing them, he withdrew from them and was carried up into heaven."*
(Luke 24:51)

**Illustration**

There is an ancient mosque built over a rock on the Mount of Olives, outside the old city of Jerusalem. It is not used for services and is completely empty except for a glass case over a place where the bare rock forms part of the floor. In the rock is an indentation of indeterminate shape, said to be the footprint left by Christ as he ascended to heaven.

Jerusalem is a holy city for the three great religions of Judaism, Christianity and Islam. The footprint in the rock is a place of pilgrimage for both Christians and Muslims, who may light a candle and worship silently at the site where Jesus was last seen on earth. For Muslims, the site gives a memory of Jesus, a great prophet, but for Christians this small, unassuming place bears witness to the continuing life of the risen Christ, God incarnate.

**Gospel Teaching**

What are we to make of the story of the ascension as told in the New Testament? Did it happen as Luke says? Is it true? Or should we regard it as a legend?

Interestingly, only Luke the storyteller gives any details about the ascension. Unlike Matthew and Mark, Luke, the writer who brings us the delightful details of the Christmas story and the excitement of the coming of the Holy Spirit at Pentecost, elaborates on the story of the ascension and adds plenty of flesh to the bare bones.

Like Mark, Luke too ends his Gospel with the briefest of statements, "While he was blessing them, he withdrew from them and was carried up into heaven." But Luke begins his second book, the Acts of the Apostles, with a much more colourful account of what might have happened. In a style reminiscent of the story of the ascension of Elijah in the Old Testament (2 Kings 2:11), Luke pictures a cloud which gathers up Jesus and removes him from the disciples' sight. The bemused disciples then see two angels in white robes, who ask enigmatically, "Men of Galilee, why do you stand looking up towards heaven? This Jesus, who has been taken up from you into heaven, will come in the same way as you saw him go into heaven." Clearly whatever happened had a profound effect upon the disciples, for they all returned to Jerusalem to the upper room and together with "the women and Mary the mother of Jesus and with his brothers" (Acts 1:14) devoted themselves to prayer.

Perhaps the disciples learned more during their weeks with the risen Jesus than they did during the years of his earthly ministry, for when Jesus disappeared for good they were no longer the shrivelled, terrified human beings that they had been after his execution. Even before the day of Pentecost and the coming of the Holy Spirit, Peter, the disciple who had denied that he ever knew Jesus, was boldly and openly preaching the Gospel (Acts 1:15-20).

**Application**

Luke may have used his imagination to fill in the gaps left by Jesus' final disappearance from earth, and to appeal to the mindset of first-century people who lived in a world of magic and myths and legends. Or the ascension may have happened exactly as described. The factual details are perhaps less important than the truths conveyed by the account, for a vivid story enables us to remember truths easily.

When Jesus died, the disciples were distraught. But after he ascended, they were full of confidence and deep spirituality. What made the difference? On both occasions Jesus had gone, apparently to be seen on earth no more. After the ascension he would definitely be seen no more, so we might perhaps have expected the disciples to be even more distraught than they were after his death. But, somehow, meeting with the risen Christ transformed their lives. Terror and anguish were replaced by prayerfulness, enthusiasm and confidence, as they realised that a new dimension of life continues after death.

Nothing changes, for meeting with the risen Christ today still transforms lives. Those who meet with the risen Christ no longer fear death. And deep prayerfulness enables God the Holy Spirit to nurture us to our full potential; and so we can blossom in confidence and enthusiasm. God loves each of us individually. Those who meet with the risen Christ know that for themselves.

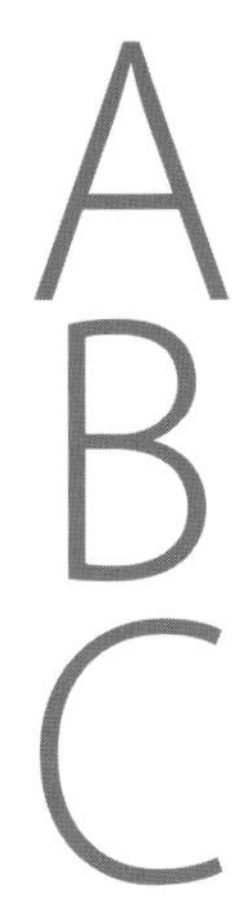

*"And see, I am sending upon you what my Father promised; so stay here in the city until you have been clothed with power from on high."*
(Luke 24:49)

Ascension Day

**Illustration**
The biblical versions of the ascension of Jesus leave him disappearing from the sight of his disciples. But what happened next? One imaginative account runs as follows:

As Jesus arrives at the gates of heaven, the angels are waiting to welcome him. Gabriel steps forward and says: "Lord, we've so admired everything you did down there. You revealed the kingdom of God; you healed the sick; you showed compassion to everyone in need; you suffered so much... But we were wondering: who's going to keep your wonderful work going?" Jesus replies: "I've given that job to my eleven followers, and to whoever joins them." Shuffling and coughing among the angels. Finally Gabriel speaks again, looking very troubled: "But Lord, do you really mean Peter, who's useless under pressure; and James and John, who're so obsessed with status; and Thomas, who's so sceptical; and Philip, who's so slow? None are reliable, well educated or well connected..." "Yes," replies Jesus, "I've given them the job." "Lord, is this wise? They're bound to make a mess of it. At least consider a back-up plan!" "No," says Jesus firmly. "No other plans."

You won't find that story in any of the Gospels, but it reminds us as we celebrate the ascension of our Lord that we are now trusted to be his body here on earth.

**Gospel Teaching**
Just as he has already done on the Emmaus road (Luke 24:27), the risen Jesus opens the scriptures to his disciples. He shows them that all that had happened to him, culminating in his death and resurrection, was no accident but rather fulfilled the deep purposes of God as these had been expressed throughout the scriptures. Going further, Jesus also teaches the disciples that the scriptures look ahead to all the nations of the world hearing of the love of God revealed through his Messiah. (No details are given, but it is natural to think of passages such as Isaiah 42:6 and 49:6.)

For the good news about Jesus to be taken out from the immediate context of Jerusalem and Judaea across frontiers of various kinds to "Samaria, and to the ends of the earth" (Acts 1:8) two things will be necessary: divine empowerment and faithful human witness. Jesus promises that God will provide the power necessary for this task in the gift of the Holy Spirit (Acts 1:4-5, 8), and because the Spirit is sheer gift the disciples can do nothing to trigger or prompt it beyond passively staying put and waiting. But this gift will not override their humanity, which will be very much at work in the acts of courageous witness described in Luke's second volume.

The minds of the disciples have been opened to grasp what God has already done through Jesus and to see that God has further work for them to do when the Spirit comes upon them. So rather than being devastated by Jesus' departure from this world, they can experience this event in a spirit of joyful trust, even worshipping him as Lord.

**Application**

The biblical writers say little that will satisfy human curiosity about what happened to Jesus' physical body when he ascended into heaven; rather they tell us that the one who was crucified is now joined to God, sharing in his authority, sitting at his right hand. And their thinking seems always to move directly from there to the implications for us, the Church. Thus in Ephesians the vision of Christ in all his ascended glory moves on naturally to the description of the Church "which is his body, the fullness of him who fills all in all" (1:23).

So where does the ascension leave us? St Teresa, addressing the ascended Lord, puts it perfectly: "You have now no body on earth but ours; no hands but ours; no feet but ours. Ours are the eyes showing your compassion to the world; ours are the feet with which you go about doing good; ours are the hands with which you are now to bless the world."

Ascension Day reveals the full extent of God's reckless plan to give his love bodily form in this world. He did this perfectly and at great cost in Jesus; but even more recklessly – and certainly less perfectly – he does so in those who try to follow Jesus. If we say "yes" to our part in God's plan we will discover that the ascended Jesus, now no longer physically visible in this world, is at work in and through us, because we are his body.

7th Sunday of Easter

*"Holy Father, protect them in your name that you have given me, so that they may be one, as we are one."*
(John 17:11)

**Illustration**
The way that people say goodbye is very personal, particularly the big goodbyes, the ones that happen when a child goes to school for the first time, or away to university. Or when a dear colleague that we find we've got so used to leaves for another job, or a good friend emigrates, or a loved one prepares to die. In short, when the people we love move on.

Some people are very expressive: it's all tears, hugs and stories. Others are deadpan, keeping it all in. Many people make sure that they say their goodbyes beforehand, when they've got time, and emotions are not quite so high. Important things can't always be said and done on the doorstep.

**Gospel Teaching**
In our Gospel reading from John, we are witnesses to just such a goodbye. In fact all of chapters 13 to the end of 17 are a goodbye – they could be called "the long goodbye", a good name for a film perhaps. Sandwiched between the raising of Lazarus – an echo of what's to come – and Jesus' betrayal and arrest in the garden of Gethsemane, these chapters are charged with the emotion of a painful but necessary farewell.

Jesus talks about what he has done, and what it all means – not always, it has to be said, with great clarity. Jesus knows that they will not have time to say goodbye later, so now he talks of how the disciples are to behave, of how they will be bound together into a community of love, and that this will give them their distinctive and attractive nature as the people of God. He tells them that things will not be easy without him, but that they will be empowered by the Holy Spirit when he leaves.

And in chapter 17, Jesus rounds it all off with a prayer. And what a prayer it is! The first part of the prayer cements Jesus' credentials. It's not just a matter of being received by God in heaven. Jesus is returning home to the glory he had with God in the beginning (remember those famous opening words to John's Gospel: "In the beginning was the Word, and the Word

was with God…"). Jesus has told them before that he and the Father are one; now he again claims God's glory as his own.

Then he prays for his followers: those who have believed that he is the Son of God, and who very soon will find themselves the keepers and tellers of the message. Jesus' oneness with God is extended to the believers. Somehow, this little band of rather unpromising humanity has become bound up with God in Christ. From that point on there is an unshakeable bond between God and humankind – something wholly different about the way that human beings relate to God.

And then it all gets much simpler: a prayer for protection. Jesus must know that the hatred that he is about to experience will soon be extended to them. They haven't always been shining examples of steady faith; how will they cope without him?

Things move on, of course, and when the time comes really to say goodbye, everything is too chaotic, too dangerous, too tortured, to say any of these things. So, over supper, Jesus says his farewells. Perhaps the disciples understand, perhaps they don't, but at least they have had the chance to hear Jesus' goodbye, and store it up as treasure for the future.

**Application**

And here we are, all these years on. Somehow, the emotion and urgency of the moment in the upper room are gone, and it's hard to imagine just what it felt like. We can but try to put ourselves in the sandals of the ones who were there; try and look into Jesus' eyes and hear his words afresh.

But that prayer still stands; still echoes across the centuries. A Palestinian peasant claims to be one with God, and something in the fabric of the universe shifts. Humankind and God are bound together when they were once set apart, and an unshakeable bond is formed that cannot be broken by human frailty and petty mistakes. Things are possible that were never possible before. Things will change that we never thought would change.

And how will it happen; how will we choose to be part of it? That's up to us, but we must always remember: whatever we do, Jesus' words of protection will ring in our ears.

*"I am not asking you to take them out of the world, but I ask you to protect them from the evil one."*
(John 17:15)

**Illustration**
There is an old Indian story which tells the tale of a woman who was so concerned that her children would be influenced for evil by the outside world that she built a huge wall around her home. Her infant children were used to their restricted world but as they grew older they became curious about life beyond the boundaries of their garden. One day, while their mother's attention was distracted, two of the children climbed over the wall. As they landed on the other side they were met by an ocean of faces of local people who laughed at their nervous expressions. The villagers had also been curious to know what existed on the other side of the great wall. The two children became very frightened and frantically searched for a way back to their home. They could not cope with the world outside the wall.

There is a very human temptation to build walls around ourselves for protection; to build boundaries around our families or communities in an effort both to guard those within and to keep others out. The worst kinds of boundaries are those around our minds: those which cling to the outmoded concepts, which limit the expansion of thought and the creative imagination which God gave us in order to do his work more effectively. Like those children escaping from their comfortably safe garden, a sudden burst of new ideas can disorientate and frighten us. But if we grow up absorbing the knowledge of Christ's confidence in us and our sanctity for which he prayed, we will have learned how to handle development and change, which is all the protection we need. We shall not need walls.

**Gospel Teaching**
Jesus did not ask his disciples to build a big wall around themselves. He was well aware of the dangers and evils of the world. He had been subjected to enough of them during his own life and ministry.

One of his concerns for them was that they should be protected from the "evil one". He does not want his followers to be removed from the world, but protected within it. The evil one takes many forms in a world like ours, perhaps even more in number and subtlety than in first-century Palestine.

In this great discourse of Jesus at the Last Supper he prays with all his might, not just for those around this Passover table, but for the whole Church, then and to come. He wants his followers to remain faithful to his teaching, as he knows that this is the way in which God's world can be renewed and made more perfect. Not an easy task in a world where many reject his message.

His disciples who accept and hand on his teaching will also receive harsh treatment. Christianity is not a cosy club. But Jesus has confidence in them and us and in our ability to keep his message alive, despite the hardships and dangers. Jesus believes in us and we can feel supported by his prayers for our protection and encouragement.

**Application**

For many of us self-doubt and lack of confidence in ourselves as Christians keep us from realising the degree of faith which God has in us. Each Christian has been given the skills and faith necessary to carry on the truths and traditions through their lives, among those with whom they come into contact. But there are dangers and we do need protection not only from our own weaknesses but against the "dark forces": those aspects of life which are not of God, which can divert or tempt us away from God's grace.

Jesus had no doubt of the quality of those he called to follow him, then and now. We are gifted just as they were. Of course we have our doubts, we struggle with questions of faith. But this is part of our gift to God, that we persist in spite of difficulty. Walls which restrict our movement or thought cannot protect us, but God can and he hears the prayers of his Son on our behalf. If Jesus has confidence in us, as individuals and as part of the Church, then we should have confidence in ourselves and each other. We are a force for tremendous good in the world. In our families and communities, in great acts of generosity and in simple acts of kindness we make the presence of God manifest. Under the protection of Christ we become confident disciples, sanctified and consecrated in the truth and ready to spread his word by our living out the example of his love.

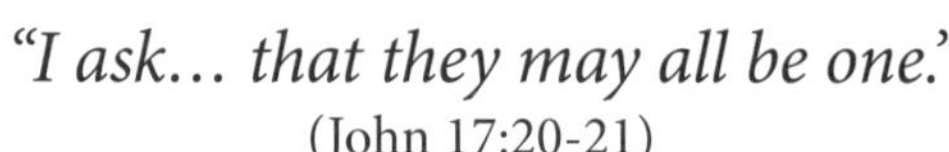

*"I ask… that they may all be one."*
(John 17:20-21)

**Illustration**

Two years ago James began attending his parish church. The welcome he received, the spirit of worship and fellowship encouraged him. He got increasingly involved in church activities and soon became a churchwarden.

Then things began to go wrong. The congregation divided over new forms of worship; financial problems became critical and friction crept in about how much people should give; there were discussions about inclusiveness (or lack of it) in the church; James became ill with depression brought on by stress in his workplace and difficulties in his marriage.

He resigned as churchwarden, a role which was becoming increasingly difficult as more differences split the congregation. He confided in a church member about his depression and the tensions in his marriage only to find his confidences broken and his problems becoming general knowledge. He was shocked when a number of people told him that, as a Christian, he should not be depressed and that a lack of faith was preventing his recovery and was also behind his marital difficulties.

James was deeply hurt. He felt let down by people he trusted, rejected by those who loved him and excluded by a once-welcoming community. He began to doubt the existence of the God of love in whom he had put his faith.

How different his experience could have been if his church had been able to live out the love and unity for which Jesus prayed.

**Gospel Teaching**

The theme of the prayer of Jesus is the indivisible unity between Father and Son. This unity is characterised by love, and Jesus prays that the glory of this loving unity will draw into itself his disciples, and those who become believers because of their witness, so that they will be one with Father and Son.

We, of course, are included in this prayer since we have come to believe because of the witness of his first disciples. It is worth listening to the words of Jesus, holding in our hearts the knowledge that we are hearing Jesus pray for each one of us and for the Church to which we belong. If we pay close attention we may suddenly feel very uncomfortable about the way we talk about each other sometimes, or the way in which we react when controversial issues arise or we find people behaving in ways that for us are difficult or unacceptable. We may ask the question of ourselves, "What are we doing to enable this prayer of Jesus to become the reality of our life together?"

We hear this prayer today in the light of Christ's "mighty resurrection and glorious ascension" and anticipating the gift of the Holy Spirit. We celebrate the victory of love over hate and life over death. But we should also hear this prayer on Maundy Thursday when betrayal, injustice, cruelty and the unspeakable agony of the cross lie ahead. If we are called to be one in the glory of the loving unity of God then we are also called to be one in the darkness and pain of this world experienced by the Son who was sent by the Father.

**Application**

There will always be differences in the Church – between denominations and within congregations. We are, after all, only human. Our calling, though, is to deal with these differences in ways which seek understanding, tolerance, acceptance and a love for one another that transcends our divisions.

Jesus prays that we will grow into unity with him and the Father for our own sakes, that we will be at one with the God who is the source of our being.

He also prays for this unity because it is through our manifestation of God's love and unity that others will come to believe in Jesus and in the Father who sent him. When we are divided and hostile in our divisions; when we offer love and support only towards those who comply with our belief system and only when things are going well; when we exclude those of whom we disapprove because of their gender or sexual orientation, then we cannot be surprised when the world rejects us and the God we claim to believe in.

When we can find healing for our divisions; when we can love all people as brothers and sisters; and when, like Jesus, we can welcome all who turn to us, then, and only then, might people come to know a God of love who wants to draw them into the glorious, loving unity of his being.

*"Receive the Holy Spirit."*
(John 20:22)

**Illustration**

For years ecologists have lobbied governments to invest in renewable energy sources, conscious of the finite nature of earth's resources of fuel. Experiments have take place harnessing the energy of the tides, using it to power generators, producing electricity for heat and light. The sun is already the principal source of energy for our planet, and scientists are constantly devising new ways of using its energy in the factory, street and home. Wind farms utilise each gust of wind to turn giant rotor arms, echoing the action of windmills, widely used by previous generations for a variety of tasks. Energy is all around us, energy sustains us, energy changes us – energy is life.

In years gone by people would hold a mirror to the mouth of a dying person. If there was breath, it would form a mist on the mirror and would show that the person was still alive. The "kiss of life" would be more appropriately designated the "breath of life".

The shortage of earth's resources has made us more conscious of what saves and sustains life, and the best example of energy indicating life is in the breath of each living person.

**Gospel Teaching**

The risen Jesus breathed on the disciples, a sign that he was sharing his life, his energy, with them. As he breathed on them he said: "Receive the Holy Spirit." The very energy and life of God was being given to them; but no one can receive the Spirit of God and remain unchanged. The disciples discovered they were able to speak in foreign tongues. They found a courage they had never known before in preaching the Good News, and they lived in a unity that only weeks before would have seemed like a dream. With the energy of God flowing through them, they showed new life and growth. This new life of the Spirit had come to them when they were at their lowest ebb, shut away in a room, paralysed by fear, confused and disillusioned.

The breath of Christ, the Holy Spirit of God, was indeed new life, energy and growth, and its gift did not simply confer new life on the disciples, but the life of Christ. In a new way Christ came close to his disciples, calling them together in communion, sending them far and wide on his mission. With his Spirit living in them the disciples became, in a new way, his people, his messengers, his body. Wherever they were, he would be, too, and this gift of the Spirit is with his disciples in every age.

**Application**

It is an enriching exercise to become aware of the energy and life in the people and the world around us. Everything we encounter is imbued with life, a life so wonderful and mysterious and complex that it defies scientific definition. The movement of the earth around the sun, the spinning of our planet, which brings us night and day, the breath of the wind across the face of the earth, the warmth of fire, the radiance of light, growing plants and flowing streams: all are signs of an energy which gives and sustains life.

Awareness of this energy and life creates awareness of the Holy Spirit of God, who moves around freely, giving life and growth to the world and the potential for peace, forgiveness and love among its people. Becoming aware of the Spirit, we become attuned to it, sensing its presence and opening ourselves to its power, to live in accordance with its force for good. We start to live in that same energy which caused the heavens and earth to be made. We, like the disciples, become energised for the work of God and dynamic messengers of the Good News.

The Christian messenger does not simply bring Christ to others, but identifies the presence of God already in existence. We demonstrate that where there is goodness, it is Christ's goodness; where there is healing and forgiveness, it is Christ's healing and forgiveness. We show people where Christ is already active in their lives and in this way, in concert with the Holy Spirit, we build up the body of Christ.

What tremendous energy was released on that first Pentecost! What tremendous energy is still released into the Church by the Holy Spirit so that we, today's disciples, may work in communion with each other, renewing the face of the earth.

*"When the Spirit of truth comes, he will guide you into all the truth."*
(John 16:13)

**Illustration**
They say that football is almost a religion these days. It certainly has its dedicated followers, vast numbers of them. And there is an almost cathedral-like atmosphere in a huge stadium on the day of a big match. The impression becomes clearer still when the crowd sings "Abide with me". Supporters identify strongly with "their" team, willing them on to glory with a fervour that puts some church congregations to shame.

On the pitch, the eleven players work as a team, putting into practice all the moves their coach has taught them. They have learned the rules of the game and, on the whole, they follow them; if only because they know the game will descend into chaos otherwise! And one person has the responsibility of ensuring that the rules are indeed followed, interpreted correctly in any given situation on the pitch, so that gifted players can produce a game worthy of them. That person is the referee.

**Gospel Teaching**
In today's Gospel reading, Jesus is preparing his team, his first eleven and the rest of the squad, for the game of their lives. The scene is the Last Supper, after Jesus has washed his disciples' feet. Judas has already set off to betray him, so Jesus is left with eleven of "the Twelve", and with those others whom John calls "the disciples", the wider group of Jesus' followers, men and women.

Although Jesus has trained his squad, coached them for the important fixture that lies ahead, although he has encouraged their talents and their dedication, he will not be with them on the pitch. His job is almost done. But he promises to send them a referee. He promises to send someone who will help them interpret what he has been teaching them, in any situation in which they might find themselves. Jesus is returning to the Father, but he will send the Spirit of truth to guide his followers.

At Pentecost, the Spirit descended upon all the disciples, just as Jesus had promised. In the vivid scene from Acts, Peter uses Joel's prophecy to make sense of what he has seen: men and women, suddenly inspired to communicate with people of all nations, to tell the world about God's mighty intervention in the destiny of human beings, through Jesus Christ. "Your sons and daughters shall prophesy," God had promised through Joel. Prophecy is not the foretelling of the future, but the interpretation of God's word in the present, for the present.

Referees are not always popular. Players do not always agree with their decisions. And in the world today, people still resist the Spirit. For the Spirit is not always a comfortable companion. He comes to jolt us out of our complacency, to challenge the world, to search our hearts. Most of all, he comes to point us once more to Jesus, to glorify him and remind us of his teaching.

**Application**

The Spirit is still moving in the Church today as the Gospel is interpreted for a third millennium. We are faced with many new situations, undreamed of in first-century Palestine: economic, social and ethical. There are dilemmas today for which no easy answers can be found in our study of scripture. We all know of arguments in which the Bible is cited by both sides, with equal conviction. We need continually to ask for the guidance of the Holy Spirit in our worship, in church meetings and in our daily lives. We need to cast aside our prejudices and presuppositions and listen to the Spirit of truth, who reminds us of the teachings of Jesus and encourages us to apply them.

Like the referee interpreting the rules of the game in specific situations, the Spirit will show us how those commandments of Jesus can be applied: love God with all your heart, and love your neighbour as yourself. A good referee allows a game to flow, stepping in only when there is conflict, and reminding players of the rules. In that way, he encourages them to use to the full the skills their coach has taught them, which in turn brings credit to the coach. If we listen to the Spirit, we can bring credit to our Teacher. We can testify on Jesus' behalf, and play the game he would want us to play.

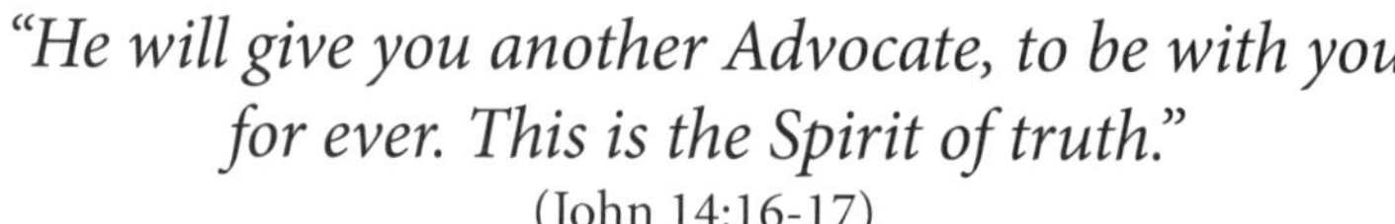

*"He will give you another Advocate, to be with you for ever. This is the Spirit of truth."*
(John 14:16-17)


**Illustration**

Some years ago, a party of British tourists was on a trip to the Holy Land. On the day they visited Bethlehem they found it strangely quiet. All the shops were shut, even the ones selling olive-wood cribs. Clearly trouble was expected. Before long, the tourists found themselves in the middle of what was clearly a demonstration of some kind. A large group of women was marching through the streets, waving placards and shouting. The tourists were curious – and a bit scared. But the placards and the shouts were in Arabic. Then one woman detached herself from the march, and came over to the tourists. In her hand was a photograph. Ignoring the men in the group, she addressed the women. She spoke no English, and they spoke no Arabic, yet they understood her. The women were the mothers, sisters, wives and daughters of men imprisoned by the occupying Israelis, demanding to know the whereabouts of their menfolk. Communication had happened across the barriers of language, race, culture and religion; communication that was mother to mother, sister to sister, human spirit to human spirit.

**Gospel Teaching**

The Bible readings at Pentecost focus on matters of communication. The Old Testament reading is the story of the Tower of Babel. The people of earth decide not to obey the intention of the creator that they should scatter far and wide and populate the earth. Rather, they will make a name for themselves by gathering together to build a tall tower, which in its size and magnificence will rival the work of the creator himself. But their attempts are thwarted. After a while, they find they can no longer communicate with one another. Cooperation becomes impossible, and the building project is left unfinished. This ancient story explains the variety of languages in the world, but it does much more; it tells us about the fundamental human need for communication, if collaboration between us is to be possible.

Acts' story of Pentecost tells of a temporary reversal of these communication difficulties. The first noticeable effect of the coming of the Holy Spirit is that Peter and the other apostles are able to communicate their Gospel message across the language barriers. Spirit speaks to spirit, God's people understand one another, because the Spirit is in them.

Talking about the presence of God is very difficult, because our words are always inadequate. Believers down the ages and across the religions have struggled to describe their experience of God. The Old Testament writers understood the difficulty. When they write of God's right arm winning the victory, or of his breath bringing the dead to life, or of his glory settling on Jerusalem, or of his name dwelling in the Temple, they are trying to find words to express the inexpressible – the sense of the intimate presence of God among them. Those who are aware of God have a sense of God out there, beyond them – and yet also a sense of God very near, so near as to be almost a part of them. Christians use the language of God as Father, Son and Holy Spirit to express this, while still recognising that anything we say about God is always going to be inadequate to express the truth of his being and his presence in the world.

Today's Gospel reading represents a stage along the way of the Church's development of the doctrine of the Trinity. But its basic message is clear enough. Jesus' departure from the world does not mean that God is no longer present with his followers. He will send "another Advocate", "the Spirit of truth", who will be with them and in them. They will experience the intimate presence of God still, no longer external to them but in their very beings. They will be held together as a community of believers, despite the opposition that will inevitably come, by the Spirit they share.



**Application**

The Church tends to be no better at communication than the rest of humanity. We are quicker to judge than to listen, quicker to condemn than to understand. The challenge of Pentecost is the recognition that God's Spirit lives in all of us. If we want to find God, we must look not only outwards, to the world he created, but inwards, into our own hearts. And we must also look into the eyes of our fellow believers, and see God there. We belong together because of the Spirit we share. If we allow spirit to speak to spirit, real communication can happen and, beyond all the Church's factions, understanding may flourish.

*"Go therefore and make disciples of all nations, baptising them in the name of the Father and of the Son and of the Holy Spirit."*
(Matthew 28:19)

Trinity Sunday

**Illustration**
Let me begin this address with a very short scriptural text: "Don't say 'Three'!" You may wonder where that comes from. Well, it's not actually from the Bible but from the Qur'an, the scripture of Islam. The Qur'an warns Christians: "Don't say 'Three'!" It's a sharp rejection of the doctrine of God as Trinity, Three-in-One.

On this Trinity Sunday it's salutary to recall that many millions of believers in God see the doctrine of the Trinity as a serious mistake. Muslims passionately defend the oneness of God. They also believe in Jesus, but as a human prophet, not as the Son of God. They believe that Jesus and his original followers simply believed in one God, but that later Christians drifted away from this pure monotheism into errors about the Son of God and the Holy Spirit and so into the seemingly contradictory idea that God is both three and one. Other religious groups (Jehovah's Witnesses, for example) also reject Trinitarian Christian faith in favour of a unitarian faith in God just as one. But for 1,400 years the challenge from Islam has posed some of the most searching questions Christians have had to face.

One response to this challenge might be to regard the doctrine of the Trinity as a problem, an obstacle in the way of good interfaith relations. ("Okay, we'll stop saying 'Three', or at least won't make so big a deal of it…") Some Christians have been drawn in that direction; but recently there has been a recovery of confident belief in the Trinity and Christians have been realising afresh that this doctrine is neither an optional add-on to our faith nor a problem to be embarrassed about. It's simply the best way of understanding what the New Testament says about Jesus and about the Christian experience of God.

**Gospel Teaching**
In today's Gospel the risen Jesus commissions the eleven to make disciples of all nations, "baptising them in the name of the Father and of the Son of the Holy Spirit". This is a pivotal moment in the Christian story: Jesus

is saying that his own relationship with God is now to be opened up to all people; they are to be baptised (or "immersed") into the life of God the Trinity.

Let's think further about Jesus' relationship with God. Throughout the story of Jesus we see his constant sense of himself as the Son, loved by the God he calls Father. And Jesus doesn't speak only of the Father; Jesus knows the love and guidance of the Father through a distinct personal presence whom he calls the Holy Spirit. Think of Jesus' baptism in the River Jordan. As the Holy Spirit comes upon Jesus he hears the Father saying, "You are my beloved Son", and is commissioned for the work which lies ahead of him. The love of the Father is poured out through the Spirit on the Son and returned in the loving obedience of the Son to the Father, again through the Spirit. This is God the Trinity, the Three-in-One, the God who is loving relationship in God's very self. And this has always been so; from eternity God has been Trinity. But in the life of Jesus, God made flesh, we see something of the Trinitarian life of God active in our world.



**Application**

Very nice for Jesus, we might think. Very nice for the Father, and for the Spirit too, but so what for us? Well, so a lot for us, actually. The point for us is that Jesus' relationship with God is opened up to us. We are invited to join in the relationship of love that flows within the life of God, that has been there from eternity and was seen in our world in Jesus. Jesus takes us by the hand and says, "Come with me and be led by the Spirit into the presence of the God I know as Father." We are to share in the life of the God who is love.

When we were baptised in the name of the Father, the Son and the Spirit, we were immersed in the life of the God who is love. And, as we see in Jesus, that life isn't static, but active, outgoing, self-giving. From his baptism onwards, Jesus' relationship with God was bound up with a mission, the life-giving, renewing, liberating mission of God in this world.

So also for us. On this Trinity Sunday may we and the whole Church of Christ be renewed in our faith in the God who is eternally love; and may we respond with joy and obedience to the call both to share in God's life and to participate in God's mission in the world.

*"Nicodemus said to Jesus, 'How can these things be?'"*
(John 3:9)

**Illustration**
Alice was moving into her very first home, and working to a tight budget. Some things she acquired second-hand, but she had spotted a new wardrobe that was absolutely right for the bedroom. The catalogue picture was beautiful – hanging space, drawers, top cupboard – so she dug into her savings and ordered it.

When the delivery van pulled up, Alice rushed to the door. "One wardrobe to sign for," said the man, but Alice's face fell. All she saw being unloaded was a long, thin, flat box. "That's my wardrobe?" she queried. "Aye, love – flat-packed. Nice and easy to put together, don't you fret." And with that he was gone.

Alice opened the box and slid out several flat pieces of wood. "How on earth can that be my lovely wardrobe?" she muttered. "I don't believe it."

**Gospel Teaching**
The picture Alice had seen was of a wardrobe in all its three-dimensional splendour. No wonder she found it difficult to understand how the pile of flat pieces in front of her could ever be much use to her. It would take a lot of imagination, a giant leap of faith, to visualise it. And it probably didn't help that the instructions seemed to be written in Japanese!

On Trinity Sunday especially, we try to make sense of how different aspects of God fit together, into an image we can use. We find it difficult to comprehend. When Jesus tried to explain the relationship between himself and God and those who were born of the Spirit, Nicodemus echoed something many of us feel about the Trinity: "How can these things be?"

Does reading the Bible's instructions help us fit the pieces together? Jesus asked Nicodemus: "Are you a teacher of Israel, and yet you do not understand these things?" He seems to imply that someone who had studied the history of God's dealings with his people, someone who worshipped God faithfully and carried out his commandments, should be able to understand. Yet it certainly isn't easy.

From his knowledge of the scriptures, Nicodemus would know about the Spirit of God having been active in creation. But here was Jesus saying that ordinary people could be born of the Spirit in a new way. Nicodemus saw Jesus as a teacher, and was sure he had come from God, a prophet perhaps. But Jesus stunned him with the announcement that he was God's only Son. Father, Son and Holy Spirit: the three Persons of the Trinity.

But the word "Trinity" doesn't appear in the Bible: it isn't in our instructions. Later centuries of Christians invented the term to describe the idea of the three-dimensional God, the way in which Father, Son and Holy Spirit together show us who God is: not separate flat pieces, but an assembly of love.

For God so loved the world, that he gave his only Son, so that everyone who believes in him may have eternal life. God created the world, created us, and loves us. Father, Son and Spirit are different dimensions of his love: creating us, rescuing us and strengthening us in faith.



**Application**
Eternal life starts here, if only we suspend our disbelief, allow the Spirit to work in our lives, and accept that Jesus can save us. If only we trust that these things might be, even if we can't quite see how.

Alice needs all parts of her wardrobe: without the sides, the top would fall down. To build these flat pieces into a wardrobe, she needs to have a good translation of the instructions, study them carefully and follow them. The same applies to our faith: a modern Bible translation with the benefit of the latest scholarship (just as Nicodemus had the benefit of Jesus' own teaching, to supplement his knowledge of the scriptures) and some study notes.

Alice will probably call on friends to help: people who have put a wardrobe together before, or are good at visualising possibilities! The same applies to us: members of a study group or friends in the congregation with stories to tell of God's love in their lives.

The wardrobe is for using. The Trinity is not just a theory. In baptism, we are born of the Spirit; as a Christian community, sharing this Holy Communion, we are part of that loving, dynamic relationship, which is the Trinity. Let's not keep God in a box, flat-packed, but share with others the height and depth and breadth of his love.

*"I still have many things to say to you."*
(John 16:12)

**Illustration**
Many of us love reading a good detective story, or watching one unfold on the television: the kind of story where the clues are carefully laid, one by one, until the mystery is eventually solved. We may have started with an Enid Blyton, such as *The Mystery of the Missing Necklace*. Later in life we are hooked by an Inspector Morse or a Brother Cadfael mystery, looking for the clues, piecing them together, until finally the whole picture emerges.

In many ways, the Bible is just such a mystery story, The mystery of the Almighty. Picture the blurb on the back of the book: "Who is this mysterious character they call God? What is he doing? And why?"

**Gospel Teaching**
Trinity Sunday is a good time to look at the Bible clues and see where they lead. In the Old Testament, the focus is mainly on God the Creator, so we only get the merest hints about the Son and the Spirit. The Wisdom of God appears as the firstborn of all creation: a glimpse of Jesus, like Isaiah's suffering servant? And the Spirit of God was occasionally active in chosen people for special tasks. On the whole, though, the first person of the Trinity takes centre stage in the Old Testament.

In the New Testament, we discover that the God who made the world loves us so much that he sent his Son to be born as a human baby, to share in our human life. God the Creator is God the Father.

We learn that, in Jesus, God loves us so much that he was prepared to die for us: a death that was not an end but a beginning, a doorway into eternal life for all of us. God the Son is God the Redeemer.

And Pentecost, which we celebrated last week, reveals yet another aspect of God's character – another dimension to his love. At Pentecost, God shared that love with us in a way that enables us to communicate with him and with one another, to make us holy, too. God the Holy Spirit is God the Sanctifier.

In the New Testament, the early Church engages with this mystery of one God who is also three. But the word "Trinity" never appears in the Bible. Later centuries of Christians invented it to describe the idea of the three-in-one God. What does emerge, in the New Testament, is a simple acceptance that there is one God, yet there are three distinct characters who each seem to be God. No clever models of triangles or intersecting circles or the leaves of a shamrock: just a simple acceptance that these three Persons relate to one another, communicate with one another and with us, yet are one.

Today's Gospel hints at a complex relationship between the Persons of God… and us. Jesus promised that the Spirit of truth would come, to tell his disciples things that he wanted them to know, but for which they were not yet prepared. And the words of his, which the Spirit would declare, are actually the Father's. The reading tells us that we, disciples of Jesus prepared by Easter and Pentecost, are on the receiving end of something which is continually being given to us by the Father, the Son and the Holy Spirit, all working together. The loving, dynamic relationship, which is the Trinity, includes all of us, individually and as a Christian community.



**Application**

If the Bible is a mystery story, "The Mystery of the Almighty", it turns out to be only the first volume. There are still many things God wants to tell us. The sequel involves us, as we seek the Spirit's guidance in our everyday lives, in a world so different from first-century Palestine. And there is to be a further episode, too, even more eagerly awaited than each successive Harry Potter. There will be a time when all the clues in The Trinity Trilogy make sense, when we see in full, though now we see only in part, through a glass, darkly.

But, for now, what's wrong with a bit of mystery? Why not simply accept that God's essential nature is a mystery? Each of us, at our baptism, became part of that mystery. And each of us, in our Holy Communion today, can share in that mystery which is the love of God. Simple acceptance of mystery: isn't that what faith is all about?

# Sundays in Ordinary Time Year A

Proper 4

(Sunday between 29 May and 4 June inclusive)

*"Jesus said, 'Not everyone who says to me, "Lord, Lord", will enter the kingdom of heaven, but only the one who does the will of my Father in heaven.'"*
(Matthew 7:21)

**Illustration**

The ark and the *Titanic*: two boats with very different stories. One survived a worldwide flood, the other sank in a calm sea on its maiden voyage, having struck an iceberg; one's cargo was an extended family and a floating zoo, the other's many passengers included some of the world's wealthiest.

The humble ark was built by Noah in response to God's instructions; the opulent *Titanic*, at the time the biggest passenger ship ever made, was constructed for the glory of humankind and the White Star Line shipping company, whose vice-president boasted that "this ship is unsinkable".

Confidence in human capability led to complacency. There were over a thousand tons of caviar on board, but no binoculars for the lookouts. As the passengers feasted, the captain enjoyed a leisurely dinner, with iceberg warnings, passed on to him that very evening, tucked away in his pocket till later.

The *Titanic* looked the sturdier option for the ocean, but it set sail towards death under man's direction; the ark headed for life under God's protection.

**Gospel Teaching**

In our passage, Jesus stresses that he needs to be at the helm of our lives if we are to enjoy an enduring destiny in God's presence.

Jesus is here completing the Sermon on the Mount, the first of five sections of teaching in Matthew's Gospel. These parallel the Pentateuch – the first five books of the Old Testament – but now Jesus is revealing the new covenant: keeping the commandments given at Mount Sinai is superseded by the call to obey God's living Word, as he speaks from the Galilean hilltop.

Matthew underlines that Jesus is not just an ethical or godly teacher, as Jesus refers to God as "my Father" for the first time in this Gospel, thus identifying himself as God's Son. The way he teaches also indicates his divine nature: usually a rabbi would instruct by drawing on quotations from other rabbis to lend weight to his own pronouncements. By not following suit, Jesus causes astonishment. Yet he has no need to refer to

mere human insight to give his words authority, for ultimate authority resides in himself as the Messiah.

Our destiny, Jesus says, does not arise from powerful deeds done in God's name, but in acts of obedience to the Son's call. We are not measured by the impressiveness of our activity for the kingdom, but on whether we are getting to know, and allowing ourselves to be known by, the king.

The distinction between personal obedience and pious action is not always immediately obvious, but in due course our Maker and Judge will call us to account for the source of our inner strength and motivation for what we have done. Those who have relied merely on outer activity, however spiritually impressive, to protect and surround them, will find the emptiness of their relationship with God exposed. Those who have heeded the words of Christ and founded everything they have built upon responsiveness to him will find themselves part of a work that is enduringly fruitful, as it flows from personal faithfulness to his call. Even if we obey the Sermon on the Mount to the letter, anything we build for God needs to be centred on a devoted attention to deepening our knowledge of the architect of the universe and the saviour of our souls, who alone brings life to our spirit.

**Application**

Jesus warns us not to be "cowboy builders" in the kingdom. We need to base our outer lives on an inner relationship with him. This means following what he has called us to do, and listening for his guidance, rather than relying on our own ideas and agenda, even if we find we are doing things differently as a result. What counts is our relationship with Jesus. It is not sufficient to say, "I don't know the Lord, I just work for him", for such work will not have eternal worth in the kingdom of heaven.

What we are like under the pressure of life's storms will reveal the degree to which we have invested our stability and security in Christ, rather than in what we do in his name. Do we dare to let God really be in charge, or do we prefer to call the shots, even when it comes to doing his work? The most impressive structure will fail if the foundations are not strong.

It's sometimes said that Christians are like tea bags: it's when they're put into hot water that their real flavour emerges. Can others taste the fragrance of Christ in us when the heat is on?

*"I have come to call not the righteous but sinners."*
(Matthew 9:13)

**Illustration**

We can be surprised when we meet people where we least expect to find them. "What are you doing here?" is our first reaction. A second – and perhaps more considered – reaction is to explain how we come to be there ourselves, and so meet people we know from other contexts in what appear to us unfamiliar surroundings.

The underlying message is how often we fall into the common human failing of putting other people into a box. We make assumptions about them. We categorise them, and then we are surprised when they do things we had not expected them to do. They have, in effect, broken out of the confines which we, in our minds, had placed upon them.

**Gospel Teaching**

This is well illustrated by today's Gospel. The narrative is all about people breaking out of boxes. In the opening verse, Jesus calls Matthew the tax collector. There are two boxes here. First, Matthew is socially unacceptable by nature of his job. He collects taxes for the Roman authorities, and no doubt deducts some for his own profit before handing the money on. So Jesus breaks open one box in calling this man from the fringe of society to share his ministry; and he breaks a second one surrounding himself. He breaks any expectations that his disciples would include only people who were respectable and orthodox. Anyone could become his follower.

As Jesus moves on, he is accosted twice in quick succession, first by the leader of the synagogue, whose daughter has just died, then by the woman suffering from haemorrhages. Both these women are subject to taboos under the Jewish law. Contact with them is severely restricted. Jesus breaks through both these boxes. The woman is healed by his touch, the girl is revived. The latter, however, only happens when Jesus reveals the falseness of one last box. The crowd, including the flute-players and professional mourners, were making their ritual lamentation. The shallowness of their action was clearly shown when their weeping turned to laughter as Jesus claimed, "the girl is not dead but sleeping". His action follows the pattern which we discern all through today's Gospel.

However, we have to be careful in approaching this passage. We could find that we are creating boxes where Jesus has broken them down. We have all watched parliamentary proceedings on TV, and watched MPs from all sides shouting "Hear, hear!" when they think their speaker has made a good point. We may find ourselves doing the same. Jesus is good. He is the leader of our party. We approve of his mission statement: "I have come to call not the righteous but sinners", and we applaud the way he puts this into practice. He calls Matthew, heals the woman, brings the girl back to life. The Pharisees form the opposition, as it were, and, together with the professional mourners, are rightly and satisfactorily put in their place by Jesus. But what we may have done, all unwittingly, is to put them all in their place. We have boxed them up, neatly and tidily, according to our own understanding of what is, and what is not acceptable to God. There is no room for those who do not quite fit. There is no margin for untidy edges.

**Application**

What applies as we read the Bible, and especially today's Gospel, applies also to our views on life in general, and to the life of our Church. We are often uncomfortable with people and situations which fail to conform to the boxes we have prepared for them. We make judgements about who people are, where they belong, what they should do, what they should be. In doing so, we fail to be aware of the limitations of the boxes in which we ourselves "live and move and have our being".

Worst of all, we confine God to a box – not that we can, of course, but we have some kind of expectation that God will behave as we want, be on our side and endorse our views. We make God in our image, and confine him to that image. We are genuinely surprised and confused, and not a little aggrieved to find that others hold, equally sincerely, a rather different image of God. This was the thrust of so much of Jesus' teaching, and he demonstrated it as clearly as he could to the people of his own time. It was difficult for them fully to comprehend and accept the meaning of his message, "I came to call not the righteous but sinners." It can be just as difficult for us.

*"Cure the sick, raise the dead, cleanse the lepers, cast out demons."*
(Matthew 10:8)



**Illustration**

Healing today is big business. Hospitals get bigger and better, equipped with the latest technology science can invent and money can buy. New treatments, new drugs, new approaches are being pioneered all the time. Such breakthroughs take time and energy. The buildings, the medicines, the research are all expensive. State-run medical services find it ever more difficult to fund the treatments which are needed and waiting lists grow longer. The private sector is being called upon to fill gaps. Morale is rarely high. Practitioners burn out or turn to other professions, frustrated by the limitations placed upon them.

Many choose to work elsewhere, sometimes in more lucrative areas of the world. But others choose poorer countries where, with many fewer resources, there can still be some sense of a job worth doing. Their patients can be met as fully human beings, combining physical and inner healing to ensure maintenance of their dignity in trying circumstances. Patients in the Western world often feel reduced to ciphers, as "cases" defined by their medical problem rather than as a person, an individual. They are reduced to feeling just the sum of their individual parts, like a car in for servicing, their emotional and spiritual needs being left to be dealt with by friends and family. Despite some forays into alternative medicine, the Western world's dominant model of healing continues to treat us like biological machines.

**Gospel Teaching**

Jesus draws an essential connection between his preaching of the kingdom and the healing of the whole person. The context for his sending out of the disciples is his distress at the state of the crowds who have come to him with their many needs. They are described, in Matthew 9:36, as "harassed and helpless", a fair description of the occupants of a modern hospital's busy ward. Jesus complains to his disciples that there are not enough labourers to work at healing their ills.

In response he calls them together and gives them a special commission. To begin with, he does not send them to the world at large, but to their

own compatriots, the people of Israel. Those to whom the promises of the Old Testament were made, promises which included that of the Father who would bear them up on eagles' wings, watch over them, guard them forever, make of them a consecrated nation.

For us today such language may seem rather detached, even ethereal, when we are faced with the problems of daily life. But what Jesus is asking of his disciples is more down to earth. In order to preach the kingdom they must first of all offer healing, whether of evil spirits or of the physical ailments which affect those they meet. To preach the kingdom is to offer healing of the *whole* person. The power to do this can only come from Christ himself, who is the fulfilment of all the Old Testament promises.

**Application**
The Church has always been involved with physical as well as spiritual healing. Medieval monasteries began the care which was later taken up by the great nursing orders, the forerunners of today's medical services. Since the State and private business have taken over the provision of physical care, the Church's role has become more directed towards the "inner" person, through chaplaincy provision and visiting. Disappointment with the depersonalisation in many areas of medicine today and the apparent split between physical and spiritual care has led to a higher profile for alternative methods of healing. Homeopathy, acupuncture, shiatsu, reflexology and others combine the two aspects of healing. The search for elements not provided by common medical practice may stem from people feeling that their whole person is not being addressed, even though we know that mind, body and spirit interact all the time.

We could say that the kingdom is not being preached as Jesus intended. Society is failing to bring people the fullest healing available to them. How do we remedy this? First by lobbying those who have the power to reassess and change the systems within our society. But also by ensuring that we treat our sisters and brothers as whole people, precious in their totality, not just the bits of them that we can cope with. Our work is to bring Christ's wholeness to all people, regardless of difference, becoming his true disciples, bringing the kingdom to all those that we meet, especially thc "harassed and helpless".

*"Those who find their life will lose it, and those who lose their life for my sake will find it."*
(Matthew 10:39)

**Illustration**
Many of us will remember the UK TV sitcom *Keeping Up Appearances*, whose heroine Hyacinth Bucket (pronounced "Bouquet"!) took to new heights the activity of being seen to be doing, wearing or saying the right thing. The reason it was funny, of course, was that nearly everyone knew someone with a bit (or a lot) of Hyacinth in them. How many of us, as children, were exhorted by our mother always to wear a clean pair of underpants in case we were knocked down? Surely children everywhere have puzzled over this concern for our underwear. Was keeping up appearances more important, even, than our health and safety?

We may feel we live in a less formal society now but, in honesty, we've all felt the pressure of keeping up appearances from time to time, whether it's trying to say the politically correct thing, or being seen by our friends to have the right type of organic, fair-traded or non-airfreighted food in our cupboards. Oh, these are all good things, but let's be honest – there is a fine and rather blurry line between being a decent and upstanding member of society and being seen to be one. The pressure to keep up appearances is still there; it always is.

**Gospel Teaching**
And so it was in first-century Palestine too. There were strict codes of behaviour that had the double-edged effect of both helping people to operate as good citizens by defining what was bad and what was good, but also excluded and labelled those who fell foul of these rules. Jesus upset the applecart, and as a result many vilified him as a lout and troublemaker. His behaviour was seen as defiantly antisocial, and he suffered both verbal and physical persecution as a result.

And so we join the story today at the point where Jesus begins to prepare his disciples to carry on his work (a foretaste, of course, of the task of every Christian), and to suffer the same things that he suffered. To their society the disciples were going to seem like fools, whingers, crackpots and inciters of antisocial behaviour – appearances were definitely not going to

be kept up. The very fabric of society would be threatened, and, as a result, they would suffer the same verbal and physical persecution that Jesus did.

Jesus' message to the disciples is that appearances are of the least concern when the integrity of the soul is at stake. Simple! But although Jesus' words are straightforward – retain your respectability and lose your soul – his call not to be afraid shows that he knew that this was not a simple or easy thing to do. The story about the sparrows is surely one of the tenderest in the Gospels, and one that assures the disciples of their worth in a community that would regard them as worthless. Jesus' careful words show that he knew and understood how much the disciples had invested in their society, and how painful it would be to change it. It was their community after all. They may have been poor and lower class, but they were still part of it all. How can it not be painful to challenge that?

**Application**

Sometimes it seems that we can't win. We do our best to be decent, upright and adhere to the rules of society, and we find ourselves having to face the challenge that all we are doing is keeping up appearances. We try reinterpreting the Gospel to apply it to our life and time and we risk watering the message down; if we take it at face value it seems impossibly disruptive, and to oppose all that we do as we try to be ordinary, decent people.

Well, sadly, there are no easy answers to this, and our challenge as Christian communities, filled with God's Spirit, is to work it out for ourselves. If there is an answer it comes from the uncomfortable place between being a good person and keeping up appearances – from a dialogue between the Pharisee and the radical that is in us all, and from honest conversation with one another about our aspirations and fears.

Jesus knew how painful it was to challenge the values of the community in which you've invested time, effort and love. He knew how much pressure there was on every decent person to keep up appearances. Let us pray for the courage to examine our own hearts honestly and to listen to our radical Lord. The pressure to keep up appearances is strong, but the loving tenderness of our saviour is stronger.

*"Whoever welcomes you welcomes me, and whoever welcomes me welcomes the one who sent me."*
(Matthew 10:40)

**Illustration**

Picture the scene. It's the final of the 4 x 400 metres relay in the Olympic Games. We're cheering our team as each of them runs their lap, pushing themselves to the very limit. The baton is handed on smoothly each time, and the exhausted runners stumble from the track to watch their team-mates complete their laps. At the finishing line they're cheering on the last runner as loudly as we are in the stands… and we've done it! All that hard work has been worth it. Our team has won. An outstanding team effort, against all the odds. And now it's time for the medal ceremony, and all four of them are on the podium. Our flag is raised, our anthem is played and our whole country celebrates.

**Gospel Teaching**

There's something of a relay race in today's Gospel. Jesus is handing the baton on. He's sending out his closest disciples to continue his own mission of both proclaiming and putting into practice the good news of the kingdom of God. In this chapter Matthew has named the twelve apostles and then recorded the instructions that Jesus gave them for their mission. They were to heal the sick, drive out evil spirits, bear witness to Jesus and announce that the kingdom was near. It would be a difficult task, and they would need to risk hardship, rifts with their loved ones and even their very lives. Why, then, should they bother?

In this final passage of the chapter, short as it is, Jesus sums up the whole purpose of their mission. The people who listen to them, the ones who welcome the good news they bring, will receive a reward: a prophet's reward, or the reward of the righteous. A prophet's reward is to see his prophecy come true, while the reward of the righteous, as Jesus made clear in the Beatitudes during the Sermon on the Mount, is nothing less than a place in the kingdom of heaven.

This, then, is the ultimate purpose of the mission: that those who are listening will know that the disciples' words come from God and that they too will be welcomed into the kingdom of heaven, where the whole company of saints will celebrate the victory that Jesus has already won for

us. There is a sequence here, almost like the handing on of a baton in a relay race. God reveals his word of love in Jesus, who passes the word to the disciples, and the disciples hand it on to those who listen to them and welcome them into their lives.

There are some important differences, of course, between the model of the relay race and the reality of mission and evangelism. When we hand on the baton of God's love, we don't lose touch with it ourselves! Love, especially the love of God, is something which can be kept and passed on. And as any Christian minister will tell you, those who listen will often hand it back, polished and shining, as a gift to enrich the minister's own life.

The relay race of revelation is one which goes on and on, round and round the track of this life. God's love flows through Jesus, through the action of the Holy Spirit, through the Church, through us as individual Christians, into the lives of those who hear about it for the first time… and back to God in our worship. We are caught up into the dynamic which is at the heart of God the Trinity: love in action.

**Application**

We are the disciples; we are the runners. The baton passed to us is so good that we want everyone to have a chance to hold it! Like dedicated athletes, we are not coerced into this race, but enter it. And the reward for this race, not earned but freely given by God, is eternal life.

Like the original disciples, we are called to spread the good news of the kingdom of God, the good news of God's love. What a privilege, what a responsibility! But talking about it isn't enough – it needs to be put into practice, like the disciples healing the sick. In this Eucharist we remember that Jesus didn't just preach about the kingdom of heaven: he opened the door to it. Here, in Jesus, is the word of God, love in action. Pass it on!

# *"...and learn from me..."*
(Matthew 11:29)

**Illustration**

Teaching has taken quite a lot of punishment in the past few years. New teaching methods are blamed for illiteracy rates. A lowering of respect for teachers by the media, and, consequently, some parents and children, has resulted in an increase in verbal and physical violence in the classroom. This is a depressing picture, which some researchers attempted to alleviate by asking a number of famous people for the names of any teacher who had inspired them.

A tidal wave of names was launched into the public eye. Apparently every person asked had the name of at least one or two teachers who had had such influence as to have changed, or certainly added to, their lives and futures. Sometimes it was their academic gifts, but it was more likely to have been their ability to inspire their pupils, to give them a special something which spurred them on to achieve their very best, even to reach heights previously unimagined. Think for a moment, who were *your* inspirational teachers?

**Gospel Teaching**

No one can overestimate the influence of a good teacher. Even if we cannot remember a thing they actually taught us, good teachers will be remembered with fondness long after their words have been forgotten. That is because people are more important than words. Qualities like kindness and generosity are always more enduring than principles or rules, and integrity is more infectious than dogma.

In today's Gospel, Jesus offers himself as a teacher: "learn from me", he says. At this point in his ministry Jesus has had to face up to being rejected by the religious hierarchy and "wise" people of his time. His message found no place in their hearts. Becoming experts in the Law had prevented them from recognising the coming of God's Messiah, the coming of God's kingdom.

Instead, Jesus found a ready audience among the people considered social outcasts. The tax collectors and sinners, those unable to keep the Law in all its rigour, all welcomed Christ's message and the hope it brought.

Unfortunately, the experts were so preoccupied with keeping the externals of the Law that they had largely lost sight of its purpose, to lead people to God. They were no longer open to *hearing* the word of God, because they did not need it. They placed the Law above every other consideration, even above people. The Law had become an end in itself.

Jesus offered a different "yoke", a simpler one. We do not have to worry about hundreds of laws, or keeping the minutiae of rules and regulations. Jesus simply offers himself as the model to follow. He alone is the way to God. Follow him and we will find God. Like a good teacher, the lasting impression he makes resides more in who he is, than anything he says. He asks us to be like him, to be gentle and to acknowledge our need for God. It is only when, like the tax collectors and sinners, we are open to the words of God, only when we admit our dependence on God, that we are able to receive God's mercy. And, like them, we experience God's love and mercy, not by mindless obedience, but by meeting a person: Jesus, God's own Son, face to face.

**Application**

Jesus says that *his* burden is light. We can be burdened with all kinds of things: the opinions of the moral watchdogs who claim superior knowledge of God, telling others how to live, what to do and think, even when and how to pray. They forget that rules in religion are only useful to the extent that they lead us to God, to the love and freedom he offers. We have burdens from our consumerist society, the burdens of others' unreasonable expectations and demands, overbearing parents, the demanding boss, the inquisitive neighbour. And then there is our own guilt, our low self-esteem, our unattainable goals. We can become overwhelmed by burdens.

Jesus' yoke is easy. It is well fitting, tailor-made to the individual. Because the task he sets us is simple – be yourself! Be the person God wants you to be, using Jesus as your teacher. Be gentle, with yourself and others. Be humble, acknowledge your need for God, don't assume you have to do it all by yourself. Resist becoming overburdened by any unreasonable demands. Resist any "system" or "rule book". Simply get to know Jesus, the person. Learn from him and you *will* find rest.

*"Other seeds fell on good soil and brought forth grain."*
(Matthew 13:8)



**Illustration**

It is well known to those of us who grow things, whether in a window box, allotment, field or garden, that we need to nourish the soil in order for plants to flourish. We dose the small potted plant with liquid feed, we replenish the soil in our window box, we hump compost onto the allotment and fertilise the fields.

In ancient China, every vestige of household waste was carried up to those garden-sized fields that climbed up the hillside. What was taken out had to be replenished and the earth could not produce good crops unless it had sufficient depth and fertility. However good the quality of seed, a rich harvest cannot be achieved without good soil in which to sow it.

**Gospel Teaching**

In Jesus' day sowing seed was haphazard. Weeds, most commonly a kind of thorn, were not cleared first, but ploughed into the ground. The paths through the fields became hard like roads, and seeds were scattered everywhere, on paths and edges and headlands where the underlying, predominantly limestone, rock came near the surface and made the soil very thin.

To his listeners Christ's description would have been instantly recognisable. He was illustrating his teaching with everyday events, through the language of work, of weather, of nature. Jesus knew that if he spoke in the dry language of the priests, of the Temple or synagogue, the people would not hear what he had to say. Jesus was a country boy and much of his teaching involved the use of symbols taken from nature; he spoke the people's own kind of language, and so they listened to him.

It is easy to become distracted when people speak in a way which does not relate to us, to our needs and our lives; to listen but not to absorb what is said, to miss the crucial heart of a message, which is what happened to many of Jesus' listeners. Some listened but did not want to know. Some heard but did not understand. Some listened and heard but were too frightened of the challenge to respond. Jesus prepared the ground in the way in which a person of the earth would do, with symbols which spoke to the experience and hearts of his listeners. He valued each person in that crowd and when we value someone we take the trouble to approach them at their own level. The harvest of response we reap is worth every moment of effort.

**Application**

And what of us? We frequently fail to listen to one another, let alone to Christ! We avert our eyes, use distracted sounds like, "Mmmm". Interrupting, not allowing others to finish. Do we really listen? How often do you telephone someone and know, by the noise in the background, that the television or radio is claiming half their attention? How often do we ask people how they are because of social convention rather than wanting the truth and the detail of their answer?

If someone listens to us attentively, we feel valued. When someone speaks to us in our own language it feeds and enhances the person that we are, making us grow in confidence and self-worth. This is how Christ listens to us and how we need to listen to him, not only in our prayers but as he speaks to us through others. By this caring we nurture the seed of his love which develops and grows into a part of his great harvest.

But if our soil is thin, what do we do? How do we compost it? By prayer, asking for enlightenment and wisdom; by a good deed, a kind word, sincere contrition for our weaknesses; not by heavy and self-congratulatory penances, but paying close attention to the ordinary events of our daily lives; by being fully present to each person, hearing his or her spoken and unspoken needs. Our compost involves facing and not avoiding life's unpalatable aspects for fear of them troubling us; it involves rising to the challenge of being fully human in the way which Jesus made transparently clear. This is the spiritual fertilisation given by God. When we accept it, it nourishes the life of God within us.

God is with us in the great and in the minute events of our lives. He speaks to us in gentle tones and in language we understand. Listen to him: he is the sower, the seed and the food for growth. Relax: the harvest will take care of itself.

*"The one who sows the good seed is the Son of Man."*
(Matthew 13:37)

**Illustration**

You can walk into some school classrooms and find a model of attentiveness, application and industry, with an atmosphere of good humour and comradeship. The teacher is respected, the rules obeyed and the examination results confirm what a good school it is. But you can walk into another classroom in the same school and discover a bedlam of noise, disturbance and an undercurrent of violence which holds no promise of success for students or the school.

The difference is in the conditions under which the young people come to the school. Within each of these classrooms we would find sincere young people, keen to learn, and others who care not one jot for education, even among students whose background and advantages predispose them to self-confidence and the desire to learn. We would find others whose poverty and lack of stability can undermine their potential and self-respect, ill preparing them for the demands of school, against which they rebel.

If we were school inspectors, how should we deal with the troublemakers? Close the school? That would be unfair to the industrious children. Weed out the nuisances? But perhaps external circumstances beyond their control are to blame for their attitudes. Perhaps we should wait until they are at the end of their education to examine their overall results, to allow for greater inspiration and the effects of a healthy, optimistic environment on their growth and ability to change; and then permit their own actions to determine their futures.

**Gospel Teaching**

There has been much discussion about this parable and to whom it applies. It would be easiest to believe that it is the world in general. It could refer to those people in Israel who would not accept Jesus as the Messiah. But others suggest that it actually refers to us, the members of Christ's own Church.

In his explanation of the parable, Jesus says that it is the Son of Man "who sows the good seed" and "the field is the world". But those whom Jesus draws into membership of his Church gather in his name and it is amongst

these, his chosen, that the weeds are sown by the evil one. There has always been evil in the world at large and it was partly to overcome such evil that Jesus came in the first place. But as this Gospel was written when the Church was in its early stages of development it may be a warning. Just because the teaching of Jesus is the perfect model to be followed, some of its adherents are not perfect, just like the errant children in school.

It would be wonderful to think that the influence of Jesus would instantly transform his followers to mirror him in every way, but life is not like that and neither are people. Spiritual opportunity, like education, can transform its participants but also may be abused; a good influence can turn rotten and can poison the whole. Even in the best surroundings, some good people change, becoming like weeds in a field of good grain. Jesus warns us against assuming that all people in his field of activity are wholesome. It is his word, his influence, his life which must guide us, or we may end up collected together with the weeds and dealt with accordingly.



**Application**
However, our next question might be, "Can a bad seed change its nature?" We need to watch out for and guard against the bad influences even where trustworthiness might be assumed. But what about those children whose disadvantaged start in life disturbs their behaviour? Or those church members who have been swayed by other influences? What about the possibility of change, for naughty children, for developing churches, and for us?

It is important to heed Jesus' warning because our eternal life depends upon it. But it is crucial that we do not become paralysed by fear. Jesus never gave up on anyone; indeed, just before his own death he forgave a criminal and promised him a place in heaven – not sometime in the future or at "the end of the age", but that very day. Leaving behind our evil ways is an opportunity we can take up every single day. Forgiveness by God is complete for those who repent.

So perhaps, then, the answer to our question is "no": a seed cannot change its own character, but God can, by his gifts and the promises which he makes clear through Jesus, promises which he keeps.

## *"The kingdom of heaven is like..."*
(Matthew 13:31)

**Illustration**

Many gardens are looking their best now, with flowerbeds in full bloom offering a magnificent profusion of colour, and vegetable gardens producing scrumptious, mouth-watering crops.

There are so many gardens to enjoy: our own (if we are keen gardeners) or, perhaps, our neighbours' (if we're not!). Then there are those truly wonderful gardens, some associated with grand houses, which deservedly draw in countless hosts of admiring visitors.

As we wander round our gardens, enjoying the rich colours and beautiful shapes and scents of flowers, or anticipating the tastes of newly cropped fruit and vegetables, perhaps questions – unspoken and marvelling – come into mind, questions like: "Does it really all begin with a small seed? How does anyone know what to sow, where, and when to sow it? Where does one start?"

**Gospel Teaching**

Today's Gospel tells of Jesus "sowing seeds" – being a gardener, if you like. In nearly all his parables he "sows seeds", seeds of wisdom and encouragement, seeds of knowledge and confidence, which will grow in the hearts and minds of his listeners – among whom we, of course, number. They are seeds that if (when!) nurtured will flourish, and be fruitful.

Typically, he uses for his "seeds" everyday examples, things his listeners would recognise and know: the tiny seed which grows to become a strong bush; the single cell of yeast helping "flat" ingredients to become a wholesome loaf. He tells of folk who, in their everyday surroundings, spot real treasure (in the field and among the pearls), treasure which they value sufficiently to give up all else to gain. And to people with fisherman-neighbours, he spoke of a huge sea harvest, fish of every kind.

The "seeds" that Jesus is sowing here are seeds about the kingdom of heaven. The kingdom is a challenging concept for many of us, but Jesus' words affirm how a smidgen of faith, a seed of love – our kingdom faith – if nurtured, will grow into something big and good. He shows that this kingdom faith is of great worth – "beyond price", one might say – something greatly to be desired, beyond our known measures of wealth. And the kingdom is all-embracing: there's a place – and room – for us all.

**Application**

In recognising Jesus sowing "seeds" here it is important to note that, whilst he may well be looking ahead to the end product – the magnificently colourful flowerbed in full bloom, or the vegetable garden heaving with prize winning crops – he is in fact, in the parables of our Gospel today, focusing on the starting point: the tiny seed which grows to become a vibrant plant, the minuscule yeast cell which acts to produce a wholesome crunchy loaf.

Sometimes gardeners will start with a seed, and watch it become a lovely flourishing plant. Sometimes they will take a well-developed strong root clump, and divide it, each small part itself growing into a thriving plant.

Who first sowed a seed of faith in us? Did our faith come through what our family and friends shared with us and rooted in us? However we received it, and however small and frail it may sometimes seem, it has brought us into the kingdom.

If we take nothing else from today's Gospel reading we must recognise that the small seed of faith in us, that small cell of faith working in us and helping us to grow, the single jewel, the small but rich treasure, is our kingdom faith. As kingdom faith, its potential to grow and grow is unlimited. And grow it will, as we grow and grow in Jesus Christ, and so enhance the kingdom.

The small seed of faith growing and working in us does indeed make us part of the kingdom – a great multiracial, multicultural, multi-generational harvest of all sizes and scents, of all colours and shapes.

The most basic of meals or the grandest of banquets is enriched by the inclusion of vegetables great or small. Our gardens and wayside hedgerows, flower arrangements at home (or in church), are all enriched by small flowers as well as large blooms, the hidden beauties as well as the bright colours.

So, too, is God's kingdom. You – we – are all part of the kingdom, God's kingdom.

Let's nurture this kingdom faith in us. Above all, let us sow and share the kingdom seeds with all around us, and so help God's kingdom flourish and grow. Let's do it – today.

*"And all ate and were filled."*
(Matthew 14:20)

**Illustration**

Much anxiety surrounds food, even in societies where food is plentiful and starvation is rare. There are regular food scares, sugars and fats are frequently seen as suspect, adverse to health. Various bacteria hit the headlines, salmonella and listeria raise their ugly heads. Medical conditions such as anorexia nervosa and bulimia affect thousands of people. Food, essential for life and meant to be enjoyed, becomes instead a threat, causing discomfort, even ill health. Where food is scarce, finding enough of anything becomes an overriding responsibility.

In the scriptures food has rich associations: from the forbidden fruit in the Garden of Eden, where food symbolised wisdom and temptation, to manna in the desert, where it symbolised God's provision for his people. The Passover meal was a vivid commemoration of rescue from slavery. The Maccabees' refusal to eat the flesh of the pig signified their faithfulness to the Law, even in the face of death. In the New Testament, Jesus is frequently shown eating: having a meal with Martha and Mary, relaxing with friends; eating with Zacchaeus, where Jesus demonstrates his regard for people often overlooked. Dining with tax collectors and sinners is a statement of who the Son of Man came to save. And in the miracles of the loaves and fishes, food is a sign of blessing and abundance.

**Gospel Teaching**

There was no absolute need to feed the people gathered by the shore of the lake. Even though they were in a lonely place the disciples suggested dispersing the crowd to the villages to buy their own food. But Jesus suggests otherwise; he responds to this need, among their other needs. Although he had intended to withdraw from the public gaze to ponder the Baptist's death, he took pity on the people and healed their sick. And, having healed them, he responded to another immediate, pressing need. They were hungry and they needed to be fed. Once again, the presence of Christ is a blessing in more ways than one. From meagre resources a huge crowd is satisfied with plenty left over. Indeed, twelve baskets, which signified abundance for each of the twelve tribes of Israel.

Where people are anxious, Jesus brings reassurance. Where they are confused, he brings enlightenment. Where they are sick, he brings healing. And where they are hungry, he brings bread. It is clear that the ministry of Christ is not just to the spirit or the soul, but to the whole person. He is not just food for the spirit, but food for the body also. The Good News is not merely an idea but a complete renewal of life.

So where there is anxiety about food, about what is safe to eat and what is not safe; when there is worry about whether there will be enough on the plate; where food seems to threaten as well as nourish, Jesus' use of food points the way. Here he brings together much of the symbolism associated with food. As in the desert of old, food here represents God's provision for people. Food represents deliverance and Jesus' concern for the marginalised, those whom the Son of Man came to save. In the taking of the bread, the blessing, breaking and distributing, food points to the sacrifice of Christ and to his abiding presence in the Eucharist.

**Application**

Food represents an opportunity in the Gospel of Christ. As in the Garden of Eden, it suggests the desirability of true wisdom and the necessity of resisting temptation. When we are anxious about the future, the provision of manna in the desert reminds us of God's generosity and care. Passover reminds us of the saving power of God, and the story of the Maccabees is an example of perseverance in the face of extreme adversity. Jesus eating with Martha and Mary demonstrates the value he placed upon friendship and fellowship. His meal with Zacchaeus, with tax collectors and sinners, makes clear that every person is worthy of respect. And the miracle of the loaves and fishes is a rich reminder of the mission of Jesus to proclaim the kingdom, to heal, to nourish and to bless.

The greatest meal of all, the Last Supper, brings together all the symbolism of food in the ministry of Jesus. When anxious, hungry, and in any kind of need, we remember how the Lord provides and how we too should provide for others in his name.

## *"You of little faith, why did you doubt?"*
(Matthew 14:31)

**Illustration**

The eighteenth-century French Jesuit priest Jean-Pierre de Caussade spent the first few years of his ministry teaching at the Jesuit college in Toulouse. In 1714 he stopped teaching, and became an itinerant missioner and preacher.

In the years that followed he developed an extensive ministry of spiritual direction based at the Jesuit retreat house in Nancy, and many of the letters on the life of prayer that he wrote during those years have been preserved for us.

His most famous work, still available today, was a longer piece entitled *Abandonment to Divine Providence*. When writing about the practice of faith in our daily lives, de Caussade had this to say: "God's will desires and can always accomplish what will contribute most to our perfection on condition that we allow God to act. Faith does not doubt this. The more our senses are faithless, revolted, uncertain and in despair, the more surely faith says: 'This is God; all is well.'"

**Gospel Teaching**

Peter's attempt to walk on the water in Matthew's Gospel follows on immediately from the feeding of the five thousand. Jesus has dismissed the crowds and sent his disciples on ahead of him, across the lake, while he goes up a mountain to pray alone.

Early in the morning the disciples see Jesus walking towards them through the battering waves, and they cry out in fear, thinking they are seeing a ghost. He calls out to reassure them, and Peter responds, "Lord, if it is you, command me to come to you on the water." When Jesus does so, Peter sets out confidently, but he is soon overcome by his fear of the wind and the waves. Jesus catches hold of Peter's outstretched hand, chiding him for his lack of faith. As they get in the boat the wind drops, and the disciples worship Jesus.

This incident is paralleled in Mark's Gospel (Mark 6:45-52), but Mark has one very significant difference: there is no mention of Peter attempting to walk on the water to Jesus. So why does Matthew record this? The usual

interpretation of this passage assumes that Peter would not have sunk in the waves if he had only had enough faith, and indeed, Jesus' words would initially seem to suggest this. But the disciples' lack of faith is also implicit in Mark's version of the incident, and has not needed a description of Peter trying to walk on the water to make it so.

The American scholar Eugene Boring has suggested that Jesus' rebuke of Peter relates not to the fact that having more faith would have made walking on the water possible, but rather that Peter was demanding proof of Jesus' presence and power, rather than relying on his faith.

Boring draws a parallel between the form of Peter's words to Jesus, "Lord, if it is you, command me to come to you on the water", and the words of Satan to Jesus in the wilderness temptations: "If you are the Son of God..." (Matthew 4:3-11).

In the wilderness experience, Jesus is repeatedly tempted to "prove" his divinity to the world and to himself by a spectacular display of signs and wonders. His threefold response to Satan indicates a refusal to be drawn into displays of supernatural pyrotechnics, and instead Jesus focuses consistently on the God who alone is worthy of trust and worship. By demanding a miracle, Peter has fallen prey to the temptation to seek physical proof for his faith, and he is consequently rebuked by Jesus.



**Application**

The message of today's Gospel passage challenges our inbuilt human tendency to demand proof for our faith; to ask that God would suspend the natural laws of his creation in order to make belief easier for us. So often we seek, not for faith, but for certainty. We have no problem when all in our lives is going smoothly; but when the "wind and waves" that are the realities of every human life threaten to swamp us – the experiences of loss, sickness and ageing that are our common lot – we find it hard to hold on to faith.

The words of de Caussade with which we began are of real encouragement here. We are urged to hold on in faith, however bleak and unpromising are our circumstances. However strong the winds or overwhelming the waves, God always wills and can do that which is for our greatest good, if only we will let him do so (cf. Romans 8:28). "This is God; all is well."

*"Then Jesus answered her, 'Woman, great is your faith! Let it be done for you as you wish.'"*
(Matthew 15:28)

Proper 15
(Sunday between 14 and 20 August inclusive)

**Illustration**
This story of a Canaanite woman's encounter with Jesus is not a comfortable one to hear, nor an easy one to understand. It seems out of character for Jesus to reject a distressed woman seeking healing for her child. It is unlike him to use such dismissive words to anyone, humiliating someone in the presence of others.

It might help us in our understanding of it to set this story in context and look at the events which lead up to it.

At the beginning of chapter 15, Matthew tells us that Pharisees and scribes come from Jerusalem to question Jesus. We can be sure these questions are not asked with minds open to a new understanding and deepening of faith. They are challenges thrown at Jesus in order to discredit and condemn him. They ask why Jesus' disciples don't follow the traditional Jewish rituals of hand-washing.

Jesus doesn't answer their question. Instead he launches a ferocious attack on the way they themselves use traditions to undermine the spirit of God's law. He calls them hypocrites – people who give the appearance of worshipping and honouring God but who in fact put their own interests first, harming others in the process.

These Pharisees, then, accuse Jesus of breaking tradition while Jesus insists that in fact he is the one calling people to live according to God's laws, not human distortions of it.

**Gospel Teaching**
After this encounter with his critics Jesus talks to his followers about what makes someone clean or unclean. He explains the teaching in more detail to his disciples who (not for the first or last time) haven't understood him. Jesus says that food we eat is processed and passes out of the body. It's a physical function having no moral implications.

However, the way we speak and act does have moral implications affecting ourselves and other people. Our words and deeds can be said to be unclean but they come from our hearts, not from our bodies and diets or the way we eat.

It is after this teaching that Jesus goes to the district of Tyre and Sidon where the Canaanite woman comes to him to beg him to heal her sick daughter.

At first Jesus ignores her. Perhaps he is struggling within himself about how to respond. His compassion and love for all suffering people would move him to respond with healing. But he is also aware of his calling as God's Chosen One from and for God's chosen people.

As he struggles, the woman continues her cries for help and the disciples suggest that the best way to silence her would be to grant her request. Perhaps partly still talking to himself and perhaps in a questioning way Jesus says, "I was sent only to the lost sheep of the house of Israel." Now the woman comes right up to him, kneels in front of him and again asks for help.

Jesus knows that his critics would reject this woman and would consider Jesus unclean for having spoken to her. He voices their thoughts, saying, "It is not fair to take the children's food and throw it to the dogs."

Her quick, witty retort that even the dogs eat what the children don't want releases the tension and we can perhaps imagine Jesus' smile and delight in finding such faith in an "outsider" when it had been missing among the "chosen people". His love and compassion flow freely once more and the daughter is healed.

Jesus demonstrates vividly that while he might be ritually unclean (by speaking to a Gentile woman) his words and actions are loving and healing, reflecting God's gracious acceptance of all people.

**Application**
This whole chapter presents us with challenges about how we live out our faith in our homes, congregations, communities and places of work.

We're powerfully reminded that we can say and do all the right things but it's what's going on in our hearts that matters and what is going on in our hearts will always somehow be shown in our lives and relationships. We're reminded that God looks to the very centre of our being but does so with love and compassion, always wanting to forgive and heal so that we can live lives free from guilt and able to love others as we have been loved.

Finally, we are reminded that we, too, are called to love beyond all boundaries, ignoring social niceties and prejudices because no one is ever outside the reach of God's love – which is for all people everywhere and always.

*"Simon Peter answered, 'You are the Messiah, the Son of the living God.'"*
(Matthew 16:16)

**Illustration**

What's in a name? Each culture has its own tradition when conferring names and there can be a mixture of tribal, family and individual meanings attached. As time goes by some of these meanings can be lost. For example, the surname "Carpenter" tells us something of a family's trade in the past, but it is by pure chance if a "Carpenter" is a carpenter today. In some Christian traditions, first names are taken from those of saints or scripture. Now a baptismal name is as likely to reflect family links, or book or film characters.

We may have strong feelings for or against our own name, but it carries power for us. An "icebreaker" activity sometimes used in the first session of a group can be to ask each person present to state their name and something about it. As well as being a useful tool to fit faces and names together, the layers of history, meaning and feelings revealed can be fascinating.

**Gospel Teaching**

Names are always significant in the Bible. They tell us much about the role the person is asked to play in the unfolding plan of salvation. Remember the importance given to the naming of Jesus and of John the Baptist in Luke's Gospel. One of the pivotal moments in the Old Testament is when Moses asks God for his name and God appears to evade the question. To know someone's name is to have power over them and no one can have that power over God.

In the Jewish tradition even God's elusive reply to Moses, often translated as "I am who I am", is never spoken aloud. Yet in today's Gospel passage Jesus asks his disciples about his own identity. To begin with he is circumspect. He asks who the crowd thinks him to be, employing the title used in Matthew's Gospel, the Son of Man. The replies are those from the past, important characters who heralded momentous shifts in the history of salvation.

But Jesus then asks his disciples who they think he is, much more direct and resonant of God's elusive self-disclosure to Moses. "But who do you say that I am?" And it is Simon Peter who answers accurately. "You are the Messiah, the Son of the living God." Jesus is recognised and named for who he is. It is a turning point in his mission and provides for a crucial change in our understanding of the nature of God. God is no longer keeping himself apart, jealously guarding his own identity, but revealing himself as one like ourselves, even subject to human power.

The immediate sequel to today's story is the proclamation by Jesus of his journey towards suffering and death. For his faith, Peter is especially blessed by Jesus and is given a new name. He is to become the rock, the source of strength and authority for the new community, the Church, the followers of this newly revealed Christ.

**Application**

Whatever our role in life, whatever our position in the Church, our starting point is the same as that of Peter and the disciples. We have to answer the same question Jesus put to them: who do we say Jesus is? Can we answer? Not just with the mind, but with the heart? We need to be ever aware of God constantly revealing himself and emptying himself for us in and through his Son. If we have the faith to do that, then we in turn receive our names. We are allowed to turn the question round and ask Jesus what name he gives us. Who does he say we are? We are all his followers but, as St Paul points out, the good of the Church and the growth of the kingdom require that we have a clear idea of what our individual contribution may be.

It is not only the clergy who are called and named in this way. Every single one of us is called by God. It is through daily prayer and reflection and the help of those who know us well that we can discern how we are to live out that calling in our everyday lives. We all have a unique contribution to make and each of our names is known to God, so it is up to us to live out that name to its fullest in the service of the kingdom.

*"Get behind me, Satan! You are a stumbling block to me."*
(Matthew 16:23)

**Introduction**

It seems to be an acknowledged truth among workers with terminally ill patients that people who are dying sometimes need "permission" from their loved ones to die. (Not by any other than natural causes, of course.) When it is clear that they are prepared, some need to know, through word or gesture, that their leaving is acceptable.

Elsie knew that she was dying and was ready to do so. We all knew that, and by every means at her disposal, apart from the actual words, Elsie was trying to ask for permission to be allowed to pass away. Except that her husband, who adored her, refused to accept that she was dying, and his inability to face the reality of what was happening prevented Elsie from a dignified and graceful death. Her physical symptoms and the sadness of her circumstances were almost overwhelming, even for the professionals. Her husband insisted upon nursing her at home. He permitted no reference to the probability of her dying and clung to her little bit of life as though it was his own.

Eventually, of course, Elsie did die. But her passing became a silent struggle with her husband, an ending which might have been avoided if he had been able to face an incontrovertible reality with fortitude. No blame attaches to him. He loved Elsie and could not bear to be parted from her. But perhaps this helps us to understand Peter's response to Jesus when the bad news became too much for him to bear.

**Gospel Teaching**

By this stage of Jesus' ministry it was clear to Peter and the other disciples that he was their Messiah, but they had yet to understand that he would not be the conquering king driving all before him and expelling Israel's enemies from the land given them by God. When Jesus rounds on him so violently we hear echoes of his very human frustration: that Peter is still thinking in the old terms and not in the radical new way of Jesus and his rule of love, not power and vengeance.

But Peter's response is our response. We do not want Jesus to suffer either, we do not want him to die. "God forbid it, Lord!" Peter says. But Jesus

knows that God will not forbid it; God will not cause his death, but will not prevent it, because the free will given to humanity means that God, too, must watch a beloved child put to death. Jesus is as scared as any of us would be. (The serene acceptance of all that is to come is some people's interpretation of Jesus' response to his fate, but this belies his full humanity.) Not only does Jesus have to deal with his own feelings, but he has these underscored by Peter's inability to understand and accept the full reality of what is to come.

Jesus did not really think Peter was Satan but simply that this title represents everything which opposes truth and is allied to worldliness, not God's kingdom. At the same time, Jesus does not want the natural anxiety and sorrow of the situation transforming into pessimism, the canker of the soul. The sister of reality is hope in Jesus' message today.

**Application**

There is a clear choice for us here. All disciples must be prepared for the worst as well as the best: this is the reality of our vocation. We take up our responsibilities and then accept the consequences – this is mature spirituality, this is dedicated commitment. The good thing about facing reality is that it unlocks us from the prison of impotent, unending fear of unknowing, and frees us to make change, to move forward and live more fully.

Yes, it is scary at first: all freedom is frightening, because everything becomes possible when one has nothing to lose. Jesus knew this. He was prepared to risk everything and did not need Peter's fussing, however well meant, or needy. He wanted Peter to grow up and face the truth and then accept what must come, so that he and Jesus could be free to pursue the next phase of their shared ministry. Jesus knew that it was a crucial step on the way to the disciples learning from where they would eventually find the strength to found and maintain the future Church: from his example, but also from within themselves. Facing reality, with hope, rarely disappoints when we undertake it with Christ.

*"For where two or three are gathered in my name, I am there among them."*
(Matthew 18:20)

**Illustration**

Imagine you lend a treasured possession to a friend, perhaps a special book or a recording of some music that's no longer available. Whatever it is, it gets damaged and when your friend returns it to you, or tells you that it's broken beyond repair, she/he doesn't seem to realise how special that particular item was to you. She/he seems quite casual in her/his apology; but you're a Christian, so through gritted teeth and with a forced smile you say, "Never mind, it doesn't matter."

But it does matter and you feel resentful whenever you think of it. That resentment simmers away until one day your friend asks if she/he can borrow something else and suddenly you flare up and make it clear to her/him in no uncertain terms that you won't lend her/him anything of value again after last time. Your friend, taken aback by this reaction, goes away to nurse her/his own new grievance against you.

Relationships can be damaged by such incidents and by others much more extreme. As Christians, we need to be realistic about this: loving others as ourselves doesn't mean pretending we never hurt or upset each other, that we never argue or that we always live peacefully together.

Our Gospel reading shows us a more loving way to deal with rifts in our relationships with our brothers and sisters in Christ.

**Gospel Teaching**

Matthew writes about the guidance Jesus gives for managing arguments and conflict within the Church.

The first step, says Jesus, is to try and sort the problem out with the other person directly, without involving anyone else at all. If that works, then the relationship begins to heal and there are no ripples from the dispute to reach and hurt others.

If this first step doesn't help, then Jesus suggests that we try again but with one or two other people present who can confirm what is said by both parties.

It's only when the rift remains that the whole Church needs to be involved, and if even that has no effect then, as a last resort, the offending person

is to be excluded from the Church and treated as a "Gentile and a tax collector" – a despised outsider.

However, although Gentiles and tax collectors were generally despised and excluded, Jesus thought of them as sinners, or lost sheep, who needed to be found, forgiven and healed with love and compassion. If we are to follow his example we need to remember that we are still to love those with whom we no longer have fellowship.

Jesus promises that whenever any of his followers meet together in his name, even if it's only two of them, he will be there with them. Remembering that Jesus is alongside us when we try to resolve difficulties in our relationships will be a powerful reminder that we are to love one another and to seek peace and reconciliation wherever there is conflict between us.

**Application**

Many of us would prefer to avoid conflict or confrontation with others. Perhaps also many of us feel guilty about being angry with someone we think we ought to love. Perhaps we feel we should "forgive and forget" a hurt or a wrong done to us.

The problem is that if self-righteousness and anger are stored up they can fester and become very destructive of our own peace of mind and our relationships with others.

The way that Jesus describes is the way towards reconciliation with other people and peace of mind within our own souls. It is the way that is healing and life-giving, and it is the way that God relates to each of us, wanting us to live rather than dying because of our refusal to accept his forgiving grace.

The way that Jesus describes is costly. It requires honesty and humility, the willingness to admit to our own failings and faults and to reach out in love to someone who has hurt us.

The way that Jesus describes can be lonely when we approach someone to seek reconciliation only to be met with a refusal to talk. That is the way of the cross, and it is perhaps when we feel most alone, rejected and hurt that Jesus is closest to us as he keeps his promise to be with us always.

When we meet in the name of Jesus to seek peace between ourselves, his Spirit moves among us to bring about the peace that the world cannot give.

*"Should you not have had mercy on your fellow-slave, as I had mercy on you?"*
(Matthew 18:33)

**Illustration**

James read his mother's letter again. "Your father doesn't have long to live. He wants to make up with you." But James seethed at the thought of his father. He remembered his coldness as a parent and his impossibly high standards. Even now his eyes moistened at the memory of punishments suffered at his hand, and belt. James had sought to erase his father's influence from his life but in reality hatred for his father had affected every major decision he had made. He had declined a place at university knowing that was against his father's wishes. He chose a wife he knew his father would dislike – the marriage was a disaster. Then there was his decision to stay abroad when all he wanted was to come home. These things were done to get back at his father, but who really suffered?

Martin Luther King said, "Hate is a boomerang that circles back and hurts you." Forgiveness is important not just for the perpetrator but for the victim, helping them to break away from anger and bitterness which could freeze them in the past and destroy their hope in the future. Today's Gospel reading is about forgiveness and shows how important it is for Christians to practise it.

**Gospel Teaching**

Jesus has been teaching his disciples about how to deal with fellow Christians who sin against them (Matthew 18:15-20). This prompts Peter, keen to impress Jesus, to suggest that he would forgive his brother seven times – a generous act, as rabbis would have limited it to three. Jesus, however, in saying that his disciples should be prepared to forgive seventy-seven times, means that Christian forgiveness should be unlimited.

Imagine the disciples' reaction – how could unlimited forgiveness be possible? Jesus explains in the parable. The servant who owed ten thousand talents was probably a high official responsible for delivering the taxes from the province he oversaw. He owed the equivalent of millions of pounds, a hopeless debt which could never be repaid. Yet when the servant begged to be given more time, the king was compassionate and went beyond his request, forgiving him the entire debt.

The king expected his generosity to affect this man's behaviour towards others, but instead the servant found someone who owed him three

months' wages (a minuscule amount compared with the servant's own debt) and demanded payment.

The key to this parable lies in the king's furious words, "Should you not have had mercy on your fellow-slave, as I had mercy on you?" If we truly understand how immeasurable a debt God has forgiven us, we will forgive others the comparably much smaller sins they commit against us.

**Application**

This is difficult teaching and there are some common misunderstandings about what forgiveness means in practice which are worth refuting:

1. To forgive you must also forget. This is not always realistic, especially when serious crimes have been committed. Forgiveness does not necessarily involve forgetting but it does affect how we take those memories into the future, preventing them consuming us with hatred and vindictiveness.
2. Forgiveness always brings reconciliation. Whilst that is often so, there are times when reconciliation simply isn't a safe or sensible option, as might be the case in abusive relationships, for instance.
3. Forgiveness involves denying that our hurt matters. We can think that forgiveness involves playing down the significance of what has happened to us. But if forgiveness is to be true and lasting it must involve confronting sin and being honest about our pain. Forgiveness is often a gradual process, one which takes time and for which we may need the help of others. To rush through it by sweeping pain under the carpet can be dangerous. By asking us to forgive, God isn't overlooking the seriousness of sin but asking us to leave any retribution up to him.
4. Forgiveness is primarily about our feelings. But actually, forgiveness is an act of the will, a choice which affects how we behave. We may well struggle with negative feelings even after forgiving someone, but God is concerned with our willingness to try, not in our instant success, and he will be there to help us.

For Jesus, forgiveness and our participation in it are fundamental signs of the kingdom of God. By practising forgiveness we show that we fully comprehend how much God has loved and forgiven us, and through it we can know the joy of working with him to pass on the grace we have experienced to others.

## *"Are you envious because I am generous?"*

(Matthew 20:15)

**Illustration**

Anyone who has anything to do with young children, whether as a parent or as a teacher or in church, knows that one of their most frequently uttered phrases is, "It's not fair!" The issue may be the amount of food on plates, or turns with the ball, or bedtime, or possession of the best crayons, or any number of things, but the cry is still the same: "It's not fair!"

Where do small children get this sense of fairness? It seems to be built into human nature, a sense that the world should be a fair place but often is not, and that human beings have the right to protest if things are not fair. And this sense stays with us as we grow up. We grumble if we feel someone else has got the promotion we deserve. We protest if our rightful needs are not met, especially if those of our neighbour are.

At its extremes, this sense of the importance of fair play can lead to horrific action. Not long ago a man who had in fact been cleared of wrongdoing was killed by his neighbours because they thought he was guilty of the crime of child molesting of which he had been accused. He should get his just deserts, they thought, and so they took matters into their own hands.

**Gospel Teaching**

This human sense of fairness is what gives the parable of the workers in the vineyard its shock value. The landowner hires some labourers at the beginning of the day, and agrees with them their pay, the normal daily wage. He goes again and hires some more at midday, some more in the middle of the afternoon, and some more still at the end of the afternoon. When pay time comes, those hired last are paid first and get the normal daily wage. The first to be hired see this, and expect more. It's only fair that they should be paid more, for more work. They are disgusted to be paid only the normal daily rate, even though that was what they had initially agreed.

I wonder whose side you are on when you hear this story. Do you think that those first workers have a point? Think of your workplace. Would it be fair for everyone to be paid the same, without regard for the effort they put in? The landowner's response to the objection is really thoroughly

unsatisfactory; he can do what he likes with his own money. True, but it does not address the issue of fairness, which is the problem here.

How might Jesus' first listeners have reacted? We can perhaps imagine the audience expressing agreement with the first workers. "It's not fair," someone in the crowd might mutter, "they should have got more for all that extra work." But perhaps a more thoughtful person in the crowd might say, "But the workers who were hired last, how were they to feed their families if they were paid only for an hour?" "Ah," someone else might reply, "but that's their own lookout if they hang around the marketplace all day instead of doing a good day's work." "But perhaps it wasn't their fault," replies our first listener, "perhaps they did their best to be hired, but there wasn't enough work to go round that day. Isn't it better that the landowner should be unfair than that children should starve?"

You see where our imaginary discussion has taken us. It has shifted the ground of the debate from issues of individual fairness, to broader issues of justice in society.

**Application**

My imaginary debate is one that we all need to have with ourselves from time to time. The example of the neighbourhood vigilantes shows how easy it is for our inbuilt human sense of fairness to get out of hand. It is good to pay attention to what is fair. But it is also right to think beyond issues of individual rights, to pay attention to broader issues of justice in society.

But this is not just a story. It is prefaced with the words, "the kingdom of heaven is like…" This is a story about God, who we suppose is represented by the landowner. "Are you envious because I am generous?" the landowner asks the workers, and by analogy God asks us. "Yes," we might reply. "We want to get what's rightfully ours." But we might then remember how little we deserve God's generosity towards us, and be willing to share that generosity with others.

## *"Which of the two did the will of his father?"*
(Matthew 21:31)

**Illustration**

Perhaps it's blindingly obvious to say that those who invest much in something have the most to lose if that something is threatened. This can be true of the stock market or the horses, but perhaps it applies most to the things even closer to our hearts. The children in whom we have invested so much love, care and money, fly the nest and leave us bereft. Longed-for retirement makes us feel lost and useless. The job that we sweated over is taken away and given to someone else. The family home that we laboured to make into a secure haven is shattered by divorce or death. The friendship that we treasured turns out to be one-sided. The Church that we are devoted to is torn apart by divisions or change.

The things we love, that we care for, or that we consider important enough to invest the best of ourselves into, these are the things that will cause the most anxiety and that stir up the most ferocious battles – and that lead, if those battles are lost, to the most dreadful hurt and despair. You invest much in something, you stand to lose much. It's one of the truths of life. If you don't invest, then you don't stand to lose so much. But what kind of life would that be?

**Gospel Teaching**

In our reading from Matthew's Gospel we are seeing the actions and words of a group of people who have invested much in their faith and community, but who are feeling increasingly threatened by looming change. Jesus has just entered Jerusalem with shouts of "Hosanna!" in his ears, and he has provocatively overthrown the tables of the money changers in the Temple.

His actions echo the message of his whole ministry: soon the establishment will come tumbling down and a new order will begin. There is trouble afoot, and the authorities know it, which is why we read today of their increasing conflict with Jesus as they try and slow him down, catch him out and eventually – in a few chapters' time – condemn him to death. They challenge Jesus' authority to do the things he is doing – a challenge which Jesus answers only indirectly, before going on the attack.

His tiny but powerful parable of the son who says he'll go and doesn't, versus the one who says he won't and does, is, as Jesus makes quite clear, a description of how the chief priests and elders – the cream of the local society and faith community – are blind to the Good News. But the prostitutes and collaborators – very much not the cream of anything – have heard the message and welcomed it.

For those who were disgraceful, failed and unacceptable, Jesus' message was one of inclusion and grace. Society invested little in these people, and they could invest little back, which is perhaps why they had the clarity of vision to enable them to see Jesus' message as uniquely good. The authorities, the respectable, the wealthy and the well-to-do had invested much in the system, and so had much, much more to lose.

Looking back on those times, it's easy to see who's right. But let's spare a thought for those people who invested much. These were not bad people. They worked towards order, stability and faithful commitment. They kept the rules – the rules given by God. How painful and confusing to find things turned on their head. Truly, those who have invested the most have the most to lose.

**Application**

Surely this is a lesson we can never afford to stop learning. We quite rightly invest time, love, attention and money in the things we consider to be the most important. Our Church and our faith are among these things. But that loving investment can also make us blind sometimes to the necessity for change, to the need to look afresh at what we do. This is particularly the case when those on the edges – the ones who don't have as much invested in the way things are – start making suggestions and changes. Or when their very presence demands that we do something different.

As faithful Christians, we should invest in good things. But the double-edged sword of the Gospel means that we can never be sure that we will not be called upon to adapt and even dismantle the very thing we treasured the most. And this is not about gathering ammunition to attack others, it's about challenging ourselves. Let's pray for the courage to face the call, when it comes.

Proper 22 (Sunday between 2 and 8 October inclusive)

*"Therefore I tell you, the kingdom of God will be taken away from you and given to a people that produces the fruits of the kingdom."*
(Matthew 21:43)

**Illustration**

The congregation had been looking forward to this particular service for a long time. It was to be their normal weekly Communion, but their guest speaker was in such popular demand that the booking had had to be made over a year ago.

The sense of eager anticipation grew as the service progressed, until all stood for the reading of the Gospel. That day, it was the parable of the Pharisee and the tax collector, praying in the Temple. The Pharisee prayed, "God, I thank you that I am not like other people…"; and the tax collector, "God, be merciful to me, a sinner!"

Slowly the preacher ascended the pulpit, praying that both he and his listeners might be open to the love and truth of God. For a moment he looked round the expectant congregation, making eye contact with each one. And then he spoke. "Hands up," he said, "anybody who didn't think, 'Thank God I'm not like that Pharisee!'" And then he returned to his seat.

**Gospel Teaching**

The parable of the wicked tenants is the third "vineyard" parable recorded by Matthew in quick succession, following those of the labourers in the vineyard (20:1-16), and a father's two sons sent to work in the vineyard (21:28-32). Today's parable and the one immediately preceding it take place in the context of the Pharisees' demand to know from where Jesus' authority comes, a demand Jesus refuses to answer directly.

There is a sense of urgency about his cryptic response: "What do you think?… Listen to another parable…" After hearing the parable of the tenants, the penny finally drops: "When the chief priests and the Pharisees heard his parables, they realised that he was speaking about them." They were prevented from arresting Jesus there and then only because of their fear of the crowds, who believed he was a prophet.

For Matthew, the slaves whom the master sends to his vineyard clearly represent the succession of prophets who were sent to a rebellious Israel. The son stands for Jesus, and the tenants represent Israel's leaders, who

kill him rather than acknowledge the master's claims. In Mark's version of this parable, the son is killed and then unceremoniously dumped outside the vineyard. In Matthew's version the son is taken outside the vineyard and then killed, corresponding to the actual sequence of events of Jesus' Passion (27:32).

Jesus reinforces the meaning of the parable by his reference to the stone that the builders rejected becoming the cornerstone, with a clear implication that he is that cornerstone. The kingdom will be taken away from those who have rejected it – Israel – and will be given to those who will faithfully produce its fruits.

**Application**

Matthew's account of this parable has caused commentators and preachers some difficulty, and indeed, previous lectionaries avoided it altogether. The human tendency to look for a scapegoat is one that is very deeply ingrained; so much so that we often don't even realise that we're doing it.

The preacher from our illustration was aware of this. We listen to the Pharisee, and Jesus' reaction to his prayer, and without even thinking about it we congratulate ourselves on not being so smugly self-righteous. Surely, we would never pray like that?

And yet it is an uncomfortable fact that many Christians throughout history have been only too willing to interpret today's text in a narrowly focused way, so fuelling the fires of anti-Judaism, anti-Semitism and all their resulting horrors. There has been a tendency to view such texts as in some way letting Christians "off the hook" ("Thank God I'm not like that Pharisee!").

It is important that we allow Matthew to speak from within his own conditioned perspective, but it is equally important that we do not accept it as the only view, allowing it to limit our own. A wider biblical perspective is offered by Paul: a Jew-become-Christian who saw that the larger plan of God embraced both Jew and Gentile, Israel and Church (Romans 9–11).

At the close of the parable Jesus speaks, not of the rejection of Israel, but of the kingdom of God being taken away from "you" and given to people who produce the fruits of the kingdom. The kingdom allows for no scapegoats: we, too, are addressed in that "you". We are weak and fallible human beings, with little of which to be proud. Our salvation comes not through finding scapegoats, but in owning our weakness and throwing ourselves on the mercy of God.

*"Go therefore into the main streets, and invite everyone you find to the wedding banquet."*
(Matthew 22:9)

Proper 23
(Sunday between 9 and 15 October inclusive)

**Illustration**

Throwing a party can be a tricky and stressful business. How many people should be invited? What if no one turns up? Then there's the reluctant guest who makes excuses – the one who says, "I've got to stay in to wash my hair," or says that they just can't find a babysitter. And there's the gatecrasher who doesn't belong.

Today's Gospel speaks of God's kingdom as a party, and the giving of it must have been about as stressful as ever. The people who were invited just would not come. Some of them wouldn't take it seriously, and went off to do their own thing – as if a person would say, "Sorry, I can't come to your party – I have to go to the superstore." And others seem to have been so insulted to be invited that they beat up and even murdered those who came to fetch them. What was it about this party that made it so unappealing?

**Gospel Teaching**

A welcoming feast for all is one of Jesus' favourite ways of speaking about the kingdom of God. But there are a few disturbing features to this particular description: Jesus really stresses God's anger at being rejected; the host in the story is absolutely furious with those who would not come. And as for the man who does come but wears the wrong clothes – he is cast out into the dark. So what on earth are we to make of this picture?

Jesus is warning us against being too complacent. Yes, God truly does offer us a place in his kingdom, promising to fulfil every one of our needs, to wipe away our tears and remove our guilt and our shame, as Isaiah said. But God deals with us as adults, not as little children. God is no magician or fairy godmother who waves a magic wand to make everything work out well in the end. He is a God who invites us not simply to take our places at his banquet, but actively to prepare it with him, to begin the work of building up his kingdom in our own lives and in the world in which we live.

St Augustine suggests that the reason the man in the story is ejected from the banquet is because the garment which he lacks is the one essential for the kingdom of heaven: love. The wedding garment is a symbol: to enter the kingdom of God, we need to repent and have a change of heart, but that is not the end of the story. This repentance must be continued in a life of love and compassion. Christians who fail to lead a life of service to others will find that merely acknowledging Christ is not enough: they run the risk of being cast out of God's kingdom into the darkness because they have failed to clothe themselves in the garment of love.

**Application**

We say that God is love and we might be tempted to use that fact to excuse any real effort on our part to bring God's love to the people we meet. If so, we are like the man without the wedding garment: he had failed to prepare and just turned up, expecting to be admitted. But the kingdom of God is not like that. We are given opportunity to choose in our lives, and the choices we make have enormous consequences. People often make light of the Christian faith – the Church tends to be seen sometimes as an ineffective body of people who hold tea parties and jumble sales. In fact, for all its faults (and there are very many) the Church, as the means of communicating the Christian faith, is certainly not something to be made light of – for if the Christian faith is true, then it is, quite literally, a matter of life and death.

Other people oppose the Church and the faith for which it stands with a real loathing and hatred, like the people who murdered the slaves in the parable. And others find themselves in it but not really knowing why – thinking they can be a Christian without letting it touch them – like the man without the wedding garment. The parable tells us that how we respond to God's invitation is vitally important – as members of the Church, and as people at the party, let us make sure that we do our part to make the invitation clear.

*"Give therefore to the emperor the things that are the emperor's, and to God the things that are God's."*
(Matthew 22:21)

Proper 24
(Sunday between 16 and 22 October inclusive)

### Illustration

The hero of *Silas Marner*, written by George Eliot in 1861, is a weaver who is forced to leave the Christian community in which he lives after he is wrongly accused of stealing. Betrayed by his best friend, separated from the woman he had hoped to marry and his whole acquaintance, all he has left is his skill as a weaver. Silas settles on the edge of the sleepy village of Raveloe where he spends his time doing only two things: making money and counting it. The twin rhythms of weaving the cloth and counting the gold dominate Silas' existence. He behaves like a machine, untouched by interaction with others or any other emotion. Silas begins to awaken from this mechanical lifestyle when his gold is stolen. But change really comes when he returns one day to find a new kind of gold by his fireside, the golden hair of an orphaned girl. As he brings up this child, whom he names Eppie, Silas regains his soul, opening his heart and his home to others, reconciling the physical and spiritual dimensions of his life.

### Gospel Teaching

In today's Gospel the Pharisees set out deliberately to set a trap for Jesus by asking him if it is right to pay taxes to Caesar. But it is the Pharisees who seem to have fallen into a trap, that of attempting to divide the physical from the spiritual. If Jesus says that paying taxes to a pagan conqueror is permissible, they can denounce him as spiritually unworthy, someone who does not respect the higher authority of God. However, if Jesus says that paying taxes is not permissible, his enemies would hope that the temporal forces of the Roman occupiers would intervene and arrest Jesus for inciting revolt.

Jesus' reply to the question is more than an intellectually deft escape. It is a profound comment on the relationship between the physical and the spiritual, between the sacred and the secular. "Give… to the emperor the things that are the emperor's, and to God the things that are God's," says Jesus. He urges us to give due attention to the secular and the material and proper attention to the sacred and spiritual in their turn. He does not suggest that we attempt to divide the two and to live either entirely in the physical, or completely in the spiritual domain, like a hermit. Rather,

Jesus warns that as human beings, with bodies and souls, we cannot afford to disregard either. To do so risks either the emptiness of Silas Marner's mechanical life of weaving and counting, or, at the other extreme, death from neglect of our bodies.

The temptation to compartmentalise our lives into physical or spiritual is strong. For some people work can become a purely physical realm where they earn money and carry out their tasks without consideration of the other dimensions of their faith which might apply. They mistakenly imagine that God is not interested in this aspect of their lives, or in the mundane household business of living. Jesus reminds us that God is interested in all that we do, asking us to deal wisely and thoughtfully with the material as well as the spiritual aspects of life. God wants us to pray and worship and do good, but he also cares about how and where we spend our money and how we go about earning it.

**Application**

We need Christ's wisdom and grace if we are to escape from the trap of compartmentalising our lives into sacred and secular. When moral or ethical dilemmas interrupt the humdrum, physical compartment we call work/home we need courage not to turn a "blind eye" or to opt for a quiet life. While we are engaged in secular activities, spiritual values, those of love and justice, still apply. Our duty to God and to God's law is paramount.

Yet such spiritual values should not lead us to despise the secular, events or people. If our religious convictions lead us to shun all that is not purely spiritual, we could end up with a life as barren as that of a miser. Jesus calls us to treat the sacred and the secular with due respect, to strive to integrate them, not to separate them. We need to be ready to find the sacred in the apparently secular and to allow our spiritual values to influence our lives in the material realm.

*"Teacher, which commandment in the law is the greatest?"*
(Matthew 22:36)

**Illustration**

Since winning an Oscar for Best Director, Clint Eastwood has been in even greater demand than usual. He's been on countless chat shows and you can bet a fistful of dollars that he'll always get asked one question in particular: "Who is the greatest actor you've ever directed?" It's a mischievous question of course. If he picks out a particular actor he risks offending all the others he's worked with. Eastwood doesn't fall into that trap. Instead, he picks out great characteristics of various actors, such as Sean Penn's intensity or Robin Williams' spontaneity, and so implies that they've all been the greatest in their own way. He could have named just one actor only if he'd ever directed a legend, such as Marlon Brando, someone whom the whole industry had already agreed was the greatest.

**Gospel Teaching**

Jesus was asked a similar question by a teacher of the law in today's Gospel. Jesus is in Jerusalem, openly available. Every Jewish sect wants to debate with him, to see how much he agrees with their views, or to see if their best speakers can catch him out. Before our passage begins, Jesus was being questioned by the Sadducees. One way that Sadducees differed from Pharisees was that they gave higher scholastic recognition to the original Mosaic Law than to all the later additions and interpretations. Seeing the Sadducees silenced by Jesus, some Pharisees couldn't wait to show their rivals how easily Jesus could be wrongfooted.

They ask Jesus, "Which is the greatest commandment in the law?" If this had been asked by Sadducees, they would probably have been referring simply to the Ten Commandments, but Pharisees would include hundreds of later accretions. They were leading Jesus into a minefield. No matter which commandment he chose, by not choosing all the rest he would offend countless sects of Judaism, upset various famous rabbis and trample all over certain well-established traditional interpretations – such as the belief that, since all the commandments are divine, none can be inferior to another.

However, the Pharisees were to be as disappointed as all those who had questioned Eastwood. Jesus used the "legend" technique. There was a Brando of the law, so to speak, a commandment in Deuteronomy 6 that everyone agreed stood head and shoulders above all the others. "Love the Lord your God with all your heart, and with all your soul, and with all your strength." But when Jesus quotes it, he deliberately embellishes the famous verse, trumping the Pharisees at their own game with his own accretion. Furthermore, the fact that he adds "and with all your mind" was perhaps a criticism of the Pharisaic approach to religion, implying that the Pharisees should use their minds for loving God rather than endlessly reinterpreting the law in such minute detail.

As if that weren't enough, Jesus goes right outside the question's parameters by introducing a second commandment, the equally famous Levitican stricture to love one's neighbour as oneself. In effect Jesus forges a totally new "compound commandment" which he believes is a summary of all that was revealed in the law and the prophets. This deals a blow to Pharisaic pretensions in two ways. Firstly because their professional lives hinge on constantly prising out more abstruse legalistic revelations in scripture and here Jesus is saying this compound summary is all that's needed. Secondly because everyone knew that Jesus' definition of "neighbour" was very different from theirs. For the Israelites, their neighbours were fellow Israelites – except sinners, who were outside the pale of the law. This exclusive kind of love is instinctive in human nature. It's a way of keeping a mate, a way of holding together a family, a tribe, or a nation.

**Application**

But Jesus taught that our neighbour is anyone in need, even our enemy. The love flowing from the throne of God knows no barriers of skin colour or tribal boundary. This love burns like hot coals on the lips of those who would cage up the alien, ostracise those who are different, or condemn those of different beliefs to eternal hellfire. This love which gives rather than takes, which forgives rather than condemns, includes rather than keeps outside, is ultimately taken outside and crucified by the nails of people who fear its inclusivity. But this love is stronger than death and lives on in our souls, hearts, bodies and minds, enabling us to follow that one, great commandment.

*"Heaven and earth will pass away, but my words will not pass away."*
(Matthew 24:35)

**Illustration**
At the end of World War II downtown Warsaw was almost totally levelled. Only one skeletal structure remained on the main street, and many devout Poles regarded it like a shrine. It was the Bible Society HQ and the words carved in its only remaining wall were clearly legible from the street: "Heaven and earth will pass away, but my words will never pass away."

Mark Twain said, "It's not the parts of the Bible I don't understand that cause me trouble, but the parts that I do!"

**Gospel Teaching**
In the Sermon on the Mount, Jesus said that until heaven and earth passed away the law would remain (Matthew 5:18). In today's passage he says his own words will outlast even heaven and earth. The law will pass away with the rest of creation, but Jesus' own words will remain. It's the sort of staggering claim that makes us ask whether Jesus is mad, manipulative, or telling the truth. And if it's true, then we must fall at his feet, learn from his teaching and follow his way.

Today is Bible Sunday and I have two questions: How do Jesus' words sit within the rest of the Bible? And can we trust that our Bibles really contain his words?

How do Jesus' words sit within the whole Bible? Although he made staggering claims for his own words, Jesus held the Old Testament in the highest regard. These sacred books were Jesus' scriptures. He revered them; he lived by them; he taught from them; he regarded them as God's word. But Jesus also interpreted these scriptures. He fulfilled the prophets and reshaped the law. This doesn't mean the Old Testament is redundant – far from it – but for Christians it must be read through the lens of Christ and his teaching.

How about the New Testament? These books comprise authoritative insights on Jesus and his teaching, written by some of his earliest followers. We believe they're inspired by the Holy Spirit and, along with the rest of the Bible, seal up in a written message all we need to know about God's

will for our lives. Notice then: Jesus is the centre. The Old Testament flows to him and the New Testament flows from him. Jesus' words interpret the old and they inspire the new.

But were Jesus' words preserved and transmitted reliably? Over the last fifty years, an enormous amount of scholarly work has shown how accurately people in non-book cultures preserve precious teachings through memory and repetition. But Jesus' disciples would also have made written notes, which were also used in the writing of the Gospels.

There are those who, according to their own criteria, claim that most of what Jesus says in the Gospels can't really be trusted to have come from him. But a recent book (*Jesus and the Eyewitnesses*, Richard Bauckham, 2006) by the former Professor of New Testament in St Andrews, Scotland, argues in depth that all four Gospels are closely based on eyewitness testimony. If that's true, we have even better reason to trust the reliability of the text.

**Application**

So what happens when you read the words of Jesus trustingly? Usually they speak to our hearts and lives: we want to pray; we feel called to live by these words. And we find that, as we pray, the one we're meeting in prayer is the same person we encounter on the Bible's written page. The Holy Spirit has brought Jesus to us by inspiring the original writers and brought us to Jesus as we seek him in prayer.

Reading the whole Bible trustingly – with Jesus at the centre – praying from it, and applying it, really is essential to Christian living. It's how we come to know Jesus better, and how we allow Jesus' words to permeate our souls. As St Paul said, "Let the word of Christ dwell in you richly."

Jesus' words were remembered because his hearers were struck by a truth they could trust. They wrote down the words of today's Gospel reading because in their own generation they saw Jerusalem destroyed and realised this was the beginning of the passing of heaven and earth, just as Jesus said. The process may take longer than any of us think, but Jesus' words stand at the heart of the Bible and in the midst of a changing, crumbling cosmos. With majesty and grace they interpret both scripture and world. Read them! Pay attention to them! Let them comfort you when you're disturbed, and disturb you when you're comfortable!

*"Blessed are the poor in spirit, for theirs is the kingdom of heaven."*
(Matthew 5:3)

**Illustration**

As we look around the church, perhaps during a dull sermon, we may well look at either statues, or the stained glass windows with images of saints. They seem very removed from our lives: perhaps a definition of saints would be "people who are not like us." They are either flat, one-dimensional, or cold and unyielding as stone. In contrast, our lives are multidimensional, and pliable – but not saintly?

Is it possible to be saintly and in a mess? Surely none of the saints had the same problems with their children, or their marriage, or their relationships or their job as I do! Actually, they probably didn't have jobs – it's hard to see how saints could have the time to be saints if they had jobs. Perhaps most importantly, to be a saint you have to be dead. We can say, with conviction, saints were not, and are not, people like us!

**Gospel Teaching**

This Gospel passage is one of the most familiar of the Bible. Jesus claims authority to teach, by assuming the seated position of the teacher. In setting this collection of teaching upon "the mountain", Matthew invites the comparison of Moses, the lawgiver, with Jesus, the giver of the new law. Although clearly significant, it is not immediately clear how to interpret Jesus' teaching. It is difficult to translate the Greek word *makarioi*, which begins each of the beatitudes. It came to be used in Greek culture to mean "how fortunate", or "how lucky". Some translations offer "happy" as an appropriate English rendition – perhaps suggesting a sense of "congratulations!" However, Jesus' use should be drawn from Hebrew tradition such as Psalm 1:1, where "happy" is used to describe being "right with God" (objective) rather than being about "how I feel" (subjective) – suggesting that "blessed" may better capture the sense of the passage.

Is this objective blessing promised for the present or the future? The other passages set for this day indicate future blessing – and, in keeping with the apocalyptic genre, future resolution of today's difficulties. (Apocalyptic writing emerges from those periods of history when the social situation appears so irredeemably bad that the only resolution imaginable is an utterly invasive act of God, bringing the existing age to a drastic end.) But

is there no present benefit of faith in Christ? There is, at least, a present assurance of a future promise, to call believers to a distinct perspective upon life.

The kingdom of heaven is found in the present and future experience and reality of peace, "shalom": a right relationship with God and one another which may only be found in Christ. It is given, not earned – it is the property of the "poor in spirit", not the confident in spirit.

"Poor in spirit" is a description of the acknowledged need at the heart of our existence, rather than a description of inherent weakness. It expresses a reliance upon God, rather than a satisfaction with ourselves. The Hebrew scriptures do speak of God's blessing upon the poor and his distaste for the rich, but riches were nonetheless the assumed sign of God's blessing. Jesus vehemently reaffirmed God's preference for the poor, who turn to him for mercy and in so doing re-establish the heart of the divine kingdom which is utterly reliant upon God.

The qualities described in these beatitudes with approval challenge many of our presuppositions of the signs of God's blessing. Each one commends those who presently suffer in weakness, for their resolution will be at the hands of God.

**Application**
On All Saints' Day we need to see that we are the saints. The beatitudes describe as "blessed" the lives of those who struggle, and suffer, and know their weakness. These are not the lives of stained glass, or plaster saints, but the lives of real people learning to rely on God in their everyday successes and failures, working together for that day when God's purposes will finally be revealed.

Our hope is not that we will live our lives like some imaginary successful life lived by one or other saint from history, but that we will know ourselves accepted by God's grace as members now of his family of saints – with our membership guaranteed not by what we have done for him, but by what he has done for us.

We are challenged to live out this truth of our lives – that we are children of God – as a response to what Christ has done for us, knowing that our present experience will be one of struggle, but encouraged by the future hope of glory.

*"The love of many will grow cold. But anyone who endures to the end will be saved."*
(Matthew 24:12-13)

**Illustration**

If you've ever ridden a roller coaster you probably wondered – as the car clicked its agonising way to the top, and your palms went sweaty in anticipation of that stomach-lurching plunge – what on earth you were doing. Why do we subject ourselves to sheer terror? That we seem to find entertainment in negative emotions is a human conundrum which has puzzled philosophers for hundreds of years.

We even pay for the dubious pleasure – whether it's taking a white-knuckle roller-coaster ride, seeing a weepie, horror or sci-fi movie, or watching a Shakespearean tragedy. The Greek philosopher Aristotle was fascinated by the tragic story of Oedipus, and wanted to know why we're drawn to it. He concluded that it has a "cathartic", or purging, effect. The fact that we've been through fictionalised fear somehow releases us from the real thing.

**Gospel Teaching**

Around Halloween, the TV schedule may be full of horror movies – and today's readings from Micah and Matthew might not look out of place among them. With their apocalyptic visions they could easily fit into the horror or sci-fi shelves of your DVD store. In Matthew's Gospel, Jesus describes collapsing buildings, war, famine, earthquakes, torture, betrayal and lawlessness. It could almost be the finale of *The Lord of the Rings*. Meanwhile, the world we glimpse in Micah is a sunless place plunged into darkness – the classic horror backdrop.

The prophecies of Jesus and Micah would also have had entertainment value for their audiences, who suffered under oppressive political systems. Jesus' Jewish listeners, living under Roman rule, were desperate for the Messiah to liberate them, although they thought it would be a political deliverance in their lifetimes. Micah came from a Judaean farming community, ruled from Jerusalem, and the people in his rural corner resented their greedy, power-hungry rulers. Indeed, much of the book of Micah is a vengeful rant against them. So these visions – no matter how awful – would have given their audiences a welcome glimpse of the justice they longed for.

**Application**

All of this throws up an uncomfortable dilemma for modern Christians. What do we draw from these passages, which are in many ways firmly rooted in the politics of their age? If we think of them as having entertainment value, akin to movies of their day, what do we think about the prophecies contained within them? Are we saying they are fiction?

It's one thing for us, children of the new covenant, to gloss over the Old Testament as having only useful instructional value, but we believe that Jesus came to set the record straight, which is why we talk about the "Gospel" truth. If we decide that his apocalyptic prophecy is an allegory, or representation, are we allowing ourselves to be purged of fear when we ought to take his words literally and be more vigilant than ever? Are we ourselves among the many who, as he prophesies, will fall away and grow cold?

Though these might not be passages you have difficulty with, there will be others which test your faith. But the point is not that we have to decide here and now what is truth and fiction, or how much danger lies ahead. Just as the human attraction to the roller coaster is something we will never fully understand, many things in life remain shrouded in mystery, and we have to accept that.

But we do make a mistake if our confused response is to discount and discard the Bible passages we find hard or unsettling. For their wisdom is just as applicable today as ever. The message that leaps out from Jesus' words is that it takes more faith, courage and determination than you can imagine to get through turbulent times. To put it in the language of the fairground: fasten your seatbelts, it's going to be a very bumpy ride.

No matter how terrifying the vision, the first step towards lasting faith is not to become overwhelmed or paralysed by fear. Rather, we need to face our difficulties in belief and confront our nagging doubts. Because if we allow them to stay in our peripheral vision they become shadowy "bogeymen" and end up gnawing away at our faith.

If, on the other hand, we turn to face our doubts and fears, and do so with humble prayer, then something truly miraculous happens – God works within us, purging us of fear and bringing us with integrity to a fuller, deeper, more peaceful faith.

*"Keep awake therefore, for you know neither the day nor the hour."*
(Matthew 25:13)

**Illustration**
The family was on holiday and the children were sleeping in a strange room. "Daddy, I can't get to sleep," came the mournful cry of the five-year-old daughter.

"Well… try counting sheep in a big field, jumping over a small hedge," came the father's tired response.

The parents stood outside the child's room and listened to their daughter say quietly, "One sheep in a big field jumping over a small hedge. Two sheep in a big field…" and so on. When the child had reached ten they crept away, smiling. After a few minutes there was another cry from the child's room. "Daddy!" by now the little girl was crying. "Daddy, I can only count up to twenty-nine!"

**Gospel Teaching**
It is only with greater wisdom and careful teaching that we, any of us, learn to count beyond twenty-nine. However, there's an element in all Christians that is like the child trying to get to sleep. The foolish bridesmaids in today's Gospel reflect this attitude – they couldn't see beyond the oil in their own lamps. They hadn't thought what would happen if the oil ran out so they had seen no need to take precautions. It is easy for us with hindsight to say they were foolish not to do so, but they didn't know how long they would have to wait.

Today we are called to wait with hope for the coming of Christ, using the wisdom brought to us by the scriptures. We are encouraged to stay awake because we don't know either the day or the hour – we don't know how long we will have to wait. It could be five minutes, or it could be five thousand years. The foolish bridesmaids are an example to us in this – they had prepared, but they hadn't prepared enough. Their horizons were limited. Perhaps they expected it to be five minutes. The wise bridesmaids, on the other hand, had brought extra reserves of oil. They were open-minded in their preparations and so they were able to light the way of the bridegroom.

Christ calls each one of us to open our eyes to all that's going on around us and be ready. We can be comforted by the words from the book of Wisdom which point out that "...one who is vigilant on her account will soon be free from care". Then the letter to the Thessalonians encourages us to remain in a state of readiness because, in that way, we will surely meet the Lord: "Therefore encourage one another with these words." We may not know the day or the hour, but what we do know is that it is within our power to be always ready to meet the Lord.

**Application**

So, how do we prepare to meet the Lord; how do we make ourselves ready? Unfortunately it isn't enough just to recite a quick prayer of repentance every night before we fall to sleep. We are called to respond with our whole lives. All of our actions can reflect a state of readiness. Every action, from driving carefully through a built-up area to reconciling differences between family and friends, needs to demonstrate our state of readiness.

Are there relationships in our lives that are in need of healing? Are there things we need to say to people that we keep putting off? We must not be fooled into thinking we have all the time in the world to sort our lives out – the message of today's Gospel is clear: we do not know how long we have got. It could be that Christ will come again today, or it could be that we will meet our own death. It is not morbid to be prepared for death; it is a sensible and faithful thing to do, because, whatever we think about it, we cannot avoid the fact that we are all going to die.

Are we like the wise bridesmaids – open-minded and fully prepared? Or like the foolish bridesmaids – with pockets of our lives untouched by the Gospel message; not prepared enough? If we are fully prepared then that extra effort in our communities, like the extra flask of oil, will transform our world – brightening all that is around us. Let us encourage one another to be so prepared and to strive to live lives of love and peace with everyone.

*"For to all those who have, more will be given."*
(Matthew 25:29)

**Illustration**

"No gain without pain" is virtually a mantra for those exercising to keep fit or lose weight – watching workout videos, following fitness regimes, jogging. We quickly become aware that the experience is not a comfortable one. We know that we have to expend effort to see results and this is the rock upon which so many of our good intentions founder. "No gain without pain" is a contemporary way of expressing a long-established tradition – the way we now describe "self-discipline", "willpower" and "application". To achieve certain objectives we have to make demands on ourselves and on others. As long as these demands are not excessive they can challenge and stretch us, allowing us to achieve even more than we might have dreamed possible.

"No gain without pain" does not mean that anything which happens more easily has no value. It is rather an observation on human life. Many of the worthwhile things in life have to be sought, worked for and repeatedly attempted. They do not happen of their own accord. It is not an absolute truth, however. "Grace" describes those things we receive as gifts, which we have not earned or deserved. The parable of the talents is clearly about responding creatively to a challenge, from God or other people, and acting responsibly.

**Gospel Teaching**

It sounds very much as though the man who was on his way abroad had a fair idea about the abilities of his servants. He entrusted the most to the servant who, eventually, was able to provide the greatest return. But the challenge was clear: to be a wise steward of the master's wealth. The master, although keen to increase his fortune, was also encouraging his servants to act responsibly and to use their initiative. As he made demands upon them, he expected them to act wisely and well. The first two are both commended, although one achieved, apparently, more than the other. The point is that they both did their best.The third servant failed in his duty because he refused to make any effort, even the most minimal of putting the money in the bank. There could be no gain, because he would risk no pain.

However, this parable is not simply about using wisely what we have been given. It is about our expectations of one another. The master could have simply banked his money himself, but that would have missed the point. If he had had no expectations of his servants, they would not have been challenged to grow in creativity and responsibility. It was important that the master did not set his sights too low, being satisfied with inactive and immature servants.

This theme has echoes in the second reading, where Paul is urging the Christians of Thessalonica to be prepared for the sudden arrival of the Day of the Lord. If they are to be ready, they must be awake and clear-headed. They cannot risk being caught off guard. Once again, there is no gain without pain. They must be alert while others sleep. But the hardship is not an end in itself; eventually it is for the well-being of those to whom the message is directed – including ourselves.

**Application**

If we expect little of our fellow human beings, we will seldom be able to see beyond our own poor expectations. If we regard others highly, seeing them as capable of greatness, we give them room to blossom and to grow. Our demands are to be for their good, however, and not simply highlight their failure in order to boost ourselves by comparison. Where we have the genuine interest of others at heart, we do well to expect much, accepting their limitations, but always encouraging growth. Exercising this creative authority is not just for managers and bosses: it is for each and every person to act responsibly with respect for their own life and the lives of others. In doing so we continue to grow into the people God created us to be.

When attempting something worthwhile for the Lord, we may find the going exceptionally tough, but this reminds us of what we will put up with for something we deeply desire. If we cannot put up with even minor hardship, it is clear that we do not want badly enough to achieve our aim. The Gospel of Christ makes demands on us. Not to satisfy an infinitely demanding God, but to challenge us to grow – to grow more like God. And that is worth some pain.

*"Then the king will say to those at his right hand, 'Come, you that are blessed by my Father, inherit the kingdom prepared for you.'"*
(Matthew 25:34)

**Illustration**
In recent years, stories about the few remaining royal families have made headlines in the newspapers. The British royal family has been under scrutiny in most countries in the world as people follow their fortunes. What emerges is that there still exist very high ideals for members of a royal family, and at the same time there is a very critical attitude towards their human weaknesses.

Today we are celebrating the feast of Christ the King. Jesus was a man who was both respected and despised. At times, it was almost impossible to see any trace of majesty in him; but even so, he was a king. He is Lord of the universe. And we are his brothers and sisters. It is important to realise that, as brothers or sisters of the king, we are also members of the royal family. So we are not only members of God's kingdom; we are royalty.

**Gospel Teaching**
Through our baptism we have become full members of the Lord's family and therefore we are truly royal people. This means of course that each one of us is due respect. Every human person deserves respect – none of us is worthless. If we were, then God would never have bothered to become one of us, and to suffer and die to save us. When we realise quite how much God cares about us, and quite how much he loves us, then we realise quite how much we are worth. The dignity of our birth as human beings has now been enhanced by our membership of the kingdom. It means that we have a role to play in the world, and it follows that we must respect the nobility of our own calling. We are to cultivate a profound respect for ourselves and for those other members of the kingdom who have been called by God to be his chosen sons and daughters.

However, we are all human. Just look at the royal families which still exist in our age. They fail, their weaknesses often emerge, at times they cannot live up to the ideals expected by those around them. Like them, we are also broken and needy people. Those around us are the same. Being part of the kingdom of God means respecting also the brokenness of others. It means

being with them in their weakness, even recognising their sovereignty in the midst of much confusion and pain. Think of the good thief hanging beside Jesus on the cross. There was not any grandeur in our Lord. Nor must he have resembled a king. Yet somehow, perhaps intuitively, the good thief recognised it. He honoured Jesus. He asked to be a member of his kingdom. And in return he was promised membership of the royal family of the Lord.

To be a Christian is to be a member of that family. That is why today's Gospel reminds us that we must care for the sick, visit the imprisoned, feed the hungry and welcome the stranger. It is the right of every member of the kingdom to have this dignity and this respect. It is also the duty of every baptised person to be truly royal: to look after those members of the family who are in difficulty, and to do all in our power to see that equality and fairness are alive in God's kingdom here on earth.

**Application**

Christ the King is in heaven at the right hand of the Father. But you and I, the members of this royal family, are here among his people. Today's feast challenges us to live out our royal responsibilities and duties as completely as we can. For the kingdom of God is not only about caring for those within it. It is about loving and seeking out those who are outside it. The passage from Ezekiel talks of God as a good shepherd searching out his sheep from all the places where they have been scattered. He seeks the lost, binds up those who are injured, and strengthens the weak. That is part of our role, too, as members of God's kingdom. But we do not have to do this alone – we do it with our King, our God.

Let us today celebrate Christ our King with great joy, and let us celebrate also the fact that we too are royal members of his kingdom.

# Sundays in Ordinary Time Year B

*"Is it lawful to do good or to do harm on the sabbath, to save life or to kill?"*
(Mark 3:4)

**Illustration**
In Jane Austen's novel *Pride and Prejudice*, the arrogant hero, Mr Darcy, judges that his friend is about to get entangled in an unsuitable relationship, and he takes steps to separate the couple.

We, the readers, know that he is wrong to do so. We know that Jane is the perfect match for Darcy's friend, Bingley, and that Darcy is causing genuine suffering to both Jane and Bingley by using his influence with his friend so improperly. Darcy himself realises this as he finds himself falling similarly inappropriately in love. He discovers that a relationship that looks unsuitable may actually be life-giving. But at the time when he was working to keep Bingley and Jane apart, Darcy was genuinely convinced that he was doing the right thing, and that it was his duty and his right to make such judgements on behalf of his friend.

**Gospel Teaching**
In today's Gospel passage, as in *Pride and Prejudice*, we the readers know who is right and who is wrong. The Pharisees may believe that they are doing what is right and defending the law, but we know that Jesus is going to the heart of the law, because he is the one who truly knows the mind of God, the lawgiver. When the Pharisees go off to plot with the Herodians at the end of today's reading, we have the luxury of seeing them as stereotyped villains, and we don't need to think about them any further.

But that lazy reading of the text creates problems. For one thing, it feeds into the terrible and shameful history of anti-Semitism, and Christian assumption of superiority. And that prevents us, the Christian readers, from hearing the true challenge of Jesus. We read this as a dispute between "them" and "us", or as something that is safely in the past, reading only with the eyes of hindsight, and with no attempt to imagine ourselves into the context.

But if we hear the story more carefully, it is much more complicated than that. Notice, for example, that the Pharisees do not dispute Jesus' reading of the law. This kind of conversation about exactly how to apply the law in different situations was very common: all rabbis did it. It was accepted that the sabbath laws could be relaxed for humane purposes. That is not the issue.

Notice, too, that Jesus is not rejecting the law. He never did. He remained a faithful, practising Jew to the end of his life. So that is not the issue, either.

So what is going on? The whole plot-line of this story seems to have come unravelled, and we are left not knowing what to think. And that is exactly where Jesus' first audience was, and exactly what Mark wants us to feel. His whole Gospel has, as its central theme, this question: who is Jesus? Mark's Gospel refuses to answer that question directly, unlike John's, for example. John tells us right at the beginning exactly who Jesus is. But in Mark's Gospel, anyone who approaches a definition of Jesus is told to keep quiet about it.

This is Mark's famous "messianic secret", and scholars have debated endlessly about the motive for this narrative device. But one thing it clearly achieves is the unsettling of us, the readers. We, too, have to ask: "Who is Jesus?" Over and over again, we see him healing, teaching, forgiving sins, claiming the right to reinterpret the law, and we use the benefit of our hindsight to say who Jesus is. And then Mark tells us that that is not enough. Knowing who Jesus is is not abstract knowledge. It isn't fiction. It's a way of life.

**Application**

Mark's Gospel wants to make disciples. It doesn't want us to stand on the sidelines and weigh up who has scored the most points. It wants us to follow Jesus. It wants us to feed and be fed, to heal and be healed, to forgive and be forgiven; to care for the poor and for the children. It wants us to live as children of our heavenly Father, in every moment and every detail of our lives, not reserving any areas where God is not king.

That is a challenge that few of us are ready to hear, and that is why today's Gospel reading is not aimed at some abstract "them", but very directly at "us".

*"He has Beelzebul, and by the ruler of the demons he casts out demons."*
(Mark 3:22)

**Illustration**

During a war, a plane transporting a group of boys out of danger crashes on an isolated island. With no adult survivors, the boys have to fend for themselves. Initially, they pull together and are resourceful, cooperative and democratic. They elect one of their number as their leader, and agree that their priorities are to have fun and attract attention. They light a fire using a pair of glasses, and take turns to keep it going. They then set about building shelters, finding water and gathering food. For a while it appears idyllic. But before long differences emerge, and a rival group – the "hunters" – is formed, led by the choirboy Jack. Fear and superstition soon start to take a grip on the boys, and some of the "littluns" become afraid of a "beast" that they imagine is lurking on the island. When they find what they suppose to be the beast, their terror intensifies, and any semblance of order quickly deteriorates, with shocking results.

At the heart of William Golding's novel *Lord of the Flies* is the premise that, if you scratch beneath the surface of man-made culture, it's not long before "civilisation" breaks down, and people regress to a primitive state of savagery.

**Gospel Teaching**

Today's Gospel reading comes early in Jesus' ministry, and it's worth setting it in context. So far in Mark's Gospel Jesus has been in a whirlwind of preaching and miracles. He has driven out unclean spirits, "convulsing and crying". He's cured Simon's mother-in-law, cleansed a leper, healed a paralysed man and a man with a withered hand. And his magnetism and charisma are as astonishing as his miracles. Huge crowds have been gathering around him and, at his command, people are leaving everything to follow him, including the fishermen Simon and Andrew, and the tax collector Levi.

There's a palpable sense of excitement, bewilderment and fear in the first three chapters of Mark. For some people it's an opportunity to seek healing, while for others, particularly the Jewish "establishment", it's very alarming. Jesus has started to meet the authorities head-on, challenging their entrenched ideas about the sabbath. By the time we catch up with him in today's reading, the beleaguered scribes have started a whispering campaign, saying: "He has Beelzebul." Beelzebul, by the way, means "Lord of the Flies".

**Application**

Often when we read the Gospels, we characterise the authorities' attitude towards Jesus as a simple power struggle. And it's true that, through heavy-handed application of the laws and petty bureaucracy, the scribes and Pharisees carved for themselves a cosy little niche, which brought them a sense of moral superiority and financial benefits.

But there's much more to it, because Jesus represents a threat on many levels. He is becoming dangerously associated with the underclass, with madness – and with convulsing, crying demons. It's terrifying stuff. And if we'd been there in the crowd, no doubt we'd have felt it too. It's that strange combination of attraction and terror that compels us to stare at a car accident, or gawp at the sight of a celebrity in "meltdown". Because Jesus is, in fact, consorting with chaos, and scratching the surface of anarchy that lies beneath civilisation. And there's something at once irresistible – and very, very frightening – about it.

So not only are the scribes afraid of having the power balance disrupted; they're also downright terrified of the turmoil that Jesus is unleashing. You can bet some of them had nightmares. And they do what many of us do – they batten down the hatches and go into defensive mode. So desperate are they to hang on to this "civilisation" which they've created around them, that their response is to become even more controlling and authoritarian.

In William Golding's novel, the "beast" turns out to be the corpse of an airman – in other words, something human. And nowadays we tend to interpret demons in the Bible as inner demons – the dark side of human nature. Because when we're up against it, we all have within us the capacity for chaos.

It's telling that, in *Lord of the Flies*, it's the formerly angelic chorister, Jack, who descends furthest into savagery – perhaps because he, like the Jewish authorities, has furthest to fall. That's not to say that we should become anarchists, but that we do well to acknowledge our own capacity for chaos. So spare a thought for the tight-lipped authorities, battling with terror in the face of demons – both external, and internal.

*"With what can we compare the kingdom of God?"*
(Mark 4:30)

**Illustration**

There's a traditional rhyme which begins, "For the want of a nail the shoe was lost, for the want of the shoe the horse was lost..." The rhyme goes on to tell how the kingdom was lost because of the lack of that horse in the army that would have made all the difference in the crucial battle. One nail missing, and a kingdom is overthrown. The poem expresses the same conventional wisdom as the saying, "Take care of the pennies and the pounds will take care of themselves." These sayings warn people not to look only at the big issues, but to keep an eye on the small things of life.

**Gospel Teaching**

Jesus too recommends that we look carefully at the small things of life, but for a different reason. For Jesus, paying attention to small things is not a way to keep a grip of our money, or to make sure that we win wars. Rather it is because it is in the little things that we can see God's kingdom.

The kingdom of God starts very small. That is the essence of the two parables Jesus tells in today's Gospel reading. The kingdom is like seed scattered on the ground which is tiny to start with, and appears to do nothing at first. But eventually, if the farmer is patient, it grows into a substantial harvest. Or the kingdom is like an acorn, which disappears into the ground but, given time and patience, grows into a huge tree.

These are familiar parables, so familiar that perhaps we forget the shock with which they might have been greeted by Jesus' first listeners. Jesus is talking about the kingdom of God, the rule of God. What would we expect the rule of God to look like? Where would we look for it? In our time we are not used to being ruled by an absolute monarch, but the people of Jesus' day were. Their king was Caesar, the Roman emperor, ruling from distant Rome through his governors, with efficient authority. Caesar was the equivalent of a god, and indeed at some times was worshipped as a god. His power was absolute, and obedience was demanded. His presence was attended by much pomp and ceremony. He lived in luxurious palaces, and enjoyed rich food and fine wine from gold vessels. The people of Jesus' day knew what a kingdom looked like. It was big and grand and powerful.

And if that was true of an earthly kingdom, how much more true would it be of the kingdom of God? When the ruler of the universe came to reign on earth, how grand and terrible his reign would be. He would be heralded by a multitude of angels, accompanied by flames of fire and crashes of thunder. The earth and sky would shake, and God would appear on the clouds, too splendid to look at.

So Jesus' parables of the kingdom come as something of a surprise. The kingdom about which Jesus speaks is altogether quieter, and smaller. It sneaks up on you like a thief in the night; it lies dormant in the ground waiting to produce a tiny sprout; it hides in ordinary working folk, farmers, shepherds, fishermen, housewives, as they go about their everyday business. God's reign is present everywhere, hidden, tiny, ordinary. It doesn't arrive with thunder and lightning for all to see. If you want to find it you have to look, very carefully and very closely, at little things.

**Application**

We live in a world that is fixated on size and success. Businesses have targets for growth. The growth of the national economy is carefully encouraged. Much of our world is ruled by huge multinational conglomerates. Churches are anxious about declining attendances. In the midst of this, Jesus' words encourage us to look for God at work in the little things: small acts of love and generosity that grow into warmth and community; the everyday kindnesses of people who serve others. Small groups of faithful people whose prayers spread over their neighbourhood. Sunshine and rainbows, buttercups and sparrows, small signs of God's creative will.

It takes commitment and patience to see in these things signs of God's reign. But it matters that we do. God's kingdom will come, Jesus said, but it is also already here. It is the task of his people to look for the signs, and to nurture them, until the whole world sees God's glory and God's love.

## *"Teacher, do you not care that we are perishing?"*

(Mark 4:38)

**Illustration**

For a time in the late 1970s, the daily news programmes on British television showed images of streets which were not cleaned, rubbish which was not collected, trains and buses which did not run. There seemed to be trouble everywhere. Everybody seemed to be on strike, even the dead were not being buried. The period was described as the "Winter of Discontent". The then Prime Minister, James Callaghan, returning from a trip abroad, was met at the airport by dozens of journalists who asked him one simple question: "What are you going to do about the crisis?"

Trying to play down the situation, the Prime Minister reportedly responded: "Crisis? What crisis?" This underestimation of the gravity of the situation very soon afterwards cost Mr Callaghan his job.

**Gospel Teaching**

In today's Gospel we hear the lovely story of the storm at sea. It had been Jesus' suggestion to take the boat across that evening. He then seems totally unconcerned when the gale gets up, and he remains fast asleep on the cushion. The first few chapters of Mark's Gospel show the whirlwind of activity that Jesus has been living in, with crowds following him everywhere. So are we perhaps meant to think that he is just tired out? Too tired to notice the storm?

At first sight it looks as though Jesus, like the politician, has a similarly cavalier and almost irresponsible attitude to the danger he and the disciples face. While the disciples struggle to save their very lives, Jesus sleeps, either unaware or unconcerned at the situation. The disciples, not surprisingly, are singularly unimpressed and ask: "Teacher, do you not care that we are perishing?" However, there is a big difference between the kind of complacency and indifference which we can often exhibit in the face of other people's suffering and Jesus' attitude here.

Jesus' apparent lack of concern comes not from indifference, or even from weariness, but from an absolute trust and confidence in the power of God to save. Such was his intimacy with God that he never once doubted his Father's love for him. This is the faith which the disciples lacked – a real, deep and personal knowledge and experience of God's total, unconditional love for them. It was this love which Christ himself came to manifest, to make present to his disciples. And Christ is the one who makes this saving relationship with God a real possibility for us, his present-day disciples.

**Application**

As a Church and as individuals, we face many storms; many things seem to threaten to overwhelm us. As a Church, we face problems over the falling numbers in our parishes, the lack of people committing themselves to the ministry, the lack of consensus on many moral and doctrinal issues, even a lack of confidence in the Church's relevance in the modern world. As individuals, we can feel swamped by depression, anger, hurts, resentments, failed relationships, jealousy, powerlessness and a sense of hopelessness. We can each add to this list.

The message of today's Gospel is not that we should meet these problems with a naive complacency or indifference. Only a lack of love could do this. Rather, as Christians, we are called to develop such a deep and intimate relationship with God that we are never truly threatened by any outside force or interior emotion. Our faith – our total trust in the power of God to save – is all that we need.

This does not insulate us against pain and loss: the cross is a reality in every Christian's life. However, as St Paul says, it is the love of Christ which overwhelms us, and only that. Once we belong to him, nothing can come between us and the love of God. Nothing else can touch us, because we are a new creation – not immune to the sufferings of this world (our own or other people's) – but secure in the knowledge that we have as our Father a God who is able to calm every evil which threatens to destroy us.

We would do well to consider what things we are afraid of and ask God, present among us, to take control of them. He will reassure us with his presence – he may even ask why our faith is frail. But most of all we can pray to gain a deeper knowledge and experience of God's love for us personally. And we can be a support to others who themselves feel threatened by some crisis and need the presence of a strengthening faith.

*"If I but touch his clothes, I will be made well."*
(Mark 5:28)

**Illustration**

Over recent years, the Church's ministry of healing has undergone a massive renewal. It has been present from the earliest times as an essential part of the pastoral ministry. Now it has been rediscovered. It receives great emphasis, and is widely practised. It is difficult to know precisely what the results are. Some spectacular claims have been made, supported by what appears to be anecdotal evidence. On the other hand, there have been disappointments, and some occasions reported when healing sessions have gone tragically wrong.

So we need to be cautious in our choice of words. Healing is not a word used in medical circles, at least not in the active sense of bringing about a beneficial change in someone's condition. Healing is something that happens from within, for example, when a wound heals. Probably no doctor would claim to have healed anyone, not, at least, in the biblical use of the word. The most a doctor would claim is to have prescribed a course of treatment which led to the patient being cured.

**Gospel Teaching**

So, as we read that Jesus actually healed people, we need to consider what it was he was doing. On some occasions his ministry seems to have been confined to curing people of their illness, for example, leprosy or epilepsy. On others, he appears to have been confronting something more deep-seated within them. He had the ability to penetrate beyond the presenting symptoms of the illness and perceive personal, spiritual and emotional malaise.

We see examples of this in today's Gospel. The crowd formed round Jesus as he responded to Jairus' request to visit and heal his daughter. In the midst of all the hustle and bustle, the woman who was suffering from chronic bleeding approached him. "If I but touch his clothes, I will be made well." Immediately, she was aware that "she was healed of her disease" and, equally, Jesus was "aware that power had gone forth from him". He challenged the crowd, "Who touched me?" and the woman "came in fear and trembling and… told him the whole truth". The moment was cathartic for her. She felt cleansed and relieved that she had been able to confront the truth about herself. She was healed not only physically, but emotionally and spiritually within herself as well.

The healing of Jairus' daughter carries much less medical detail, about either the cause of the illness, or what Jesus actually did. We only know that he took her by the hand, and told her to get up. We have no clue as to whether this brought about an inner as well as an outer healing. The really significant change seems to have occurred amongst the bystanders. Their jeers and laughter when Jesus first appeared turned to amazement when the child got up and walked. Whatever happened to her, it was those around her who were healed.

So today's Gospel gives an example of healing in the person cured, and an example of a cure with others being healed. For a third alternative, we need to look, not at the Gospels, but at people facing illness amongst us today, whether at home or in hospital. Probably most of us can think of someone who is not going to get better, for whom nothing more can be done. From a medical point of view, no further treatment is available, a cure is out of the question. Yet such a person can be, and often is, a source of hope and inspiration to their friends, family and carers. Facing death, they know resurrection. Embracing death, they are healed.



**Application**
One final thought. The words healing and wholeness stem from the same word in Old English, and are closely related. None of us is whole. None of us is what we could be, or should be, or, indeed, want to be, on our better days. All of us suffer from dis-ease. All of us are in need of healing. When we have the courage to see ourselves as we are, to acknowledge our shortcomings, and our need of forgiveness and acceptance, we open ourselves to the healing touch of Christ. "If I but touch his clothes, I will be made well." Jesus replied, "Your faith has made you well; go in peace and be healed of your disease."

*"So they went out and proclaimed that all should repent."*
(Mark 6:12)

**Illustration**
When it comes to sport, the home team is agreed to have the upper hand in any match. There will be more locals in the crowd, willing them on, cheering their attacks, celebrating every point scored and commiserating with their misfortunes. Travelling to another team's ground may prove to be a rather less comfortable experience, for there the crowd will probably be indifferent, at best, to the players' efforts, while at home the majority are right behind them. It's a different matter when the name of the game is "imparting a message". Instead of cheering on one of their own, the crowd may well turn on them.

**Gospel Teaching**
This is precisely the situation in which Jesus found himself. The problem was, he could not deliver only messages the crowd wanted to hear – it was as though he was scoring goals for the other side. No matter if his genius was still obvious in the manoeuvres he executed, what he was doing was not what the many desired or expected – their minds were narrowed by habit and prejudice. For this reason Jesus achieved little in the way of miraculous works on home territory: the conditions were simply not favourable. His fellow townspeople were too affronted by his presumptuousness to be receptive to any works of power he might perform in their community. The problem with prophets, which you never find in sporting heroes, was that they would insist on challenging the audience; the crowd's response was more important than the action.

Voicing a familiar proverb, Jesus notes the impossibility of being an honoured prophet among one's own people, and, consequently, he adopts a different strategy in commissioning the disciples for their prophetic and pastoral ministry. He sends them out, to places where they are literally and metaphorically unencumbered by baggage, although not entirely alone. The reaction of the hearers elsewhere should be less prejudiced by familiarity – the disciples will play on a "level field". The message itself is all-important, and the Lord wants it to be plain, undisguised by the livery or identity of its presenters.

**Application**
As we think about this story, should we perhaps consider where we are when the Lord's message is spoken to us? Are we at the "home" or "away" ground? Too often we tend to become the insiders, the partisan crowd. Many of us have grown up with Jesus and he – and his disciples – have almost become "ours": the domesticated home team. They are at our disposal, their job is to please us and not challenge us, their targets should be the "outsiders" rather than us. The more we hear the words of scripture, the more we become comfortable with what they say: we practically know Jesus too well. So we must try to be foreigners in our listening, to hear the Gospel as if it were new every time.

Initiating a response in their audience was what the disciples, John the Baptist and the Old Testament prophets had in common with Jesus. Their vital proclamation was enhanced by plainness and strangeness, it was not the crowd-pleasing of the home team, but a stark wake-up call from somewhere else. Yet it is not only a change of heart which is required of those who hear the Gospel. For we are less obviously challenged in turn to bear the message ourselves, like the disciples, without baggage or additional protection: we too must carry the kingdom abroad.

You may be thinking that you couldn't possibly be a prophet, standing up and speaking out; or the kind of travelling preachers or healers that the apostles were, let alone another John crying in the wilderness, a Paul or even an Ezekiel, but you can. For there are two fundamental elements which are essential to Christian discipleship: how you pray and how you live.

Through diligent prayer you may become attuned to the words and ways of God. Then perhaps you may adopt values and behaviour somewhat different from those of your immediate neighbours. Thus your whole life can become part of God's message and you will find that you make a difference simply by being "on the pitch", both home and away, without ever resorting to your soapbox! Essentially re-evaluating your life in the alien light of Jesus' teaching, and changing your ways accordingly, amounts to "repentance" and, by thoughtful living, you will be proclaiming his teaching to others.

*"Herod feared John, knowing that he was a righteous and holy man... When he heard him, he was greatly perplexed."*
(Mark 6:20)

**Illustration**

Imagine you are in the supermarket, doing your weekly shop on a busy Saturday morning. As you reach second place in the queue, the unremarkable person in front of you starts ripping the packaging off all the things in their trolley and throwing it in a heap on the floor. As they begin loading their undressed purchases onto the conveyor belt, they also start to proclaim loudly the dreadful wastefulness of our society. "All these plastic containers are made with oil we cannot spare; they will pollute the ground for centuries; and all this time God's precious children are lost and starving. I want the food, but not the packaging; you are killing our planet and all you care about is making money, no matter who gets hurt."

It's not just embarrassing and disruptive; it makes you uncomfortable. Your trolley suddenly seems full of packaging, too. You look anxiously for another checkout; you try to stand apart from the rumpus. Then the manager appears, and the security staff; they manhandle the miscreant out of the way and try to clear up the mess.

**Gospel Teaching**

Herod may have had similar feelings about John the Baptist. He was torn between the position of the supermarket manager and the discomfited fellow-shopper. In a position of authority he could not allow John to damage his reputation. He has vested interests in the way that things are, whether he thinks John is right or not. Then again, despite his sneaking suspicion that John may have God on his side, he realises that his own behaviour cannot escape John's criticism. He personally has too much to lose from sparing the Baptiser. He has the power to silence John's protests and lets himself be forced into doing so by someone who is more resentful and less scrupulous.

Mark, by careful ordering of his material, hints that the same fate awaits Jesus, who has still greater authority than John, the prophet who has prepared his way. The people are too stubborn and self-willed to listen to the voice of God. They are too preoccupied with worldly matters and self-interest to repent. Changing their mind about past and present behaviour would be humiliating – there is simply too much to lose. So the uncomfortable disturbances must be silenced.

**Application**

The prophets who revealed God's insight into contemporary behaviour were members of a long tradition in ancient Israel. They were rarely welcomed, not only because their behaviour was often bizarre, but because people did not want to hear the truth. Yet with the benefit of hindsight their message was better understood, their divine inspiration perceived and their words respected.

As Christians we are called both to heed the voice of the prophets and to be like them – speaking out for God. It is not a prospect we relish because it may make us stand out in ways we will find uncomfortable. Influenced by our liberal, rights-orientated times, perhaps we are more prepared to tolerate what is clearly unacceptable. But, like the uncomfortable shopper, we sometimes recognise underlying issues and know we should not remain silent.

Yet we are not alone in our calling: being a Christian is not so much about lone voices crying in the wilderness, as being a God-centred community. We can choose to live according to different values from the rest of the world. To do this we must be self-aware and honest about our own behaviour. We must pray: always seeking the guidance of the Holy Spirit when faced with moral dilemmas. We must use well the rich resources of scripture, tradition and reason. We must think carefully about the issues which face humanity and we must do our best to agree on ways to respond. We should be prepared to change our minds and our behaviour, and not afraid of ridicule or criticism.

It seems far simpler to keep well away from people who make a scene, however much we secretly admire their motives. Yet apathy and inaction may have been just as crucial in bringing John and Jesus to their deaths as aggression and fear. If we do not have the "gift of prophecy" ourselves – the insight and ability to communicate – perhaps, as Christ's body on earth, we should associate ourselves with those who do. For only with our active participation can the kingdom of God be realised.

*"He had compassion for them, because they were like sheep without a shepherd."*
(Mark 6:34)



**Illustration**

This is the age of the expert. And television has been responsible for a whole new breed of them: the armchair expert. Whether it is the couch potato who can see exactly where the professional footballer is going wrong, or the viewer who criticises the TV chef's technique, we probably all know an armchair expert. Armchair experts are very good on the theory, but never put it into practice. They remain in front of the television set, pontificating, while the real expert gets on with the job.

A similar phenomenon occurs in churches, if people confine their Christianity to Sunday worship. How many of us are guilty, from time to time, of joining together in the familiar words of creeds or hymns, but not taking that message out into the rest of the week and the rest of the world? And we all know people who can quote scripture, but seem to have missed the practical application of it. Sunday Christians are pew experts and, like armchair experts, rarely practise what they preach.

**Gospel Teaching**

Today's Gospel reading illustrates that Christianity demands practice as well as theory. The apostles, returning from their mission, report "all that they had done and taught". Their mission of teaching and healing mirrors that of Jesus himself. Here Jesus teaches the crowd many things and heals their sick friends and relatives. In the verses omitted from today's reading, Jesus feeds the five thousand: another very practical outworking of his compassion for "sheep without a shepherd".

The image of Jesus as Good Shepherd, occurring throughout the New Testament, continues an Old Testament theme depicting God in these terms. Just as Jesus entrusts this task to his followers, to share in his own role as shepherd of the people, so in the Old Testament the leaders of Israel are described as shepherds. It is no accident that both Moses and David actually were shepherds.

An armchair shepherd is of no use to the sheep; shepherds need to be with their sheep, to protect them from harm and lead them in the right direction. Biblical images of shepherds leading their flock contrast with the modern British image of walking behind them with a border collie, but in biblical times a shepherd needed to go first into dangerous situations. Instead of our own rural idyll of green pastures and rolling hills, biblical shepherds were faced with craggy outcrops and ravening wolves. Today's shepherds in Britain return to a warm bed each night; biblical shepherds slept with their flocks, ready to act if danger threatened.

Jesus, God with us, lived with his flock. He did not preach the kingdom of God during the day and retreat to a heavenly palace at night. He did not set up a permanent pulpit in temple or synagogue, or restrict his teaching ministry to the sabbath, but combined his teaching with practical demonstration of it, out in the everyday world. Like a good shepherd he was prepared to risk his life for his sheep, and in the Eucharist especially we recall how he sacrificed himself to save us from the sin that preys on us. Jesus practised what he preached, and he sent his followers to do likewise.



**Application**
Like the first disciples, we are sent to continue Jesus' mission in the world: a mission that involves theory and practice, faith and works, evangelism and pastoral care. These elements of Christianity must not be separated if we are to remain faithful to the example Jesus himself set us. The very word "pastoral" comes from the word for a shepherd, and it is often used to distinguish practical Christian ministry, the service of others, from what is seen as a higher calling: evangelism. If we remember that the Good Shepherd himself combined teaching and doing, we will not fall into that trap.

We can carry our faith out into the world, in ways that are best suited to our own gifts and situations. Some are ambitious community projects, others are much simpler: visiting, helping and praying for others. Whatever form it takes, practical support of others, when carried out in the name of Jesus Christ, is effective evangelism. Sunday Christianity, unaccompanied by compassion in action, is no better than the ranting of the armchair expert.

*"He looked up and saw a large crowd coming towards him."*
(John 6:5)

**Illustration**

Towards the end of the film of *The Railway Children*, from the book written in 1906, by Edith Nesbit, the young people hurry through the countryside to the railway station, wondering at some momentous event which they suspect is in the offing. When the train comes to a standstill, through the steam issuing from the engine, they see a figure standing alone. Roberta, the eldest child, can hardly believe her eyes. After all this long time without him… there he is… she hurls herself along the platform shouting, "Daddy…!" All her dreams had come to fruition, her faith rewarded, all her anxieties could be put aside. There he was, at last, her Daddy. No more need to worry about him and his fate, and their family's future. They would be together again. Her mother would no longer be lonely, the little children no longer lost without him and Roberta herself would feel secure. Daddy would make their lives complete, he would ensure that they never went hungry again and fill the empty space that his absence had created in their hearts and in their lives. In spite of his long absence, he had not forgotten them.

**Gospel Teaching**

The people of Israel longed for the Messiah to come, but expected only prophets, because they were all that God had sent to them so far. But how could the Messiah come when the Romans inhabited the land God had given them? Elisha had provided for God's people through miraculous actions. Numerous other prophets had drawn the people back to God when other diversions had arisen and they had taken other paths, mostly leading to conflict and pain. In this period of cruel occupation people had run to John the Baptist for reassurance and evidence that God had not forgotten his people, but then John was killed.

To whom could they turn, but to the man who seemed so much more than just another prophet? Here was one who could rescue the diseased from their ailments, who offered reassurance of God's love for them and security to those rejected by the religious authorities as unfit for Temple worship. And Jesus fed them. He fed their minds with the truth, fed their hearts with the compassion he preached and lived, and fed their bodies with nourishment created by a miracle.

They ran to this man expecting a prophet as of old but, because they were prepared to believe, they received the gifts which only God could give them. This was the God whom Jesus referred to as his Father, and who then proved through Jesus that he was indeed the Father of all. Later, with his friends, Jesus would also demonstrate his power over the elements of water, time and space, but the crowd would not be present then. But for the time being they had received what they needed: the reassurance that, in spite of all that had gone before and the present burden of foreign invasion, God had not forgotten them. Their continuing faith had brought this man to them and his availability to them in their dire need was their proof.

**Application**

Where do we find our comfort, our reassurance, in these days of increasing secularism and continuing conflict? We now know more about God than the crowds fed by Jesus because our knowledge is filtered through the wonder of the resurrection. We know what God is really like because Jesus told us and showed the extent of God's love for us in all of his actions. Jesus told us to call his Father "Abba", which means "Daddy". No longer is God to be the stern and authoritarian patriarch of the ancient times, one who filled the world with awe and anxiety. God became the Father upon whose knee the insecure might find comfort, the weary would find rest and the hungry would be fed from his hand. While remaining the Lord of all creation, in majesty and power, God demonstrated a loving parenthood more encompassing than anything we could even imagine, bending to earth to nurture the little and the lost and give hope to all who turn their faces heavenwards.

Since Jesus, we are no longer alone. Our strength comes not only from bread, hope and guesswork. We have seen the face of God, and the actions of the Almighty, in the person of Jesus. To know him is to know the extent of God, to have the totality of God and the kingdom of heaven among us.

*"Whoever comes to me will never be hungry, and whoever believes in me will never be thirsty."*
(John 6:35)

**Illustration**

For years Maura had been trying to educate her children in the skills of housekeeping such as cleaning, shopping, washing, ironing and cooking. One of the boys, Michael, who could turn his hand to most tasks, placed housekeeping low on his list of priorities. No amount of persuasion from Maura could convince him of the usefulness of such skills when he left home. But he had more interesting things to do. He did the minimum demanded of him and then disappeared.

Going away to college gave him a different perspective. He shared a house with other students and found it difficult to live in a messy and disorganised environment. He was obliged to use instant foods while wishing that he could cook more substantial meals. Admitting this to Maura was uncomfortable, but subsequent visits home taught him what he needed to know in order to grow more self-sufficient and to enjoy using his skills.

Maura was delighted at the transformation. Michael had discovered through experience a new vision, one of what life could be like by using his strength of character to admit his needs and with the motivation of a messy house. Thanks to Maura's willingness to teach him, Michael grew up into a greater maturity. His boundaries extended, his horizons became more exciting and the quality of his life changed for the better and for ever.

**Gospel Teaching**

The crowds who came searching for Jesus in today's Gospel reading brought with them a confused set of questions and desires. They wanted to find out more about God; they wanted to see signs of God's presence among them; they wanted help in understanding the relationship between Jesus' teaching and the teaching they had grown up with.

Jesus was surprisingly gentle with them. He knew he was making headway in his ministry when the people began asking him questions about their lives and how the way they lived related to his teaching. They had discovered their need for a teacher.

The sick, always in need of healing, began to realise that this man Jesus might be a source of their desire. Sinners had come to see him as one with spiritual authority who could see into hearts, could understand the motivations and circumstances of their lives, one who might grant them God's forgiveness. Lonely people, outcasts from the Temple or society, saw in him a friend who would not let them down, one who, in bringing them together with one another, would also share their exile.

Jesus came to his followers according to their need. Jesus knew them well and recognised their motives but did not judge them accordingly. Instead he offered them a new vision of life and its expectations, a new vision of God. They had originally followed him because they were physically hungry. Now they were ready for something beyond the physical. He offered himself as their salvation, which he spoke of in terms they would understand. Their new hunger could only be met by a new bread. Jesus would be this bread. With him as their bread, he would not only satisfy their temporary needs but would fill them with a new life.

When the people recognised their needs, Jesus was ready to satisfy them and bring them into a deeper relationship with God through himself.

**Application**

We too must try to understand where our own lives are impoverished: to look at ourselves honestly in order to discover our weaknesses and strengths so that we know what to pray for in order to become more perfect before God.

We are already strengthened and blessed by our baptism, so we are partly prepared. We may have gifts which are underused; ideals as yet unfulfilled; longings for life to be different, a desire to change ourselves and the world more in keeping with God's will.

When we experience these feelings we are beginning to grow in maturity. We see that we can change and we reach for a greater wholeness in our lives. This is the moment for us to ask: "Jesus, what must we do, to be doing the works of God?" Being aware that we need to be told will open our eyes and ears and hearts to the answers. But an earnest desire to grow and to change for God's purposes will give us a clearer vision of Christ and his teaching. He will feed us with the manna from heaven that we need.

## *"Whoever comes to me will never be hungry."*
(John 6:35)

**Illustration**

Perhaps you have seen the film *The Shawshank Redemption*. Set in an American prison, it deals with themes of redemption and hope and what it means to be free. At one point in it, the character Red describes what it means to be institutionalised: "These walls are funny. First you hate them, then you get used to them, and then you depend on them; that's institutionalised." When Red is finally released he finds, as he feared, that freedom is unnerving and cruel. His mind is so shaped by the years of imprisonment that it is difficult for him to act as a free man. He even considers reoffending in order to get back to the relative security of institutional life. Red finds that even when his body is free, his mind is telling him that he is still in prison.

**Gospel Teaching**

Freedom, redemption and hope are also at the heart of Christ's message, and it is no less tricky for us to understand what it is to be free than it was for Red in *The Shawshank Redemption*. There are many things that oppress and imprison us, but perhaps the thing that represents our captivity most completely is our need for food and drink. Even if we are not held behind bars, or made to work as slaves, we can never be free from the fact that before we do anything else, we need to make sure that we and our families have enough to eat. So when Jesus announces himself to be the bread of life, he strikes right at the heart of that which holds us captive as human beings. He declares that the bottom line of our existence is not our need for food and drink, but our need for Christ.

This was a daring statement to make, and, not surprisingly, it was followed by cries of protest: who on earth was this local boy, after all, to say such outrageous things? In the verses following our reading, we learn that even those who had supported him began to drift away. John crafts his Gospel to help his readers to see who Jesus is, and to put their faith in him; but it was never going to be an easy decision. Through faith in Christ we have unimaginable gifts, but they are not always easy gifts to receive. For starters, even the most committed believers still have to feed themselves. We are all still captive to our human needs; they still shape how we think and act.

So what kind of freedom is it that we have through Christ? Is it a spiritual freedom that exists despite our physical and mental constraints? Or is it a freedom that comes into effect only when we are finally free of our earthly bodies after we die? It is both these things, and yet more. A freedom that exists only in a spiritual realm does not have the completeness of the kind of freedom Christ meant to bring. When Jesus declares himself to be the bread of life, he is effectively saying that his freedom operates at the heart of our everyday lives; at the heart of what it means to be human. It is a freedom that changes how we live in the here and now, and not just one that exists only on a spiritual level, or only in the hereafter.

**Application**

As Christians we all know what it is to struggle with the contradiction of our human constraints and our spiritual freedom. It may be that we are amply provided with food and drink; but we all know what it means to have to pay bills on time, please the boss, complete assignments and care for our family and friends.

And as Red found in *The Shawshank Redemption*, years of captivity shape your mind. The trick is not just to live differently, but to think differently. And for Christians, the means to achieve this is to feed on the bread of life. Christ has set us free; he has opened the prison doors. In this world we can live as if we are free, or we can live as if we are captive. Let's pray that we may find the courage to feed on Christ (and courageous it is), and in doing so to be truly free, even in the midst of the captivity of the humdrum constraints of our everyday lives.

*"Those who eat my flesh and drink my blood abide in me, and I in them."*
(John 6:56)

**Illustration**

A newly married couple, thrilled with the automatic bread-maker given them as a wedding present, looked forward expectantly to waking to the smell of freshly baked bread wafting from the kitchen.

They quickly became accustomed to that delicious homely aroma as they put their present to immediate use. The wonderful smell of newly baked bread, however, was never quite matched by the quality of the bread itself. They followed the instructions meticulously but somehow the bread seldom came out as intended. The loaves barely rose, and were sometimes a soggy mess. Oh dear!

Determined not to be beaten, they reread the instructions and (in the small print!) discovered some helpful hints, among them a firm recommendation that a special sort of yeast should be used in bread-makers.

Thereafter they woke to the smell, and the taste, of excellent, wonderful crusty loaves – and marvelled at how a small amount of one simple ingredient could be so important, so vital, and make such a difference.

**Gospel Teaching**

John, as so often, is not seeking to report Jesus' words with strict accuracy, but to convey the real significance of what Jesus said. In our Gospel reading today he recounts Jesus' teaching about spiritual food.

Jesus uses bread – a symbol of daily life, a very simple, basic but vital commodity – to make his point. He describes himself as the "living bread", bread that "came down from heaven", and he emphasises that whoever eats this bread will live for ever. His listeners, perhaps not surprisingly, challenge this, thus giving Jesus the chance to reiterate that he is talking about spiritual food, and about eternal life, life beyond the frontier of death. It is the eternal life of Jesus within those who believe which holds out the promise of life for ever.

The Jews would have had some understanding of the concept of "bread from heaven" for they knew of the manna that had sustained their ancestors during their desert exodus (even if it had not extended their lifespan beyond the normal expectation). What was this bread from heaven Jesus was talking about, that would enable them to live for ever?

If this was not sufficiently challenging to them, Jesus' listeners were thrown by his talk of "those who eat my flesh". He wasn't advocating cannibalism, was he? And as for drinking blood, did he not know that the strict Jewish food rules and rituals forbade this?

Of course Jesus knew these rules, but his challenge was intended to get his listeners to look beyond their earthly needs, beyond their stomachs to their spiritual needs, and beyond their restricting rituals to new life within each of them.

**Application**

Jesus most certainly is not advocating cannibalism and the eating of his actual flesh but is inviting his listeners then – and us today – to feed on his humanity. "Fill your heart, your mind, your soul, your very inner being, with me." is what he is saying.

Reworking an image sketched by the much-loved and respected theologian William Barclay, try to imagine a man surrounded by well-stocked bookcases. Much knowledge is available to him in those books, but as long as they remain on the shelves – unread – all this array of knowledge is outside him, beyond him. But when he takes a book from the shelves, opens it and reads it, it becomes part of him. It fills his mind and his imagination; some parts fire his heart; others lift his spirits. Thereafter, whether the book is in his hand or on the shelves, he is able to feed on it, on its wisdom, knowledge, inspiration.

So it is with Jesus. When we take him into our hearts, consume him, then we are able to feed on him, and all that he offers. So, too, with his blood. Jesus' divinity was to take him beyond death, beyond the cross, to new life, and all who drink of him share this life, everlasting life with Jesus himself.

In our re-enactment of Jesus' command at the communion table we eat bread and drink wine, representing the broken body of Jesus and the blood he spilled for us. The bread remains bread, the wine remains wine, but by consuming it in faith, we take Jesus' body and blood, his humanity and his divinity, into ourselves, into our very being. He becomes part of us, as we become part of him.

A small piece of bread, and the merest sip of wine, simple, natural everyday things – and yet so important, so vital, and they make such a difference.

*"Those who eat my flesh and drink my blood abide in me, and I in them."*
(John 6:56)

**Illustration**
Long ago in a faraway land, a boy left home to seek his fortune. Before he left, his father gave him a key. The boy was not impressed. "What use is this key," he asked his father, "without the door it opens?" His father replied, "It's all I have to give you, so please take it."

Unfortunately, the boy failed to make his fortune. One day, not having eaten for days, he stole an apple. The stallholder caught him. This country had a very strict legal system and for this theft he was thrown into a Chinese box of cells, each one unlocked by a different key, and each one more unpleasant than the last. He ended up in the deepest dungeon, little removed from hell itself.

The boy was in despair, when he remembered the key his father had given him. "At least," he thought, "if it fits the first door, I can remove myself from this deepest pit, which has the largest rats I've ever seen." So he tried the key and, to his surprise and joy, it opened the door. Feeling he had nothing to lose, though he knew it wouldn't work, he tried the key in the next door, and amazingly it opened that door too!

And so he went from door to door and found every one was opened by that one key his father had given him. Freed from prison, he made his way back home and threw himself at his father's feet in gratitude, repenting that he'd ever doubted him.

**Gospel Teaching**
St John's Gospel doesn't contain an account of the institution of Holy Communion, but this passage in chapter 6 is surely John's version. Christ is saying we have to feed off him to live the abundant life. His body and blood are the true bread and the true vine which ensure we remain in God. Since the true bread and the true vine are spiritual phenomena, they could be represented in the physical realm by anything we chose, as long as we were perceiving the spiritual reality within them, which is Christ himself. Christ chose bread and wine – bread was a staple of survival and wine a staple of celebration.

Thus every Communion is a statement of our dependence on Christ for spiritual survival, but also a celebration of the richness of the spiritual life we share, which is a million times greater than simple survival. It's as if we're given a food voucher, but then find its purchasing power is limitless. It's as if we are given a day to live and then find it is the first day of the rest of our life. It's as if we get a job as a cleaner in a large company, only to find we get the same pay as the chairman.

Communion is so basic, so primitive. We are invited to feed off another person, like babies at the breast. And just like children who will discover that their mothers have a bottomless treasure-trove of love, that will feed them long after the milk has dried up, we learn that the new life in Jesus, as lived out in a fellowship of faith, is more than merely a piece of bread and sip of wine. It's as if we come to light a candle and then find it's a floodlight shining on the rest of our week.

Communion is so physical, standing or kneeling side by side, rubbing elbows, chewing bread and holding the cold metal cup, and yet its effects are so spiritual, proclaiming our spiritual unity in the one body of Christ. We commemorate Christ's painfully physical death on the cross of two thousand years ago and, in the same act, celebrate, in the here and now, his rising again in our hearts and souls.

**Application**
As we follow the sacred round of the Church's year, let us not hold back from the table. Rather let us gather regularly, even when it feels more like a duty than a joy. We don't come just for our own sakes.

Hear what Paul says in Ephesians 5: "make the most of every opportunity, because the days are evil". By joining other pilgrims in the upper room, we are expressing solidarity with all that is holy, all that is good in the whole world: more than that, we are helping God to create the antidote to evil, by embodying Christ in the world.

*"You abandon the commandment of God and hold to human tradition."*
(Mark 7:8)

**Illustration**
It was a filthy Sunday morning – rain and strong winds. Meg Smith, the vicar, slipped inside the church door an hour before the service was due to start, to be sure the boiler was working.

She was followed in by Jim Markham, who organised their small town's monthly farmers' market. He was distraught. It was going to be impossible to hold the market in these conditions but he was reluctant to cancel because the market had become a lifeline for local farmers. Would Meg use her local knowledge to find a building where the market could find a refuge?

She rang the caretaker of every large building in the town, but no one could help. Just then John Stocks, churchwarden, arrived. Meg took John aside and the two of them spoke in low voices for a few moments, with John nodding vigorously. Then Meg turned to Jim and pinched herself as she heard herself say: "Jim, would it be possible for you to hold the farmers' market here in church?" It was – and they did.

**Gospel Teaching**
Pharisees from Jerusalem were shocked to see how people in the provinces disregarded the Law of Moses. They asked Jesus to explain how he could let his disciples so blatantly disregard the traditions of their religion.

The Pharisees probably weren't trying to trick Jesus here. They were genuinely troubled. And they were right to be, for an institution can become so dependent on its traditions for its sense of identity and worth that if they were all stripped away, like barnacles off a ship's hull, it might reveal so many holes that the ship would sink.

Jesus cleverly draws on the words of one of their "elders" that the Pharisees are invoking and he quotes Isaiah 29, where God deplores the hypocrisy of Israel. It is a devastating prophecy and cuts right to the quick of the Pharisees' complaint. For God calls the worship of Israel a vain show and her doctrines merely based on human precepts. There can be no more crushing critique of a religion than for its worship to be judged as show and its teaching a human invention.

What added to the power of this quote is that it was eight hundred years old! If Judaism had barnacles of tradition clinging to its hull all those centuries ago, what must its condition have been like as Jesus debated the point with these religious leaders? How was it able to stay afloat?

Jesus is ruthless in answering this implicit question: "You abandon", he says, "the commandment of God and hold to human tradition." What is left of a religion once it has abandoned God and replaced him with human traditions? Nothing! According to Jesus' judgement, therefore, the ship had sunk beneath the waters long ago. No wonder he was crucified.

Jesus then calls the people around him to hear his answer to the specific complaint of the Pharisees concerning dietary and cooking traditions: nothing that goes into a person's stomach will defile them, only what comes out of their heart. In that one brilliant statement Jesus places all religion where it should be: within our beliefs, desires, thoughts and intentions – and the actions that result from them. God only ever wanted contrite hearts and a people that treated the weak and the stranger justly. Jesus in this instance is repeating the age-old message of the prophets.

**Application**

Jesus accused the religious leaders of using human traditions to enslave people with the excessive demands of institutionalised religion, but ironically the same process has happened in the Christian religion.

We have to spend so much time just keeping the Church afloat and yet how willing are we to take a knife to the barnacles of tradition that weigh us down? Maybe we need to be more willing to listen to the prophetic voices of unchurched newcomers? Sometimes the only way is for change to be forced upon us: for instance, when their building undergoes a major repair and they have to worship elsewhere, congregations often find a new spiritual life granted them in the new environment.

Fortunately there are plenty of good signs: for example, the growing involvement of congregations in issues of peace and fair trade; our reduced dependence on service books, allowing for more creativity and spontaneity in worship; and the reordering of our churches to make them more suitable for community use – though it will probably be a while before the farmers' market is traditionally held in the parish church!

*"He has done everything well; he even makes the deaf to hear and the mute to speak."*
(Mark 7:37)

**Illustration**

Most of us take our five senses for granted. We cannot remember what it is like to be without the forms of communication which we learned so early on. Going abroad and being unable to speak the language returns us to our infantile state as we struggle to make ourselves understood. We again become vulnerable and exhausted with our efforts and understand better the trials experienced by those living with disability.

But God's miracles extend into our scientific age to assist those more permanently disabled by their sensual loss. For example, there are now cochlear implants which allow some deaf people to hear through a series of electronic impulses. There is the possibility that one day retina implants will enable those blind from birth to see, even if only for a short time: time to see their loved ones' faces and some of the wonders of which they have only heard.

God's miracles are all around us: gifts that delight us and guide us towards a greater understanding of his love. This reassurance frees us to become more fully the people he made, whether or not our bodies or minds are physically complete.

**Gospel Teaching**

During Jesus' ministry the miracles he performed always pointed beyond themselves. At a straightforward level he heals. Not just by what he says but by what he does. He is not afraid to touch people and puts his fingers in the man's ears, touching his tongue with his own spittle. He gives of himself, physically and in terms of concentration and energy, and, as a result, the man discovers the freedom of hearing and speech.

At another level this process illustrates the concern which Jesus has to free the hearing and speech of all who listen to him, whether or not they experience disability, including us today. It is only when we hear him clearly that we can, in turn, live out and proclaim the truth of his message.

Some people are disabled by poverty or by discrimination against outsiders or foreigners, like the Syrophoenician woman, alien to Jewish culture. But yet it was she who recognised Jesus' true status. When she challenged him with her depth of faith he realised that his ministry was for all people. Both she and the deaf man were completely open to Jesus, vulnerable in their total faith. Unlike the cynical, well-informed Pharisees, they did not presume they had the answers to life's questions.

We are sometimes hampered by our complicated knowledge: it can blind and deafen us. True wisdom is being conscious of what we do not know and remaining open to being taught. Jesus works hard to clarify our hearing and our sight, our understanding and our insight, so that with or without perfect physical senses our discipleship is of the best, God's truth is heard and God's will is done.

**Application**

Deafness and blindness are not necessarily physical conditions. The scribes were deaf to the full meaning of Jesus' teaching while hearing his words perfectly. Some of Jesus' disciples were blind to events which seem obvious to us in retrospect.

We are more likely to develop our sense of God and his working through us if we can recognise how deaf to his word we can become. When people believe they have all the answers, a monopoly of the truth, there is a danger that they reinforce their blindness and inability to hear.

Jesus will free us today, just as he freed the deaf man in the Gospel, when we are open and vulnerable, available to be approached and do not assume that we know everything. Jesus told us that to love God well we must become like little children; not childish, but childlike. With their ability to trust implicitly, children listen with open ears and see with unclouded vision.

And when we recognise our poverty, our littleness and our need for God, Jesus can work in us: to heal us in all our disabilities, to include us despite our differences and foreignness, and to teach us what we need to know in order to hear the word and act upon it.

These gifts are given to those who ask. This is how the kingdom of God is extended upon earth – by disciples attentive to their master. We are those disciples and Christ's Church relies upon our wisdom, insight and vision.

*"He asked them, 'But who do you say that I am?'"*
(Mark 8:29)

**Illustration**

Gossip makes the world go round. None of us can resist the latest rumours and scandals, as newspaper and magazine sales figures make clear. Even if we have ourselves been the victim of false rumours, we can't quite help believing stories about other people. "No smoke without fire" must be one of the most depressing maxims in existence, when applied to gossip. We even manage to pass on gossip with a clear conscience. We say, "I have heard… but of course I've no idea if it's true or not." We seldom expect to be confronted with the person whose reputation is under the microscope, or to be held accountable for the truth or otherwise of the story we are helping to spread.

**Gospel Teaching**

Jesus' ministry was attended by a great many rumours. For a lot of the time, he was followed about by large groups of people who had heard stories about him and, in those pre-newspaper days, could only join in the gossip by being there. In the Gospels, we hear the stories of those who come into direct contact with Jesus, but we hear very little about these others, this shadowy mass of people hanging round the edges of all the action. In the tremendous whirlwind of Jesus' ministry, there isn't really time to worry about those who are just looking for a sensation. Jesus and the disciples have their hands full with potential friends and enemies, without bothering with those who don't really want anything in particular.

But in today's Gospel reading, Jesus suddenly asks his disciples what people are saying about him. The disciples answer so quickly and with so many options that it sounds as though this was a discussion they had been longing for. After all, their own reputations were bound up with Jesus'. They are thoughtful friends. They do not pass on the unkind rumours, the doubts about Jesus' sanity, the suggestions about his paternity and so on. They only pass on the acceptable gossip, and wait to hear what Jesus has to say.

But then Jesus goes to the heart of it. "Who do you say that I am?" And the disciples go quiet. It is so much easier to pass on gossip, taking no responsibility for it, than to stand up for their own opinions. Only Peter is prepared to risk an answer, and gets very little reward for it. Technically, Peter is right. Jesus is the Messiah. But he is just as much wrong as right, because what Peter thinks is a Messiah is not at all what Jesus is going to be. Jesus is going to free his people and lead them to victory, just like a good Messiah should, but he is going to do it through suffering, and, even then, it might not end up as the kind of triumph his disciples have in mind. Peter has been so influenced by what "everyone says" a Messiah should be that he even tries to contradict Jesus. Perhaps Jesus just hasn't read the right books and newspapers, Peter thinks, as he tries to teach Jesus what his mission should be.

But centuries of history have shown what comes of trying to do things the way "everyone knows" they should be done. In Jesus, God has come to make plain that there is only one way to change everything, and that is the way that Jesus is walking.

**Application**

Like the disciples, we would usually rather live with borrowed opinions than venture our own. We would prefer not to stand out against the crowd, and declare what we believe. We, too, would prefer our God to be strong and victorious, so that our own reputations can be vindicated along with his.

How very hard it is to allow God to make his own definitions. But that is just what God does in Jesus. God shows us how he defines himself, what his nature is and how he chooses to act. We can reject God, but we cannot make him be a different kind of divinity. This is God, take it or leave it. Jesus is not swayed by what others say about him, or by what his disciples long for him to be. He knows what he must do and be, for our salvation. As his followers, we must keep our eyes fixed on him, and resist any other rumours or definitions of God.

*"Whoever welcomes one such child in my name welcomes me, and whoever welcomes me welcomes not me but the one who sent me."*
(Mark 9:37)

**Illustration**

One of the many things which has changed dramatically over the centuries is the way in which we treat our children. It is a popular misconception that children have always been treated as separate entities within the family or community, or that a period of infancy is followed by a childhood without any responsibility leading to carefree youth and a rebellious adolescence easing them into adulthood.

But this does not accord with history. Children have usually been valued as extensions of the family, ensuring the continuation of the family line, more especially in the case of a son.

But as with some cultures today, children in first-century Palestine had no economic or social status. Though loved and cherished by their extended families, they had no special treatment partly because so many of them died in infancy. They became a viable part of the household when they could begin working, tending flocks, fetching water etc. Their education, usually only for boys, entailed becoming a good Jew, learning the Torah, the Jewish Law. Girls assisted their mothers in learning the skills they would need in running a household. Not for these children the toys, fashions and accessories which are designed for children today. Children were at the very bottom of the pecking order, occupying a minor area of activity with no voice.

**Gospel Teaching**

The disciples were assailed by confusion and misunderstanding, seeming unable to grasp their role within their own group, let alone in the wider community. They were concerned with questions of status and role because much of what Jesus taught confused the accepted social and religious rules of the day, as well as turning the (then) class system on its head.

For example, rich people were understood to be not just lucky or clever, but especially blessed by God, richly rewarded for their "good" life. But Jesus taught that God loves everyone equally, even the poverty-stricken and sinners.

The disciples ached to discover where they fitted into it all. In using a little child to illustrate his point about his disciples' service to the community, Jesus was choosing a stratum of society which had no voice, no influence, no material wealth, no power: the littlest people in all respects. But this is not sentimentality. To be his disciple, then and now, means serving the needs of those who have nothing to give back, for which there is likely to be no reward, except from the "one who sent me".

Jesus also makes another point. Elsewhere he refers to his disciples as "little ones" and "my children". He is not being patronising but not only describing the fact of their innocence of life's potential but showing them clearly how, in choosing them, God has already chosen the humblest: these are the ones whom God will uplift to greater things, beyond their imagining. But still the message remains the same. Even while being exalted by their new learning, experiences and miracle-working, they not only remain the "children" whose simplicity is so pleasing to God, but they must continue to serve the humblest, among themselves and in the wider world. Because this is Jesus' model for the new Church: being, and serving, the humblest.

**Application**

Being childlike is different from being childish. Children accept God easily and trustingly. God our parent longs to teach us what we need to be happy, to become fulfilled and authentic human beings. But children are also Jesus' metaphor for those whom society regards as at the "bottom of the heap": asylum seekers (whether economic migrants or not), drug addicts, people who sleep rough, who sell sex, etc.

As our society becomes richer, more and more weak, vulnerable or demanding groups are relegated to the back of our minds. But just as we have a duty to our children, so, Jesus tells us, do we have a duty towards the less fragrant members of society. He gives us no escape from his example. He consorted with outcasts just as despised as our list. His clarity of vision of the kingdom remained constant in its simplicity, his trust in his Father was absolute. Jesus modelled childlike love and uncritical service. Children are integral to the present and future Church, but then so are we and so is everyone we meet, however demanding or smelly.

*"Whoever is not against us is for us."*
(Mark 9:40)

**Illustration**

One familiar theme in many great stories throughout literary history is that of the impossibility of loving, or even giving credibility to, someone who does not belong to your group. Shakespeare's *Romeo and Juliet* and *West Side Story,* its modern interpretation in musical form, are good examples. Problems often arise when people look beyond their own immediate circle of family and friendship allegiances towards those who do not seem to fit.

The intentions of the person reaching out may be of the best. Their minds, unencumbered by the limitations set upon them by their particular tradition, may have become broadened by experience and developed a greater tolerance than their peers. It takes a boldness and courage to step outside acceptable norms. It can take a grand passion (like *Romeo and Juliet*) or great faith to impel us into such risky behaviour. But this course can provoke such fear and anxiety in those around that the likely outcome can range from our own exclusion from the group to violence and even death for one or more participants. Conventional wisdom tells us to stick to our own.

Fortunately for us, Jesus and his disciples and the saints who followed them were foolhardy and trusting, and anything but conventional.

**Gospel Teaching**

The disciples had tried to stop someone from casting out devils in Jesus' name because "he's not one of us". John obviously expected Jesus to be pleased with them for doing this. Why should he derive credit for miracles which were the work of Jesus and his particular disciples? Surely, he must be prevented, for everyone's protection? As we know, without any hesitation, Jesus went against this conventional wisdom. It does not matter to him that the man was not a part of his immediate followers. His overriding concern always was that good should be done, whenever and wherever possible. If this was being credited to his power, which was really God's power, then no harm would be done and evil would have found another enemy.

Jesus stresses the importance of each of us deciding on whose side we are prepared to stand and fight, and what we are willing to defend. But he also asks us to think about who will suffer for it. God will never ask us to sacrifice the "little ones", Jesus says. If we are defending our "in-group" at the cost of the vulnerable, we are not working with Jesus. Over and above this there are no restrictions upon the good actions of anyone. God's kingdom is not a club requiring membership fees, but the free gift of the Father to all his children. There is only one rule in God's kingdom, that of love. When it permeates our whole being, dedication to God becomes the central driving force of our life and the pivot upon which turns our hope of eternal joy to come.

**Application**

If we are open to the Spirit of God and recognise the existence of the Spirit within others, then we will rejoice to find God's work being done, no matter where it is happening and who is conducting it. It is very tempting to allow ourselves to believe that we belong to a privileged "in-group". This, after all, can give us a sense of identity, a belief in our self-worth. But we have long passed the time when membership of a particular denomination was seen as the only passport to heaven, to the exclusion of everyone else.

We now know that God's truth is found everywhere, amongst all peoples. Even among those who claim not to know God, we find God at work. The Spirit does not need permission to flood the heart with good intentions. In our fight against evil in its many forms, in the struggle to free people from slavery, from injustice and poverty the important question is not "Are they one of us?" but "Are they doing God's work and can we help?"

Today, the Gospel reiterates the vital question. Do we truly desire to dedicate ourselves to God's will and God's work? If so, let us rejoice that those who take up the challenge are so infinitely varied and sometimes unexpected. Our God of great surprises calls each by name, and the Spirit we share and which draws us into unity is one for all time.

*"So they are no longer two, but one flesh. Therefore what God has joined together, let no one separate."*
(Mark 10:8-9)

**Illustration**
Rabbi Lionel Blue, the well-known British religious writer and broadcaster, commented that honesty is essential if morality is not to become mere moralising. The assertion is true and the distinction is an important one. Morality seeks to discern what is right and what is wrong and to live by what we find to be the truth. It is a way of finding freedom, for ourselves and others.

In contrast, moralising is about judging others' behaviour and seeking to impose our moral values on them while sometimes exempting ourselves from our own moral legislation. It is generally an attempt to limit others, either because we can, which becomes a crude exertion of power over them; or because in seeking to limit them we are recognising that we ourselves are not free. It is difficult for some people to watch others fly in freedom when they have neither the will nor the courage to do so.

Introducing honesty into the equation enables us to examine our motives, something the Pharisees were not very good at. But moralising and legalism make cosy bedfellows. They produce a blanket of security for people who never take risks with imagination or life. It is easy to forget that laws are made for the people's guidance, protection and well-being, not to trip them up, especially those given by God to his well-loved children.

**Gospel Teaching**
The Pharisees were not primarily interested in the question of divorce. Their main purpose was to test Jesus, to catch him out, to see if he was prepared to acknowledge the Mosaic Law as they themselves taught it. Their question was an attempt to find a weapon which they could use against him.

The divorce law as it stood then sought to moralise. It laid down firm rules but was very one-sided in favour of men who could put away women at will, leaving them destitute.

Jesus was fully aware of the Pharisees' intentions. But as he had done before, Jesus turned their trickery into an opportunity to teach them and us a moral truth. In describing the unity of both partners becoming one flesh he is implying that they are not just indivisible as human beings but that they are to be equal in their treatment of each other, and their union is to be similarly respected by the outside world. There is not to be one set of rights for men and another for women. God made them, joined them and loves them equally. This is a model for vowed relationships.

Jesus was overwhelmingly concerned about justice, especially in relationships. Women and children in his day came low on the status ratings. Yet, following his teaching on marriage, he sternly ordered that the little children should not be prevented from equal status with adults in their right to approach him. He even chooses them as the model of perfection needed by adults to achieve heaven. So, in one short exchange, he diplomatically handles the Pharisees, then highlights and raises up the status of ordinary men, women and children to take their rightful place as equals, in society, under the moral law, as properly befits a people made by God.



**Application**
This attitude of Jesus' is extremely important for us today in a world which places a greater emphasis upon what people produce than on their intrinsic worth. It is a foundation stone of his moral teaching about justice in relationships, not just marriage, but amongst neighbours, in communities, in the Church, between nations.

Jesus wants people to be free, not to condemn them. Free people are people with a purpose, moving forward in life and relationships, keen to grow, to change, to live in a constant state of becoming more authentically who God made them to be.

Most importantly, people who themselves live with a sense of God-given freedom are far more likely to help to free others. Free people are happy people and happy people are far better able to do God's will with quiet determination and a light heart. But freedom can be a hard road, much harder than the security of legalism and moralising. Jesus' teaching gives us the tools for the job and a yardstick by which to measure our natural responses to life's questions. Its essence is clear-sighted honesty. Honesty is the key to morality. Rabbi Blue, that other Jewish teacher, is right!

Proper 23
(Sunday between 9 and 15 October inclusive)

*"As he was setting out on a journey..."*
(Mark 10:17)

**Illustration**
Why is it that, however big the suitcase, there is never enough room for that last pair of shoes? Perhaps there is a scientific principle that the volume of holiday clothes expands to fill the capacity of the available suitcase – and then some! Most of us take far more luggage on holiday than we really need. At any airport, we see fellow tourists with their bulging suitcases, most of them with wheels these days for easy transfer from taxi to aeroplane to taxi. But we also see the backpackers, mainly young people, eager to do some serious travelling, to see the real world and not just the tourist hotels. When it comes to packing, the backpacker's principle is a simple one: I shall have to carry this on my journey, so do I really need it?

**Gospel Teaching**
Two people were setting out on a journey in today's Gospel reading: Jesus and the rich man. Jesus knew where he was going; the rich man was unaware that he was even setting out. Jesus the backpacker was travelling light, on his journey towards the cross. The rich man was setting out on a spiritual journey, a pilgrimage of discovery, as he turned away from Jesus, grieving, carrying his bulging suitcase of material possessions.

The rich man was not a bad man. He had obeyed all the commandments, and we are specifically told that Jesus, an excellent judge of character, looked at him and loved him! To the man's question about how to inherit eternal life, Jesus replies with an amazing invitation: "Follow me." But first he must sell his possessions and give to the poor. All that stood between the rich man and a life of discipleship, all that stood between him and eternal life, was the wealth that was weighing him down. With that bulging suitcase, he would not be able to keep up with Jesus and his backpacking disciples.

Wealth itself is not evil. But it can get in the way. It is not something we need on our journey. Wealth, or the pursuit of it, can provide a focus for our lives, which should instead focus on the needs of others and a relationship with God, in the pilgrimage towards eternal life. We do not know where the rich man's spiritual journey took him, but perhaps those words from Jesus pierced his soul. Perhaps he emptied his suitcase on the way, handing out his possessions to those he passed who had little of their own. Perhaps he followed the advice Jesus gave, and then returned to follow Jesus himself. God may have helped him through the eye of the needle.

But in the meantime, those who were already following Jesus were wondering about the things which they had given up. Peter reminds Jesus that the travelling band of disciples had left homes, families and occupations to follow him. Jesus reassures him that the rewards will far outweigh the sacrifice, but also warns that the journey will be a difficult one: there will be persecutions along the way.

**Application**

Those of us who are not wealthy may feel smug on reading this Gospel story. Perhaps we congratulate ourselves that it is easier for us to inherit eternal life because we are not weighed down by material possessions. But what is there in our own lives that is surplus to requirements? What can we leave out of our backpack, once we decide to abandon the suitcase and undertake some serious travelling? Following Jesus along the path to eternal life entails sacrifice on our part, the giving up of anything which prevents us from seeing the needs of others or gets in the way of a living, loving relationship with God. Ambition, pride, laziness and self-satisfaction are among the items we can remove from our packing list.

It is all too easy to feel smug as a Christian. After all, every Eucharist reminds us that Jesus has already made the ultimate sacrifice, dying for our sins on the cross. His death and resurrection have earned for us the eternal life which that rich man sought to inherit. Jesus has passed through the heavens and opened the way for us into the Father's presence. But if we seek to follow him there, let us not risk being turned away from the flight because our baggage is too heavy.

*"The Son of Man came not to be served but to serve."*
(Mark 10:45)



**Illustration**

Philip Pullman's trilogy *His Dark Materials* tells the story of Lyra, a girl with an important destiny. As the story of Lyra and her adventures unfolds, as she journeys to worlds other than her own, meets witches, angels and talking bears, finds out the identity of her parents, and travels in the world of the dead, we gradually discover what that destiny is. Lyra is the new Eve, the one who will re-enact the fall of humanity, lose her innocence, and bring the world to new consciousness and understanding. The ultimate task of Lyra and her friends is to overthrow the Ancient of Days, the authority in heaven; to abolish the kingdom of heaven and replace it with a republic, in which human beings will decide their own destiny, free of divine intervention and church interference. In some ways the books are anti-Christian. Philip Pullman is certainly opposed to the structures of the institutional Church, and has no love for Christianity. But in another way, the truths about which he writes are profoundly Christian, as today's Gospel reading shows.

**Gospel Teaching**

In the Gospel reading Jesus and his disciples discuss the nature of power in the Christian community that is to be. James and John want to make sure of their places, but incur the wrath of the other disciples for getting above themselves. The argument provides Jesus with an opportunity to talk about relationships among his followers. The author of the Gospel knows that Jesus is addressing those who, in the author's own time, are the leaders of the new Christian Church. They have come from humble backgrounds, from a subject people, into a position of authority. One might expect them to enjoy finally having some power, with the best intentions of exercising it for good. They have travelled with Jesus, endured hardships, worked at understanding his mission; they have earned their position of leadership and intend to use it well. But Jesus will not allow it.

What Jesus does is to redefine the nature of power relationships within the community. The Christian Church is not to behave as if it were any other organisation, he insists. Christian leaders are not to lord it over other members of the Church. On the contrary, those who are in a position of leadership must set an example of humble service. They must even, in effect, be slaves to other members of the community. They must do this in order to follow the example of their one true leader, Jesus himself, who, the Gospel says, "came not to be served but to serve, and to give his life a ransom for many".

The whole of Jesus' life, ministry and death was an expression of submission, of service to the human race. He modelled a new kind of leadership. His kingship is one gained through the ultimate act of service, his death on the cross. If his followers are to be true to him, they must adopt the same patterns of leadership and relationships. The Christian community is to be a community of mutual service and love.

**Application**

There is perhaps no other teaching of Jesus that has been harder for the Church to follow. We human beings find it hard to live without structures and hierarchies. We enjoy our own importance. We like to be honoured by others. We work hard for recognition, and enjoy receiving our due reward.

And Christians are not immune to these natural human instincts. Very soon after Jesus' death and resurrection, the Church had developed structures of leadership and ministry – and perhaps it could not have survived without them. If we think about it, we can see that an attitude of service modelled on that of Jesus would transform all our relationships, from international politics to family life. Only God can bring about that transformation; but that does not excuse us from trying to follow Jesus' example in our local churches and in our personal lives. How many of those quarrels between church members could be avoided if everyone adopted an attitude of mutuality and service?

The Son of Man came not to be served but to serve. As we try to build the kingdom of heaven in our place and time, may it rather be a republic of heaven, in which all are equal and all both serve and are served.

*"Jesus said to him, 'Go; your faith has made you well.' Immediately he regained his sight and followed him on the way."*
(Mark 10:52)

**Illustration**
*The Three Trees* is a Scandinavian folktale. It is the story of three young pine trees growing together on a hilltop. Each one of them had a different dream for its life.

The first wanted to be made into a beautiful treasure box, to hold the most valuable jewels in the world. The second wanted to become a wonderful ship, and carry the most important people on the oceans of the world. The third tree had a more simple and (he thought) humble dream: to stay right there on the hillside and grow tall and strong, pointing everyone towards God in heaven.

When the big day for felling these trees came, they all were disappointed – the first was made into an animal's feeding trough, the second into a small fishing boat, and the third was left just as logs in a lumber yard. What had happened to their dreams?

But, with time, all three came to see how they were caught up into the story of God in very special ways not of their own making. The first tree became the feeding trough that held the newly born Son of God, the second tree became the fishing boat from where the man of God stilled the storm, and the third – he became the cross on which Jesus the Messiah was crucified, pointing the way to God for all generations.

**Gospel Teaching**
Our prayers so often reflect our question: "Can I get God to do this for me?" Today's reading about blind Bartimaeus asks another question: "Can God enlist me in his service?" When Bartimaeus calls out to Jesus the Messiah, Son of David, to have mercy on him, we "see" with him that it wasn't what he did – his call, his prayer – that was the powerful thing that brought change, but rather the fact that his prayerful call was to Jesus, who has the power.

Yet this story is also part of the theme of drawing near to Jerusalem, to the entry of the king and then the suffering of the Messiah there. Jesus' question to Bartimaeus may seem a little obvious – clearly, we say, Bartimaeus wants to be healed of blindness – but the healing will bring new responsibilities, new risk, new life. Bartimaeus would need to trust Jesus even as he declares his sovereignty. He would need to refocus his life, not just as he lives with renewed sight, but as he re-centres himself to live out his declaration of who Jesus is, to see God's kingdom, know God's will, and be remembered as one of the followers of Jesus. To follow Jesus at this point was to bring healing and joy, but also to risk suffering and trouble with all that was to happen to the Messiah in Jerusalem. Bartimaeus' faith brought healing, but faith also was to sustain him as he followed the way. In ways he could never have "seen", Bartimaeus' faith brought him into the service of God and the kingdom.

**Application**

Being Christian is being God's stewards within God's new creation. As God's creation, we are called to gather ourselves in ways which bring not only our own healing, but also wholeness to all of humanity. Our prayers will become more than calls to God for our survival and healing when we see, not that we control God, but that God can do far more abundantly than we can ask or even think.

God seeks our re-creation and renewal in the kingdom, not just for our survival, but for our wholeness: for all that will bring celebration, the peace of consolation and the creativity of love to the world. Whether we come to good or difficult times, quiet or tragic times, the way of faith and wholeness in God will mean that we are free and able to reach into the depths and heights of knowing and seeing Jesus, and trust in the reality of mercy, joy and compassion. Then, being re-centred on those truths, we are ready to be part of that long journey towards renewed creation and recreated humanity.

The giving, receiving, strengthening that we see in Eucharist-shaped prayer and praise celebrated within our churches, the consolation of prayer and enjoyment of fellowship – all remind us of the framing of our lives in the knowledge of God, and of our Messiah and priest, Jesus. And we are reminded as we go out, with Jesus, to be part of God's ongoing story with creation, and to bring glory to God.

*"You search the scriptures because you think that in them you have eternal life; and it is they that testify on my behalf."*
(John 5:39)

**Illustration**

Many of us have a deep longing for certainty. This is not necessarily wrong. So much of our lives and our world is in flux, and there seems so little that we can really rely on that it is hardly surprising if we want assurance that some things will never change. Nor is it surprising that, for many people, this place of assurance and certainty is their religious faith. God does not change, after all, so surely this eternal changelessness should be reflected in the Church? Even people who never set foot inside a church can get surprisingly angry and upset when there is news that their local parish church might close, or that there is to be a new translation of the Bible or the Lord's Prayer. Some things just must not change.

But the trouble is that sometimes, if things are to continue to serve their original purpose, they have to change their form. Parish churches are built to house a worshipping community, and if the community has moved, then so must the building. It is not the building itself that matters, but the purpose for which it was designed.

**Gospel Teaching**

This is what Jesus is painstakingly trying to explain to his accusers in today's Gospel, and it is part of a struggle for understanding that goes on throughout his ministry. In the earlier part of chapter 5 of John's Gospel, Jesus has performed a miracle on the sabbath. He has healed a lame man, and caused great controversy by doing so. According to the strict letter of the Jewish scriptures, as they were then interpreted, Jesus should not have been doing this kind of thing on the official day of rest, and, in doing so, he was challenging the unchanging certainties by which his accusers lived.

But Jesus is trying to argue that, on the contrary, it is they who have changed what they inherited by refusing to allow it to adapt. The Law of Moses, handed down through generations, was designed to build a distinctive people, whose whole lifestyle and society would demonstrate the nature of God. The Law, and the scriptures that bear witness to it, are not ends in themselves, Jesus is arguing, but means to an end.

And, he says, with fierce clarity, they clearly are not serving the ends for which they were designed, because God's people do not know what God is like. If they did, they would recognise Jesus. They would recognise that what he did, what he taught, all that he was, was continuous with all that God's chosen people have always known about the nature of God, through their laws and their scriptures. Instead, they have allowed the laws to mask God, when they were designed to reveal him. They have become so attached to the letter of the Law that they have forgotten that the Law serves God, and that it will not act out of character. The Law must not be allowed to dictate the nature of God and what God will or will not do for his people. Jesus' accusers say that he is changing the Law, but really it is they who have changed it by applying it so strictly, so inhumanly, that it cannot any longer reveal the God who shaped it.

**Application**

It is a terrifying thought that we might be betraying God by what we see to be our faithfulness. Yet if we cling to certainties, rather than to God, that is almost bound to happen. The Bible, like the Law, bears witness to God. It is designed to show us the shape of lives lived in obedience to God. Scripture will not act in a way that is not characteristic of God, because it is God's tool. If we make it into a weapon of hatred, or division, or false reassurance, then we will be in danger of losing the ability to discern God.

Throughout the Bible, we see the nature of God displayed, culminating in Jesus. It is the Bible's job to help shape us into God's likeness, and we must not make it serve any other ends. The most damning thing that Jesus says to his questioners in today's Gospel is that it is Moses himself, the one they thought they were serving, who would condemn them for not recognising Jesus. How awful it would be if we found that we had used the scriptures, which we think we love, to hide the face of Jesus for our generation.

*"Did I not tell you that if you believed, you would see the glory of God?"*
(John 11:40)

**Illustration**

Do you remember your first encounter with the reality of death? For many of us it may be that the death of a pet was the first time that the finality of death really dawned on us. Others of us will have more traumatic memories of facing the death of someone we loved, and facing our own lives without them. As we get older, that experience will become more common, but never easier. Even when death comes to someone as a blessed relief from suffering or dementia, it is hard for those left behind to view that death with simple gratitude, unaffected by our own grief and loss. When we think about our own inevitable death, uppermost among our fears is what impact it will have on the people who love us.

Christian teaching about life after death can sometimes sound like a mindless optimism that refuses to face reality. We cannot bear to think of life without the people we love, and we are sure that they cannot manage without us, either, so we simply invent a comforting story that allows us to believe that, even after death, we can still be together.

But actually, the Christian belief in life after death is not so much based on what we would like to believe about ourselves, but on what we know to be true about God. It is the love, power and sheer vitality of God that underpin our belief in life after death.

**Gospel Teaching**

The people who are sitting and mourning the death of Lazarus have begun to know something of God's power, as it is expressed in Jesus. They have seen him perform astounding healing miracles and Mary, at least, firmly believes that if Jesus had been there when Lazarus was ill, Jesus would have been able to heal him. But even she has not yet grasped the fullness of what Jesus is capable of, while some of the others who are keeping her company are openly sceptical. They see Lazarus' death as a sign that Jesus' power is either waning, or perhaps was never as great as people made out. Perhaps, they guess, Lazarus was too seriously ill for Jesus to heal him. Perhaps Jesus really isn't all that special.

Certainly, Jesus seems very vulnerable and shaken as he faces this death of a friend. He is not different from the rest of us in feeling the awful separation. Although he speaks to Mary with absolute confidence, and acts decisively, still we are told that he is "greatly disturbed". But his sense of loss does not prevent him from trusting in God and acting for God. Even Martha and Mary, two of Jesus' most ardent supporters, do not believe that he can do anything for their brother now that he is actually dead. Already, the processes of decay are starting, and Martha and Mary expect nothing from Jesus, except that he will share their grief.

And, indeed, he does share their grief, but not so strongly that he loses touch with God. Moved and saddened as he is, he steps up to Lazarus' tomb and calls his friend back to life. And instantly, Lazarus responds. This is, after all, the voice that called all creation into being.

**Application**

It is hard not to envy Jesus his power to bring his friend back to life. How we have longed to be able to do the same for someone we love. But Jesus tells Mary that he is doing this so that she – and all the watching crowds – "would see the glory of God". Jesus calls Lazarus back from death, not because he cannot bear to be without him. Jesus knows that soon enough he himself will face death, and that his ordinary human relationships will change for ever. Lazarus is alive again to show the power of God. Mary and Martha believed that death was the end, but Jesus showed them that there is no end to the love of God. This is the glory of God; it is the very nature of God, that God is life and that nothing, not even death itself, can separate us from the overwhelming life of God.



So the Christian belief in life after death is a belief in the never-ending vitality of God. It is not a sentimental and unrealistic desire to maintain unchanged our precious human relationships, but a realisation that our love for each other is a small and imperfect symbol of God's love for creation. We can trust this God absolutely with those we love.

*"The first is... 'love the Lord your God with all your heart, and with all your soul, and with all your mind, and with all your strength.' The second is this: 'You shall love your neighbour as yourself.'"*
(Mark 12:29-31)

**Illustration**

Pascal wrote, "Men never do evil so completely and cheerfully as when they do it from a religious conviction." When we look at events throughout history and the world today, we see many examples of peoples of all religions causing suffering, pain and death to their fellow human beings. In such cases, the carrying out of what some believe to be God's will has terrible consequences for others, others who are counted as expendable in this "higher" purpose. Tragically, in such cases, a wholehearted dedication to God seems to reduce people's compassion for others.

In contrast, many take an opposite position: instead of focusing upon God's will above everything else, they disregard God and concentrate upon the needs of humanity. Those who think this way see no need for God, reasoning that we can look after each other well enough, if not better, without religion.

Today's Gospel reading reflects what Jesus believed about the compatibility of a wholehearted devotion to God with a desire to serve humanity.

**Gospel Teaching**

Jesus has faced a series of trick questions from both Sadducees and Pharisees attempting to catch him out before the crowd. The teacher of the law in our Gospel reading, though, appears to be sincere in what he asks. His question, "Which commandment is the first of all?", reflected an issue over which there was much disagreement. It was held that there were 613 commandments and there was argument over whether some commandments were more significant than others and whether it was possible to sum them all up in one general principle.

In answering the scribe, Jesus made reference to two separate pieces of scripture which he linked together. He quoted Deuteronomy 6:4-5 (part of the creed known as the *Shema* and recited daily by Jews) and Leviticus 19:18. He was only asked to cite one commandment but instead chose two, the implication being that he saw a strong connection between them.

To love God with all our "heart", "soul", "mind" and "strength" is a reminder that this love involves not just emotion but everything about us – our thoughts, energy, will, ability and understanding – and is a love which includes action and obedience. Our need to make God central in our lives is reinforced in Mark's version of the event where Jesus' quote from Deuteronomy also includes the words, "the Lord is one", which emphasises that only God is worthy of our worship and devotion.

In the original quotation from Leviticus the word "neighbour" would have referred to Israelites alone, but the parable of the good Samaritan (Luke 10:25-37) suggests that Jesus' definition of neighbour was much wider, embracing all humanity, including one's enemies.

**Application**

For Jesus, there was no clash between focusing upon God and meeting the needs of humanity. In fact, naming these two commandments as greater than the others shows that Jesus saw them as interconnected. The teaching of 1 John 4:21 sums up this connection: "those who love God must love their brothers and sisters also". If we truly love God we will also love God's creation, humanity. Indeed 1 John goes as far as to say that if we hate our brother or sister then we cannot love God (1 John 4:20): the two things are mutually exclusive.

Jesus also believed there was no place for neglecting God to focus solely upon humanity: after all, he names the love of God as the first commandment. Of course, humanists are right that much good can be done without any reference to religion, but recognising the unconditional nature of God's care for us brings a new depth to our own understanding of, and ability to, love. 1 John 4:19 says, "We love because he first loved us." Only in Christ's death on the cross do we see what love really is: love goes beyond caring for those who love us and from whom we get something back. It involves loving those, too, whom Jesus viewed as our neighbours: those we dislike, those we don't understand and those we don't approve of. His example gives us the motivation and strength to take love beyond its usual human limitations.

So making God central in our lives shouldn't distance us from others but encourage us to value each individual. The love of God and the love of humanity are inseparably bound together. Indeed, Jesus made this point very strongly in his parable of the sheep and goats (Matthew 25:31-46) in which he taught that it is in caring for others that we serve Christ himself.

*"And Jesus said to them, 'Follow me...' And immediately they left their nets and followed him."*
(Mark 1:17-18)

**Illustration**

Many of us will be familiar with the business of moving house. Perhaps the reason was a change of job, financial necessity or the need for more or less space. Moving is always a stressful time, but it can be exciting looking forward to new spaces and new opportunities. Equally, however, we may be leaving behind a much-loved home which holds precious memories. We cannot keep the old and the new; we have to make our choice.

**Gospel Teaching**

According to today's passage from Mark's Gospel, John the Baptist has just died, and as his work comes to an end so Jesus' ministry begins. But this very clear positioning in time, plain for anyone to see, is echoed by Jesus' words, "The time is fulfilled..." Jesus looks beyond the march of purely human history to God's timing, which has now come or "is fulfilled". So as he walks by the Sea of Galilee he carries a sense of divine destiny and calls certain fishermen to "follow" him in his mission.

Since Jesus and the fishermen were all local boys, it seems likely they already knew each other, though the passage does not actually say so. Perhaps Mark expresses it as he does to emphasise the authority of Jesus' call and the immediacy and willingness of the men's obedience. But to appreciate the significance of this response we must consider not only what they are taking on but what they were prepared to leave behind.

Since the Sea of Galilee was well known for its fish, which were sold far beyond the local region, these fishermen probably had a stake in prosperous family firms, yet they were prepared to abandon them to follow Jesus. Mark tells us that the brothers Simon and Andrew leave their nets and so turn their backs on a major business investment. Meanwhile James and John respond in a similar way, leaving their "father Zebedee in the boat with the hired men". For them Jesus represents a cause for which it is worth disrupting both business and family. How Zebedee felt about his sons' departure we are not told, but could the presence of only "hired hands" with him suggest that all his hopes for the continuation of his business within the family had rested on James and John? Their decision must surely have created waves, if not rocked the boat!

What was it, then, that Jesus was calling these new disciples to do? The expressions “fish for people” and the traditional “fishers of men” fit in with the narrative, but both have a rather uncomfortable feel of entrapment in English. The meaning, however, is plain: they were to join Jesus in calling others into the kingdom of God. Theirs would be an evangelistic role, drawing women and men to Christ and his kingdom in a way that firmly established the faith and the Church and enabled it to hold fast and develop over the last two thousand years.

**Application**

While those fishermen were called to a unique foundational ministry, some Christians today are called to devote their lives to evangelism, and all believers should be ready to give account of their faith to whoever may take an interest. But we should not be too surprised if God calls us into areas that we never imagined: serving the Church in some capacity in a country other than our own, for example. Or we may sense that God wants us to use our professional or trade skills in new ways, perhaps teaching the underprivileged, or setting up a community project.

No matter what the challenge may be, the question is how we will respond. The first disciples had to make decisions which would to some extent loosen the ties that had secured their lives thus far – the “network” of family and business. In the same way, our response to God involves the same decisions over family and money and probably other factors as well. In spite of Mark’s picture of this move as a quick and impulsive one, we must doubt that it really was; more likely it was the product of extended heart-searching, a heart-searching that we too may have to experience at some point in our Christian lives.

One thing we can be sure of is that the fishermen of Galilee would have been amazed at where their decision took them in later years, and although some of them had a very tough death they certainly had exciting and eventful lives, and the knowledge that their work took place within God’s time. Are we ready for the challenge?

*"... the end is still to come."*
(Mark 13:7)

**Illustration**
A favourite subject of cartoons is the man wearing a sandwich board which boldly proclaims, "The end of the world is nigh." The caption generally refers to him taking out an insurance policy or booking a holiday – anything to show that he does not really believe the message he is carrying around the streets. "The end of the world" has become a standing joke, only believed in by members of weird sects.

From time to time, groups of such people gather together to await the end of the world as we know it. Very often, they have calculated the exact time from a biblical text, taken out of context. Apocalyptic writings, such as Daniel or Revelation, have always provided fertile ground for the imagination. Yet the dates pass, and the world remains.

**Gospel Teaching**
In today's Gospel, Jesus mentions the destruction of the Temple, and his four closest disciples ask for the sign that will precede this calamity. His reply shows that he has read their minds: they are not asking merely about the destruction of a building, but about the end of time. Jesus knows that they have been influenced by prophecies of the end time found in their Hebrew scriptures.

To a first-century Jew, it seemed perfectly logical to connect the destruction of the Temple with the end of time. The Temple was the very heart of Jewish religion, culture and politics, the embodiment of their national identity. If the Temple were to be destroyed, then the world itself must be coming to an end. In a similar way, the 11th September terrorist attacks on the World Trade Centre and the Pentagon in 2001 seemed an assault on American, even "Western", civilisation. A building can represent much more than bricks and mortar.

The Temple was indeed destroyed, in AD 70, yet the world did not end. The reply Jesus gives to his disciples is the same encouragement we give to someone whose world seems to be falling apart: "Don't worry. It's not the end of the world." Before the end, he says, there will be catastrophes: wars, earthquakes, famines. But these are not to be understood as signalling the end. They are, rather, signs of this age: of a world which still flouts God's will, channelling vast amounts of money into war, which could be used to support agriculture in the developing world or build homes away from fault lines.

When Jesus spoke about the stones of the Temple being thrown down, he was quite probably not making any specific forecast about its destruction. He was almost certainly not talking about the end of time. He was replying to the awe in which the disciples held the Temple building itself. For Jesus himself, not the Temple, is now the embodiment of God's dealings with his people; his is the new priesthood. He was reminding them that buildings come and go, national institutions come and go, but God remains for ever. In God's good time, this age will end, and he will make all things new: there will be a new creation, a new birth. But it is not for us to know the day or the hour.

**Application**
The preoccupation with visible signs of organised religion remains today. It is too easy to think of "church" as the building in which we gather on a Sunday, rather than as the body of Christ, the people of God. It is too easy to invest all our religious feelings in this building, rather than in the life that it represents. We are called to be living stones in the temple of which Christ himself is the cornerstone.

For the end of the age starts now, as we live out the teaching of Jesus in the world, loving God and loving our neighbour. Rather than bother ourselves with calculating dates, rather than look for signs, let us simply accept that the end will come in God's good time. Our Saviour will come again in glory. Until then, our best preparation for the end is to heed the hymn's advice and live each day as if it were our last. Jesus spoke of those catastrophes as the beginning of the birth pangs of a new creation; we can act as midwives, helping the world through its pain and working towards the joy which it promises, however long the labour may turn out to be. For the end, like the best, is yet to come.

*"You say that I am a king."*
(John 18:37)

**Illustration**
The cathedral was busy when the fire alarm went off. The office staff were expecting an evacuation practice, but not till the following week. So they had not quite got around to reading their instructions. In the Chapter House, the Mothers' Union coffee morning was in full swing. Anxious heads poked out of doors into the corridor. Were the alarm bells being tested? Was it a drill? What were they to do?

Then the head verger appeared. "Evacuate the building," he announced very clearly and calmly. At once people grabbed their coats and headed outside. Someone was in charge, so it was all right. And pretty soon the DJ practising for a wedding reception later that day in the Cathedral Centre had been told to turn his smoke machine off, and life was back to normal.

**Gospel Teaching**
In the world, with all its alarms, who is in charge? Today the Church makes a bold assertion. Today we celebrate the feast of Christ the King. Who is in charge of the world? Christ is, we proclaim.

When the Gospels discuss the kingship of Christ, they do it in a very particular context. The land where Jesus lived was occupied and ruled by the Romans. And the Romans had an emperor whose rule was absolute. Tiberius ruled by force and by fear. Under his rule, Roman citizens lived secure, knowing that no one would dare to attack them, so great would be the reprisals. But for subject peoples like the Jews things were very different. The emperor was their lord and master, and they had better keep quiet and obey him. For anyone else to claim authority was treason of the most dangerous kind, and would be punished immediately and severely.

This is what lies behind Jesus' conversation with Pilate, the Roman governor, running Judaea on behalf of Tiberius. If Jesus has indeed claimed to be a king, as Pilate has been told, he will immediately be executed. There is room for only one king in this empire, and the divine emperor already has that position. Pilate wants to find out whether Jesus is setting himself up over against the emperor, because, if he is, that makes his life easy. He can just sign the death warrant, get the Jewish leadership off his back, and get on with oppressing the people and making money out of them. Jesus, however, does not want to talk about the kind of kingship Pilate is thinking of. He wants to talk about truth.

The account of this conversation is written long after the events it describes, after the resurrection. The author of the Fourth Gospel knows that Tiberius is dead but Jesus is alive. He knows that there is a power here which has much more claim to rule the world than does the Roman emperor. The emperor may have the power of life and death, but Jesus has power over death. "My kingdom is not from this world," Jesus says to Pilate. Jesus is the king of a very different kind of kingdom, ruled by peace not force, by love not fear. Soon this king will be fastened to an instrument of execution which will come to be recognised as his throne for ages to come.

**Application**

There is no emperor ruling our world. There are dictators still, but they are on a rather smaller scale. Our need is not for someone to offer an alternative to the rule of the empire. Our need is for someone to provide security in our chaos.

Is Christ the king? Look around you. Does it seem like it? The world appears to be in the grip of financial, political and natural forces completely beyond our control. Can the world survive? Will it be nuclear war that destroys us? Or global warming? Or the collapse of all our financial systems? Or a flu pandemic? It is difficult to find evidence that Christ really is king of the world.

And yet we say it. Whatever the evidence, whatever we feel, today we say that Christ is king. We assert the truth which is deeper than appearances. We reaffirm the truth that at the heart of the universe is a force for peace and justice and love which is stronger than all human forces, which has been from eternity and will be to the end of time.

It is part of human nature to search for meaning in the chaos of life, and to want there to be a structure and a purpose. We want to know that someone is in charge. Today we remind ourselves that someone is.

# Sundays in Ordinary Time Year C

*"Not even in Israel have I found such faith."*
(Luke 7:9)

**Illustration**

Never, perhaps, has a war been so effectively chronicled as the conflict in Iraq. Television cameras and reporters were with the British and American troops from the moment of invasion, through the search for Saddam Hussein, the struggles to restore and maintain order, and the gradual withdrawal.

Some of the most memorable images involved the interaction between the soldiers and the Iraqi people. To some Iraqis the troops were welcome liberators, to some they were hated oppressors to be driven out. Divided from the people by language and culture, unable to read the subtle signs, it was hard for the soldiers to know who was likely to shoot or bomb them. So we saw soldiers walking through the streets of a town and coming under fire. And we saw smiling children greeting the soldiers as friends. But even on the television screen, it was possible to sense the tension, the feeling that anything could happen at any moment.

**Gospel Teaching**

When we hear stories of Jesus travelling with his disciples, teaching and healing, it is easy to forget that the context for Jesus' ministry is life in an occupied country. Judaea is occupied by the Roman Empire, and the Romans are not squeamish about doing whatever it takes to maintain order, as Pontius Pilate later shows. Between the Jews and the Romans there is an atmosphere of fear and mistrust. At any moment there could be a rebellion, or a clampdown. At the higher political levels there is a necessary accommodation; no doubt the top Jewish officials have learned enough Latin to do business, and the governor knows some Aramaic, or at least has an interpreter on his staff. At the local level, the two communities probably ignore each other as much as they can.

So the centurion in our story is a bit of a surprise. He is a soldier in the occupying army. We can imagine that he has been in Judaea some time, long enough to settle down and get to know some of the locals. In particular, he has explored something of their religion.

Religion in Rome is a state affair. The emperor is a god, and you take part in his cult as part of civic duty. Jewish faith is very different. Perhaps the centurion has asked questions of his Jewish neighbours. Perhaps he has heard stories of the heroes of Israel's past: Solomon who built the original version of the Temple which is now in Roman hands; Moses who rescued the people from an earlier oppressive empire; the great prophets who interpreted the politics of their day and promised that God would act to save his people.

Perhaps the centurion thinks it would be a good idea to be on the right side of this God who has a history of destroying oppressors. Or perhaps he is drawn to the faith. Whatever it is, we are told that he builds a synagogue, a local place for Jews to gather and worship. And so he hears news of the travelling rabbi who heals, just at the point when his household is in trouble. There is no need for the rabbi to come, a word will suffice. The centurion knows authority when he sees it, and he doesn't want to get the rabbi into trouble with his own people by having him enter a Roman house.

The centurion talks about being under authority, and that is the truth. The Roman army did not allow for any disobedience to orders from above. If the centurion had been ordered to destroy the synagogue he had helped to build he would have had no choice but to do it. The people know this, and yet they commend him to Jesus. Somehow, here, a wall has been broken down, and enemies have become neighbours. There is faith and trust where once there was only fear and hatred, and Jesus the Jew accepts faith expressed in a Roman soldier's language.

**Application**
There is faith outside the Church as well as inside. There are people who give money for our church buildings, and people who are willing to work alongside the Church on social projects. There are those who worship in mosques or temples, who are people of faith in their own way. Jesus encourages us to welcome faith wherever we find it and however it is expressed.

## *"A great prophet has risen among us!"*
(Luke 7:16)

**Illustration**

In 1969, people on earth watched a miracle happening. People gathered round their television sets and watched as a man stepped onto the surface of the moon. They looked out of their windows across the unimaginable distance through the darkness of space, and they knew that what they were witnessing was as much magic as it was science, something that only a short time before would have seemed quite impossible. They were seeing the miracle of Apollo 11.

The following year there was another miracle. Apollo 13 also made the journey across space to the moon, but the astronauts did not land. Instead a terrible accident to their spacecraft left them struggling to survive. To the horrified television audiences it looked as though the crew of Apollo 13 would die in space. Only a lot of courage, quick thinking and creative improvisation brought them back to earth. The mission had still failed. But the failure was even more of a miracle than Apollo 11's success, because it snatched victory out of utter defeat.

**Gospel Teaching**

In our Gospel reading Jesus performs a miracle. The only son of a widow has died, and the whole town has turned out to support her in her grief. They know what it means to her, to lose the child she so loves and depends upon. Jesus, too, is touched by her sorrow. He goes across to the funeral bier and tells the young man to get up. A miracle happens. The dead boy sits up, alive.

Naturally there is a reaction. The crowd knows first and foremost to praise God for what has happened. But they also know their scriptures and are probably reminded of a story of something like this happening before. They may remember the story of the prophet Elijah doing something similar. Elijah had been lodging with a widow, whose son became ill and died. Elijah, the story tells us, stretched himself out on the boy three times and prayed, and so restored the child to life. Elijah's successor, Elisha, performed the same kind of miracle too. So the crowd who see the miracle Jesus performs know how to interpret it. They are seeing the work of a prophet.

If we saw a dead person coming back to life, we would probably suspect trickery. Or we might think that the person had only really been in a coma. Or we would know that a first-aider had performed the necessary resuscitation techniques. But the people of Jesus' day have their own explanation. "A great prophet has risen among us!" they exclaim. There's a new Elijah walking the earth. That's what prophets do, perform miracles. So that's what Jesus is.

Some time later, there are crowds again. But this time it is the prophet who is dying. The crowds are expecting a miracle. Elijah, after all, did not die, but went off to heaven in a chariot. Surely this new prophet who can raise the dead will save himself from execution.

But this is a different kind of miracle. This is the kind of miracle that snatches victory from defeat. This miracle will not bring just one young man back to life. This miracle will defeat death for ever. This is no new Elijah. This is God's servant and Son, the one who knows that victory can only be won when death has done its worst. The greatest miracle the world has ever seen begins in disaster.

**Application**
It can sometimes be tempting to ask God to work miracles for us. And sometimes miracles happen. Sometimes the bad things we are expecting don't come about. Sometimes people recover from illness, or children are born, or nations make peace. But sometimes when we wish for a miracle, nothing happens.

The people of his time thought Jesus was a miracle worker. And that was not so unusual. There had been great prophets before, who performed miracles. There were magicians, whose skills looked more impressive when scientific knowledge was less advanced.

But we know better. We know that the true miracle Jesus performed was to be defeated, and to die. Only on the other side of death could the miracle of eternal life be seen. That miracle offers life not just to one young man but to the whole of humanity. And it offers it not just for a few years, but for the whole of eternity.

*"Your sins are forgiven."*
(Luke 7:48)

**Illustration**
There are some wonderful attention-grabbing – and thought-provoking – church noticeboards, aren't there? Sometimes, too, a simple entry in a church's visitors' book may make us stop and think in a very profound way. One church noticeboard, advertising its forthcoming healing service, announced: "Try our Healing Service – you won't get better."

Another notice, displayed by a New York church, could well be adopted by every church and should be read by every passer-by: "Do come in – trespassers will be forgiven."

That particular notice can, perhaps, be set alongside a very revealing entry in the visitors' book in the tiny church at Capel-y-ffin in the Brecon Beacons, a beautiful jewel of a church in the Gospel Pass leading from Llanthony to Hay-on-Wye.

Browsing through its visitors' book a visiting clergyman was very taken with an entry written appreciatively, earlier that day: "In a world that is all rush, a moment of stillness and quiet. Thank you for being open."

Reflecting on that, and sensing the deep gratitude of its writer, the clergyman reflected that the Church is indeed always open – or it should be! And it is open to all – or it should be!

**Gospel Teaching**
In our Gospel reading today Luke recounts an occasion where Jesus is at supper with Simon, a Pharisee, who, almost certainly, is well established (perhaps even well regarded) in the community. With Jesus, the "man of the moment", at his supper it is likely Simon has invited his friends, along with others he would like to influence.

It seems to have been the custom then that such an occasion was "open house" for poorer folk, who would drift in to see what they might find to eat.

The woman in Luke's story – he calls her "a sinner", other commentators refer to her as an immoral woman, others say she is a prostitute – has slipped in to the meal and, not content with sitting quietly in the background, in a very intimate and yet loving way she takes centre stage.

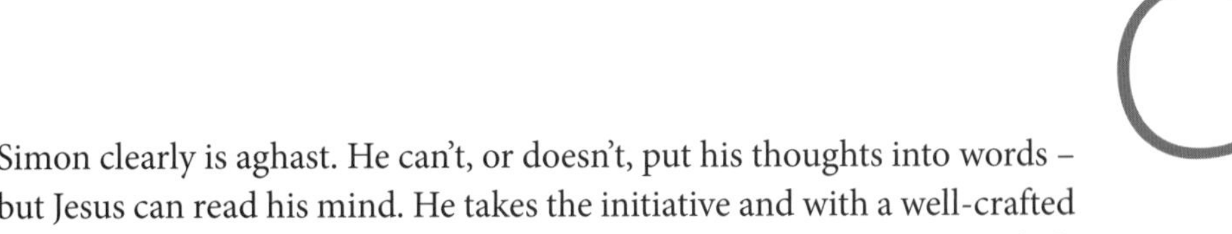


Simon clearly is aghast. He can't, or doesn't, put his thoughts into words – but Jesus can read his mind. He takes the initiative and with a well-crafted parable makes Simon aware of just how easy it is to be blinded by one fault in a person, to be one-eyed and prejudiced. Above all he makes abundantly clear that God's love is for everyone – and so, too, is his forgiveness.

**Application**

Are we ever "sniffy" about some of those who come into church? Do we consider we are more "holy", more faithful, more Christian, than others in the congregation because we attend more regularly than they do? And what about those who don't ever come to church ("but jolly well need to!") – some of them neighbours and friends? Do we ever feel "better" than them because we are churchgoers; we are Christians (aren't we?), and they are not? How easy, and tempting, it would be to answer "No". But wait a moment – have we never trespassed? Are we not trespassers too?

Jesus makes unequivocally clear that his love is for all. His forgiveness is open to all, no matter how great their trespasses. His forgiveness is for all who recognise their need for it, and seek it – as that amazing woman recognised her need for forgiveness and recognised his willingness to give her his unconditional love.

We are all sinners. We need his love and his forgiveness today and every day of our lives. When, like the woman in today's Gospel account, we recognise that we too are trespassers, and that we need his forgiveness and love, we shall find our gratitude is so great that, like the woman's, it will overflow. We shall not feel in any way inhibited in responding lovingly to the love which Jesus holds out to each one of us.

Jesus is not "sniffy". Nor should we be, for if we are to be faithful, if we are to be more Christ-like, if we are to be better (than we are, not better than others!), we must recognise Jesus offers his forgiveness and love to everyone, us included. He, like his Church, welcomes trespassers – trespassers like the woman in Luke's report, trespassers like you and like me.

*"Return to your home, and declare how much God has done for you."*
(Luke 8:39)

**Illustration**
Joanna was a devout Christian who, out of the blue, experienced a real sense of the presence of God; she overflowed with gratitude and it changed her life. She did not tell many people, guessing that most of her friends would not understand what she was talking about. But after some inner prompting she was drawn to talk to a priest who, after hearing her story, agreed to become her spiritual counsellor. For a time she was on a spiritual "high" and could talk of little else than her new awakening.

Then one day her spiritual guide said: "Jo, isn't it time you came down from the mountain?" When she queried this, he reminded her about Moses who, having seen the face of God, returned to the desert plain to continue leading the people of Israel.

When Jesus had exposed his disciples to his transfiguration on the mountain, they all returned to continue their journey towards Jerusalem. And even now, in our own day, the lovers of Christ who gather at Taizé or other places of Christian community and experience the openness, vision and spiritual renewal are reminded that they cannot stay there. However, they are encouraged to take Taizé back to their own countries and homes. And so it was with the "Gerasene demoniac".

**Gospel Teaching**
Jesus, even though among foreigners, was confronted by someone whose insight and loosened tongue announced him to be the Son of God. In those days, such a declaration and behaviour would always have been regarded as madness. Today we might diagnose these as symptoms of a psychiatric illness possibly engendered by anxiety, environment, or even the Roman occupation of his country.

Jesus is not concerned with reasons for distress, but only by the distress itself. Jesus never concerns himself with the minutiae of illness or, indeed, sin. Jesus knows our weakness and vulnerability and it is these he addresses and heals. He does not delve for detail. It is the fundamentals of someone's life and their degree of pain which absorb him.

It is easy to imagine the degree of wonder and gratitude that the man felt at being healed so completely by Jesus. After being deprived of his liberty, shunned by his family and excluded from religious life, his freedom must have made his heart sing. No wonder he wanted to drop everything and follow Jesus! The life which had been returned to him was his gift to his Lord.

But Jesus knew that the good news of salvation, which was intended to release millions of others from their own shackles through the ages, would not be effective if everyone who received his healing during his earthly ministry travelled with him. Seeds have to be planted wherever people are. In sending the healed man away, he was committing him to take up the work in his own place, among his own people. Jesus knew how hard this would be. But the man went and did it because he believed and trusted Jesus.

**Application**

Anyone who has ever been healed from a debilitating illness, released from any kind of prison, or relieved of a crushing burden will know how our Gerasene brother must have felt. Joanna certainly would! To become aware of God's action in the world at a very personal level becomes the yeast which enlivens the world around us. It is so tempting to remain upon the mountain, forever to live within the moment, or memory of, the moments of God's presence which so graced us and inspired us. Who wouldn't choose to remain with Jesus, following, listening, sharing? But this is not active Christianity. God gives these moments of intimacy to strengthen us for the task. He places his hand upon us for a moment, to remind us that he is God and we are his people.

But we are his people with a purpose, his purpose. However tempting it is to "remain on the mountain", we have to come down to the desert plain and begin to talk, to work, to share what God's inspiration has given us. We each become a channel of God's grace. His gift provides eloquence and energy to speak the words of justice, of peace, of equality, of righteousness, and the courage to do this where we are, where we live and work. It is where God wants us to be, where we belong, where his will is truly done by those who truly love him.

*"But as for you, go and proclaim the kingdom of God."*
(Luke 9:60)

**Illustration**

A letter once arrived on a bishop's desk containing a cheque for several million pounds. The letter was from a rich businessman who wanted to pay for a cathedral to be built in the poor city in which he had grown up. He was prepared to give this vast sum of money to ensure that the shabby place at least had a magnificent monument which generations of people would come to visit and appreciate; its beauty, if not its location.

The bishop hesitated for just a moment as he contemplated what a beautiful building it could be. What a gift to honour God. But then he thought of the thousands of people living in overcrowded, makeshift homes in the slum area within the city. These places were unfit for living, let alone raising children. Children lived on the street, prey to abuse from adults and the increasing drug culture, which deadened their hopelessness for a few hours. The bishop carefully placed the cheque in an envelope with a handwritten note. He thanked the businessman kindly for his generosity, which God would surely reward, but politely explained that the city needed many things before a cathedral.

**Gospel Teaching**

In today's Gospel we are introduced to three people who were potential followers of Jesus, all of whom are presented with options concerning discipleship: to make a decision between two different "goods", between what is good and what is best. These are sincere people who are worthy to be called as disciples; Jesus recognised their potential. They had work, families and the usual responsibilities to which they wanted to remain loyal.

The first needed to know that physical hardship was probably part of discipleship: Jesus' movement had no money apart from donations, no secure base, no comfortable bed. For the second, burying a dead parent was the solemn duty of a Jewish son, no one else. Failing to do so would be regarded as a gross act of betrayal. For the third, it was only natural to expect an expression of farewell to loved ones before an epic change of life, into an unknown future.

In the way that Jesus responds to these three people, it can almost sound as though he is trying to put them off. Does he not, then, want them to be his followers? They thought they were doing him a favour by offering to join him, but Jesus seems dubious.

Jesus did not mean to be as heartless as he sounded; he was simply being truthful with his followers – making it quite clear that the life upon which they were embarking would be unlike anything previously experienced. It would take courage and daring, superseding even the power of family ties – the greatest of all Jewish responsibilities. To follow Christ is to be prepared to sacrifice those things held most dear to us, even though we may not be called to do so very often – to choose between the good and what Jesus offers: the very best there is.

**Application**

Many of the things which God calls us to do these days as Christians do not involve such sacrifices. We are not often called upon to choose between the good and the best. Our decisions are more likely to be in our actions, how we speak, what we say, how we apportion our resources, how we conduct relationships. Sometimes these may prove to be difficult choices, to the extent of even giving things up when it is a decision between right and wrong behaviour, based on what we know are Christian values: performing works of love instead of snapping at each other; rejecting the kind of behaviour which only benefits ourselves; being generous with self as well as resources. Christian life is not easy, especially in the world as it is. We all need God's strength if we are to remain free from sin. But right and wrong are fairly clear.

But how do we choose between, let us say, going to church or remaining at home to care for an elderly, infirm person who appreciates our company? We may not always find what appears at first sight to be the right answer. But if our decision after prayer is based on what Jesus taught about self-offering love, we shall not be wrong. And we, like the bishop in his tough decision, shall be following Jesus in the best way we know, by actions which proclaim the kingdom of God.

Proper 9

(Sunday between 3 and 9 July inclusive)

*"He said to them, 'The harvest is plentiful, but the labourers are few; therefore ask the Lord of the harvest to send out labourers into his harvest.'"*

(Luke 10:2)

**Illustration**

As runners crowd excitedly towards the start of the London marathon, there's an atmosphere of celebration – the perspiration comes later! Yet it's also a culmination of many months of training. Such training is costly: the recommended four runs a week (three forty-minute jogs and a longer one at the weekend) will have their impact on a runner's diet, social life and other interests, as well as their comfort. After all, who wants to step out on a wet, cold evening? As race day approaches, it increasingly influences the runner's daily life. Yet for the dedicated, the marathon is worth the sacrifice.

Fr Pedro Arrupe, SJ, observed that "What you are in love with, what seizes your imagination, will affect everything." Whatever our passion, from sporting activity to another person, an ideal or a cherished ambition, it claims our full attention, putting other things into perspective. And it needs to: if we are too easily distracted away from our goal, we may lose out on what is really important. Marathon runners cannot afford to train casually if they want to stay the course on the day.

**Gospel Teaching**

When it comes to what matters, what could be more vital than spreading the good news of God's kingdom? As Jesus sends out the seventy, their mission is as urgent as it is important. He is now well on his way to Jerusalem and the climax of his ministry: sealing God's ultimate victory over evil through his death and resurrection. Jesus instructs his disciples to devote themselves to their task. They are not to be distracted by lengthy greetings on the road or indulgent socialising at their destination: they are to stay in one house only. They are not to carry possessions, wealth, or even a spare pair of sandals, but merely go as they are. Such simplicity will not only keep the disciples focused, but also remind them of their dependence on God's provision.

Jesus is fully aware of his disciples' vulnerability, describing them as lambs going out amongst wolves, but the need to rely on divine rather than human resources is vital. The disciples are to be engaged in urgent kingdom work, proclaiming God's salvation for all. The message of the prince of peace, who offers reconciliation at every level, will be life-giving for those who respond, whilst those who choose to turn their backs on the living God will face the deathly consequences. The disciples are to underline any rejection of God's invitation by "shaking the dust off their feet". In Jesus' day, strict Jews returning to Palestine from abroad would rid their footwear of any defiling Gentile mud picked up on their journey. Thus the disciples' action will illustrate that those who spurn God's message are placing themselves outside the company of his people.

The disciples are not just one more group of itinerant preachers: the inauguration of God's kingdom is now imminent, and they are its appointed heralds. As they preach, heal and cast out demons, they will express Christ's victory over the evil one, whom Jesus sees being defeated even as they exercise their ministry. Perhaps the disciples glimpse this glory on their mission, as they return in delighted amazement at their first-hand experience of God's power and authority. But Jesus warns them not to let the excitement go to their heads: however dazzling their temporary spiritual achievements, their eternal citizenship in heaven is the real cause for rejoicing.

**Application**

Do we get distracted in our discipleship? We often have good intentions as we seek to follow our Saviour. Yet we can so easily find ourselves sidetracked on the way. Our Gospel passage reminds us that the work of God's kingdom is of supreme importance – ultimately a matter of life and death. We need to take time to attend to eternal priorities amidst our everyday pressures.

If we feel daunted by our call to proclaim Christ's love and salvation, we are in good company. The disciples, too, were ordinary, frail folk. Serving Christ will take us out of our comfort zone, where we become all too aware of our human limitations. Yet that can be the very place where we are ready to draw upon God's resources, and discover just what he can do through us when we have the courage to go for him as we are, not as we'd like to be.

*"But wanting to justify himself, he asked Jesus, 'And who is my neighbour?'"*
(Luke 10:29)



**Illustration**

One night British writer and broadcaster Libby Purves got out of her new car beside a busy main road, leaving the engine and lights on. To her horror, the car locked itself. Her keys, mobile phone and coat were inside. Commuters rushed past, paying no heed to her waves for help. One battered vehicle did stop. Inside were two rough-looking young women, members of a minor pop band. She asked to be taken to the nearest phone box, but they, concerned at her waiting alone for some time while her husband drove out with the spare keys, insisted on taking her all the way home. In age, lifestyle and outlook they were poles apart. But in a moment of crisis, they were just three women together.

Stories like that provide light relief to newspapers and newscasts. Schoolchildren comfort an elderly person who has fallen, while another calls an ambulance. A teenager dives into a swollen river to rescue someone older. It warms the heart; there's still good in the human race. But what strikes us most is the contrast between the person in need and their "good Samaritan". It brings Jesus' parable closer to home.

**Gospel Teaching**

He may have based it on a real event – the road to Jericho was notorious for its bandits. But the characters represented an extreme contrast. Samaritans were religiously and ethnically related to the Jews but accepted only the first five books of the Bible. They had once built a temple on Mount Gerizim to rival that of Jerusalem. Sometimes there was open hostility. About two hundred years before Christ, a Jewish reformer destroyed the Samaritan temple. Sometime between 6 and 4 BC Samaritans scattered bones in the Jerusalem temple, desecrating it. So to orthodox Jews, Samaritans were outsiders, traitors, heretics. They could neither agree to disagree, nor live alongside each other. Most Jews practised a kind of apartheid by taking a long detour to avoid walking on Samaritan soil – a convention Jesus broke.

So the idea of a Samaritan being a good neighbour to a Jew, or a Jew being neighbourly to a Samaritan, horrified the lawyer. He asked, "Who is my neighbour?" because he was looking for a let-out clause which defined "neighbour" as "someone like me". Instead, he got a spiritual knockout punch. Jesus laid bare the biblical teaching that all people are neighbours made in God's image. Before God all are equal – equal in dignity, and equal in sin. Colour, class, race and creed are for practical purposes irrelevant. There are no second-class or inferior people, just people, like us. The two great commandments, which the lawyer knew by heart, ruled that wholehearted love for God was to be expressed by selfless and practical love for our neighbour. The two laws were completely inseparable. Break one, and you've broken the other. We are to be like God: he gave himself for us, so we are to give ourselves for others.

**Application**

We can feel the lawyer's pain. We also like to choose whom we help and whom we ignore. Like the priest and the Levite in the story, we look for excuses not to get involved. Fear of consequences may be one. Being dragged into more than we can cope with is another. Or we may feel sorry but conclude it's someone else's responsibility to help. But the beggar in the street who needs medical attention is my neighbour even if he does make me late and my car dirty. The noisy, rude and disruptive family down the road whose house is damaged by fire or flood leaving them homeless are my neighbours even if I wouldn't invite them to camp out in my house by choice. Of course, when we see pictures of starving children, we reach for our small change; but it would be more neighbourly to change our way of life so that people everywhere had a fairer deal.



This is not comfortable teaching. But it is not impossible either. Jesus never asked us to do the impossible. We need only the will to obey; he'll give us the strength to act and he'll sort out the complications. And who knows? As we love God with heart, soul and strength and our neighbour as ourselves, others may be drawn to God too. We never know what one good turn can achieve when it's done in Jesus' name. So let's serve him by serving others.

*"Lord, do you not care that my sister has left me to do all the work by myself? Tell her then to help me."*
(Luke 10:40)

**Illustration**

Louisa M. Alcott's book *Little Women* is essentially a morality tale. But it is told with great liveliness, and it centres around the relationships between four sisters, each of them very different. They do not always get on with each other, but they love and trust each other enough to learn from each other. If they had been more alike in character, the story would have been far less amusing, and there would have been far fewer opportunities for each to grow. Their differences are essential to the plot.

**Gospel Teaching**

Martha and Mary are clearly very different characters, too, but today's Gospel reading suggests that the learning is all one-way: Mary is right and Martha is wrong. But probably most of us, particularly, perhaps, the women here today, have a sneaking sense of sympathy for Martha, and a feeling that Jesus is being less than just. After all, somebody has to make preparations for guests, get dinner ready, clean up and so on. We can't all sit about in a contemplative daze.

This story about Martha and Mary is one that we tend to think we know quite well, only to realise that what we think we know is actually an amalgam of several different stories. We tend to associate Mary with the sinful woman who anointed Jesus with costly perfume, and who had a brother named Lazarus, whom Jesus raised from the dead. But Mark tells us the bare facts that a nameless woman anointed Jesus' head; Luke says she was a sinner and that she anointed his feet, but still gives no name, and John tells us that Mary anointed Jesus' feet, but says nothing about her sinfulness. It is also John who tells us about Lazarus.

So let us look with more care at the passage set for us today, and see what it actually says, rather than what we think it does.

It says, for one thing, that this all happens in Martha's house. There is no mention of any male relative. All Luke's first readers would have known instantly that this was an example of Jesus' famed radical stance towards women. He is doing something very daring by being in that house at all, when they are not his family.

But Martha and Mary are also doing something daring by welcoming this man into their home. Their reputations are definitely going to suffer. No wonder Martha is in a bit of a flap: if it is her home, she is the one who has taken the bold decision to invite Jesus in.

If Paul's letters are anything to go by, Luke's first readers, the earliest Christians, would have been meeting in just such homes, and would have been debating whether or not women could be hosts and leaders of their gatherings. Luke, with his well-known interest in women, is suggesting that Jesus set them a precedent here.

Luke goes on to show Jesus specifically commending Mary for sitting at his feet and listening to him. Students might sit at the feet of rabbis to learn, but women didn't. If women were present at all, it was simply to provide food and drink, and to remain quietly out of sight. Once again, for Luke's first readers this would have played into the discussion about women disciples. Were they just here to enable and facilitate the men's vocations, or could they be true disciples themselves? Luke is saying that Jesus has already answered that question.

It is ironic that this vignette of the full participation of women in the mission of Jesus should have turned into a story about a fallen woman and her harassed sister! If we take the context seriously, Jesus' words to Martha are a clear call: women, like men, need to put discipleship above everything else.

**Application**

And that is surely the point. Like Martha, we are all "worried and distracted by many things". There are so many things that have real claim upon our time and our hearts, where we feel justified in saying with indignation, "We can't all be contemplatives. Someone has to do the work!"

And, of course, that is true. But we must not let our worries and duties mask our real nature, or most important task, which is to be disciples of Jesus.

*"How much more will the heavenly Father give the Holy Spirit to those who ask him!"*
(Luke 11:13)

**Illustration**

Each one of us is a unique child of God. So each of us prays in our own way – expressing our relationship to God in the way that comes most easily to us. But sometimes we are lost for words. Sometimes we are depressed, not sure of ourselves, anxious, fearful and we know we need to pray but find we can't. It is then that the promise mentioned in the letter to the Romans comes to our rescue (Romans 8:26). The Holy Spirit of God dwells in us, so we can let the Holy Spirit pray in us. Jesus himself shows us the way. And when the disciples need to know more, he teaches them how to pray.

**Gospel Teaching**

Today we hear Jesus leading his disciples into greater awareness of discipleship. They were with him, talking, listening, eating, sleeping in his company, but they understood prayer to be something different from their direct interaction with him. They had a model of prayer which fitted their Jewish culture and time: formal, precise and fitting a required format. They were familiar, as Jesus was, with the prayers of the Psalms.

But they were to understand that God is flexible in his listening and that presence is as important as words. They were in Jesus' company and yet did not recognise this as prayer. They were preaching the good news and healing but still they wanted what John's followers had: a formula, a set of words which said what they thought was missing from their lives. They were searching for something lost, or not yet discovered.

As usual, Jesus offered them much more than they expected. He did not give them a theory about how to pray, or a lecture on the nature and purpose of prayer. He didn't rebuke them for their lack of insight into the nature of their fellowship with him. He didn't give them techniques for breathing and for concentration, or ways of avoiding distraction, so that they could become "professional" in their prayers. Instead, he inducted them into his own relationship with God.

He gave them a new insight into the nature of our God, "Abba", (Daddy) in place of the formal term for a mighty and distant God. He showed them a side to the Almighty, to his relationship with God and their own, which they had never before experienced, one of intimacy and intensity and all-embracing love, the kind of love and sacrifice which offered them all that a loving parent gives to a beloved child and much greater than that which friends share. The prayer he gave them contains everything which human beings need for their well-being, but which God knows even before we utter it. In their search for God, Jesus gave the disciples the perfect formula until they fully recognised the full reality of who it was that gave it to them.

**Application**

To want to search for God is, in itself, a gift of God. To search is to find because Jesus, who is the bridge between heaven and earth, and the Holy Spirit, at the heart of all prayer, provide the practical teaching and the spiritual inspiration which draw us towards the truth. We often search in the vain hope of finding our lost something when the uncertain world cannot provide the security we need. Frequently it is in this state of vulnerability that we find God, because our reaching out is sincere and usually in the complete faith which can risk everything, because there is nothing to lose.

It is for times like these that we were given what we know as the Lord's Prayer. It is all we need, if needing words at all. For it has been said that one minute with our full attention given to God with our whole presence is enough; God is not limited by our notions of time. Jesus understood our reliance on concrete terms, the recognisable formula and our need to express our yearnings in ways which convince us – and it is our needs that we are thinking of.

The Lord's Prayer says everything we need to say in words and brings us into God's presence as surely as the disciples were present to the person of Jesus. We can pray with confidence, certain that our prayer is heard.

*"One's life does not consist in the abundance of possessions."*
(Luke 12:15)

**Illustration**

In Bach's Cantata 82, the bass soloist repeats the haunting refrain that gives the song its title: "Ich habe genug." I have enough. Composed for the feast of the Purification of the Virgin Mary in 1727, the cantata expands on Simeon's words as he holds the infant Jesus, the words Christians still say as the Nunc Dimittis at evening prayer: "Now, Lord, you let your servant go in peace: your word has been fulfilled."

In the cantata, we hear: "I have enough, for I have taken the Saviour into my arms. I have enough; I have seen him, my faith has held Jesus to my heart. I have enough!"

And at that point, as in Simeon's original praise, the singer is happy to die. Music critics call this a gloomy song, with its focus on death: a description also applied by some commentators to today's reading from Luke's Gospel. Are they perhaps missing the point?

**Gospel Teaching**

The parable Jesus tells of the rich fool and his barns is not about death, but about life: about the way to live, not about the need to die. Jesus tells it in answer to an interruption from someone in the crowd while he was talking to his disciples about his identity and their mission to tell others about him. Into this discourse comes the jarring demand for Jesus to arbitrate in a property dispute.

Jesus replies first with a question: "Who set me to be judge over you?" Not a rhetorical question, for there's irony here: it was God who appointed Jesus, as we say in the creed, to judge the living and the dead, when he comes again in glory. For the moment, though, Jesus was not there to judge, least of all to settle family squabbles over land or goods.

Cautioning his listeners to shun greed of any kind, Jesus reminds them that life is more than possessions: life is a loving relationship with God. That is what we were made for. When our earthly life is over, our possessions are left behind; but if we have cultivated our relationship with God, then life goes on in God's eternal kingdom. Faith in God, in God's love for us as revealed in Jesus, is all we need. It is enough.

Jesus isn't saying that we should have no material possessions at all, shouldn't enjoy the good things God has given us – or that we should focus entirely on the one apparent certainty in our lives: their end! For there is another certainty: the love of God, a love that teaches us the value of giving, rather than receiving.

The rich fool had enough, and to spare, of material possessions. Specifically, he had food – so much that he couldn't store it all. Did others around him have enough food? Did he bother to find out? Did he call to mind God's frequent insistence through the prophets that we should feed the hungry, clothe the naked, give to the poor?

**Application**

We do not know the hour of our own death, or of Christ's coming again in glory, so all our carefully laid plans for increasing our material wealth in this world may come to nothing. If the investment we make is in our spiritual wealth, however, we can be sure of a rich dividend. If we seek the Spirit's treasures of love, joy and peace, they will be multiplied in the next life.

Let us look this week at the needs of others, and be prepared to give of our own abundance to those who do not have enough: to give our time, our talents, our money to help those in need; to share our faith with those who have yet to recognise God's love. This is not a way of earning our salvation, but simply helps us appreciate it. The more we absorb the commandments to love God and our neighbour, and the more we allow our lives to be guided by those precepts, the less preoccupied we will become with our own possessions and the less we need fear death.

Enough, they say, is as good as a feast. And the feast we have come together to share today is a reminder of God's all-sufficient love and a taster of that feast we will share in heaven. Feed on him in your hearts, by faith, with thanksgiving. For if we have faith, we have enough.

*"Be like those who are waiting for their master to return from the wedding banquet, so that they may open the door for him as soon as he comes and knocks."*
(Luke 12:36)

**Illustration**
Sally is looking forward to her birthday in a fortnight's time; in two weeks she'll be nine years old; in fourteen days she hopes she will be given the birthday present of her dreams. What she's longing for with such passion is for her parents to give her riding lessons at last. But mixed with that hope and expectation is an awful uncertainty. What if her parents, who promised to think about it, have decided against it? How will she cope with the disappointment and sadness? How can she dare to hope when there's the chance it won't happen?

It's two weeks later: it seemed to take for ever, but her birthday has arrived and here are her presents. She only now wonders how you would wrap up riding lessons – what would that parcel look like, surely not like any of these in front of her? She opens the card her parents give her and there on the inside is the message: "Your first riding lesson will be on Saturday 8th September at 11 o'clock." Her joy and excitement are more than thanks enough for Mum and Dad!

Now Sally's looking forward with a hope and excitement that she knows will not be extinguished – gone is that uncertainty and fear that haunted her before. She has the assurance that what she has hoped for will be hers.

**Gospel Teaching**
What a difference it makes when we look forward to something exciting that we know is going to happen. We can enjoy that delicious feeling of certain anticipation without the tension of doubt and anxiety.

In today's Gospel reading Jesus is encouraging his disciples to enjoy that sort of hope. He wants them to have the faith that is "the assurance of things hoped for, the conviction of things not seen".

He speaks to them of the Father's pleasure in giving them the kingdom; he talks about the unfailing treasures kept safely in heaven. He encourages them to be ready like servants who know for certain that their master will come back, they just don't know when. He tries to make them understand that the Son of Man will certainly come – the only doubt is in the timing of that coming.

The words of Jesus also suggest that God, too, waits in the hopeful expectation that his people will be ready for him, that they will be waiting eagerly for his arrival. Jesus talks of the master returning from the wedding banquet and finding such joy in his servants who are prepared that he actually gets them to sit down for a meal and serves them himself!

While we long for God's kingdom and do our best to prepare ourselves and keep alert, it may encourage us if we also have a picture of God longing for us to come home, to be at peace and to live in true fellowship with him.

**Application**

If we are to live our lives with the faith that is "the assurance of things hoped for, the conviction of things not seen" we need to allow that faith to take root and grow within us so that we no longer put our trust in treasures that don't belong in God's eternal kingdom.

To build a foundation for that faith we can look back at the long tradition of God's promises to his people and of the faith that has sustained generations of believers from the time of Abraham to the present day. It can often be the faith of people we admire that kindles faith in us, or the desire to have the sort of assurance they have.

We will each need to find our own ways of building our faith on these foundations. Some of us may want to spend more time with the scriptures and in prayer alone with God; some may prefer the fellowship of other people and discussions around faith that can feed and nourish all who take part; others may need to express their thoughts through writing, art or music. Perhaps some of us need all these things.

One thing we can be sure of is that as much as we are searching and longing for a richer experience of God's presence with us, God's longing for true fellowship with us is stronger than death itself, and he will find ways of reaching us – we just need to be ready to welcome him.

*"I came to bring fire to the earth."*
(Luke 12:49)

**Illustration**
In 1939 the British Prime Minister, Neville Chamberlain, came back from his meeting with Hitler in Munich, announcing "peace in our time". Everyone, apart from those near the seat of Government, breathed a sigh of relief and carried on.

But peace does not come that cheaply. Peace is something which needs careful thought and often some sacrifice. The price of that particular peace was in giving way to Hitler's territorial demands. Our momentary peace came at the cost of someone else. It was not even enough to hold back the tide of war, as had been hoped, as shortly afterwards war was declared.

Whatever we might think about the rights and wrongs of war, this incident stands as a tragic memorial to the failure of the policy of appeasement, the meaning of which is agreement to anything simply in order to keep the peace. It is interesting to contemplate what might have happened to the progress of what became the Second World War if the British Government had stood its ground, if it had supported those already under threat from Hitler rather than taking the soft option, if it had spoken the words of justice and truth rather than expediency. We can only guess.

**Gospel Teaching**
Today's readings give us an unusual insight into the people charged with bringing God's word to his people. The last thing on their minds was appeasement. The prophets, who were wedded to the truth and spoke it, did so despite threats. Jesus, who, in this instance, was far from being gentle and meek, told his listeners precisely what the consequences were: far removed from the peace and reconciliation which are the hallmark of the Gospels, and a million miles from appeasement.

Indeed, division and strife are to be expected when families differ in their spiritual allegiance. It can be hard for us to accommodate this apparently violent language from the Prince of Peace. The fact is that the word of God is not always welcome and neither are God's messengers. It is true that peace is a Gospel value, but peace is not the same thing as appeasement. Appeasement is about compromise, anything for a quiet life. This kind of

pseudo-peace costs too much, bought at the expense of justice, freedom and truth.

Peace without justice simply supports the forces of evil by cloaking the injustice. Dom Hélder Câmara said: "When I give the poor bread, they call me a saint. When I ask why the poor have no bread, they call me a communist." Wherever the Gospel is proclaimed, injustice, oppression and falsehood are challenged and this is bound to lead to division and strife because we live in a world where selfishness is regarded as strength and compassion is a sign of weakness. Jesus spoke of the division caused by his Gospel because sin goes deep.

Recognising and acting against injustice can disrupt families and communities when the world's values are in control.

**Application**

There is no doubt that the Gospel of Christ is a tough manifesto to live up to, telling things we would rather not know. It makes us read items in the newspaper reminding us of our Christian duty, feeding those who are poor, educating those who are illiterate, housing those who are homeless, campaigning for the rights of strangers because they, too, are children of God.

While we long to grasp the ultimate freedom of becoming the people God wants us to be, we are still drawn to the easy, popular and socially acceptable life, even though we know this way involves doing things of which we really disapprove and which we know are self-destructive. We are so easily tempted to chase after what leads to death and not life.

The Gospel message challenges us, our churches and communities to stand up and be counted, to become part of the solution, not remaining as part of the problem. The Gospel message will not be silenced while injustice, lies and oppression abound. The fire which Jesus wishes to light is a purifying fire, the fire of his Spirit, a flame which illuminates the forces of evil for all to see the paltry shallowness of sin, a fire which gives healing light and life.

This can be very painful, for we see ourselves reflected within those flames. The struggle against the forces of evil is not without cost. The cross cannot be evaded, but it is where the proof of love becomes evident.

*"Woman, you are set free from your ailment."*
(Luke 13:12)

**Illustration**
Have you ever thought about what it must be like to be in a wheelchair or to have to live with physical disability? The woman in today's Gospel story is bent over so much that she cannot straighten herself at all. She cannot turn herself to see the face of the one who calls her. She hears only the sneering, or pitying, or pitiless voices of people in too much of a hurry to care, and sees only their scurrying feet. Her bent figure, like that of an over-courteous servant, serves only to invite the scorn of the already haughty. She is good for very little; it is quite possible that she survives only by begging alms from fellow Jews on their way to worship.

And yet she is not bitter. Though her perspective is awry, it is not distorted with respect to her neighbour. For all the neglect she has suffered she does not cry out for grief, nor does she give voice to her complaint; though she is bent and twisted, she has resisted the temptation to gratify her anger. She does not presume to beg of the Teacher; instead he calls her over to him. When Jesus places his hands on her, she straightens up immediately, and praises God.

**Gospel Teaching**
What was it about that poor woman that moved Jesus so? Surrounded by throngs of people, in the midst of such controversy, he saw her. Was it the poverty of her spirit, the humility of her demeanour? Possibly she has understood something that few understand about themselves. "Woman, you are set free from your ailment." Jesus does more for this woman than simply heal her; he accepts and forgives. This is the healing she hoped for; this the peace she has longed for through the many years she has begged alms in the vicinity of the synagogue. Could it be that she alone among the people knows that the Lord lives among the poor in spirit and the contrite of heart, that the kingdom of God belongs to such as these?

And so came Jesus among the people of Israel, bringing good news to the poor and healing to the infirm. We have already wondered what it is about the woman that moved Jesus. But what was it about Jesus, we might ask, that moved him to have compassion on the woman obscured by the questioning crowd? More remarkable even than the woman's faith is that

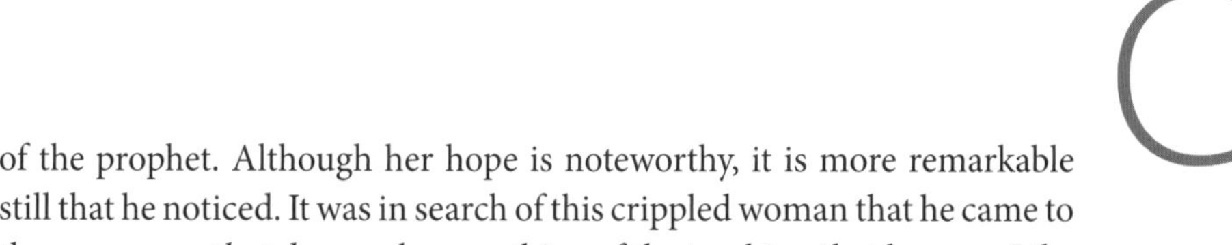

of the prophet. Although her hope is noteworthy, it is more remarkable still that he noticed. It was in search of this crippled woman that he came to the synagogue that day; we hear nothing of the teaching that he gave. Like Jeremiah, "the child among the nations", Jesus is but a "foolish carpenter" from the provinces, yet his foolishness shames the wise. His opponents are humiliated, but the people are full of wonder.

**Application**

Jesus came to the synagogue in search of a crippled woman who was despised. She was the last person that anyone else would have been thinking of on their way to worship – let alone the speaker – the most unlikely person to single out from the crowd. He must have sought her face in his prayers to have found her out. This was his remarkable faith: that this woman in her poverty was worth far more to God than the "acceptable worship" of the synagogue ruler and his pharisaical followers.

Jesus' remarkable faith is to be ours also. How often do we pray that the Lord will guide us to the most unlikely recipient of our love? How often are we prepared to pay attention when he answers us? Do we have ears to hear? Do we have hearts to hear? We want to be loved, but we are less ready to give the love that others also need. Like the woman in the Gospel story we all feel neglected, some more justifiably than others. Jesus is able to love because he has more than enough to share. Secure in the knowledge of his Father's love, he loves and loves. Let us pray that, in recognition of his great sacrifice for us, and of the abundance of the Father's love in giving so costly a gift, we too might love, even as he has loved us.

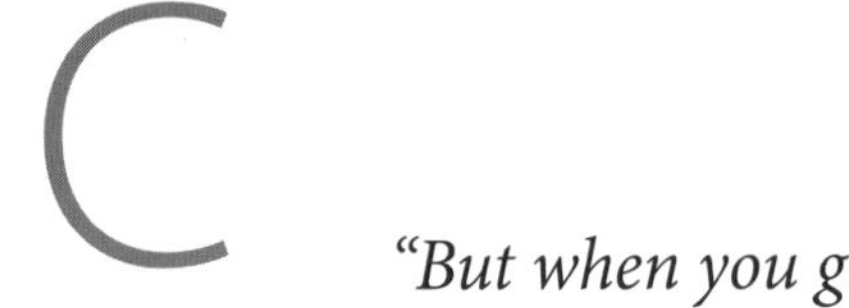



*"But when you give a banquet, invite the poor, the crippled, the lame, and the blind."*
(Luke 14:13)

**Illustration**

"Elbows off the table"; "don't scoop your peas with your fork"; "it's a napkin, not a serviette"; "don't lick your knife"; "don't talk with your mouth full". Most of us remember being taught a particular set of table manners as children; it was a way to show that you were part of polite society, not down with the riff-raff.

But the funny thing is that it's a good bet that most of us have changed our habits over the years. Why? Well, because times change and people mix. The gentle slurping of soup by someone we love proves not so shocking, after all. Table manners are good; they help us to fit in, and avoid making other people sick. But they have limitations too. There are those who have crumpled with embarrassment as they gazed at a line of different forks and wondered which one to use for the soup course. We're thinking about table manners here, but this two-sided nature to the rules in society has broader implications, and it's just this that Jesus is dealing with in his own stories about table manners.

**Gospel Teaching**

In Jesus' hands, tales about simple things are often also tales about universal truths, and our Gospel reading gives us two tales about table manners that are also pointing to much, much more serious concerns. In the first tale, Jesus is at a party with the great and the good. In those days, everyone had their place around the table, and hoped to get as near the top as possible, causing a bit of a scramble for the best seats. Jesus encourages them to aim low, and then enjoy the attention of their host as they are moved to the best seats in the house.

This is absolutely not a signal to everyone to deliberately pick the lowest place at either the table or in life, just so that they can be raised up. No, the point is that Jesus stands for a revolution, not just at the table, but in life in general. Rules are good, but they are also bad: they separate and divide. For Jesus, those who don't know how to work the system and which fork to use with the salad course are as respectable in God's eyes as the decent and well-to-do.

The second tale is again about someone throwing a party. In those days, as in our own, you tended to invite people rather like you. And why not? There's nothing nicer than a group of like-minded people getting together. Sometimes a little business is hatched, or an important introduction is made, but most of all it's just about pleasantness and mutual respect. Again, Jesus turns the rules on their head. "Invite people who can never repay you," he says. This doesn't mean inviting the disadvantaged and unlovable just to feel sorry for them and make the host feel good about themselves, but is about everyone being open to learning new things from unexpected people when Jesus turns the tables; about the shifting and changing of attitudes because of the mixing of people who are usually separated in life.

**Application**

You see, it's all about rules. Not just the obvious ones, like table manners, but those visible and invisible rules of society that determine how we live together. They are good in many ways. They help us to be sure of ourselves in unfamiliar situations, and they pave the way for getting on together. They are how our communities work. But they also create barriers and set people apart. They determine that we value some kinds of people more than others. They make it so that some people are in and some people are out.

When the rules break down we feel confused and frustrated, but, in reality, this may be a gift from God. Just as accepted table manners have slowly changed, so we need to be open to the possibility that the rules that define us can be changed. We can get together with people who are not "our kind of people", and be changed ourselves. Every time we break one of these rules to forge relationships we didn't think possible, get to know people we don't really have much in common with, a barrier begins to crumble, and the kingdom of heaven moves a step or two closer to becoming reality.

*"Whoever does not carry the cross and follow me cannot be my disciple."*
(Luke 14:27)

**Illustration**

Early in the last century two groups of explorers, one British, led by Captain R.F. Scott, and one Norwegian, led by Roald Amundsen, set out to race to the South Pole. The Norwegians got there first, one month before the British. When Captain Scott arrived he found the Norwegian flag firmly planted where he had hoped to place the British flag. It was a moment of deep disappointment for him and his team. They faced not only the burden of returning without the victor's crown but a journey beset by appalling weather conditions and reduced rations. Lawrence Oates, a member of the party, developed severe frostbite. He was anxious that his condition would slow down the progress of the team and endanger their lives. One night when they were weatherbound and unable to move, Oates left the safety of the tent and walked out into the blizzard, thus sacrificing his life for his friends.

**Gospel Teaching**

It is this kind of loyalty and self-sacrifice which Jesus asks us to consider as part of our own Christian witness in today's Gospel. He uses very dramatic language which demonstrates true commitment and dedication. Jesus always used strong and descriptive language to ensure his disciples understood their vocations. No half-measures: tough decisions and hard lives need proper emphasis and this is what he gave them. It may be that ultimate sacrifices will not have to be made, but it is our *preparedness* to make them that becomes our responsibility. In the end, nothing and no one must come between us and our vocation: nothing can ever be more important than carrying out the will of the God to whom we have pledged our lives.

Jesus wants us to be without doubt about the commitment's furthest extent. We are told by Luke that great crowds were accompanying Jesus. He knew that he was on the way to Jerusalem in order to be put on trial and made to suffer, even die. But the people had seen his miracles, witnessed the healing, heard him offer the promise of joy and glory to the downtrodden and oppressed. They wanted to become part of the next piece of action, to share the immediacy of events, touching his glory. So he lays bare the truth of what will happen. He wants *followers,* not hangers-on; sincere disciples, not opportunists. Can they pay the price and risk having to make the sacrifices? Are they equal to the challenge, can they face the cross?

**Application**
Christ poses the same question to us although we seem very far from the circumstances of his earthly ministry. Following Christ can demand a kind of heroism, willingness to endure pain, rejection, misunderstanding and hostility. If we follow our crucified Lord we will at times have to make painful choices and decisions about our lifestyles, attitudes, friendships, activities and jobs.

If our discipleship does not contain questions about these elements of our lives, perhaps we are living more like hangers-on, missing the point. Are we following Christ for the rewards, security, community, consolation, rather than because we are committed to him and to his values? Jesus asks us to commit ourselves to him and to take all the risks, to make the tough decisions because, in the end, this way of life will bring us greater joy than we can imagine. Christians should not be masochists, seeking pain for its own sake, Jesus has done that suffering for us. But we may have to face it with courage when it is imposed upon us. If we live in constant fear, if we are scared of the risk and do nothing, then our lives are like an unopened gift, like salt that has lost its saltiness: useless.

For Jesus, life is about more than safety and security. A life worth living is one which is not afraid of commitment to our ideals and taking the consequences of them. It is risking derision by offering ourselves by effort and money to enhance the lives of others. It may even take us to the furthest boundary of human giving, like Captain Oates, the offering of our lives that others might live. We must not fear the cross, in whatever form it takes in our lives. Jesus has been there first, he shows us the way and is the perfect example if, however imperfectly, we too have the courage to follow him.

*"There is joy in the presence of the angels of God over one sinner who repents."*
(Luke 15:10)

**Illustration**

In recent years, the music industry has witnessed a phenomenon described as "popera" or crossover music. Modern love songs are performed by classically trained voices: soloists like Andrea Bocelli and Katherine Jenkins, or groups such as Amici Forever and G4. By far the most successful act is the international quartet Il Divo: four men from Spain, France, Switzerland and America, whose first three studio albums knocked even the most famous pop star off the top spot in the charts.

A fourth, less well-known, album features a collection of music for Christmas. Among obvious favourites (like "O Holy Night") is a modern offering called simply "Rejoice", about returning to faith. Like all Il Divo numbers, it begins gently, with each tenor or baritone voice taking a line or two, before building to a soaring climax of harmony and power. And the chorus is: "Come and rejoice! What was lost is found!"

To their fans, this rousing finale is like a taste of heaven. Purists grumble, claiming that pop and classical don't mix, but there is something other-worldly about the sound of voices in harmony, which has been denied to those who shy away from classical music.

**Gospel Teaching**

Purists grumble in today's Gospel reading, too, as the Pharisees complain about Jesus socialising with "sinners". If "this fellow" were really a prophet, if he were really the Messiah, if he were really the Son of God, what is he doing mixing with such people? In reply, Jesus tells two parables, each echoing that same wonderful chorus: "Come and rejoice! What was lost is found!"

Both stories, however, challenge our received wisdom. If you were a shepherd, would you really leave ninety-nine sheep at the mercy of wolves and weather, and dash off into the wilderness to look for one silly stray? If you lost a coin, would you go to such extravagant lengths as that woman, calling friends together to celebrate finding it?

But that, of course, is the point of a parable. Jesus told stories to make people think, make them question their assumptions, and, most importantly, to tell us something about the nature of God and God's dealings with us. To God, every sheep is important, however silly, whatever scrapes they get themselves into. Every single human being is loved by God, however far they may have wandered from the path, and God will go to any lengths to rescue us.

We might not like to think of ourselves as sheep (silly creatures with no mind of their own). We might not even like to think of ourselves as sinners (they're the yobs, the rapists, the dictators). But the story is aimed at all those who, like the Pharisees, think themselves above reproach: at all those who cultivate a them-and-us attitude, and put other people into the "sinner" category because they're different, because they don't match up to our standards, because they're of another race, creed, "class", sexuality or gender.

Of these two parables, the story of the lost sheep gives us the traditional picture of God as a shepherd, familiar to the first listeners from Hebrew scriptures, our Old Testament, and one of the many male images of God. Only Luke, with his interest in women's faith, records the parable of the lost coin. The women around Jesus would surely have treasured up this story and passed it down, this story that wonderfully includes a woman as the God-figure, this story that uses an illustration from the household. They would not think the woman mercenary or foolish. Had she been saving for years for her daughter's wedding? What joy she would feel on finding that coin!



**Application**

God has been saving for years, too. God has been saving since the beginning of creation, loving us extravagantly, forgiving us unconditionally, patiently waiting. God saved the chosen people from slavery in Egypt and, as we recall in this Eucharist, God saves all people from sin and death, through the cross. We are all sinners but, in Jesus, God's love reaches out to us, searching for us until we're found. We only need to repent, which simply means to recognise that we're lost and to listen for the voice that's calling us (in prayer, Bible study, worship and everyday life) to a joyful reunion.

The name Il Divo was coined by analogy with opera divas, but of course "Il Divo" means the divine one. Jesus himself is our divine one, who came into the world to save sinners. The ultimate crossover act. God's love song.

*"You cannot serve God and wealth."*
(Luke 16:13)

**Illustration**
Monkeys are greedy and selfish. If they find food, they hold on to it. So here's how to catch a monkey. Put a big, tasty morsel inside a heavy stone jar that has a narrow top. The monkey smells the morsel, puts his hand in the jar and grabs it. Now he's trapped. He can't pull his hand out. The narrow neck of the jar will allow an open hand to pass but not a clenched fist that is clutching something. The monkey's only chance of freedom is to let go of the morsel, open his hand and pull it out. But he won't do that. He won't let go. He is imprisoned by his own greed.

**Gospel Teaching**
What is the subject of at least sixteen of Jesus' parables? Incredibly, it is money, and the possessions we buy with money. Jesus gives a lot more teaching about money than about prayer. Sometimes he sounds more like an investment banker than a spiritual teacher! How can this be?

Today's parable answers that question by making it clear that the way we handle our earthly wealth will go a long way to determining our spiritual wealth, in several ways.

Firstly, because our physical actions are a kind of enacted parable of our spiritual life. If we are irresponsible or lazy in financial matters, which are trivial in the grand scheme of things, we will behave in a similar way with our soul – a pearl of infinite value. In today's parable, we can assume that the steward's soul is in mortal danger – he has neglected his material duty, and so this steward will be equally lax in saying his prayers, forgiving others, and such.

Secondly, the way we treat what other people have entrusted to us reflects how we treat the spiritual treasure that God has entrusted to us – salvation for our souls through Jesus Christ. The steward has got somebody else in debt, and so is clearly incapable of looking after his own soul. He is fired – literally, if you believe in the flames of hell.

Thirdly, our earthly possessions are a wonderful opportunity for us to be generous. The more we give in the physical dimension, the more blessings we will receive in the spiritual realm. This is what Jesus is getting at when he gives what at first sounds like rather dubious spiritual advice: "Make friends for yourselves by means of dishonest wealth so that when it is gone, they may welcome you into the eternal homes." However, note that Jesus is not in fact recommending what the steward did. The steward was generous (with his master's money!) so that he'd be welcomed into the homes of the recipients of his generosity, whereas Jesus is recommending earthly generosity so we will be welcomed into eternal homes.

And this is the whole point of the parable, that "children of light" should be as shrewd as the "children of this age". The children of this age, like the steward, know the rules, and play the system to their benefit. They give and expect a return in kind. It makes good business sense. Hence companies who invest in quality products, with excellent customer services, earn their customers' loyalty in return.

Now, since giving and expecting nothing in return brings a heavenly reward, it is shrewd "spiritual business" to do exactly that. It is a proven fact that generous people have more friends, forgiving people are more forgiven, and loving people are more loved. This is the way the spiritual universe works, the laws by which it functions, and only very unshrewd people would ignore that fact and behave in a mean, grasping way, like the monkey who was trapped by his unwillingness to let go.

**Application**

Fortunately, we're not monkeys, although we live in a society run by people all clinging on to their wealth, and waving their fancy lives in our faces like so many stone jars. We have hope in the life-giving words of Jesus: "You cannot serve God and wealth."

Who is the servant, you or your money? If money is your master, making decisions for you about lifestyle, choice of work and relationships, then you cannot claim to be serving God. You may have a fuller supermarket trolley but an emptier heart.

If, on the other hand, you are serving God and not your money, then the way you use your money will have divine qualities. You will be a shrewd servant, as Jesus recommends, and so will be welcomed into eternal dwellings.

*"And at his gate lay a poor man."*
(Luke 16:20)

**Illustration**

Sometimes we simply get used to the unthinkable. Familiarity makes the unimaginable seem normal. The film *Schindler's List* presented us with a very stark contrast. On the one hand there was the Kommandant's sumptuous house: a house where there took place parties, feasting, merrymaking and fun – an altogether delightful place to live. Then on the other, outside the walls of the house, in the wider camp area, was the horror which was the life of the Jews imprisoned in the concentration camp: a life of hunger, cruelty, deprivation and sheer inhumanity, never knowing at any moment whether they would become the target for playful retribution when the Kommandant needed an escape from boredom. It was as though the house and its surrounding camp were a million miles from each other. Two sets of lives existing side by side, one oblivious of the other until sport was required and the guns brought out; the other only too aware of their parlous position; but neither knowing the other as human beings.

**Gospel Teaching**

Today's Gospel presents us with a similar, though less violent, contrast. The rich man enjoys every comfort and luxury life has to offer, while at his gate is Lazarus, hungry, suffering, degraded, dehumanised and, in this case, unnoticed. The rich man's sin was not intentional and purposeful – he simply lived only for himself. He was not deliberately cruel to Lazarus – his eyes and his mind were closed, he just did not notice him. The rich man was not wicked, like the Kommandant – he did not order Lazarus to be cleared away from his gate or treat him unkindly. After all, even in the agony of hell he loved his brothers, and was thoughtful for their care enough to try to save them from sharing his own fate.

The rich man found himself in hell not because of his actions, but because of his inaction, his blindness, both toward the world outside his own narrow sphere and to the word of God. He was indifferent to both. He was blind and unable to *see* Lazarus, and deaf, unable to hear the word of God, just like his brothers; unheeding of the warning and instructive words of the prophets. He was unthinking and uncritical of his own actions, unable to consider and calculate the obvious differences between himself and those around him. Jesus warns us that there can be a time limit within which we may see, understand and act. After that we have to rely on God's vision, understanding and action!

**Application**

When we hear this story it is tempting for us in the developed world to feel guilty about our lifestyles, for we are the "rich man" here. Faced with the complex problems of world debt, hunger and underdevelopment, we often feel unable to do much except give money to charity. For some people this amounts to paying for the scenes of deprivation to go away. We escape from the awfulness of our sense of impotence with a chequebook.

But do we even see those who are poor at our own gates, or are we deaf and blind to their needs? Do we recognise the poverty in our own cities: the homeless sleeping rough? The people trapped in their homes because they have no means of going out, either because of disability or age or lack of money? Do we recognise the poverty of the people who are perhaps sitting in the pew in front of us? Not just the material poverty, but emotional poverty, the loneliness, depression, the helplessness of the young mother trapped at home with small children. The isolation of the person who cannot read, the young person's desperation to find a job, the refugee far from home in a hostile and unwelcoming environment.

There is real poverty at our own gates. We cannot do everything for everyone, but if we choose to do nothing and refuse to become involved then we risk sharing the fate of the rich man. But when we are alert to the needs of the people close by, we shall also become more sensitive to poverty beyond our immediate community. And once seen with the clear vision of Gospel values our blindness will clear, our ears become attuned and the words of Jesus will take on a new resonance and imperative.

Proper 22

(Sunday between 2 and 8 October inclusive)

*"The apostles said to the Lord, 'Increase our faith!'"*
(Luke 17:5)

**Illustration**

In 1997, a student called Peter spent part of his gap year building chicken runs in Zimbabwe. One day he had the chance to do something he'd never done before: go skydiving. After the usual training, he was taken to a hangar to pick up a parachute. He was confronted by a long table upon which some youths were laying out parachutes for packing – for a derisory wage. Peter gulped. If these poorly paid youths made a mistake while packing his parachute, he would die. In that moment he knew what it meant to have faith. It wasn't a feeling, or an abstract proposition. Faith was stepping forward to take a life-saving parachute. Peter did. Another in his group did not. That is how faith works.

**Gospel Teaching**

However, most of us probably think of faith as coming in various levels of intensity. Thus the saints and martyrs had the most faith, then it descends in intensity to ourselves who are always, like the pleading apostles, in need of more faith. While this is ostensibly a humble attitude, it can also be a self-serving view of faith, allowing us to live a pale shadow of the Christian life, using our "little faith" as an excuse.

Jesus will have none of it, and rebukes the apostles. Using the example of the mustard seed's worth of faith, he says in effect that they don't need more faith. They just need faith!

How can this be? What is the nature of this faith that is either there or not? Surely it is natural to feel more believing sometimes than others? By no means, because the faith that Jesus describes isn't at the mercy of feelings. It is, quite simply, a matter of will. Just like the love he orders us to have for one another, faith is an act of will.

It is something we decide upon, and, once decided, act upon. If we sat around waiting to "feel" love for our enemies, we'd never do it – and in all honesty how many of us actually do? Likewise with faith. If we sit in our pews pleading with God to increase our faith sufficiently for us to revive his Church, sufficiently for us to take up our twenty-first-century crosses and live the Gospel life, we will wait for ever. We either believe or we don't.

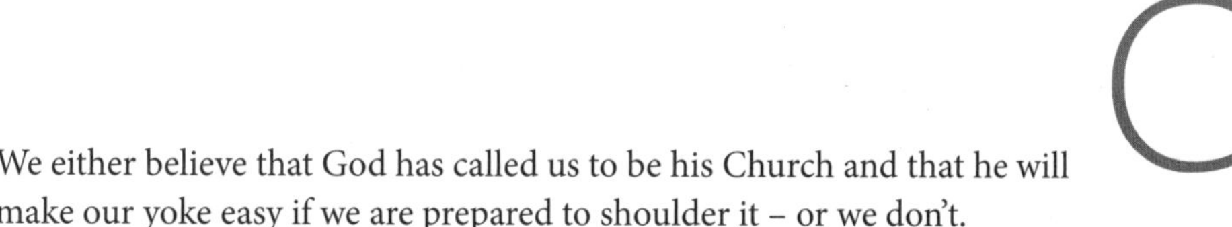

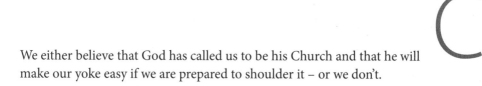

We either believe that God has called us to be his Church and that he will make our yoke easy if we are prepared to shoulder it – or we don't.

If we look more closely at how Jesus describes to the disciples the nature of faith, this will become clear. As earlier in Luke (ch. 7), when he heals the centurion's servant, faith is here explained in terms of obedience. The slave obeys his master. He wouldn't dream of eating at the master's table and the master would never ask him to. There is an order to life; faith means knowing that order works.

What is that order? Jesus never made any bones about it. God is the master and we are his slaves. Once we accept that order, then we have faith. We can't "half-accept" his lordship over us. There are no degrees of servitude. And there are no degrees of faith.

**Application**

If we have faith it means we have volunteered for God's army, which means we follow orders without expecting a big "thank you" when we do so; it means we take on the tough challenges as well as the comfy ones. But it also means we are guaranteed all kinds of benefits – salvation in Christ; the power of the Holy Spirit in our lives; the fellowship of God's Church.

Ah, but can we give orders in our turn? To mulberry trees and mountains? We can indeed. We can order mountains of hate to leave our hearts to make room for acts of reconciliation and forgiveness. We can command whole forests of fear to uproot themselves and be swallowed up in the sea of hope. We can command our dealings with other people to be based on justice and fair play, both in our personal relationships and in our treatment of poorer nations.

And we will give all these orders to ourselves in the confidence that they will be obeyed because we in our turn are obeying the one, the only one, who makes these impossible things possible.

## *"Jesus, Master, have mercy on us!"*
(Luke 17:13)

**Illustration**

Every winter the flu has us reaching for our hot-water bottles, aspirins and cough remedies. We crawl to our beds, afflicted with a high temperature and aching muscles. It's at times like this that we welcome the presence of another human being who will care for us. Simple gestures like making a cup of tea or preparing some soup help to raise our spirits. We don't expect our families or friends to provide a miracle cure for us, but their kindness and support can help us to recover from our illness. The goodness and support of a kind friend who is willing to be close to us when we are at our weakest can be healing and truly affirming.

**Gospel Teaching**

When the ten lepers in today's Gospel approached Jesus, they were not looking for a miracle cure. They simply wanted to be acknowledged by Jesus in their plight. They wanted to be accepted by Jesus, that is all. Because of their infectious condition the lepers stood some way off from Jesus to shout, "Have mercy on us!" Lepers were the untouchables of society; they remained always on the fringes of a community – shunned by everyone.

Through his actions, Jesus shows his followers the importance of accepting and embracing those who live on the fringes, those who are shunned, those who have become untouchables. Like the lepers, those who live at the edge of society don't have the confidence to walk forwards to meet others. They stand some way off. They had to shout at Jesus in order to make themselves heard, but Jesus didn't shout back at them. He drew near to them and spoke to them, treating them with all the respect that any human being deserves. His words gave them the ability and the confidence to re-enter society when he said, "Go and show yourselves to the priests."

For nine that may have been the end of the story. We do not know what happened to them. Perhaps they were so shocked to be healed that they simply forgot to say thank you. Or, more likely from the tone of the passage, they took what was on offer and revealed their bitter ingratitude by their hardhearted response. But there was another way. One of the former lepers, on seeing what had happened to him, was filled with praise for God. Jesus' love and acceptance had touched him at more than a superficial level. It had changed his heart, and he wanted everyone to know about God's mercy to him.

The response of this one man was what Jesus had hoped would be the response of the others. Their inability to see what had really happened to them saddened Jesus, and his words reveal his humanity, his capacity to be disappointed. "The other nine, where are they? Was none of them found to return and give praise to God except this foreigner?" He didn't want thanks for himself, but wanted the lepers to acknowledge the mercy and love of his Father. Jesus healed people not simply for the sake of it, but in order to show them how much God loved them. It was only the Samaritan, one of many despised by the Jews, who came back to thank Jesus. Once again, we are reminded that the healing power of Jesus extends to all.

**Application**

There are few lepers around today perhaps, but in our parishes there may be many who feel shunned. There may be many who feel unwelcome and isolated: single parents, divorcees, the elderly, the homeless and perhaps those who are ill.

We are called to embrace those who feel they are outsiders, to give them the confidence to be active members of our communities. We are called to accept people, not to exclude them. Like the Samaritan, those who live on the edges of society are not only looking for healing; they seek understanding and acceptance.

Jesus has shown us that his love and concern were not restricted to those of a particular race or class. God's love and mercy are given freely and are never-ending. They are available for everyone. And so our kindness, friendship and acceptance should also be available for those who feel that they don't belong anywhere. Like Jesus, there may be disappointments for us along the way, but the cultivation of real love, friendship and acceptance will do wonders for our community at every level.

*"Will not God grant justice to his chosen ones who cry to him day and night?"*
(Luke 18:7)



**Illustration**
Mozambique is just one of the countries that have known long-term conflict to be at the root of their poverty and isolation in the world. First, it was bush warfare against the Portuguese colonialists, then it was guerrilla warfare against an internal force supported by right-wing outsiders. For almost thirty years, Mozambicans suffered destruction, insecurity, dislocation and isolation from the world community.

Whilst all the political powers met for discussions for peace, the churches came together in prayer for peace. Every Friday was a day of prayer and fasting. The Mozambican churches were courageously led by their peace-seeking and peacemaking leaders of all denominations. The Christian Council member churches began to plan for peace with workshops on conflict resolution, and proposals for a project to "beat swords into ploughshares". Despite the delay, never did the churches doubt that their prayers would be answered.

And they were miraculously answered in October 1992, with the signing of a peace agreement. Onlookers were nervous that the road after the agreement would be rocky, or that peace might be impossible, but ordinary faithful Mozambicans were rewarded. In the years that followed, Mozambique celebrated continued peace, increasing prosperity – and popular creative art displays of recovered weapons!

**Gospel Teaching**
This is an odd parable, because it seems to equate God with an unjust judge. But that is why Luke is careful to tell us that it is actually a story about the importance of persistence in prayer. Some things can only be achieved by faithful, dogged persistence. Prayer like this begins to shape the one who prays. It becomes more than just a passing whim: it becomes a real vocation.

The Bible often uses the image of the weakness of widows to signify loneliness and dependency on the Lord, and in Israel widows were those who had a particular claim for justice. The character of the unjust judge seems to be painted darkly for us, but this is to highlight the contrast between him and our righteous judge. We are encouraged to consider how much our loving God will judge justly, and will act for those persistent prayers of faithful believers. Augustine once wrote that every soul that knows itself lonely and helpless, except in God alone, is like a widow. The destination and nature of the Church is to be the Bride of Christ, but in darker times the prayers of those who know their "widowhood" will see God's justice come.

This parable draws out a lesson for those struggling to survive in difficult times, whether individuals or communities: God will not abandon them and they must remain faithful, continuing in prayer until God answers. It is faithfulness to God that provides the power of our prayers. But the parable leaves a question for the disciples of Jesus – not a question of whether God hears and responds, or whether Jesus will come again, but rather a question of whether the disciples of Christ will remain faithful during a delay in a response of God, and during the long haul caused by the delay in his return.



**Application**

Dark times come to our world and to all of us at times. Today we are not talking about the darkness that comes from sin in our lives, but the darkness that comes from evil in the world. It is important to know and make the distinction, so that our prayers may be more far-reaching and real.

In our world today, with mass media and communications, we are easily brought in touch with tragedies and disasters of all kinds. We daily have many reasons for prayer for injustices of all kinds, personally, locally, nationally and globally. Daily, we are required to remember who God is, hold on to what we know from experience of the unchanging character of our loving, embracing God, get involved and keep on praying for justice. The world needs our prayers. We need to be faithful disciples, bringing our prayers unceasingly before our God who listens and responds so graciously.

God is not like the unjust judge who grudgingly deals with the widow – God is committed and involved with creation and with us, his people, in all that life brings, good and bad – but it is by our persistent prayer that we show our trust and participation in God's activity in our world and our lives. So, keep on keeping on!

*"God, be merciful to me, a sinner!"*
(Luke 18:13)

**Illustration**
Have you noticed how the most compelling heroes and heroines are those who get things wrong? Take the delightful Elizabeth Bennet, for example, in Jane Austen's masterpiece, *Pride and Prejudice*. She initially dislikes Mr Darcy because he seems to think himself better than other people, yet she prides herself on having a better understanding of human nature than other people do. This combination of pride and prejudice on both sides gives the novel its depth, as well as its title.

Both Elizabeth and Darcy learn lessons, and we end up loving them both. Neither of them is perfect, but we love them all the same. Is it because, deep down, we recognise that we, too, are less than perfect? Perhaps that's why we usually identify with the tax collector in the parable Jesus tells in today's Gospel. Yet our response should not echo the apocryphal Sunday school teacher, who finished reading this story to her class with the words, "Let's thank God we're not like that naughty Pharisee."

Nor should we say, "Thank God I'm not like that silly teacher." This could go on for ever!

**Gospel Teaching**
So what is Jesus teaching us here? If the Pharisee did not steal or commit adultery, if he fasted regularly and gave a tenth of his income back to God, should we not identify with him, rather than the tax collector who admits to being a sinner? Tax collectors were collaborators with the Roman occupiers, habitually charging extra for their own gain. A Pharisee was a model of good behaviour, a tax collector the epitome of evil. The parable's first audience must have been horrified when Jesus announced that the tax collector, not the Pharisee, was justified – restored to a right relationship with God. Nobody, it seems, is too good to need forgiveness, nobody too bad to be forgiven.

Two other important messages emerge from this parable. First, that it is not what we do, or do not do, that restores our relationship with God ... but what he does. God alone can give us the forgiveness we all need. The Pharisee, like some Christians in the course of history, thought that salvation could be earned by doing good deeds. The tax collector recognised that salvation comes through the grace and mercy of God.

The second message is equally important: we must not judge others. The Pharisee, in his pride and prejudice, considered himself superior to other people. Yet Jesus vindicated the tax collector, who saw only his own sin and recognised that only God could wipe that clean. When we stand before God, we answer for our own shortcomings. There is no point in making comparisons with other people, even if we could know the secrets of their hearts, which we cannot: only God knows those.

Jesus tells us that those who exalt themselves, those who do not give God his due but rely on their own strength, will be humbled. He tells us that those who humble themselves, those who recognise that God is in charge, will be exalted. A dominant theme runs through Luke's Gospel like a golden thread: the proud will be cast down and the humble lifted up, until both are brought to a point where they can accept God's loving purpose for them.



**Application**

All of us are sinners. Just like Elizabeth and Darcy in *Pride and Prejudice*, just like the Pharisee and the tax collector in the parable, we all have our faults and failings – but we all have our good points, too. None of us is perfect, all have fallen short, yet Jesus died for us all. Each of us is made in the image of God, and God is longing to restore the clarity of that image in each of us, if we simply turn to him and ask.

Jesus tells us not to compare ourselves with others, whether it's "God, I thank you that I am not like other people" or "She's such a good Christian, she makes me feel really guilty." In our dealings with others, let's remember the old rhyme:

> "There's so much good in the worst of us
> and so much bad in the best of us
> that it ill behoves any one of us
> to talk about the rest of us."

None of us is perfect, but God loves us all the same. God, and God alone, knows exactly who we are. And loves us still.

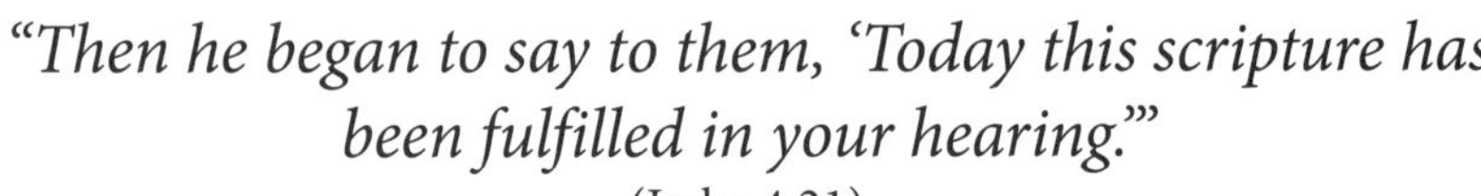

*"Then he began to say to them, 'Today this scripture has been fulfilled in your hearing.'"*
(Luke 4:21)

**Introduction**
The encounter between Islam and Christianity, recently so much in the news, brings various challenges to Christians, not least the challenge to grow in understanding of our own faith. Within Christian–Muslim dialogue a recurrent question is that of the nature and purpose of scripture – a good question to ponder on Bible Sunday. A brief look at how Muslims understand their scripture, the Qur'an, may help us think afresh about the place of the Bible in our faith. The Bible and the Qur'an make for an illuminating comparison.

The Qur'an is at the very heart of Islam. Muslims believe that every Arabic word of the Qur'an was revealed by God to Muhammad. For Muslims, the Qur'an is therefore in an absolute sense the Word of God. It contains the messages which God dictated through Muhammad, who was not in any sense the source of these messages but simply passed on the divine words entrusted to him. When quoting the Qur'an, Muslims do not say, "as Muhammad says...", but "as God says..."

The Qur'an is seen as a mercy from God, a miracle bringing God's eternal, uncreated speech into this world and providing a straight path to God. The Qur'an was revealed in Arabic and is strictly speaking untranslatable; translations into other languages are useful guides to the Qur'an's meaning, but they are not the Qur'an itself. God has spoken in Arabic words, which have been collected together in the Qur'an, after which no further divine revelation is needed.

Christians are sometimes known by Muslims as "People of the Book". We too have a scripture, which we treasure and to which we listen to hear God's word. But the place occupied by the Qur'an within Islam is akin not to that of the Bible within Christianity but to that of Jesus himself. Both faiths proclaim a definitive act of merciful divine communication which brings into this world an eternal and uncreated reality: for Muslims this is the Word made book in the Qur'an; for Christians it is the Word made flesh in Jesus of Nazareth.

So if Jesus is the heart of our faith, where does that put the Bible? Encounter with Islam can clarify things helpfully, because, however vital the Bible is, it is not orthodox Christian doctrine to claim for the Bible what Islam claims for the Qur'an. For example, the biblical authors were inspired by the Holy Spirit, but their humanity was fully engaged, which gives us a rich diversity of scriptural witness to God's ways. This is a reality not to be wished away but to enjoy and to learn from.

Another deeply embedded feature of the Bible is its translatability. Consider that it was only in translation that the vast majority of the words of Jesus came to be in the Gospels. So in contrast to Islamic confidence about God's very words in the Arabic of the Qur'an, the Bible may seem to offer a rather dilute form of revelation. But this is no cause for Christian defensiveness, because the Bible can be the Bible in every human language; the history of its translation is one of the glories of the story of the Church.

The fundamental contrast is that whereas the Qur'an is to a very significant degree a scripture about itself, proclaiming itself, the Bible has no such sense of its own centrality. The Bible is not about itself, but (from a Christian perspective) about Jesus. The written word points in a great variety of ways to the living Word. The Bible tells us that the language of God's deepest communication is not ultimately scriptural words, but rather flesh and blood.

**Gospel Teaching and Application**

So in today's Gospel we hear how, in the synagogue at Nazareth, Jesus reads aloud words from the prophet Isaiah and then declares that this scripture has been fulfilled – fulfilled in him, the one who has just been anointed at his baptism with the Spirit of the Lord to bring good news to the poor. The Word made flesh takes up the written word and declares that it is to him and his healing power that it points.

So we pray that in the Church and in our own lives the Bible may do the job that God has assigned to it. It is vital to our faith but it is not its centre. As we attend more closely to the words of scripture may they constantly point us beyond themselves to the presence of Jesus and all that his coming means for the world.

*"Blessed are you who are poor, for yours is the kingdom of God... But woe to you who are rich, for you have received your consolation."*
(Luke 6:20, 24)

**Illustration**
Many years ago, an anonymous letter was sent from a prisoner in a Soviet concentration camp. Many of the prisoners had been incarcerated because of their religious convictions, and the letter spoke of their experience of Easter in the camp. The conditions in which the men were kept were grim but, against all natural expectations, they found themselves united in the joy of Christ. There was no outward encouragement for this; on the contrary, the prison guards seemed to go out of their way to be even more difficult and obstructive than usual. The letter continues:

> "Yet Easter was there: great, holy, spiritual, unforgettable. It was blessed by the presence of our risen God among us – blessed by the silent Siberian stars and our sorrows. How our hearts beat joyfully in communion with the great Resurrection! Death is conquered, fear no more, an eternal Easter is given to us! Full of this marvellous Easter, we send you from our prison camp the victorious and joyful tidings: Christ is risen!"



**Gospel Teaching**
Today's Gospel presents us with Luke's harsh and uncompromising version of the beatitudes: it is the materially poor who will inherit the kingdom; the rich have already received their reward. As citizens of the wealthy West we find it hard to accept that Jesus may have meant exactly what he says here: that God favours the poor, not for any super-spiritual qualities they may possess, but simply on account of their poverty, which is an offence against the justice of a righteous and holy God. Such an attitude challenges our natural greed and acquisitiveness, and in our discomfort we tend to prefer Matthew's more spiritual form of the beatitudes – "Blessed are the poor in spirit, for theirs is the kingdom of heaven."

But the spiritual and material cannot be separated, and today's Gospel forms part of a consistent thread running through the whole of Jesus' teaching: "You cannot serve God and wealth" (Matthew 6:24). "Not everyone who says to me, 'Lord, Lord,' will enter the kingdom of heaven, but only the one who does the will of my Father in heaven" (Matthew 7:21). And in today's reading: "Do to others as you would have them do to you."

Jesus is talking here, not so much of any intrinsic evil in material wealth, but of the dangers of our distorted attitudes towards it. When wealth and possessions take priority, we become blind to the fact of our total dependence on God and careless of the suffering of our brothers and sisters. But with priorities correctly ordered, the seemingly impossible becomes possible: "Love your enemies, do good to those who hate you, bless those who curse you… If anyone strikes you on the cheek, offer the other also… Give to everyone who begs from you; and if anyone takes away your goods, do not ask for them again."

**Application**

The prisoners in our illustration suffered involuntary poverty: they were unjustly deprived of their liberty, treated with gratuitous cruelty, separated from their loved ones, robbed of money and possessions, and had no guarantee that they would emerge from their incarceration alive. And yet the letter spoke of Easter being "blessed by the silent Siberian stars and our sorrows". Their deep faith enabled them to see beyond the dark appearance of things, and to experience the profound joy and mystery of the risen Christ in their midst. That joy could not be contained, and overflowed even to those outside the camp. They were able to bless where they were cursed, and love where they were hated.

We need to resist the temptation to live in spiritually watertight compartments, and allow ourselves to be confronted by the words of Jesus in all their raw challenge. A life that seriously seeks after God will inevitably be engaged with the world, and will be unable to help expressing itself in ways of justice and compassion. Conversely, a spirituality that is essentially self-seeking will never be able to reach outwards to the world.

The beatitudes in Luke focus first on the need for right action; those in Matthew give priority to a right spirit. In both, Jesus calls us to re-examine our priorities and our attitude to the riches we have been given. We are challenged to allow our consumer mentality to be transformed into that of a steward, reaching out in love to all humanity, holding all things in trust and available for God's purposes in the furthering of his kingdom on earth. We are challenged to be saints, with Jesus as our pattern.

*"For the Son of Man came to seek out and to save the lost."*
(Luke 19:10)

**Illustration**
Losing things is very frustrating. You know quite well that you have put four pairs of socks in the washing machine, and yet two pairs and four odd ones come out. Or you put something away in a safe place, and then haven't the faintest idea where that place is. Or you can't find your credit card or your car keys. Whether the loss is minor or really worrying, we have all had those times of searching feverishly for something that we just know is there, but we simply can't find it. Very often, we just have to tell ourselves to calm down and think of something else, and then suddenly the precious object turns up, somewhere we know we looked several times already.

**Gospel Teaching**
In today's Gospel reading, there is a lot of searching going on. Obviously, Zacchaeus is searching for a way to see Jesus. So desperate is he that he's even prepared to climb a tree just to get a glimpse. He isn't expecting any more than that. Quite the contrary, probably. Climbing up a tree removes him from any chance encounter with Jesus. He isn't going to be jostled by the crowd and pushed forward accidentally into Jesus' path. He isn't going to be one of the crowd reaching out to touch Jesus or shout to him or hold their children out to him.

Zacchaeus has, without consciously realising it, chosen himself a position that perfectly expresses what he thinks he deserves. He is an outsider, an onlooker, removed from the excited crowd below him, seeing what they see, but not sharing their lively interchanges about what is going on. Zacchaeus' way of life has ensured that that will always be the case. He has made himself an outsider, buying himself security but at the cost of being an outcast, just as the sycamore tree buys him a view, but guarantees that he is removed from the emotion that goes with it.

But Jesus is searching, too. Jesus is searching for the lost. And his search and Zacchaeus' search come together. Zacchaeus may have thought he was just looking for a good view, but Jesus knows at once that Zacchaeus longs for much more than that. He longs to be found and to be taken home, back to his own people and his own community. As soon as Jesus looks up into the tree and finds Zacchaeus, Zacchaeus knows that he has found what he is looking for and been found by the one who was searching for him. He had not realised, before now, that anyone cared enough even to notice that he was lost, let alone to search for him. He had not realised that he himself had lost something so precious that no money could buy it back. But now, instantly and joyfully, he is willing to pay everything for it, to give back all his ill-gotten gains, because he knows he is loved and valued, and that he has come home.

Jesus knows he is searching, and Zacchaeus comes to realise that he is, too, but they are not the only seekers in this story. The people who grumble as Jesus brings Zacchaeus home are also searching. They are searching for a way to go on excluding Zacchaeus. They are searching for a way to keep their home to themselves. They are trying to make Jesus behave like a proper teacher and condemn Zacchaeus and all the other collaborators who have wilfully got themselves lost. They are looking for ways to keep God in his proper place, in church, not out here in the crowd, finding all the lost and bringing them home. Their search is doomed, because God just will be God. But that means that God is searching for them, too, searching for their generosity, their vision, their love and their compassion: God's never-ending search, in them and in us, for the human beings we are made to be.

**Application**
In this Gospel story, Jesus gives us one of the central definitions of his ministry: he comes to find the lost. Those of us who call ourselves his disciples are required to join in the search, and to seek out the lost and bring them home, to God's people, God's house, God's love. The home we share is God's, not ours, and we are all God's beloved guests.

*"He is God not of the dead, but of the living; for to him all of them are alive."*
(Luke 20:38)

**Illustration**
Recent years have seen considerable development in the care of the dying. Most areas now have access to a hospice, providing care for those who are dying and support for their families. Hospices accept people of all faiths and encourage them to approach death with confidence. There is no attempt to pretend that recovery is on its way, only an imaginative determination to approach death with dignity and without fear. Quite often residents will take the time to arrange their own funeral service and choose beautiful music that reflects this spirit of calm acceptance of death and celebration of the life drawing to its close.

Even fit and healthy individuals often comment after hearing an inspiring or uplifting hymn: "I'd like that to be played at my funeral." In the secular world this used to be considered a rather morbid thought, but now society has a more healthy attitude to dying.

For Christians it has always been appropriate to think of these last things, to prepare for our passing from this life to the next, because we share the life of Christ, just as he shared ours, and as he rose from the dead, so shall we. We have Jesus' own assurance about this. Therefore, as we believe there is more to death than an ending, indeed, beyond it a better life awaits us, we can prepare our funerals with their joyful music secure in confidence and faith.

**Gospel Teaching**
The Sadducees, who did not believe in the resurrection, may not have been able to face death with our confidence. They asked Jesus how death would affect a woman who had been married to successive brothers after each of their deaths, which was the custom at that time. Which man could claim her? This was a kind of test of Jesus, seeing how his teaching would stand up in comparison with orthodox Jewish belief. And Jesus passed the test, for no one could argue further with him.

But for us, Jesus' response brings more than just confirmation that he knew the right answers, within the Law. He brings hope and confidence to all those who believe in him as the Messiah of God. He reminds us that, before him, Moses in the Hebrew scriptures had implied that the dead would rise again. For us, Jesus presents a vision of heaven which is very different from our present world. Accordingly, the structures of our earthly condition will not exist in heaven. It is hard for us, as it was for the Sadducees, to understand how things will be when we die. Yet the words of Jesus in today's Gospel are very simple and direct. He tells us that God is God of the living and the dead: all are alive to him.

This seems to imply that our life continues but in a different and transfigured form. But one thing is certain. Jesus never expressed any anxiety for the future of the disciples he loved. He assumed that their relationship would continue for ever, and this is our hope when we adopt discipleship of Christ as our life.

**Application**

It is consoling for us who may have lost dear friends and relations through death to be reminded that all are alive to God. Our God and their God, there is no division. All that separates us from our loved ones is our limited human vision and understanding, not God's. This should give us courage.

As Christians who try to live accordingly, we are already living the life of God. And this life in Christ which we enjoy now we shall also share with those who have gone before us. Death is an ending of this life before we move into that other dimension where the fullness of God will be made known to us.

At the moment, we have crucial tasks to accomplish on earth: primarily, to reveal the love of God to those around us who do not believe. We are God's hands and feet in the world, and are being used to draw people to him; to live his presence, to be his voice of reassurance and hope. We are here to transform what has been spoiled by human nature into what God intended. Although this task seems well beyond the capacity of human beings we must remember that we do not toil alone. We are accompanied and empowered by the Holy Spirit; we are resurrection people and our song is hope.

*"This will give you an opportunity to testify."*
(Luke 21:13)

**Illustration**
On British television not long ago there was an intriguing documentary about what is often called "The Rapture". The narrator was partly interested in where in the Bible the idea came from, but much more interested in how the people who believe it to be imminent are preparing themselves for it. He went into a shop in America to ask for advice on what would be suitable equipment with which to await the Rapture and was ushered towards a shelf of guns. This is not recommended by any of the Bible texts that talk about the turmoil before the end of the world!

**Gospel Teaching**
Most commentaries on today's Gospel reading, and the similar ones found in Matthew 24 and Mark 13, are agreed that what Jesus is predicting is the terrible war that took place in AD 70, when the Roman occupying force decimated the Jewish people and razed the Temple to the ground. Even though this doesn't seem to do justice to everything in the passage, it certainly makes more sense than the theory of the Rapture, which has to be forcibly read into the passages. It might be comforting to think that God's chosen ones are airlifted out of the worst of the chaos and devastation and taken to sit with the Son of Man and watch the nasty things happening to those who are left behind, but it just isn't in the text.

But the passage is certainly sombre and baffling. The sequence of events is not clear, and neither is the timescale. It is entirely understandable that we tend to want to focus on the crossword-puzzle aspect of it, trying to guess exactly what is to happen when and to whom, rather than focusing on the advice being given to the disciples and us. In the midst of all this chaos and terror, they are given two concrete instructions. One is not to be too easily swayed by simple solutions, and the other is not to be over-prepared. This is very strange advice, and terribly hard to follow, under the circumstances.

They are not to follow people who say, "I'm the one to bring all this to an end. I know how to fix things. I'm the one you need." They know that the only one they need has already come and is with them, namely, Jesus. However tempted they are to look around at the world of war, earthquake, famine and betrayal and doubt God, they must simply keep on keeping on. By sheer dogged persistence, they are to bear witness to the truth that everything is in the hands of God, despite all evidence to the contrary. And when this resistance to the panic of the moment gets them into trouble – as it certainly will – that, too, must be met with the same calm. They are not to prepare their defences as though this human trial is the most important thing in the world, because they know it isn't. It is simply something that happens to all followers of Jesus.

So through all the uproar and the terror around them, Jesus' followers are to bear witness to the reality of God's world and God's rule. Everything that happens to them just gives them the chance to testify to God's reign. There is real anguish in the words of the Gospel, as it describes how all those the disciples thought they could most trust to love them would betray them. But through it all, they are never to begin to believe that their persecutors are right. That is the testimony that they have to offer to the world, steadily, faithfully, even with the tears streaming down their faces – the world is good and belongs to God. However counter-intuitive it may seem at times, however much the circumstances might seem to contradict their witness, they must continue to testify to what the world most needs to know.

**Application**

That is our testimony, too. It is too easy to become gloomy and depressed about the state of the world, and to doubt that God is really the ruler of the world. But that gives us an opportunity to testify. It gives us the chance to point to the God whose Son suffered all that we are suffering, so that he could be with us in everything, and bring the power of his resurrection life into the dead world. There is a reality greater than any chaos or war or terror, and that is God. Let our lives tell that out.

*"There was also an inscription over him:*
*'This is the King of the Jews.'"*
(Luke 23:38)

**Illustration**
Each of us has our own feast day, our birthday. It's a day when we celebrate being alive. Cards, flowers, gifts, a special meal and phone calls tell us that our friends are glad to know us and that we make a difference to their lives.

Today we celebrate the feast of Christ the King. We celebrate Christ, risen, ascended and glorified. We give thanks to God for all he has done for us through Jesus and for the difference Jesus makes to our lives.

We celebrate the kingship of Christ, but what sort of kingship is it that we're celebrating? Our Gospel reading gives us a vivid picture to reflect on.



**Gospel Teaching**
The picture is certainly not what we would expect to see illustrating kingship, power and authority. Here are no fine robes but a naked and scarred body. His crown has no jewels, only vicious thorns. On his hands there are no rings of power, just the nails which fix him to a wooden cross – no golden throne. There are no courtiers or servants around him – just two criminals sharing his fate, and an assorted crowd of soldiers and ghoulish spectators who taunt and mock him.

But before we turn away from this ghastly picture of cruelty and humiliation we see the words "This is the King of the Jews" and we hear the voice of an unlikely believer, "remember me when you come into your kingdom". Someone here has caught a glimpse of the glory that is hidden by the awfulness of this torture. And we hear another voice, the voice of authority coming from the defeat of the cross, "Today you will be with me in Paradise."

We heard the voices of mockery and hate. Now we hear the voices of faith and compassion and it makes us stop and wonder.

Is it possible that in this picture we are getting a glimpse of the sort of kingship that can meet our deepest inner needs, the needs we sometimes daren't even face ourselves and which certainly aren't met by the rulers of this world?

Here is a king who is prepared to suffer alongside us. This is not a king who holds himself aloof from ordinary folk. This is a king who experiences betrayal, savage injustice, brutal cruelty and utter humiliation, and yet maintains his dignity and integrity. This is a king who has lived life as we live it, who has died as we must die but who now lives a new resurrection life. He reassures us and welcomes us into that same resurrection life in his kingdom, where we will know the peace and healing for which we have longed.

**Application**

The picture of kingship in our Gospel story turns traditional kingship upside down. It reaches out to us, calling us to offer ourselves to Christ the King, and we can perhaps sense what a difference this would make to our lives.

Next week we will begin again to tell the story of the coming of Jesus into the world as a baby and we will again start looking forward to Jesus returning as Christ the King. As we journey through the year, hearing again the stories of Jesus' birth and life, his ministry and teaching, his death and resurrection, we too will be travelling on our own journeys. We too will go through wilderness times of doubt and anxiety. We may enter the Gethsemane of anguish and despair. We will have mountain-top experiences of excitement and good news. We will plod along through the everyday life of ordinary times.

As we travel we will also have a companion alongside us and a vision to give meaning and purpose to our lives. Our companion will be Christ, the Son of Man, who knows what it is to be human and who will show understanding and compassion when the going gets tough. His presence will make all the difference when we feel most alone and isolated. Our vision will be that of love's victory over death and of Christ the King who will draw us into his eternal kingdom. His kingship will make all the difference when things seem out of control, chaotic and heading from bad to worse.

Today we celebrate the eternal presence of Christ the King in bread and wine. Let us pray that his spirit will make a difference in our lives, bringing us refreshment, peace, the power of love and whatever else our hearts need for the journey that lies ahead.

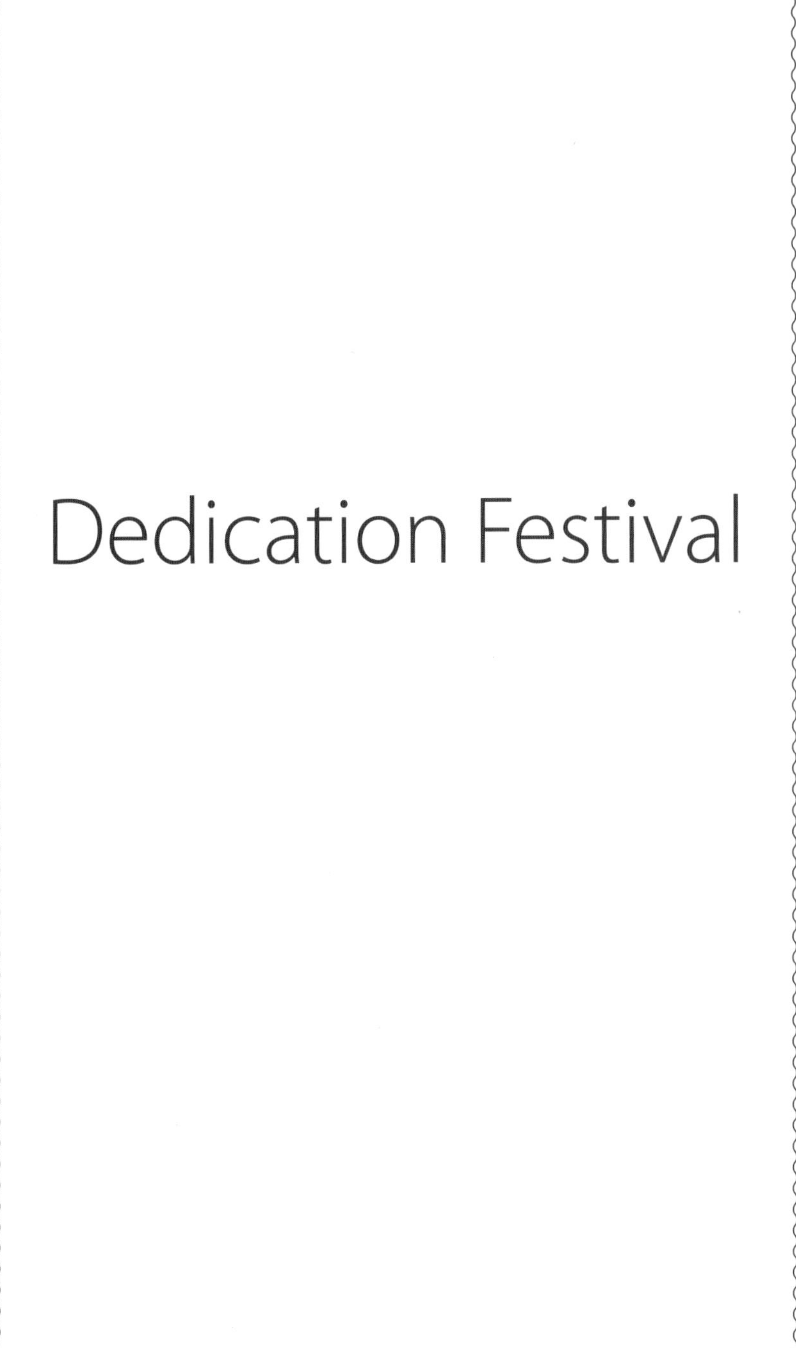

# Dedication Festival

*"'My house shall be called a house of prayer'; but you are making it a den of robbers."*
(Matthew 21:13)

**Illustration**

Most of us remember, if we are honest, at least one occasion where we didn't want to admit our faith. Christian youngsters coming out of a nightclub in the early hours of the morning and being met by kindly, patronising, pamphlet-waving Christians, explaining the folly of the nightclub lifestyle, might well creep away without greeting their brothers and sisters in Christ. Or if listening to a well-meaning but simplisitic street-evangelist, few of us go up and lend our support. It isn't necessarily, even, that we disagree with what these other Christians are saying; it's just that they are being embarrassing. Surely faith doesn't have to be embarrassing?

**Gospel Teaching**

On the face of it, this is a rather dampening Gospel passage for those of us gathered here to celebrate the life of the Church in this building. The uncompromising story of Jesus rounding on the comfortable routine of the Temple doesn't seem fair or appropriate for us. We may have a bookstall, but that hardly qualifies us as a "robbers' den", does it?

Matthew doesn't tell us what Jesus' followers made of his actions, but it is hard to imagine that they weren't at least slightly embarrassed by such apparently disproportionate behaviour. They must have had friends and relations working or worshipping in the Temple that day. They themselves must have been as used to the Temple system as anyone else. They understood that this commerce was part of the everyday working of the Temple, the necessary price to be paid. Why was Jesus overreacting like that?

Matthew's Gospel gives us less than Luke's does of the relationship between Jesus and the Temple. Luke shows us the boy Jesus going instinctively to the Temple, his Father's house, and finding understanding and respect there. That was the place where God dwelt, and so it was the place any devout Israelite would expect to feel closest to God.

But all the Gospels detail the growing conflict between Jesus and the religious leaders of the day. Where Jesus might have hoped to find himself at home, given a hearing, at the very least, he finds instead that he and his teaching are rejected, and his whole relationship with God considered suspect. He found that people preferred to take refuge in the Temple, and in the whole carefully constructed edifice of religious life that regulated God and God's demands, and enabled people to know the limits of their obedience. There is a bitter and terrible irony about the fact that the very people and place best equipped to support Jesus and his mission preferred to stay well away.

**Application**

It is very easy for us to sit in judgement on the people of the past. With the benefit of hindsight, we read the Gospels and we know the goodies and the baddies. We know which side to take.

But that dangerously sidelines the challenge of this passage for us. This is not just about what some people did two thousand years ago. It is about a universal human instinct. We do not like change; we want to do good, but not for God to make disproportionate demands upon our lives, our time, our money, our relationships. We believe in God, of course, but we do not want to have to make embarrassing public displays of our faith. We don't want to be classed with the overzealous street-preacher, or the cringe-making do-gooders outside the nightclubs. Or with the man making a public disturbance in the Temple?

What we are celebrating today is worthy of celebration. We are remembering and thanking God for the faith of a community that has been here for so many years; we are rejoicing at the generosity and commitment of all those who helped to build this church all those years ago, and who help to keep it going today. What has this story of Jesus and the money changers to do with us?

Perhaps it is only a lesson to be filed away in case of future need. But it is worth just double-checking that it has no more immediate relevance. This building is beautiful and helpful, but it is not God. It isn't even where God lives. No house made by human hands can house our God. Let us by all means give thanks for everything this building has enabled, all the opportunities it has offered, all the lives that have been changed here, the marriages, the baptisms, the funerals, the day-by-day, week-by-week offering of worship to our God. But let us never think that God's embarrassing, over-the-top claims on us stop when we walk out of this building.

*"The works that I do in my Father's name testify to me."*
(John 10:25)

**Illustration**

How do we know if something is true? Well, that is, of course, a more complicated question than it sounds, because different criteria apply to different kinds of knowledge. We will have different ways of judging whether it is true that our spouse loves us and whether it is true that we have some money left in our bank accounts. It is possible to be wrong about both of those things, but we have a rough idea of how to go about finding an answer. It is a perfectly valid question to ask how we know if something is true.

**Gospel Teaching**

So the people who come to Jesus in today's Gospel reading are doing something both recognisable and sensible. They are trying to find out if it is true that Jesus is the Messiah. They really need to know, because all kinds of other things follow from it. If Jesus is the Messiah, their lives will have to change.

But Jesus gives them an answer that they do not know how to measure. Jesus suggests that their question is one they may not have understood, because they do not recognise that they already have the answer in their hands. Everything they know about Jesus and what he has been doing ought to have made it clear to them. Why otherwise are they asking? The very fact that he has provoked them to ask the question ought to make them begin to recognise the answer.

So why doesn't it? Why do they not know how to measure the truth of Jesus? The passage seems to suggest two possible answers.

The first is that, at some level at least, they do know the answer to their question but they don't like it. They do not want to recognise who Jesus is precisely because they would then have to acknowledge his claim to their obedience, they would have to change. They are hoping that he will give them an answer that they can weigh up, find wanting and reject.

But Jesus also seems to be implying something else, as well, which is a different approach to knowledge. He tells his questioners that they do not know the answer to their question because they do not belong to his "sheep". They want uncommitted, risk-free knowledge, but the only way to find out who Jesus is is to risk following him.

This may sound like an odd theory of knowledge, but it has parallels. For example, you can't really find out how to play football without doing it. However good you are at the theory of it, no one will believe you are a footballer if you never move out of your armchair. Similarly, the only way you can find out whether or not you believe in marriage is to be married. Otherwise you are just theorising on the basis of other people's experience, and you'll never know if it applies to you or not. Of course, you are more likely to take the risk if other people generally report a positive experience than if you see misery to be the more usual outcome of marriage! But there is no risk-free, experiment-free method of finding the answer to some of these kinds of question.

**Application**
Those of us gathered here today for this Dedication Festival have the benefit of many other people's experience of God, many other people's answer to the question that Jesus is asked today. We have trusted them and our own experience and taken the risk of following Jesus. We have found that belonging to Jesus' flock has made us better able to hear his voice, to know him and be known by him. We have found the method for answering this question about who Jesus is.

But the method and the answer are not just for us. If this is something that we have found to work, we need to share it. We need to help other people to take this risk. Something about our lives together should be challenging enough and attractive enough for people to see that this is a possible answer to the questions they are asking. Not all will accept. For some, it will be the answer that they refuse to recognise. But we need to be sure that we have lives that reflect our shepherd, and faithfully pass on the possibility of belonging, just as this place and its people have done for us.

*"Making a whip of cords, he drove all of them out of the temple... He also poured out the coins of the money-changers and overturned their tables."*
(John 2:15)

**Illustration**
In *The Silver Chair,* one of C.S. Lewis' Narnia stories, the children, Jill and Eustace, are given all the signs they will need to recognise in order to fulfil their mission and save the Narnian prince from the wicked queen who is trying to use him to get control of Narnia. Jill and Eustace faithfully memorise the signs and, to begin with, they repeat them very regularly. But soon they start to forget, as they get busy and distracted, and anyway, they keep finding they have failed to recognise one sign after another because it wasn't as clear as their simple memorised list had suggested.

Finally, when they have missed all the signs but the very last, they are faced with a terrible dilemma as they come across the last sign in a very dangerous situation. In case there are still some here who have not yet had the pleasure of reading the Narnia series, we had better not give any more away. But the book is, among other things, a subtle exploration of the difference between symbol and reality, between things learned parrot-fashion and things so memorised that they become recognisable in whatever form they appear.

**Gospel Teaching**
Today's Gospel reading is the harsh, uncompromising story of Jesus' rage with those involved in trade in the Temple. All of the Gospels tell this story, although John has it near the beginning of Jesus' ministry, while the others have it near the end, as part of the escalating hatred between Jesus and the religious authorities of his day.

At the heart of this conflict is Jesus' perception that these religious people have been given all the signs they need and yet they do not recognise what the signs point to. They have been given scriptures, laws, the Temple itself, and they have learned them all faithfully by heart. But they have allowed themselves to forget that the signs are not just a way of life; they point to something. They have domesticated the signs, and started to weave them into ordinary life, even making money out of them, and they have forgotten the urgency of their mission.

All of these signs were supposed to prepare them to recognise God. Yet, as John's Gospel tells us absolutely without compromise in its opening chapter, they signally failed to do so. The Word, Jesus, lived among them unrecognised by all but a tiny minority.

**Application**

It is very easy for us to read these stories and feel smug. It is easy to assume that we have understood the signs correctly and recognised Jesus. But that is dangerous complacency. This kind of taming of God's signs and symbols is common to all religious traditions. We get on with our life, occasionally repeating by rote the sacred signs that we have memorised. We try, of course, to be faithful witnesses, to continue to look out for God among us, but we can't spend the whole of our lives doing that, can we? We have to live.

As we celebrate this Dedication Festival, we also need to ask ourselves some hard questions about the role that this much-loved building plays in our lives. It is a profoundly important symbol, one that helps to ground our memory of God, one that helps us to repeat the signs of our salvation, but we need to be very sure that we have not confused the sign with the reality. This building is not God; serving it, caring for it, visiting it regularly is not the sum total of the Christian life. It is part of what can and should equip us for our real task, which is to recognise the presence and activity of God when we encounter it. It should help us to bear witness to the reality of God.

So what we are celebrating today is a symbol of our calling. It is fine to feel loyalty to this building, to thank God for all those who helped to make it the powerful, attractive sign that it is of the work of God in this place. The time we spend here, repeating and relearning and deepening our understanding of what we have been given, is vital. But it is only preparation for the real mission. We need to go out and recognise Jesus, with the help of all that we have learned here. Then this symbol will have served its purpose for us, as it has for so many before us, and as we pray that it will for the many who come after us.

# Index of Gospel Readings

**MATTHEW** **Page**

**MARK** *continued* **Page**

**LUKE** *continued* **Page**



**JOHN**